Formulation in Psych(
Psychotherapy

The first edition of *Formulation in Psychology and Psychotherapy* caught the wave of growing interest in formulation in a clinical context. This completely updated and revised edition summarises recent practice, research, developments and debates while retaining the features that made the first a leading text in the field. It contains new chapters on personal construct formulation, formulation in health settings and the innovative practice of using formulation in teams.

The book sees formulation as a dynamic process which explores personal meaning collaboratively and reflectively, taking account of relational and social contexts. Two case studies, one adult and one child, illustrate the use of formulation from the perspectives of expert clinicians from six different theoretical positions. The book encourages the reader to take a constructively critical perspective on the many philosophical, professional and ethical debates raised by the process of formulating people's problems. Among the issues explored are:

- the social and political context of formulation;
- formulation in relation to psychiatric diagnosis;
- the limitations of formulation;
- controversies and debates about formulation.

This readable and comprehensive guide to the field provides a clear, up-to-date and thought-provoking overview of formulation from a number of perspectives, essential for clinicians working in all areas of mental health and social care, psychology, therapy and counselling.

Lucy Johnstone is a consultant clinical psychologist and a former Programme Director of the Bristol Clinical Psychology Doctorate. She has worked in adult mental health settings for many years.

Rudi Dallos is the Research Director on the Clinical Psychology training programme at the University of Plymouth. He also works as a clinical psychologist specialising in work with adolescents and their families.

Formulation in Psychology and Psychotherapy

Making sense of people's problems

Second edition

Edited by Lucy Johnstone and Rudi Dallos

Routledge
Taylor & Francis Group

LONDON AND NEW YORK

First published 2014
by Routledge
27 Church Road, Hove, East Sussex BN3 2FA

Simultaneously published in the USA and Canada
by Routledge
711 Third Avenue, New York, NY 10017

Routledge is an imprint of the Taylor & Francis Group, an informa business

© 2014 Lucy Johnstone and Rudi Dallos

British Library Cataloguing in Publication Data
A catalogue record for this book is available from the British
Library

Library of Congress Cataloging in Publication Data
Formulation in psychology and psychotherapy : understanding
people's problems / edited by Lucy Johnstone and Rudi Dallos.
-- Second edition.
pages cm
Includes bibliographical references and index.
1. Psychology--Methodology. 2. Psychotherapy--Methodology. I.
Johnstone, Lucy, editor of compilation. II. Dallos, Rudi, 1948-
editor of compilation.
BF38.5.J64 2013
616.89'14--dc23
2012048131

ISBN: 978-0-415-68230-5 (hbk)
ISBN: 978-0-415-68231-2 (pbk)
ISBN: 978-0-203-38057-4 (ebk)

Typeset in Garamond 3
by Saxon Graphics Ltd, Derby

Printed and bound by CPI Group (UK) Ltd, Croydon, CR0 4YY

This book is dedicated to the memory of the Bristol Clinical Psychology Doctorate 2001–2010 and the staff, trainees and supervisors who contributed to its critical and reflective ethos.

Contents

    a principle-driven approach   18
    ROBERT DUDLEY AND WILLEM KUYKEN

    A principled approach to CBT case conceptualisation 18
    Jack 20
        Principle 1: levels of conceptualisation 20
        Presenting issues 20
        Perpetuating factors 23
        Precipitating factors 27
        Predisposing factors: quantity of events 30
        Predisposing factors: quality of events 30
        Principle 2: collaborative empiricism 33
        Principle 3: include client strengths and conceptualise resilience 34
    Janet 37
        Levels of conceptualisation 37
        Collaborative empiricism 38
        Strengths and resilience 38
    Reflections 40
    Conclusions 41
    Key characteristics of CBT formulation 42
    Acknowledgements 42
    References 42

3   Psychodynamic formulation: looking beneath the surface   45
    ROB LEIPER

    What is a psychodynamic approach? 45
    Core features of a psychodynamic approach 46
    The dynamic perspective 46
    The developmental perspective 49
    The structural perspective 52
    The adaptive perspective 54
    Jack: a psychodynamic formulation 57
        A prince betrayed and disinherited 57
    Reflection on the formulation 59
    Towards intervention 59
    Janet: a psychodynamic formulation 61
        A girl unheld 61
    Reflections 62
    Key characteristics of a psychodynamic formulation 64
    References 65

Figures and tables

Figures

Table

Contributors

Samantha Cole is a clinical psychologist working across the lifespan in acute hospitals in Bristol. Her main interests are in psychological approaches to pain management, health-related appearance concerns, procedural anxiety and end-of-life issues. She has conducted research in formulation and contributed to conferences, workshops and professional guidelines related to integrated formulation with healthcare teams.

Rudi Dallos is Professor and Research Director on the Plymouth University Doctorate in Clinical Psychology. He works as a clinical psychologist and family therapist in an early intervention family therapy service. He has developed an integrative therapeutic model combining systemic, attachment and narrative frameworks (Attachment Narrative Therapy, 2006). His research includes explorations of family dynamics and attachment themes and process of triangulation in families. He has also authored several books, including 'Reflective Practice in Psychotherapy and Counselling' with Jacqui Stedmon.

Robert Dudley is the Degree Programme Director for the Doctorate of Clinical Psychology course at Newcastle University, and a Consultant Clinical Psychologist and he also works in an Early Intervention in Psychosis service. As a researcher he is interested in improving our understanding of the processes that lead a person to experience distressing psychotic symptoms like voices or visual hallucinations, and in using CBT formulation to aid the selection of the optimal interventions. This work on formulation has been shaped by a rewarding collaboration with colleagues Willem Kuyken and Christine Padesky.

David Harper worked as a clinician in the NHS for a decade before moving, in 2000, to the University of East London where he is currently Reader in Clinical Psychology. He has published a number of articles and book chapters. In addition he co-authored *Deconstructing Psychopathology* (Sage, 1995), co-edited *Qualitative Research Methods in Mental Health and Psychotherapy* (Wiley, 2012) and co-authored *Psychology, Mental Health and*

Distress (Palgrave MacMillan, 2013). He also works as a Consultant Clinical Psychologist in Newham as part of the Systemic Consultation Service.

Lucy Johnstone is a consultant clinical psychologist in an Adult Mental Health service in South Wales and former Programme Director of the Bristol Clinical Psychology Doctorate. She is the author of *Users and Abusers of Psychiatry: A critical look at psychiatric practice* (Routledge 2000) and a number of other articles and chapters taking a critical perspective on psychiatric practice. She is lead author of the Division of Clinical Psychology *Good Practice Guidelines on the Use of Psychological Formulation* (DCP, 2011) and a regular trainer and conference speaker.

Willem Kuyken works as a researcher, trainer and clinician at the Mood Disorders Centre in Exeter. His research and clinical work specialise in CBT approaches to recurrent depression. A particular theme of his work is exploring how therapists develop and share conceptualisations. After completing his PhD and clinical training he worked as a Postdoctoral Fellow at the Center for Cognitive Therapy, University of Pennsylvania for two years with Aaron T. Beck (1997–1999). Since 1999 he has worked in Exeter, England where he co-founded the Mood Disorders Centre, a research, clinical and training centre. He has published widely on case conceptualisation, including co-authoring the book *Collaborative Case Conceptualization* with Christine Padesky and Rob Dudley.

Rob Leiper is a Consultant Clinical Psychologist and Psychoanalytic Psychotherapist. His career has focussed clinically on the development of integrative specialist psychotherapy services. He has recently retired from leading a pilot project on the treatment of personality disordered offenders in Oxleas NHS Trust and is in private practice in Scotland and South Africa.

Lynn McClelland is a Clinical Psychologist working in Torbay CAMHS and teaching on the Exeter DClinPsy programme. She teaches and supervises clinical and research work in the area of critical community psychology, diversity, and reflexive organisational practice.

Harry Procter retired from the NHS seven years ago; he has continued to devote his time to developing and teaching his constructivist approach to working with children and adults and their families, teams and organisations. Recently he has completed papers on the nature of the construct, reflective practice, developing the theory underlying Qualitative Grids and their application in different settings and different clinical problems as well as in exploration of poetry and drama. He is interested in the philosophical background of constructivism and is researching the work of Charles S. Peirce whose work provides a fascinating meta-framework for looking at and understanding constructivist approaches.

Dave Spellman is a Consultant Clinical Psychologist with Lancashire Care NHS Foundation Trust. He qualified in Liverpool in 1988 and works in a multi-agency team with children who are looked after, adopted and their families and carers across East Lancashire.

Jacqui Stedmon is Programme Director for the Doctoral Training Programme in Clinical Psychology at the University of Plymouth. She has a clinical interest in paediatric psychology and bereavement in children and young people. As well as working with systems and families she is keen to promote reflective practice in clinical psychology.

David Winter is Professor of Clinical Psychology and Programme Director of the Doctorate in Clinical Psychology at the University of Hertfordshire. He has applied personal construct psychology in National Health Service settings for many years, and has published extensively in this area and on psychotherapy research. His books include *Personal Construct Psychology in Clinical Practice* (Routledge, 1992) and *Personal Construct Psychotherapy: Advances in Theory, Practice and Research* (with Linda Viney, Whurr, 2005). He is a Fellow of the British Psychological Society, and has chaired its Psychotherapy Section, as well as the Experiential Constructivist Section and Research Committee of the UK Council for Psychotherapy.

Preface to the second edition

A formulation draws upon psychological theory in order to create a working hypothesis or 'best guess' about the reasons for a client's difficulties, in the light of their relationships and social contexts and the sense they have made of the events in their lives. Formulations are co-constructed with clients, and their main purpose is to inform the intervention.

Formulation has become one of the central emerging issues in psychotherapy and mental health practice, and the contributors are all experienced clinicians who are at the leading edge of developments in theory and practice. The first edition has become a standard text for clinical psychologists and widely read by other professionals, both in training and qualified. This new edition formulates two client stories from six different theoretical traditions: CBT, systemic, psychodynamic, narrative and social inequalities, as before, with personal construct psychology as an addition. The two completely revised chapters on Integrative Formulation explore the issue of combining models through the framework of the evolving therapeutic relationship. This edition is the first book to provide an overview of the innovative practice of using formulation in teamwork. There is a new chapter on formulating in physical health settings. The final chapter is a thought-provoking update and overview of emerging issues such as formulation and culture, formulation and research, benefits and limitations of formulation, and formulation in relation to psychiatric diagnosis.

Feedback from the first edition suggests that it has succeeded in its aim of being accessible and comprehensive while encouraging the reader to take a constructively critical perspective on the many philosophical, professional, clinical and ethical debates raised by formulation. It provides a lively, challenging and clinically informed overview of the subject, enabling both experienced and novice clinicians to enhance their knowledge and skills.

Chapter 1

Introduction to formulation

Lucy Johnstone and Rudi Dallos

Formulation in psychology and psychotherapy

Formulation is a topic that is continuing to attract attention in psychology, psychotherapy, counselling and psychiatry. It is a defining competency of the profession of clinical psychology (Division of Clinical Psychology, 2010), which has recently published best practice guidelines for its members (DCP, 2011.) It is also listed as a skill in the Health and Care Professions Council regulations for health, educational, forensic, counselling, and sports and exercise psychologists (Health Professions Council, 2009), and in the curriculum for psychiatrists' training in the UK (Royal College of Psychiatrists, 2010). However, although it is arguably central to the implementation of any psychological intervention, its conceptual and empirical basis remains to be firmly established. It has until recently been a neglected area of research, training and publication, especially in the areas of complex and integrative formulation.

The most relevant early publications are Persons (1989) *Cognitive Therapy in Practice*; Bruch and Bond (1998) *Beyond Diagnosis: Case Formulation Approaches in Cognitive Behaviour Therapy*; Eells (2006a) *Handbook of Psychotherapy Case Formulation*; Weerasekera (1996) *Multiperspective Case Formulation*; and Lombardo and Nezu (2004) *Cognitive-Behavioral Case Formulation and Treatment Design*. Since the first edition of this book, they have been joined by other texts including *Clinical Case Formulations* (Ingram, 2006); *Case Formulation in Cognitive Behaviour Therapy* (Tarrier, 2006); *Assessment and Case Formulation in Cognitive Behavioural Therapy* (Grant et al., 2008); *Behavioural Case Formulation and Intervention* (Sturmey, 2008); *Collaborative Case Conceptualization* (Kuyken et al., 2009); and *Constructing Stories, Telling Tales* (Corrie and Lane, 2010). All of these are useful texts, but are written by psychiatrists with a medical readership in mind (Weerasekera); are oriented towards an American audience and healthcare system (Eells, Weerasekera, Ingram); or are written from a CBT perspective only (Bruch and Bond; Persons; Tarrier; Sturmey; Kuyken et al.). With the exception of Corrie and Lane, none of them covers the newer therapeutic traditions, and nor do they give a critical overview of the wider issues raised by the theory and practice of formulation. This book is an attempt to fill those gaps. Feedback from the first edition suggests that it has been useful to trainee and qualified clinicians from a wide range of helping professions and therapeutic orientations.

We have organised the book around a number of central themes which run through the various chapters, and are brought together in the chapter on Integration and in the final overview and reflection. The themes are detailed below.

Formulation and collaboration. Is formulation something that we do to, or with, clients? If formulation is the starting point for the whole process of therapy, this has crucial implications for the whole way in which the therapy proceeds. How important is it to ensure the client's genuine involvement right from the start, and how can we promote this in the process of formulation?

Formulation and reflective practice. The notion of reflective practice is becoming increasingly important in all therapeutic traditions; that is, the necessity of being aware of one's own thoughts, feelings and reactions as a therapist as well as one's own position in terms of professional status, gender, class, ethnicity and so on, and how these impact upon the therapeutic process. How might these ideas be taken on board in formulation? What kind of biases is formulation open to, and how can we minimise them? How much overlap is there between formulation and reflective practice?

Formulation and the therapeutic relationship. Linked to the above are general questions about power and control in therapy, and in whose interests the therapy, or the formulation, operates. This leads us to ask questions such as who has the 'problem', how and when we share formulations with clients, and whether it is advisable to do so or perhaps not to do so in particular clinical situations. It also highlights an important distinction between formulation as an object or event, and formulating as a process which is embedded within the therapeutic relationship itself.

Formulation and ethical practice. Questions about power, bias, confidentiality and so on raise the issue of ethics and best practice. They imply that formulations can be harmful, as well as simply not helpful. How can we take steps to avoid this possibility, and what best practice guidelines might we draw up in relation to both formulation and formulating?

Formulation and integration. As the following chapters will show, there are as many different approaches to formulation as there are therapies, although there is also a recent trend towards therapeutic integration, with all traditions being more open to borrowing ideas and concepts from each other. Is it possible to combine the strengths of various different approaches in order to develop integrated formulations, and how might this be done?

Formulation and psychiatric diagnosis. There is an ongoing debate about how formulation differs from psychiatric diagnosis. Is it a replacement for, or an addition to, the more traditional way of matching clients to treatments? Or is it trying to achieve something rather different, perhaps a more individualised and tentative working hypothesis?

Formulation and context. Different therapies take different positions on what is included in the formulation. Do we refer mainly to individual thoughts, feelings and behaviours; do we include family and institutional settings as well; and/or do we also look at much broader social and political contexts? And if the latter, how do we integrate these into our understandings of our clients' difficulties? Where does the 'problem' reside, and how can we come to a shared view about this which will allow constructive work to be carried out?

Formulation and culture. One aspect of formulation is, of course, ethnicity and culture. How can we ensure that cultural identities and values are fully incorporated into the process of formulation? What constitutes a 'problem' as opposed to a cultural variation in acceptable behaviour? More generally, formulation is itself a concept that has arisen within a particular culture. To what extent does this limit its usefulness beyond that culture, and is there any way of compensating for this?

Formulation, evaluation and evidence. This brings us on to some more fundamental debates about the nature and scientific status of formulations. Can they in some sense be described as 'correct' or 'true', or are they best viewed in terms of their usefulness to the client? In either case, how might we evaluate this, and whose view (therapist or client) counts most? What kind of research has been carried out to date and what kind is needed in the future?

Do we need formulation at all? Finally, we should not be afraid to ask fundamental questions about the value and place of formulation. As will be seen in the chapters on social inequalities and social constructionism, not everyone is convinced that formulation is an essential part of therapeutic work. Is it simply rhetoric, politically useful as part of a claim to expertise and professional status? Could any non-professional do as well – or perhaps better? Indeed, is it possible not to formulate – in our work and in our everyday lives? Can we take anything meaningful and valuable from the debates that all parties would be able to agree with, and if so what might that be?

Our themes, then, are threads running throughout the chapters, which are organised around the stories of two clients – Jack, a young man in his mid-twenties, and Janet, a child aged nine. Their difficulties are formulated from a number of different perspectives in turn: CBT, psychodynamic and systemic, which represent mainstream therapeutic approaches; and social inequality and social constructionist viewpoints, which are more recent developments. This edition also includes a chapter on formulating within Personal Construct Therapy, which emerged from within the constructivist tradition, or in other words 'the study of how human beings create systems of meaning in making sense of and acting in the world'. Readers will be able to gain a clear sense of how to formulate within each tradition, and the respective strengths and limitations of the different approaches.

There then follows a chapter on the general principles underpinning integrated formulations. Integration is a key theme in two other new chapters, one on 'Using integrative formulation in health settings' and one on an innovative use of formulation which is rapidly growing in popularity, 'Using formulation in teams'. Finally, we present a summary and critical overview of the themes of the book, in order to come to some tentative conclusions about the place of formulation in therapeutic work.

What do we mean by formulation?

Approaches such as CBT, psychodynamic theory and so on, are broad, general sets of explanations that draw on their own characteristic ideas and concepts; for example, negative automatic thoughts in CBT or the unconscious in psychodynamic therapy. A formulation takes these general theories and applies them to a particular individual and their difficulties.

As already discussed, the term 'formulation' can be understood as both an event and a process. In the former sense, which is commonly assumed on training programmes and in the literature, the formulation is an 'object' or event that often takes a concrete form – for example, a written assignment, a letter to the referrer, or a diagram given to the service user. Most of the research into formulation is based on this understanding (see chapter 12). However, formulation as a recursive process of suggestion, discussion, reflection, feedback and revision that is part of the moment-to-moment process of therapy may be the more common clinical reality.

Most of the definitions are, like the ones below, based on the assumption of 'formulation-as-an-event'. (See Corrie and Lane, 2010: 10–12 for a fuller list.) It may be useful to bear in mind the themes outlined above as we reflect on them:

> Formulation is ... a provisional explanation or hypothesis of how an individual comes to present with a certain disorder or circumstance at a particular point in time.
>
> (Weerasekera, 1996: 4)

> A formulation is the tool used by clinicians to relate theory to practice ... It is the lynchpin that holds theory and practice together ... Formulations can best be understood as hypotheses to be tested.
>
> (Butler, 1998: 2, 4)

> A psychotherapy case formulation is a hypothesis about the causes, precipitants and maintaining influences of a person's psychological, interpersonal and behavioral problems.
>
> (Eells, 2006b: 4)

> Psychological formulation is the summation and integration of the knowledge that is acquired by the assessment process that may involve psychological, biological and systemic factors and procedures. The

formulation will draw on psychological theory and research to provide a framework for describing a client's problems or needs, how it developed and is being maintained.

(Division of Clinical Psychology, 2010: 5)

A psychodynamic formulation: makes a statement about the nature of the patient's problems or difficulties, usually in terms of repeated maladaptive patterns occurring in relationships ... Makes an inference as to how these are related to the patient's internal world, including unconscious conflicts ... Links the above (if possible) with historical information in an explanatory model.

(McGrath and Margison, 2000: 2)

Thus, the common elements are that a formulation provides a *hypothesis about a person's difficulties*, which *draws from psychological theory*.

We may wish to note that what seems to be missing from these definitions is the viewpoint and role of the service user in developing the formulation – in other words, formulation as a *shared* production that is based on *personal meaning*. These aspects, along with the sense of 'formulation-as-a-process', are captured by Harper and Moss's phrase 'a process of ongoing collaborative sense-making' (2003: 8); and by Corrie and Lane's phrase 'the co-construction of a narrative that provides a specific focus for a learning journey' (2010: 24). The Division of Clinical Psychology Good Practice Guidelines have a similar definition (DCP, 2011: 2):

Formulation ... summarises and integrates a broad range of biopsychosocial causal factors. It is based on personal meaning and constructed collaboratively with service users and teams.

Team formulation

A recent development is the use of formulation in teamwork, in order to facilitate a group or team of professionals to develop a shared understanding of a service user's difficulties. Team formulations can, like individual ones, be based either on specific therapeutic approaches or on an integrative model. The slightly different emphases and uses of this approach are discussed further in chapter 10.

Differences and common factors in formulation

Formulations from the various therapeutic traditions differ in terms of:

- the factors they see as most relevant (thoughts, feelings, behaviours, social circumstances, etc.)

- the explanatory concepts they draw on (schemas, the unconscious, discourses, etc);
- the emphasis they place on reflexivity;
- the degree to which they adopt an expert as opposed to a collaborative stance;
- their position in relation to psychiatric diagnosis;
- their position about the 'truth' versus 'usefulness' of the formulation;
- the way that the formulation is developed, shared and used within therapy.

These differences are explored more fully in the subsequent chapters, each of which concludes with a bullet-point summary of the characteristic features of formulation within that particular therapeutic tradition.

However, all formulations have the following features in common, in that they:

- summarise the client's core problems;
- indicate how the client's difficulties may relate to one another, by drawing on psychological theories and principles;
- suggest, on the basis of psychological theory, why the client has developed these difficulties, at this time and in these situations;
- give rise to a plan of intervention which is based in the psychological processes and principles already identified;
- are open to revision and re-formulation.

In addition, as already noted, the DCP (2011) guidelines emphasise that 'These unique individual stories are centrally concerned with the *personal meaning* to the service user of the events and experiences of their lives'. As well as drawing on the evidence, formulations 'require a kind of artistry that also involves intuition, flexibility and critical evaluation of one's experience'. The clinician is thus required to balance 'psychological theory/principles/ evidence on the one hand, and personal thoughts, feelings and meanings on the other ... in order to develop a shared account that indicates the most helpful way forward' (DCP, 2011: 7). The assumption is that this process will demonstrate that however unusual, distressing, overwhelming or confusing a service user's experiences are, 'at some level it all makes sense' (Butler, 1998: 2).

What is the purpose of a formulation?

Again, there are a number of different but complementary views on this.

Psychodynamic

The formulation explains how and why the patient's equilibrium has become disturbed and how the problems or symptoms have arisen and are maintained. From it, a logical course of therapy can be deduced, taking into account the probable consequences of change (losses and gains) and the likelihood of achieving change. The formulation, therefore, serves both as a map for therapy and a guide to which map to choose (Aveline, 1999: 202).

Cognitive-behavioural

A formulation ... 1. relates all the client's complaints to one another, 2. explains why the individual developed these difficulties, and 3. provides predictions concerning the client's behaviour given any stimulus.

(Meyer and Turkat, 1979: 261)

(Case formulation's) purpose is both to provide an accurate overview and explanation of the patient's problems that is open to verification through hypothesis testing, and to arrive collaboratively with the patient at a useful understanding of their problem that is meaningful to them ... The case formulation is then used to inform treatment or intervention by identifying key targets for change.

(Tarrier and Calam, 2002: 312)

Systemic

By hypothesising we refer to the formulation by the therapist of a hypothesis based upon the information he possesses regarding the family he is interviewing. The hypothesis establishes a starting point for his investigation as well as his verification of the validity of the hypothesis. If the hypothesis is proved false, the therapist may form a second hypothesis based upon the information gathered during the testing of the first.

(Palazzoli et al., 1980: 4)

Formulation ... is not seen as something that the therapist *does to* the family but as something that they *do with* the family ... a co-constructional process whereby the therapist, supervision team and the family members come to jointly develop new formulations of their problems. The process of formulation itself is seen not as an objective process, but as a perturbation which starts to change the family system. The process of how formulation is undertaken, the questions that are asked, when and how they are asked, are all seen as having the potential to bring about significant changes.

(Dallos and Stedmon, this book, chapter 4)

Integrative

> Formulation ... is defined as a provisional explanation or hypothesis of how an individual comes to present with a certain disorder or circumstances at a particular point in time. A number of factors may be involved in understanding the etiology of the disorder or condition. These include biological, psychological and systemic factors ... All these variables interact under certain conditions to produce a specific condition or phenomenon ... A comprehensive formulation then needs to examine all three models carefully.
>
> (Weerasekera, 1996: 4)

Butler (1998: 9) gives a detailed summary of the purposes of formulation:

- Clarifying hypotheses and questions: 'Therapists should work with a formulation in mind right from the start ... they guide questioning, and open the therapist's mind to the kind of understanding from which effective treatment strategies can be derived, applied, and evaluated.'
- Understanding: 'Providing an overall picture or map: formulations, just like maps, provide an overall view ... of something that it is not possible to see all at once.'
- Prioritising issues and problems: 'Formulation ... helps to differentiate what is essential from what is secondary in a general sense. It also helps in a more particular sense to decide which issues or problems should be prioritised.'
- Planning treatment strategies and selecting specific interventions: 'The way in which a problem is formulated determines what should be done about it.'
- Predicting responses to strategies and interventions: predicting difficulties. 'Formulation ... helps to predict the effect of the intervention ... and to predict the stumbling blocks and difficulties that will be encountered during therapy.'
- Determining criteria for successful outcome: 'A formulation provides the basis for hypotheses about what needs to change for someone to feel better, or the goals of therapy in the broad sense of the term.'
- Thinking about lack of progress; trouble-shooting: 'When lack of progress lead to frustration, and the reactions of both the patient and the therapist interfere with subsequent progress, including these factors in the reformulation can reveal ways of overcoming them.'
- Overcoming bias: 'Working with a formulation that can be explained to others provides a check on the use of too much speculation and too many far-fetched inferences.'

The essential elements here would seem to be *helping to select and guide the interventions*. Again, this raises the questions of who draws up the formulation and in whose interests it operates. Is formulation something done by the therapist to the client, and how does this fit in with the broader therapeutic relationship? We might also want to ask about the role of reflexivity – the therapist's awareness of their own process and position – and the wider social context within which the client lives and the problem is construed.

We should also remember that a formulation may indicate that no intervention is required – or that the identified client is not the location of the 'problem'. Formulation can also be a powerful intervention in its own right, and may be sufficient to enable a client to move forward with a richer understanding of their dilemmas and difficulties and without professional support.

Recent work suggests that formulation may serve other purposes including:

- Noticing gaps in the information
- Framing medical interventions
- Ensuring that a cultural understanding has been incorporated
- Helping the service user (and carer) to feel understood and contained
- Helping the therapist to feel contained
- Strengthening the therapeutic alliance
- Encouraging collaborative work with the service user (and carer)
- Emphasising strengths as well as needs
- Normalising problems; reducing service user (and carer) self-blame
- Increasing the service user's sense of agency, meaning and hope

(DCP, 2011:8)

Additional benefits have been reported from the use of formulation in teamwork, including achieving a consistent team approach to intervention; drawing on the expertise of all team members; minimising disagreement and blame within teams; raising staff morale; and facilitating culture change (DCP, 2011: 9; and see chapter 10).

How did the concept of formulation arise?

The answer to this question varies according to the therapeutic tradition in question.

Psychodynamic approaches

The earliest psychotherapy formulations originate from Freud's case studies, and draw on the psychoanalytic concepts of the unconscious, the transference, defence mechanisms, and the id, ego and superego (Bateman and Holmes, 1995). Although Freud did not use the term formulation, this was a way of explaining symptoms in psychological terms as having both a meaning (often symbolic) and a function (classically, meeting instinctual needs).

'Psychodynamic' is a general term for approaches that draw on psychoanalytic ideas and assumptions, but the field is a very wide one, and includes significant later developments such as object relations theory, self psychology and attachment theory (see chapter 3). Each of these brings its own characteristic emphasis, which is reflected in the process of formulation.

During the initial assessment interview, which is seen as being of crucial importance, the psychodynamic therapist will be gathering information and looking for the client's ability to form a good working alliance, to make use of interpretations, and to be in touch with their feelings (Bateman and Holmes, 1995). He or she will be looking for important factors in the past, for patterns in relationships, and for the key defences used by the client. From this, a psychodynamic formulation of the client's difficulties, which would typically be based on the 'triangle of person' (see chapter 3) – that is, the links between the client's current relationships, the relationship with their parents, and the relationship with the therapist – will be developed. Elements of this may be shared with the client at the end of the first meeting in order to assess their response and hence their ability to work psychodynamically.

The scientific status of psychoanalysis and its derivatives has been a subject of heated debate for many years, and was part of the impetus for the emergence of the more experimentally verifiable behavioural schools of therapy. For the purposes of this book, it is worth noting that a number of recent attempts have been made to evaluate psychodynamic formulations scientifically (see chapter 12).

Cognitive-behavioural approaches

Most current writing and research on formulation comes from the cognitive-behavioural tradition, where it is usually referred to as 'case formulation'. Bruch and Bond (1998) describe how the approach was pioneered at the Maudsley Hospital from the 1950s onwards by clinical psychologists such as Hans Eysenck, Victor Meyer, Monte Shapiro and Ira Turkat (who coined the term 'case formulation'), key figures in the development of the then new approach of behaviour therapy. In its earlier form of functional analysis, case formulation was seen as a more useful alternative to psychiatric diagnosis, aiming to describe problem behaviour in terms of environmental stimuli and response contingencies (Hayes and Follette, 1992). For example, agoraphobia might serve the purpose, or function, of helping someone to avoid anxiety-provoking situations, or alleviating the possessive jealousy of an insecure partner. This kind of analysis was said to provide a much more useful guide to treatment than psychiatric diagnosis.

Cognitive therapists such as Aaron Beck (1976) have, from the 1970s onwards, made significant additions to early behavioural analysis by including the role of thought processes in the development and maintenance of mental distress, and there is now a very large literature on the subject (see chapter 2).

The term 'formulation' first appears in the regulations governing the profession of clinical psychology, which traditionally specialises in CBT, in 1969 (Crellin, 1998). Crellin has argued that the concept of formulation (and its earlier versions of functional analysis) played a crucial political role in establishing the expert status and independence of the fledgling profession, which was at that time over-shadowed by psychiatry and also in competition with a number of other professions with a claim to alleviate mental distress. Indeed the profession still claims, contrary to Health Professions Council (2009) regulations, that 'this activity (is) unique to clinical psychologists' (Division of Clinical Psychology, 2010: 6).

In CBT, formulation is located firmly within a scientific, experimental framework as 'a central process in the role of the scientific practitioner' (Tarrier and Calam, 2002: 311). It is 'an elegant application of science' (Kinderman, 2001: 9). Similarly, clinical psychologists are described as using 'psychological science to help solve human problems' (Division of Clinical Psychology, 2010: 3).

Systemic approaches

The concept of working hypotheses has been central to the practice of family therapy from the late 1970s (Palazzoli et al., 1980). In the early years of family therapy there was an emphasis on making 'objective' and 'scientific' assessments and formulations of a family 'out there', and mapping their dysfunctions (Dallos and Draper, 2000). The 'symptoms' displayed by one member were seen as part of an attempted solution that was serving a function for the whole family. More recently there has been a recognition that the therapist's values and assumptions are inevitably part of the process of formulating, and that there is no such thing as 'the truth' about a given family. This represented a shift from a position of certainty, from which the families were assessed in terms of their 'dysfunctions', to one in which it is recognised that there are multiple realities in any given situation; there is no one way of viewing a family and thus the therapist holds 'working hypotheses' not truths. This frees the therapist to allow new and different ideas to enter their thinking. Later still, the emphasis moved towards the holding of a position of 'curiosity' rather than hypotheses or formulations.

Systemic formulations, or working hypotheses, must therefore retain an 'as if' quality, and be constantly open to revision ('progressive hypothesising'). Their worth is best judged not in terms of 'truth' but by their usefulness in helping to bring about change.

A social constructionist perspective is influential in current systemic thinking, leading to an increasing awareness of the wider socio-cultural context in which therapists and clients exist, and the variety of assumptions that shape our understandings of what, and whose, the problem is. Systemic approaches have always drawn on social and relational, rather than medical, factors for their hypotheses. The process of hypothesising might nowadays include questions about the role of social inequalities; of competing views of the problem that may be held by agencies such as social services, psychiatry, the school and so on; the role of therapists as employees of the state; and the more general cultural assumptions about how families 'should be'.

Other therapeutic traditions

As noted above, not all therapeutic approaches use formulation as a starting point. Humanistic therapists have been reluctant to engage in a process that Carl Rogers (1951) saw as an unhelpful imposition of an expert view on the client's experience, a theme that has been taken up in different ways by social constructionist and social inequality writers (see chapters 5 and 6). In the case of social constructionist and social inequalities perspectives, the distinctive characteristic is a reluctance to engage in a traditional process of psychological formulation and a preference for alternative ways of generating useful ideas or narratives. Further possibilities are introduced by the increasing tendency for therapists to work integratively; that is, to draw from a number of different models in their formulation and intervention, as described in chapter 8.

Best practice in formulation

As already noted, any therapeutic practice or procedure can be harmful as well as helpful depending on how it is used, and formulation is no exception. The issue of potential damage is discussed further in chapter 12. It is also addressed in the DCP Guidelines (2011), which includes checklists of best practice for formulation (as an event) and formulating (as a process). The former list specifies that formulation should, along with serving the purposes listed by Butler (1998), meet the following criteria:

- Grounded in an appropriate level and breadth of assessment (chapters 2, 3 and 7);
- Culturally sensitive (chapters 4, 5, 6 and 12);
- Expressed in accessible language (chapters 5 and 10);
- Considers the possible role of trauma and abuse (chapters 6 and 10);
- Includes the impact and personal meaning of medical and other healthcare interventions (chapters 4, 6,10 and 11);
- Considers possible role of services in compounding the difficulties (chapters 4, 5, 6 and 10);
- Informed by service/organisational factors (chapters 4, 10 and 11);
- Informed by awareness of social/societal factors (chapters 5 and 6).

These aspects are discussed in more detail in the DCP Guidelines. They are also explored throughout this book, especially in the indicated chapters.

In addition, the Guidelines include two criteria which may be controversial outside the particular profession for which they were developed (and to some extent within it). These are: 'Informed by a range of models and causal factors' and 'Is not premised on a functional psychiatric diagnosis', which are discussed in depth in chapters 10 and 12 respectively.

The checklist of best practice in formulating (formulation-as-a-process) specifies that the clinician:

- is clear about who the formulation is for (individual, family, team, etc;)
- is clear about who has the 'problem';
- is clear about who are the stakeholders and their interests;
- is respectful of the service user's/team's view about what is accurate/helpful;
- constructs the formulation collaboratively with the service user/team;
- paces the development and sharing of the formulation appropriately;
- can provide a rationale for choices within formulation (integrative, single model or partial);
- is reflective about their own values and assumptions.

These aspects are also explored in more detail throughout the book.

Conclusion

Psychological formulation has been used under various synonyms for many years, but has recently attained new prominence. The editors of this book see formulation as having many strengths, but at the same time take a constructively critical view of its limitations. Both viewpoints will be explored thoroughly in the following chapters, which illustrate the very different, although sometimes overlapping, formulations that could be relevant to our two clients, Jack and Janet. Their stories are outlined below.

Jack

Jack is 25 and was referred to a clinical psychology department shortly after his admission to an acute inpatient unit, because nursing staff felt that unresolved issues in his life were contributing to his distress. He was quite 'high' in mood for much of the time, talking non-stop about music, but at other times would lapse into tears and say that he and his life were a hopeless mess.

Jack was born and brought up in Swindon. His father, who came to England in 1979 from Southern Italy, had worked his way up from humble origins to become head of a chain of shops, and the family was well off and comfortably settled as part of the community. His mother stayed at home to bring up the family, which consisted of Jack and his three younger sisters. Jack did well at school and was popular and sociable, with a talent for music, and there were strong expectations that as the only son he would carry on the family business.

Jack's father was an alcoholic and was violent to his wife and children. Both the drinking and the violence worsened as his business began to run into trouble, when Jack was about 10. When Jack was 14, he took on a Saturday delivery job and was sexually abused on several occasions by the male boss. He felt unable to confide in his family and was still very reluctant to discuss these events at the time of referral; no other details are known.

Jack himself started drinking from the age of 15, and failed his GCSEs. Around this time his parents divorced and his father moved back to Italy and has not kept in contact. Jack has very mixed feelings of love and hate towards his father, although his sisters seem to believe they are better off without him. The effect on the family was disastrous; they had to sell their comfortable house, lose contact with the Italian community in Swindon and move to central Bristol, where Jack's mother tried to make ends meet by various low-paid jobs. The family were harassed and burgled on a number of occasions.

Meanwhile, Jack continued to go off the rails, drinking, taking drugs and becoming involved in petty theft. A pattern developed in which he would hold down a job for a few months, but invariably slip back into drinking. Eventually, after some violent rows at home, his mother threw him out and he slept rough for a few months. At around this time he was first referred to the psychiatric services for outpatient appointments and was diagnosed as depressed. He was put in touch with a project for the homeless and appeared to settle for a while.

About two years later, Jack's mother developed some serious health problems and finances became even more stretched. At around the same time Jack began to develop the first signs of what was diagnosed variously as 'paranoia' and 'persistent delusional disorder', when he started to complain that Robbie Williams (the pop singer) had stolen his songs and his royalties and that Robbie's friends were out to beat him up or kill him. He also believed that Robbie had raped one of his sisters. He described the frightening experience of looking in the mirror and seeing his father's face reflected back at him.

Eventually Jack was admitted to hospital at his family's request, where he became a little more settled, but still convinced of the truth of his ideas and reluctant to address the problem of how he was going to put his life back on track, because he was anticipating a huge royalty cheque any day. He was compliant with medication and said he found it helpful.

It was hard for the psychologist to get a clear agreement about what to work on, given Jack's tendency to escape into fantasy. Problem areas identified by Jack were:

- He was desperate to get hold of the royalties that were, he believed, due to him.
- He was afraid to go out in case he was attacked by Robbie Williams' minders.
- He was very concerned about and protective of his family, especially the sister who, he believed, had been raped (although the sister said that no such event had taken place).
- He missed his father and was confused about his feelings for him. When he saw his father's face in the mirror he was filled with fear and self-loathing.

Janet

Janet, aged 9, was referred by a school nurse to the primary care therapy service serving GPs in an inner city locality. Social services had previously been alerted about a number of contacts with the Accident and Emergency department of the local hospital, although no evidence of abuse had been found. Mary, Janet's mother, had also contacted social services for various reasons including a request for a wheelchair to help with Janet's mobility problems. She was concerned that Janet was not developing properly and wondered if this was linked to Janet's reluctance to travel or use public transport. In addition, Mary and the school nurse had concerns about Janet's low weight. Janet was already being reviewed at yearly intervals by the paediatric consultant because of worries about her development as an infant. On assessment, no physical problems were evident.

Mary, in her late forties, separated from Janet's father, Colin, when Janet was 3. He still lives nearby, and was until recently having overnight contact with Janet at his home. Janet has now said she does not want this to continue, although she still sees her father. Colin is a heavy drinker and was violent towards Mary. Colin and Mary's older child, Andrew, aged 12, is doing well at school, both academically and socially. He also lives with Mary and Janet, and hopes to join the police force when he grows up.

Mary says that she found it 'hard to bond' with Janet when she was born, and felt sad and depressed for a long time after the birth. At times she wished Janet could be taken away, although she did not feel this way about her other children. This is hard for her to understand, and makes her feel guilty.

Mary has four older children from an earlier relationship, two of whom live in the same street, and Mary is very involved with her two infant grandchildren. She is particularly proud of the son who has done well educationally and become a schoolteacher. Mary is also close to her sister, Cindy, who lives locally and has no children of her own, but has a special relationship with Janet and takes a close interest in her.

The family have always lived in a very socially deprived location in local authority accommodation, alongside some of the most 'difficult' families in the area. The estate is due for demolition and the family has been waiting to be re-housed for the last two years. They are a Romany family and this is a central part of their identity, expressed in a strong interest in spiritualism and clairvoyance. A clairvoyant had told Mary about a 'white car', which Mary connected with Janet's nightmare about a 'white van' and her fear of using any form of transport.

At the time of referral, Mary was awaiting a heart operation, having suffered from angina and arrhythmia for a number of years. This means that she easily becomes exhausted.

The referral letter documented Mary's many concerns about Janet, including her weight loss, behaviour at home and refusal to use transport, although she will walk to school, town and therapy sessions. This is paralleled by her mother's limited mobility, which is resulting in them both becoming more withdrawn and isolated, especially from their extended family. Mary describes Janet as being a prisoner in her own home.

Janet was also described as being unable to sleep in her own bed because of night terrors, so that she often ends up sharing Mary's bed; losing her temper (including once setting the dog on her mother); and refusing to eat food prepared for her by Mary, so that she is now seriously underweight. However, she has friends at school, joins in quite enthusiastically, and is achieving adequately for her age.

References

Aveline, M. (1999) 'The advantages of formulation over categorical diagnosis in explorative psychotherapy and psychodynamic management', *European Journal of Psychotherapy, Counselling and Health*, 2 (2), 199–216.

Bateman, A. and Holmes, J. (1995) *Introduction to Psychoanalysis: Contemporary Theory and Practice*. London, New York: Routledge.

Beck, A. T. (1976) *Cognitive Therapy and Emotional Disorders*. New York: Meridian.

Bruch, M. and Bond, F.W. (1998) *Beyond Diagnosis: Case Formulation Approaches in Cognitive – Behavioural Therapy*. London: Wiley.

Butler, G. (1998) 'Clinical formulation' in A.S. Bellack and M. Hersen (eds) *Comprehensive Clinical Psychology*. Oxford: Pergamon, pp. 1–23.

Corrie, S. and Lane, D. (eds) (2010) *Constructing Stories, Telling Tales: A Guide to Formulation in Applied Psychology*. London: Karnac Books.

Crellin, C. (1998) 'Origins and social contexts of the term "formulation" in psychological case reports', *Clinical Psychology Forum*, 112, 18–28.

Dallos, R. and Draper, R. (2000) *Introduction to Family Therapy: Systemic Theory and Practice*. Maidenhead: Oxford University Press.

Division of Clinical Psychology (2010) *The Core Purpose and Philosophy of the Profession*. Leicester: The British Psychological Society.

——(2011) *Good Practice Guidelines on the Use of Psychological Formulation*. Leicester: The British Psychological Society.

Eells, T.D. (2006a) (ed.) *Handbook of Psychotherapy Case Formulation*, 2nd edn, New York, London: The Guilford Press.

——(2006b) 'History and current status of psychotherapy case formulation' in T.D. Eells (ed.) *Handbook of Psychotherapy Case Formulation*, 2nd edn, New York, London: The Guilford Press, pp. 3–32.

Grant, A., Townend, M., Mill, J. and Cockx, A. (2008) *Assessment and Case Formulation in Cognitive Behavioural Therapy*. London: Sage.

Harper, D. and Moss, D. (2003) 'A different kind of chemistry? Re-formulating formulation', *Clinical Psychology*, 25, 6–10.

Hayes, S.C. and Follette, W.C. (1992) 'Can functional analysis provide a substitute for syndromal classification?', *Behavioral Assessment*, 14, 345–365.

Health Professions Council (2009) *Standards of Proficiency: Practitioner Psychologists*. London: Health Professions Council.

Ingram, B.L. (2006) *Clinical Case Formulations: Matching the Integrative Treatment Plan to the Client*. Hoboken, New Jersey: John Wiley and Sons.

Kinderman, P. (2001) 'The future of clinical psychology training', *Clinical Psychology*, 8, 6–10.

Kuyken, W., Padesky, C. and Dudley, R. (2009) *Collaborative Case Conceptualization: Working Effectively with Clients in Cognitive-Behavioral Therapy*. New York, London: The Guilford Press.

Lombardo, E. and Nezu, A.M. (2004) *Cognitive-Behavioral Case Formulation and Treatment Design*. New York: Springer Publishing Company.

McGrath, G. and Margison. M. (2000) 'The dynamic formulation'. Online. Available http://www.geocities.com/~nwidp/course/dyn_form.htm (accessed 19 October 2004).

Meyer, V. and Turkat, I.D. (1979) 'Behavioural analysis of clinical cases', *Journal of Behavioural Assessment*, 1, 259–269.

Palazzoli, M.S., Boscolo, L., Cecchin, G. and Prata, G. (1980) 'Hypothesising – circularity – neutrality: three guidelines for the conductor of the session', *Family Process*, 19, 3–12.

Persons, J.B. (1989) *Cognitive Therapy in Practice: A Case Formulation Approach*. New York, London: W.W. Norton & Company.

Rogers, C. (1951) *Client-Centered Therapy: Its Current Practice, Implications and Theory*. Boston: Houghton Mifflin.

Royal College of Psychiatrists (2010) *A Competency-based Curriculum for Specialist Core Training in Psychiatry*. Available www.rcpsych.ac.uk/training/curriculum2010.aspx (accessed 5 August 2012).

Sturmey, P. (2008) *Behavioural Case Formulation and Intervention: A Functional Analytic Approach*. Chichester: John Wiley and Sons.

Tarrier, N. (2006) (ed.) *Case Formulation in Cognitive Behaviour Therapy: The Treatment of Challenging and Complex Cases*. Hove, New York: Routledge.

Tarrier, N. and Calam, R. (2002) 'New developments in cognitive-behavioural case formulation', *Behavioural and Cognitive Psychotherapy*, 30, 311–328.

Weerasekera, P. (1996) *Multiperspective Case Formulation: A Step Towards Treatment Integration*, Malabar, Florida: Krieger.

Chapter 2

Case formulation in cognitive behavioural therapy

A principle-driven approach

Robert Dudley and Willem Kuyken

A principled approach to CBT case conceptualisation

Case formulation is described as the 'lynchpin' of Cognitive Behavioural Therapy (CBT) (Butler, 1998). This is because it improves practice by explaining clients' presentations in a theoretically informed, coherent and meaningful way which leads to effective interventions. Essentially formulation helps marry the unique experience of the client with the skills, theory and knowledge we bring as therapists to help us understand and alleviate the client's presenting issues. Given this, it is understandable why formulation is seen as one of the key elements of CBT (Beck, 2011). In this chapter we describe principles that underpin effective CBT case formulation. We illustrate this process with reference to the cases of Jack and Janet.

CBT has an established evidence base for helping a wide variety of presenting issues. Consequently, there is now an abundance of treatment manuals for clinicians to base their therapy on. However, this can leave the clinician with the daunting challenge of drawing on a vast range of resources whilst at the same time attending to the very human and important task of engaging with, understanding and helping the individual client.

A second challenge is that clients rarely present with one single disorder (Dudley et al., 2010). Co-morbidity is the norm but the evidence base demonstrating the effectiveness of CBT largely reflects the results of research on single disorders. In such instances there may not be a treatment manual that fits the client's unique presenting features. So whilst CBT prides itself on its scientific foundations there is considerable art in its application. For these reasons we advocate a principle-based approach to formulation rather than recommending a specific template or manual. This ensures that the formulation is tailored to the client rather than vice versa.

Kuyken, Padesky and Dudley (2008, 2009) use the metaphor of a crucible to illustrate the process of CBT case conceptualisation. A crucible is a robust vessel for combining different substances so that they are synthesised into something new. In the same way, the case conceptualisation process synthesises a person's presenting issues and experiences with CBT theory and research to form a new understanding, personal and specific to the client. CBT theory and research are key ingredients in the crucible.

The crucible metaphor further illustrates three defining principles of case conceptualisation. First, the process of change is facilitated by heating the vessel to drive the reactions. In our model, collaborative empiricism produces the heat that encourages the process of conceptualisation and accelerates the transformation. In a collaborative approach, the perspectives of therapist and client are combined to develop a shared understanding that accounts for the development and maintenance of the presenting issues. Working together increases the likelihood that the outcome is acceptable and useful to the client, and informs the selection of helpful interventions.

Second, like the reaction in a crucible, a conceptualisation develops over time. Typically it begins at more descriptive levels (e.g. describing presenting issues in cognitive and behavioural terms), moves to include explanatory models (e.g. a theory-based understanding of how the symptoms are maintained or perpetuated) and, if necessary, develops further to include a historical explanation of how pre-disposing and protective factors played a role in the development of the issues (e.g. the developmental history). In this way formulations can be built up layer upon layer over the course of therapy.

Third, what is formed in the crucible depends on the properties of the ingredients placed into it – including the client's experiences and CBT theory and research. Historically there has been an emphasis on clients' problems and distress, but while these are naturally included in our model it also incorporates client strengths at every stage. This helps both to alleviate distress and build client resilience. Their personal and social resources are protective factors which have prevented problems from escalating; have enabled clients to build up a repertoire of resources and successes; and suggest an intervention strategy of 'least resistance' that builds on strengths. Protective factors can be described as 'all that is right with a person', including personal resources (e.g. intellectual ability, physical health, hobbies and interests, financial resources, etc.) and social resources (e.g. a close and confiding friendship or relationship). Accordingly, client strengths are an essential part of the crucible's ingredients.

We illustrate the three key principles of case conceptualisation, which are levels of conceptualisation, collaborative empiricism and incorporation of client strengths, with particular reference to the case of Jack. In this way we demonstrate how the principles help inform the decision as to which cognitive model to select as the basis of the formulation, how to develop the understanding with the client and then how to utilise this shared understanding to help the client optimally. Before we do this, it is important to note that the authors of this chapter have not spoken to the real Jack (or Janet). Normally within CBT there would be detailed eliciting of the client's perspective and the thoughts, feelings and behaviours associated with the presenting issues. Moreover, collaboration means that conceptualisations are co-created by client and therapist which clearly has not been possible in this instance. However, in the spirit of the book we will illustrate the process of cognitive formulation for Jack using the available material.

Jack

Principle 1: levels of conceptualisation

As a starting point it is helpful to understand that a CBT formulation is developed from the cognitive model. The cognitive model is based on the deceptively simple idea that how we view ourselves, the world and the future shapes our emotions and behaviours. People are thought to develop emotional disorders when they are locked into unhelpful patterns of interpretation and behaviours (Beck, 2011). These moment-to-moment appraisals or interpretations of current experience are shaped by more enduring beliefs that we hold about ourselves, other people and the world around us. From this comes the idea that if we evaluate and modify unrealistic or unhelpful thinking, we can profoundly affect our emotional wellbeing. Lasting changes occur when people are able to modify dysfunctional beliefs and learn healthier and more adaptive beliefs. This helps prevent relapse and enables people to remain well in the future.

We suggest a framework for CBT formulation that helps link the person's experiences to the cognitive model using the five Ps: presenting issues, precipitating, perpetuating, predisposing, and protective factors. We examine the Ps in turn, outlining how each relates to therapy (Table 2.1). They are presented as we might typically expect them to unfold in the course of therapy, from description to inference.

We begin with the presenting issues, as preliminary conceptualisations are usually quite descriptive and should be closely mapped onto the experiences and difficulties that clients report.

Presenting issues

When people come to therapy they are usually looking for help with specific problems, even if these may not initially be well articulated in their own minds. They may feel sad, lack energy or be anxious when around people. The assessment phase seeks to generate a list of presenting issues that is specific, clear and useful to the client and therapist. For instance, instead of writing the problem as 'depression', the person might be asked, 'In what way does depression show itself in your day, or your life?' This may indicate very specific and individual problems like not getting out of bed. A comprehensive assessment in terms of cognition, affect and behaviour in the context of relevant psychosocial factors helps us better understand the needs of the client and address the question of where to start working when faced with a multitude of presenting problems. A

Table 2.1 The five Ps of CBT formulation

The five Ps	Relationship to therapy
Presenting issues. Statement of the client's presenting problems in terms of emotions, thoughts and behaviours.	This process goes beyond diagnosis in that we begin to define the current problems the person faces. This introduces specificity and individualisation. We also define short-, medium- and long-term goals that can help identify the likely end point of therapy. This process helps to develop the therapeutic relationship, clarifies problems and instils hope.
Precipitating factors. The proximal external and internal factors that triggered the current presenting issues.	Introduces the cognitive model and provides initial focus for CBT interventions. If successful builds clients' confidence in themselves, therapy and therapist.
Perpetuating factors. The internal and external factors that maintain the current problems.	Provides a focus for intervention by breaking the maintenance cycle.
Predisposing factors. The distal external and internal factors that increased the person's vulnerability to their current problems.	Provides a longitudinal understanding of the problems and a focus for more in-depth interventions that aim to maintain change and prevent relapse.
Protective factors. The person's resiliency and strengths that help maintain emotional health.	Provides a path of least resistance by suggesting interventions that build on existing resiliency and strengths. Also provides pathways to long-term recovery.

clear description of the issues helps establish the goals of treatment. Agreement of goals is a key process in the development of an effective therapeutic alliance, which is a robust predictor of outcome (Martin et al., 2000).

Despite the initial focus on *current* problems and goals, CBT is also interested in the developmental origins of the difficulties. Hence, an initial assessment would normally include relevant background and context to the presenting issues (onset of the problems, family, educational, occupational and psychiatric history, personal and social resources and so on), which in the later stages of formulation enable a more in-depth understanding. While the assessment process is not strictly formulation, it is essential groundwork for a CBT formulation.

Jack is described as experiencing a number of problems including periods of mania and low mood, anger and anxiety that seems to result from persistent delusional beliefs with both persecutory and grandiose themes. He has had problems with substance misuse and had a period of inpatient admission.

We would ask Jack for concrete and specific examples of how his presenting problems affect him. He may identify his difficulties as feeling low, lacking in motivation, feeling afraid when out or having no money. From this initial description, goals of treatment are articulated (Greenberger and Padesky, 1995). Jack and his therapist may agree to focus on trying to feel better in mood, to have more money and to be able to go out without fear of being beaten up. If he were more able to go out, we would ask how he would like to spend his time and with whom (which may reveal something about his strengths and his values; see principle three).

Having constructed a list of presenting issues and goals the therapist would work collaboratively with Jack to identify the area that caused greatest distress or had greatest impact on his life. Thus, low mood or his fear of being attacked may become the initial focus of therapy. Generating a presenting issues list that is collaboratively reviewed and prioritised is an important initial task of treatment.

The next level of CBT formulation involves articulating the external and internal factors that tend to trigger the presenting issues. On closer questioning it is usually the case that people experience some variation in their presenting problems according to time and place. As already described, the cognitive model emphasises that it is not the events themselves, but a person's view of the events, that explains their reaction. When people are asked what has led to them being anxious or sad they often describe events: 'I am unhappy because I am divorced/bankrupt/out of a job'. It goes without saying that these situations can be distressing to us all. However, it is also obvious we do not all respond to stressful events in the same way. To begin the process of socialisation to the cognitive model we might draw upon a simple four factor version that differentiates situation, thoughts, feelings and behaviour. This helps separate out the original event from the interpretation and consequences. The person may say 'I am sad because I spilled my coffee'. The simplified model helps illustrate the importance of thoughts (or Negative Automatic Thoughts as they are referred to) and images (Hackmann et al., 2011) in determining distress by explicitly introducing the notion of an appraisal between the situation and the emotion (see Figure 2.1).

Such specific and personalised examples help illustrate the fact that there may be different ways of seeing any situation and that thoughts and images are not necessarily facts or truths, but points of view. Using the collaborative but questioning style of CBT we can ask whether everyone would feel sad on spilling coffee, would others react differently, would the person him or herself have thought and reacted differently before they became depressed.

Jack seems to meet the diagnostic criteria for a psychotic illness characterised by persecutory beliefs. Whilst disorder-specific approaches exist for such difficulties (Freeman, 2007), the common starting point is to map the presenting issues, and develop an initial understanding that is not limited by a specific model. The key point is that the model is not pre-selected and the client is not fitted to the model.

In Jack's case (Figure 2.2), a simple descriptive model may help to reveal that his low mood, anger and anxiety are intimately tied to his persecutory

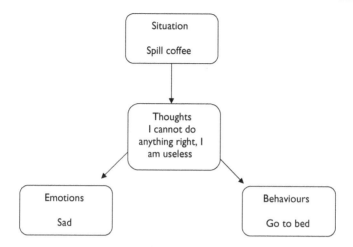

Figure 2.1 Illustration of an initial cognitive model

concerns. We may initially build up a series of such descriptive formulations using recent examples from Jack's life. In this way we can identify common triggering factors, common appraisals and common reactions that help us understand his experience. These could be summarised as in the last example in Figure 2.2.

Perpetuating factors

Although the descriptive model is a useful heuristic device it does not really explain what maintains the issues in the long term. Hence, we draw on an expanded model that articulates the relationship between the elements, and helps to show the reinforcing nature of the problems. This model often includes more explicit information about the physiological responses to a situation (Greenberger and Padesky, 1995). This cross-sectional or maintenance model emphasises the perpetuating features that add inferential hypotheses about how the problem is maintained by cognitive and behavioural factors (see Figure 2.3). This is the classic maintenance or vicious cycle of Cognitive Therapy.

In such a model, the direction of the arrows is important and the initial phase of therapy must provide a defensible rationale for the links between components. For instance, we need to consider the way that behaviour in a given model might maintain an appraisal.

Within the CBT research literature there is an increasing emphasis on understanding the specific and key features unique to each different disorder (see Wells, 1996). However, there are several core cognitive and behavioural mechanisms that are common to a range of different types of psychopathology (Harvey et al., 2004). These include various forms of emotional and behavioural

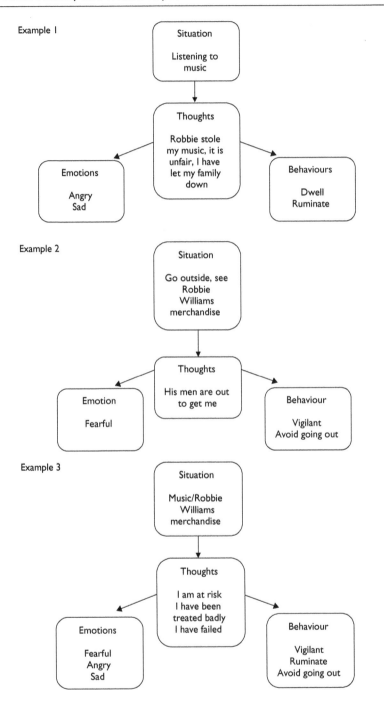

Figure 2.2 Jack's presenting problems mapped onto a simple descriptive formulation

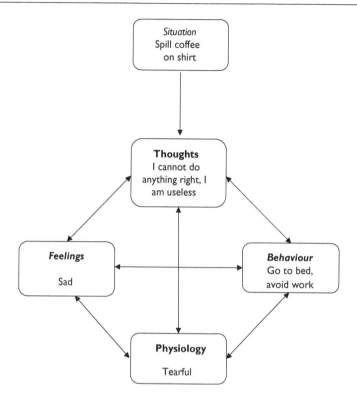

Figure 2.3 Perpetuating factors

avoidance, attentional processes such as vigilance for threat, and cognitive processes like rumination and worry (Dudley et al., 2010).

An important perpetuating mechanism in many CBT formulations is avoidance, which prevents the person finding out whether a feared consequence will occur. In the case above (Figure 2.3), by avoiding going to work the person may actually confirm a view of him or herself as useless. Avoiding situations can also lead to a loss of rewarding and pleasurable behaviours, and thus help to maintain problems like depression. However, problems may continue even without avoidance. It seems that when people do go into difficult situations, they may engage in subtle behaviours that serve to keep them safe, or 'safety-seeking behaviours' (Salkovskis et al., 1996). For instance, Jack may be worried about being noticed and attacked when he leaves home, and so he may keep his sweatshirt hood up to stop people recognising him. These behaviours, intended to help, prevent disconfirmation of the belief, and maintain it. Paradoxically, they can even make things worse; for instance, by masking his face Jack may be more scrutinised by shop staff or security guards when he goes out, thereby increasing his belief that he is being watched.

A cognitive behavioural model of maintenance provides a rationale for a number of interventions, since change in any of the maintenance elements will create change in the others. Clients will be encouraged to identify, evaluate and challenge their thoughts, which in turn means that they are likely to appraise situations differently and thus feel and behave differently. Behavioural methods may help overcome avoidance and prompt change in feeling and thoughts. The main behavioural approaches involve increasing positively reinforcing behaviours (e.g. behaviours that are pleasurable and generate a sense of mastery in people diagnosed with depression) and extinguishing or replacing negative behaviours (e.g. 'safety behaviours').

Maintenance formulations or cross-sectional formulations capture the reinforcing and spiralling nature of Jack's current difficulties (Figure 2.4) in which avoidance and vigilance seem to be important factors.

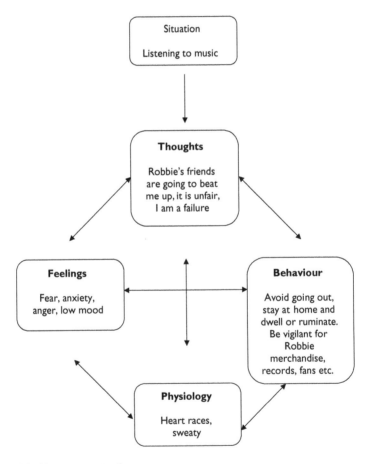

Figure 2.4 Jack's perpetuating factors

Jack also reports using rumination and this would be incorporated into the developing conceptualisation as well. This provides a strong rationale for targeting these processes with specific interventions for overcoming avoidance, and rumination (Watkins et al., 2007).

Precipitating factors

Although cross-sectional or maintenance models help us understand what may be perpetuating a problem we may still be unclear what led to the onset of the difficulties. To understand this we introduce the notion of a longitudinal or historical formulation that identifies a precipitant or trigger to the onset of the difficulties, which commonly turns out to be a particularly stressful event or time.

Quantity of stressors

Stress-vulnerability models help us to understand the onset of difficulties (e.g. Neuchterlain and Dawson, 1984) by emphasising that we are all susceptible to stressors in our lives and our vulnerability specifies the point at which we can no longer function or cope. Although this broad model specifies the likelihood that a breakdown will occur, it is less specific on what may lead one person to develop depression and another anxiety. Here, we need to consider the meaning of the events to the person and whether there were specific risks for that person that made those events particularly stressful; in other words, the quality rather than the quantity of events, their particular and unique meaning to the person, and whether they carried a specific vulnerability or predisposition.

Quality of stressors

To account for potential predisposition or vulnerabilities we draw upon a longitudinal model (see Figure 2.5). In this (Beck 2011; Persons 2008), precipitating factors trigger access to a deeply seated view of oneself (core beliefs or schema, or internal predisposing factors) that was learned through formative developmental experiences (external predisposing factors). For instance, a person may see him or herself as fundamentally unlovable (core belief) owing to early experiences of neglect. This basic belief is highly emotionally charged and deeply ingrained. Before the triggering event occurred, the person has managed or coped by employing a rule or assumption of some sort that has prevented accessing this affect-laden view of oneself (e.g. 'If I am in a relationship then I am OK'). Rules, assumptions or conditional beliefs are often phrased in this style of 'if ... then'; or sometimes as imperatives such as 'I must', 'I should'; or as 'I ought'; for example, 'I must always be in a relationship'. The rules, assumptions and conditional beliefs in turn are directly linked to a repertoire of compensatory strategies that keep the person living within their belief system (e.g. working hard to maintain relationships and avoid perceived abandonment, perhaps by being unfailingly attentive and loyal to their partner). Here we can see that the developmental experiences, core beliefs, conditional assumptions and compensatory strategies are related to each other in understandable ways. At the end of the relationship the rule is broken and accesses the very affect-laden core belief. This event acts as the trigger or precipitant for the presentation. Once started, the presentation is perpetuated through the patterns of relationships outlined in the maintenance models.

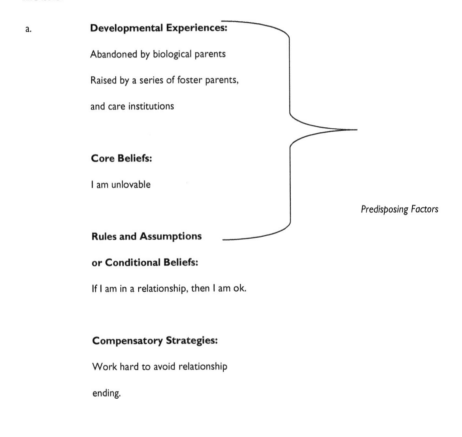

a.

Developmental Experiences:

Abandoned by biological parents

Raised by a series of foster parents,

and care institutions

Core Beliefs:

I am unlovable

Predisposing Factors

Rules and Assumptions

or Conditional Beliefs:

If I am in a relationship, then I am ok.

Compensatory Strategies:

Work hard to avoid relationship

ending.

Triggering events   *Precipitating Factors*

End of the relationship

b.   **Maintenance Cycles**

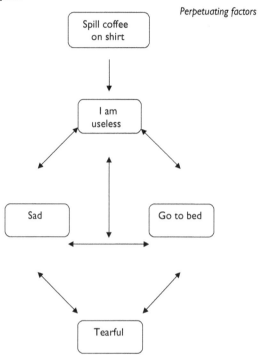

c.   **Problems**   *Presenting issues*

Difficulty concentrating,
Problems attending work
Feeling lonely
Not ringing people to arrange to go out
Not answering the phone
Avoiding people in case I cry
Not being able to sleep
Feeling sad and low

Resilience and strengths   *Protective factors*

Supportive adoptive mother and sister
Good friend
Good job, well paid
Interest in sports, and plays badminton every week
Good sense of humour

Figure 2.5 An illustration of a longitudinal formulation

In the middle and later stages of CBT, conceptualisations increasingly draw on theory and inference to explain how predisposing and protective factors contribute to clients' presenting issues. Each disorder-specific model indicates the key processes, beliefs and assumptions that are thought to help account for the particular disorder.

Predisposing factors: quantity of events

When working with people with psychosis a very common process is to generate an understanding of the events leading to the emergence of the first psychotic symptoms, using a stress-vulnerability model (Brabban and Turkington, 2002). The particular stressors for Jack appeared to consist of a series of difficult life events, perhaps precipitated by sexual abuse. Trauma experiences are increasingly being recognised as important in the onset and maintenance of psychosis (Callcott et al., 2010; Dudley et al., 2010). For Jack, the trauma seemed to have led to drinking and drug taking, and resulted in him failing his GCSEs. These experiences, combined with moving house to a less affluent area where the family was burgled, his father leaving following the parental separation, and loss of contact with his friends, left Jack increasingly isolated. This is very much a quantity model, in that we can see Jack was under considerable stress in the time preceding the development of his depression and eventual psychotic breakdown. Understanding the precipitants would allow the provision of information about the role of sleep deprivation, trauma, drug use and so on in the onset of persecutory beliefs. This could help normalise the onset of psychosis (Dudley and Turkington, 2010) and help Jack to identify triggers and risk factors. Thus, a longitudinal formulation may help us understand Jack's particular vulnerabilities and what it was about the triggering events that was so very upsetting for him.

Predisposing factors: quality of events

Jack's history indicates that he was subject to physical and presumably verbal abuse when his father was drunk. He may have seen himself as to blame for his father's anger, and may have believed that he was a disappointment in his father's eyes: 'not good enough'. He may also have internalised the notion that men cope with their distress by drinking alcohol. Hence, we have a hypothetical and provisional core belief, as well as some possible rules. Jack's early experiences may also have led him to internalise a view of himself as having to provide for and protect his sisters and mother. This is the role his father undertook, and possibly a view shared by the community he comes from. This would probably give Jack a view of success as consisting of working hard, being financially successful and fulfilling the roles expected of a man. As a result Jack may once again see himself as weak or as not good enough. Also, given his experiences of abuse he may well view others as untrustworthy, cruel and unkind. Negative beliefs about others are characteristic of people with paranoia in the context of psychosis (Freeman, 2007). His compensatory strategies are to cope with difficult emotions with drugs, and to work hard to achieve success and financial security. However, alcohol abuse eventually led to losing his job. This increased the pressure on him to succeed, and hence increased the pressure to cope by drinking.

Trauma such as sexual abuse can manifest itself as a post-traumatic stress disorder (PTSD), or as a damaged view of self (Callcott et al., 2010). In the absence of overt PTSD symptomatology we would consider the possible meaning of these events for Jack: perhaps he concluded that he is in some way a bad person; or that he should not have let this happen; or he may have questioned his own sexuality. Given the role of masculinity in Jack's community, an experience like this would probably be difficult to discuss, thus denying him the opportunity to consider alternative perspectives on abuse. All of these hypotheses would be examined by questioning Jack gently about what he understood to have happened to him, what this says about him as a person and what it means about other people.

These experiences and beliefs help us understand the importance of the triggering events: Jack's parents' relationship deteriorating and his father leaving and losing contact. Faced with this pressure, Jack began to drink as presumably this was his model of how men coped with stress. He failed his GCSEs, the family moved, and his mother had to go to work, further reminding Jack that he was not providing for the family. It is likely that he was depressed from around this time. His mother's ill health presumably increased the pressure on Jack even more, and he began to develop psychotic and persecutory beliefs. People with paranoia have a tendency to blame others for negative events (Freeman, 2007) and consequently when Jack was trying to make sense of his lack of success he may have been drawn to an explanation that blamed another person rather than himself or the situation.

Jack's lifestyle of sleeping rough and using drink and drugs will have dysregulated his basic self-care (e.g. sleep, diet), increasing the chance of abnormal ideation and experiences such as seeing his father's face in the mirror (Collerton et al., 2012).

At this level of conceptualisation, a number of interventions may help to interrupt the maintenance processes and also encourage Jack to consider the usefulness of his strategies and the helpfulness of his beliefs about himself and other people (Beck, 2011). Owing to the speculative nature of this formulation (see Figure 2.6) there is no way in which we can determine its accuracy. However, in the clinical setting we would use the principle of collaborative empiricism to help us establish its accuracy and utility.

The therapist and client would work together to co-create the formulation using the questioning style of cognitive therapy (see Kuyken et al., 2009: 193–195 for illustrations of this process). Hence we now consider the second principle of collaborative empiricism.

Early Experiences:

Father physically and verbally abusive when drunk

Only son in a family in which the expectations are men will provide for the family

Successful father works hard and provides a high standard of living

Core Beliefs:

I am not good enough/I am a failure/weak

Others are cruel and rejecting

Rules and Assumptions or Conditional Beliefs:

If I work hard and provide for others then I am ok and not a failure

If I show my emotions others will be cruel and reject me

Compensatory Strategies:

Work hard to achieve and provide for others through work

Do not show emotions, mask them with drink or drugs

Triggering events:

Sexual abuse, end of the parental relationship, social changes, change in house and lifestyle

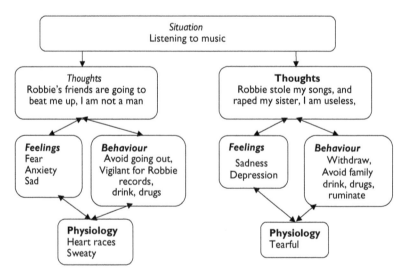

Protective factors:

    Music, school, previous community, mother and sisters

Figure 2.6 Jack's longitudinal formulation

Principle 2: collaborative empiricism

Collaboration refers to both therapist and client bringing their respective knowledge and expertise together in the joint task of describing, explaining and helping ameliorate the client's presenting issues. The therapist brings his/her relevant knowledge and skills of CBT theory, research and practice. The client brings his/her in-depth knowledge of the presenting issues, relevant background and the factors that he or she feels contribute to vulnerability and resilience.

Empiricism within therapy is evident in two main ways. First, the therapist draws on the research on CBT to determine its appropriateness for the particular presenting issue. Cognitive therapy was first developed to help people with mood disorders (Clark and Beck, 1999), but has been increasingly applied to a range of presenting problems and disorders. The breadth of application results from a commitment to empiricism, and the careful observation of specific diagnostically based disorders. This has helped to elucidate the cognitive and behavioural processes that characterise and maintain each presentation. These unique differences are empirically tested between people with the disorder and those without and are targeted with specific interventions (Wells, 1996) which are in turn evaluated using manualised treatments in Randomised Controlled Trials (RCTs). CBT has thus established an evidence base for a range of psychological and emotional difficulties (Butler et al., 2006; Wykes et al., 2008). CBT therapists use conceptualisation to adapt these manualised disorder-specific models and treatments and incorporate client-specific information and direct treatment with real world impact, equivalent to that seen in RCTs (Kuyken, 2006; Persons, 2008).

Given the substantial evidence base for many disorder-specific CBT approaches, a relatively straightforward mapping of client experience and theory may be possible with many clients. Nonetheless, it is always important to derive the case conceptualisation collaboratively so the client understands the applicability of the model to his or her issue. When clients experience multiple or more complex presenting issues it is often helpful to attend to trans-diagnostic processes like rumination, vigilance and avoidance (see Figures 2.1 and 2.2).

Another aspect of empiricism in therapy is the emphasis on observation and evaluation of experience. Therapists and clients develop hypotheses, devise adequate tests for these hypotheses and then adapt the hypotheses based on feedback from therapy interventions. This makes CBT an active and dynamic process, in which the conceptualisation guides and is corrected by feedback.

Since clients often do not have experience of CBT, in the early stages it can help to offer a rationale for collaborative working and to follow this up with actual experience of working together on a task. For instance the therapist may say to Jack: 'I find it best if we can work together to try and understand

and help your problems. It helps if we combine our efforts, so I need you to tell me what is important for you to cover, and I will have some ideas about what I think we should cover in our sessions together. How does that sound?' This would then be followed up by asking Jack what particular questions or issues he would like to work on in the session. This openness about collaboration would also be extended to the process of developing a formulation. The therapist may say: 'You know a lot about your situation and what has helped or not helped in the past, and I know what has helped other people. Perhaps if we can put this together we will find that we can share some ideas that may help you. How does that sound?'

Similarly, the therapist may introduce an element of a model, such as the potential maintaining role of vigilance, rumination or use of safety-seeking behaviours and then encourage Jack to gather evidence of whether this plays a contributory role in his case. The therapist may ask Jack to record over the coming week how often he finds himself dwelling on the idea that his music has been stolen and to note what effect it has on his mood. By jointly reviewing the outcome of this task using Socratic questioning, the therapist could establish whether vigilance has a legitimate role in the emerging conceptualisation of his concerns. Disorder-specific models of paranoia (Freeman, 2007) emphasise that people with delusions may have a tendency to 'jump to conclusions', blame others for negative events, or find it difficult to generate or consider alternative explanations for their experiences. These processes may be introduced and tested with Jack as well. This curiosity acts as a check and balance on the development of the formulation and to ensure its accuracy and usefulness.

Principle 3: include client strengths and conceptualise resilience

As discussed, we argue that a strengths-focused approach at every stage of conceptualisation helps to alleviate client distress and builds a person's resilience (Kuyken et al., 2008). For example, goals may include not just reducing distress (e.g. for Jack, to feel less anxious being around people) but increasing strengths or positive values (e.g. to be more able to enjoy time with my mother and sisters) as well. Accordingly, clinicians can routinely ask in early therapy sessions about positive goals and aspirations and add these to the client's presenting issues and goals list.

Specific discussion of positive areas of a person's life may reveal alternative coping strategies to those used in problem areas. These presumably more adaptive coping strategies can be identified as part of the same process that identifies triggers and maintenance factors for problems.

Owing to Jack's low mood it is possible that he easily overlooks or undervalues his strengths, but in the early stages of assessment and treatment the therapist can purposefully ask about those areas of his life which he manages more effectively, and even enjoys, and how he copes with his low mood and persecutory ideas. For example, Jack may notice that he becomes less upset when he spends time with his family. His love of music could be utilised to help interrupt maintenance processes and to help increase positively valued activities and interests (Beck, 2011) and to disrupt the maintenance cycle as illustrated in Figure 2.7.

It is also important to enquire about cultural values or identity that can serve as potential sources of strength (Padesky and Mooney, 2012). People's values may derive from their faith, sexual orientation, or other cultural, leisure or sporting activities, and can help us to understand some of the vulnerability for the onset of the difficulties (in Jack's case that men are valued for their ability to provide for others, and that men do not show emotions) as well as indicating resources for change. Throughout therapy, client values, longer-term goals and positive qualities can serve as a foundation to build toward long-term recovery and full participation in life.

Jack's ruminations may be a key maintaining factor of his low mood and persecutory ideation. However, the content of these thoughts reveals much about the areas he invests in, and about his strengths and values. These beliefs about what is most important in life are typically relatively enduring across situations and shape a person's choices and behaviours. Incorporating values into conceptualisations enables us to better understand clients' reactions across different situations. People may worry about work, family, attractiveness

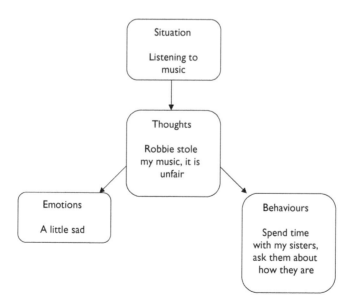

Figure 2.7 Use of cognitive framework to identify use of strengths to overcome difficulties

or health according to how these are valued. Jack is worried about not providing for and not protecting his sisters as it represents an important domain in which he is heavily invested, in part owing to the abandonment of the family by his father.

Discussion of the events leading to the person seeking help often reveals a person trying to achieve important and valued goals by utilising previously helpful strategies to an excessive degree and/or in the context of too many additional demands (Neuchterlain and Dawson, 1984). Clearly, one goal of successful treatment is to find more adaptive ways to engage constructively with these valued domains. For Jack, this was defined as his ability to take care of his family, but without the crippling paranoia and sadness that this was causing. A second important goal for Jack was to remain well even if faced with further potentially excessive demands. In short, the goal was to help Jack be more resilient.

Resilience is a broad concept referring to how people negotiate adversity. It describes the processes of psychological adaptation through which people draw on their strengths to respond to challenges and thereby maintain their well-being (Padesky and Mooney, 2012). It has multiple dimensions, and people do not need strengths in all areas to be resilient. Masten (2007) draws an important distinction between strengths and resilience. Strengths refer to attributes such as good problem-solving abilities or protective circumstances such as a supportive partner. Resilience refers to the processes whereby these strengths enable adaptation during times of challenge. Thus, once therapists help clients to identify strengths, they can be incorporated into conceptualisations to help understand client resilience.

Among Jack's strengths are his ability to form and make good use of a number of family relationships in the past, notably with his sisters; and his positive engagement with mental health services, which bodes well for considering integrated interventions. In Jack's case we might try and encourage him to revisit some of his previous strengths such as playing music, rebuilding his relationship with his sisters, and other activities that indicate he is a good person. Such approaches have been shown to both increase self esteem and reduce psychotic symptoms (Hall and Tarrier, 2003).

Clearly, the acid test of a formulation is whether it leads to helpful interventions. Chadwick and colleagues (2003) have demonstrated that people with psychosis do not necessarily report that formulations increase therapeutic alliance or alleviate distress in themselves. This is not surprising as CBT is not just an insight-oriented therapy. We consider increased understanding as valuable if it leads to a change in cognitions and a change in behaviour. The formulation can be helpful in providing an alternative explanation that can be tested to see if it accounts for the experiences. In addition, the formulation should direct us to appropriate interventions. Discussion of all of the appropriate interventions is well beyond the scope of this chapter, but readers are directed to the work of Morrison et al. (2004).

Janet

Formulation of Janet's presenting issues from a cognitive perspective would also draw on the principles represented in the crucible. A crucial first step would be to undertake a comprehensive assessment. The groin injuries, refusal to visit her father overnight and the night terrors could all be regarded as signs of serious assaults and/or abuse of Janet. However, without more detail, and in the absence of converging sources of information it would be out of keeping with the CBT formulation to speculate on such events and their impact on Janet. There are many people involved in this case and we would draw on all these sources (school nurse, school reports, CAMHS reports, Social Services, paediatricians, health visitors, etc.) in our assessment as well as on Janet's and her mother's views. Such an assessment would help determine if there is evidence of historic abuse, provide information about current risk and ensure proper safeguards are in place. During this process we would spend time with Janet, building a therapeutic relationship and ensuring she feels safe and comfortable with the therapist.

Levels of conceptualisation

Following assessment we would begin in the same way as with Jack and define a presenting issues list. This would help to identify the issues to work on. For Janet we may identify travelling on public transport, having nightmares, feeling angry, and problems with eating and low weight. Then the therapist would enquire about each of these areas and tentatively describe them within a cognitive behavioural framework and crucially begin to get a sense of Janet's point of view. This may be achieved with questions such as 'What do you think, Janet, when your mum puts food on the table?' or 'What do you think to yourself when you are most upset at bedtime?' Such questions and the use of techniques like family trees, or genograms, may be used to help determine Janet's view of the problems as well as her family relationships and hence provide the beginnings of a window into her world.

Outlining the issues within a simple descriptive cognitive behavioural framework is a helpful starting point. By gathering examples over time and across situations we can identify themes or commonalities that may help understand the issues better and also direct us to potential treatment options. If we do not understand her issues we may choose inappropriate interventions. For example, we may conclude that Janet is avoiding transport owing to being bullied because of her Romany heritage. It is a hypothesis but one that needs to be tested against the evidence. In discussion, it may emerge that Janet will not travel by transport as her mother is dependent on it and that this reflects her anger towards her mother. Equally, if Janet states that she refuses food prepared by her mother for the same reason, then we may have identified anger as a common theme that fits with the evidence (frequent temper outbursts and setting the dog on her mother). Understanding the precipitating and perpetuating factors may then direct us towards an intervention addressing anger.

It is a pertinent to ask whether longitudinal conceptualisations can be developed for very young children. Beck's cognitive model of emotional disorders is increasingly being applied to this age group. However, our understanding of how to adapt the model for a 5-, 8- or 15-year-old is still limited. Where we are able to set goals using descriptive and maintenance formulations we may not need to develop a longitudinal formulation. Of course, if we were to do so, we would draw on the principle of collaborative empiricism as with adult clients.

Collaborative empiricism

Through the process of collaboration we would agree with Janet what areas to work on and then begin to develop an understanding of the maintenance of the presenting issues using five factor models. This will also help us to assess how able Janet is to describe and label thoughts and emotions – clearly an important process when considering whether CBT is a good match to the issues she faces (Braswell and Kendall, 2001).

Careful consideration will need to be given to whether there is an evidence base for the use of CBT with a child of this age. We do not know if Janet meets diagnostic criteria for a particular disorder. However, a number of reviews have indicated that CBT is an effective treatment for problems such as depression and anxiety disorders (Cartwright-Hatton et al., 2004). There is a general assumption that children from around eight years of age may benefit from CBT but this is largely untested. It may need to be adapted so that it is acceptable, understandable and helpful to young children (Cresswell and O'Connor, 2011).

With a very young child, there is evidence that involving the family in the form of family-based CBT may well be helpful for anxiety disorders such as obsessive compulsive disorder (Freeman et al., 2008), although whether family-based CBT is as effective clinically as individual work or is cost effective for older children is disputed (Bodden et al., 2008). So, if Janet's assessment indicated she experienced anxiety or depression problems there would be a rationale for offering CBT.

Strengths and resilience

Given Janet's age and developmental stage it would be important to avoid pathologising her feelings or behaviour. Even if individual work was offered, throughout treatment there would be an emphasis on recognising and harnessing her strengths. Careful enquiry about areas of her life in which she feels she is doing well (perhaps at school, with friendships, or in an ability such as a sport) would enable such factors to be woven into intervention strategies. Humour and play would be particularly helpful in working with Janet and her family. Her Aunty Cindy seems to be a particular source of support and it may be that her close interest in Janet can be utilised, possibly to help with the eating concerns as Janet seems to eat food prepared by others, and possibly in helping establish a consistent sleeping pattern.

Of course another potential strength in Janet's life may be her mother. It may be possible to use a formulation of Janet's presenting issues but not directly work with Janet. As with carers of people with dementia, difficult behaviours (such as the refusal to use transport, or food refusal) can be conceptualised within a CBT framework and suggested to the carers as a different, alternative explanation to the potentially unhelpful explanation the carer has come up with (DCP, 2011: 19). For example, Mary may see Janet's food refusal as a sign that Janet hates her because of a failure in bonding. This attribution will probably make Mary feel very sad. However, the formulation may come up with an alternative explanation that does not attribute blame to Mary, and thus increases the chance of her trying to help Janet. Similar methods can be used when working with families of people with psychotic illness (Barrowclough and Tarrier, 1992) and may be an option for Jack's family.

This issue of working indirectly with resources in Janet's life raises an obvious question of who is the client and what is the most effective route to creating change? It is clear that Mary herself has experienced and continues to experience very difficult circumstances. A cognitive approach may be useful in helping understand Mary's reported depression. A perpetuating model of Mary's postnatal difficulties might start with Mary looking at Janet and thinking, 'I don't feel close to my baby'. This may lead Mary to think that she is a bad mother as she did not feel this way with her other children, and she may then feel guilty and depressed. This in turn may lead her to withdraw from Janet, hence reinforcing the sense of being distant and not caring. The loss of energy and tiredness associated with depression make it even harder to motivate herself to care for Janet, and means that it is likely that other people such as her husband will assume responsibility for Janet, hence increasing Mary's guilt. Mary now involves herself heavily in the care of her grandchildren, perhaps as compensation, but this may serve to remind her that she did not do the same with Janet, and hence perpetuate her guilt even some years on. A provisional formulation (Figure 2.8) such as this could form the basis of an intervention designed to improve Mary's functioning, and hence indirectly lead to improvements in Janet's perceived problems as Mary becomes better able to manage these difficulties.

In summary, there are four potential ways that work with Janet could be informed by a CBT formulation. First, there is direct work with Janet. It is difficult to develop a CBT formulation for Janet owing to the lack of detailed information about her perspective and developmental ability. However, we

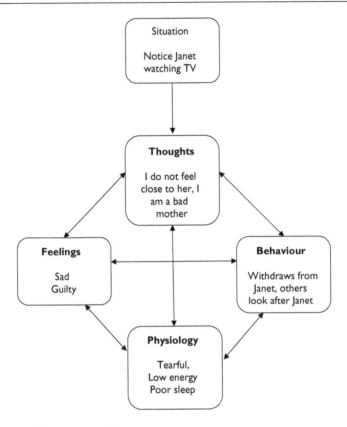

Figure 2.8 Mary's perpetuating factors

have indicated some potential routes to this information. Second, the formulation could be used as part of family-based CBT in which Mary and possibly Cindy are key contributors. Third, the formulation may be used indirectly with Mary to help her better understand and consider how to help Janet. Fourth, it may be that Mary needs help with her own mood difficulties for which CBT may be useful.

Reflections

We have made some suggestions for CBT formulations based on the available information about Jack and to a lesser extent Janet. It is important to re-emphasise that what would make this a CBT formulation are the principles set out earlier, which can be used with a range of presenting problems and clients of different ages and socio-cultural backgrounds. We have elected to draw on a generic CBT model to describe and explain Jack's presentation. Other models, for example of PTSD, trauma and psychosis (Callcott et al., 2010) or mania (Basco and Rush, 1996) could have been credible alternative frameworks. The only way of establishing the value of a formulation is to develop it in the spirit of collaborative empiricism, changing it as new understandings emerge from the assessment and therapy. Done well, this leads to strengthening of the therapeutic relationship and better-targeted interventions.

Formulation also has an important role in supervision and self-reflective practice. A key question for a practitioner is: 'If I thought the same as the client in those situations, would I be likely to feel and act in the same way?' If the answer is yes, then there is a good chance that the formulation has captured the distress experienced by the client and has provided the therapist with a glimpse of the world as if seen through the client's eyes. Where the answer to the question is no, then a frequent focus of supervision will be in the development of the formulation and identification of strategies to elicit this information collaboratively, perhaps by the development of behavioural experiments that will help identify the missing pieces of the jigsaw.

Gillian Butler (1998) outlines ten tests for a formulation (see p. 264), including whether it demonstrates logical coherence across the levels and whether it accounts for the onset and maintenance of the difficulties. Clinicians and supervisors may find it helpful to consider the formulation against these criteria.

Conclusions

In this introductory chapter we have indicated that CBT, like other psychotherapeutic approaches, places a strong emphasis on formulation. We liken CBT formulation to a crucible where the individual particularities of a given case, relevant theory and research synthesise into an understanding of the person's presenting issues in CBT terms that informs the intervention. As such, formulation is considered to be central to the process of undertaking effective CBT, mirroring its intrinsic orientation to evidence-based practice. We have argued that what makes CBT formulation distinct is its use of CBT theory, its emphasis on collaborative empiricism, its emphasis on the current problems and goals and its evolving status as new understandings come to light throughout therapy. We have suggested a framework for CBT formulation that moves from descriptive frameworks in CBT terms, to simple inferential models (ie five factor models), to more complex explanatory models starting from what maintains the presentation and leading onto what may have made the person vulnerable. These principles and frameworks are illustrated through case examples.

Key characteristics of CBT formulation

- Based on the cognitive model.
- Utilises core concepts of schemas/beliefs, conditional assumptions and rules, and maintenance cycles to explain onset and maintenance of emotional difficulties.
- Formulation developed in levels from presenting issues to more predisposing factors.
- Client and therapist work as a partnership or team to co-create a formulation.
- Strong emphasis on evidence-base for the effectiveness of the intervention.
- Strong emphasis on empiricism in session so that appraisals are treated as ideas to be tested and alternatives considered.
- CBT is closely associated with diagnostic frameworks in that RCTs are usually based on diagnostic categories. CBT formulation is complementary to psychiatric diagnosis. Diagnosis may be a reason to consider a hypothesis or intervention strategy, but the diagnosis will probably only have marginal bearing on the process of formulation.

Acknowledgements

Many people have contributed to the shaping of the ideas in this chapter. We are indebted to the valuable contributions of many colleagues including Aaron Beck, Peter Bieling, Paul Chadwick, Mark Freeston, Kathleen Mooney and particularly Christine Padesky. RD would also like to express his thanks to Stephen Westgarth who provided valuable thoughts on the case of Janet. However, the ideas expressed remain the responsibility of the authors.

References

Barrowclough, C. and Tarrier, N. (1992) *Families of Schizophrenic Patients: Cognitive Behavioural Intervention.* London: Chapman and Hall.

Basco, A.G. and Rush, A.J. (1996) *Cognitive Behavioural Therapy For Bipolar Disorder.* London: Guilford Press.

Beck, J.S. (2011) *Cognitive Therapy: Basics and Beyond.* London: Guilford Press.

Bodden, D.H., Bögels, S.M., Nauta, M.H., De Haan, E., Ringrose, J., Appelboom, C., et al. (2008) Child versus family cognitive-behavioral therapy in clinically anxious youth: an efficacy and partial effectiveness study. *Journal of the American Academy of Child & Adolescent Psychiatry,* 47(12), 1384–1394.

Brabban, A. and Turkington, D. (2002) The search for meaning: detecting congruence between life events, underlying schema and psychotic symptoms. In Morrison, P.M. (ed.) *A Casebook of Cognitive Therapy for Psychosis.* East Sussex: Brunner-Routledge, pp. 59–77.

Braswell, L. and Kendall, P.C. (2001) Cognitive behavioral therapy with youth. In K. Dobson (ed.) *Handbook of Cognitive Behavioral Therapies*. New York: Guilford Press, pp. 246–294.

Butler, G. (1998) Clinical formulation. *Comprehensive Psychology*, 6(1), 1–23.

Butler, A.C., Chapman, J.E., Forman, E.M. and Beck, A.T. (2006) The empirical status of cognitive-behavioural therapy: a review of meta-analyses. *Clinical Psychology Review*, 26(1), 17–31.

Callcott, P., Dudley, R., Standardt, S., Freeston, M. and Turkington, D. (2010) Treating trauma in the context of psychosis: a case series. In Hagen, R., Turkington, D., Berge, T. and Grawe, R.W. (eds) *CBT for Psychosis: A Symptom-based Approach*. East Sussex: Routledge, pp.175–192.

Cartwright-Hatton, S., Roberts, C., Chitsabesan, P., Fothergill, C. and Harrington, R. (2004) Systematic review of the efficacy of cognitive behavior therapies for childhood and adolescent anxiety disorders. *British Journal of Clinical Psychology*, 43, 421–436.

Chadwick, P., Williams, C. and MacKenzie, J. (2003) Impact of case formulation in cognitive behavioural therapy for psychosis. *Behaviour Research and Therapy*, 41(6), 671-680.

Clark, D.M. and Beck, A.T. (1999) *Scientific Foundations of Cognitive Theory and Therapy of Depression*. Chichester: Wiley & Sons.

Collerton, D., Dudley, R. and Mossiman, U. (2012) Visual hallucinations. In Blom, J. and Somner, I. (eds) *Hallucinations: Research and Practice*. New York: Springer, pp 75–90.

Creswell, C. and O'Connor, T.G. (2011) Cognitive-behavioural therapy for children and adolescents. In Skuse, D., Bruce, H., Dowdney, L. and Mrazek, D. (eds) *Child Psychology and Psychiatry: Frameworks for Practice*. 2nd edn. Oxford: Wiley-Blackwell, pp. 265–270.

Division of Clinical Psychology (2011) *Good Practice Guidelines on the Use of Psychological Formulation*. Leicester: The British Psychological Society.

Dudley, R., Kuyken, W. and Padesky, C.A. (2010) Disorder specific and trans-diagnostic case conceptualisation. *Clinical Psychology Review*, 31, 213–224.

Dudley, R. and Turkington, D. (2010) Using normalising in cognitive behavioural therapy for schizophrenia. In Hagen, R., Turkington, D., Berge, T. and Grawe, R.W. (eds) *CBT for Psychosis: A Symptom-Based Approach*. East Sussex: Routledge, pp. 77–85.

Freeman, D. (2007) Suspicious minds: the psychology of persecutory delusions. *Clinical Psychology Review*, 27, 425–457.

Freeman, J.B., Garcia, A.M., Coyne, L., Ale, C., Przeworski, A., Himle, M., et al. (2008) Early childhood OCD: preliminary findings from a family-based cognitive-behavioral approach. *Journal of the American Academy of Child and Adolescent Psychiatry*, 47(5): 593–602.

Greenberger, D. and Padesky, C.A. (1995) *Mind Over Mood: Change How You Feel by Changing the Way You Think*. New York: Guilford Press.

Hackmann, A., Bennett-Levy, J. and Holmes, E. (2011) *Oxford Guide to Imagery in Cognitive Therapy*. Oxford: Oxford University Press.

Hall, P.L. and Tarrier, N. (2003) The cognitive-behavioural treatment of low self-esteem in psychotic patients: a pilot study. *Behaviour Research and Therapy*, 41(3), 317–320.

Harvey, A.G., Watkins, E., Mansell, W. and Shafran, R. (2004) *Cognitive Behavioural Processes Across Psychological Disorders: A Transdiagnostic Approach to Research and Treatment*. London: Oxford University Press.

Kuyken, W. (2006) Evidence-based case formulation: is the emperor clothed? In Tarrier, N. (ed.) *Case Formulation in Cognitive Behaviour Therapy: The Treatment of Challenging and Complex Clinical Cases*. London: Brunner-Routledge, pp 12–35.

Kuyken, W., Padesky, C. and Dudley, R. (2008) The science and practice of case conceptualisation. *Behavioural and Cognitive Psychotherapy*, 36, Special Issue 06, 757–768.

——(2009) *Collaborative Case Conceptualization. Working Effectively with Clients in Cognitive Behavioural Therapy*. New York, London: Guilford Press.

Martin, D.J., Garske, J.P. and Davis, M.K. (2000) Relation of the therapeutic alliance with outcome and other variables: a meta-analytic review. *Journal of Consulting Clinical Psychology*, 68 (3), 438–50.

Masten, A.S. (2007) Resilience in developing systems: progress and promise as the fourth wave rises. *Development and Psychopathology*, 19, 921–930.

Morrison, A.P., Renton, J.C., Dunn, H., Bentall, R.P. and Williams, C. (eds) (2004) *Cognitive Therapy For Psychosis, A Formulation-Based Approach*. London: Brunner-Routledge.

Neuchterlein, K.H., and Dawson, M.E. (1984) Vulnerability and stress factors in the developmental course of schizophrenic disorders. *Schizophrenia Bulletin*, 10 (2), 158–159.

Padesky, C.A. and Mooney, K.A. (2012) Strengths-based cognitive–behavioural therapy: a four-step model to build resilience. *Clinical Psychology and Psychotherapy*, DOI: 10.1002/cpp.1795.

Persons, J.B. (2008) *Cognitive-Therapy in Practice: A Case Formulation Approach*. New York: Norton.

Salkovskis, P.M., Clark, D.M. and Gelder, M.G. (1996) Cognition-behaviour links in the persistence of panic. *Behaviour Research and Therapy*, 34(6), 453–458.

Watkins, E., Scott, J., Wingrove, J., Rimes, K., Bathurst, N., Steiner, H., et al. (2007) Rumination-focused cognitive-behaviour therapy for residual depression: a case series. *Behaviour Research and Therapy*, 45, 2144–2154.

Wells, A. (1996) *Cognitive Therapy of Anxiety Disorders: A Practice Manual and Conceptual Guide*. Chichester: John Wiley and Sons Ltd.

Wykes, T., Steel, C., Everitt, B. and Tarrier, N. (2008) Cognitive behavior therapy for schizophrenia: effect sizes, clinical models, and methodological rigor. *Schizophrenia Bulletin*, 34, 523–537.

Chapter 3

Psychodynamic formulation
Looking beneath the surface

Rob Leiper

What is a psychodynamic approach?

There is no single psychodynamic theory and hence no single way of constructing a psychodynamic formulation. Psychoanalysis has reproduced within itself many of the controversies of the entire field. It contains a multiplicity of ideas and approaches: there are competing visions, differing assumptions and a wide variety of possible conceptualisations which have led to an endless debate. The term psychodynamic is now used generically to encompass the many theoretical approaches that remain connected to these psychoanalytic roots. A key feature of the psychodynamic use of formulation can be related to this confusing multiplicity: that sustaining a sense of uncertainty is in itself a value that has come to be held very close to the heart of the modern psychodynamic stance. In the realm of unconscious processes one should not presume to know too much. No form or formula can be clung to as a secure guide – except perhaps that of 'not knowing'!

Within the array of ideas and approaches that constitutes the psychodynamic tradition, there is, nonetheless, a commonality of outlook which holds the different strands together (Leiper and Maltby, 2004; Wallerstein, 2002). This is not the enforced unity of ideas that Freud once thought was essential to protect the analytic ideal from watered-down versions or wild practitioners. However, certain key perspectives and shared values constitute the essentials of a coherent approach. At its most basic, what is held in common exists at the level of the perception of the human condition rather than its conceptualisation: it is, in a sense, pre-theoretical. This shared vision forms the basis of a recognizable clinical orientation – a sensibility about the nature of therapeutic practice – rather than an articulated psychological paradigm. Such a general way of looking at clinical material leaves a lot of scope for diversity in what an 'accurate', or even a simply useful, formulation might look like.

Core features of a psychodynamic approach

What ideas constitute the core of the psychodynamic approach? Perhaps the most fundamental one is the focus on psychological or emotional pain. Life is thought of as a difficult and demanding process and the psyche is constructed in the struggle to deal with it. What is 'dynamic' is the turbulence created in the currents of mental life by these struggles. Means of avoiding pain are developed: ways of seeing, thinking, feeling and behaving can all serve this purpose. Much of this activity takes place out of awareness. There is an 'internal world' constituted differently from external reality, the unconscious elements of which have a fundamental influence on the way we live our lives. These unconscious attempts to avoid pain often fail, but since our awareness is limited, they are nonetheless repeated again and again. Failing defences are what give form to and maintain patterns of psychological disorder. Therapy is about getting in touch with thoughts and feelings which were previously 'warded off', kept hidden from the conscious mind because they seemed to be too much to deal with. Psychodynamic therapy is about helping the client to 're-formulate' what they are experiencing in a more inclusive way, and to tolerate the discomfort that this involves. The understanding that the therapist and client develop about these difficulties expands the client's awareness and opens up new options for managing conflict. The client's capacity to bear emotional pain and cope constructively with dissatisfaction is enhanced, and the ability to reflect on and be curious about their experience is developed.

This view of human life, personal development and psychological functioning underpins the 'clinical theory' of psychodynamics, and informs and guides the therapist's thinking and actions (Wallerstein, 1988). At this level of theory, it is possible to pull together (to some extent at least) the competing psychodynamic versions of psychological development and structure and establish the elements of an approach to formulation. Several complementary 'points of view' (Rappaport, 1959) can help to systematise our understanding both of the general theory and of a particular individual clinical situation. I will emphasise four main perspectives: the *dynamic*, the *developmental,* the *structural* and the *adaptive*. These can be used to organise the diverse array of information that needs to be integrated into a coherent narrative to arrive at a useful formulation. (Compare McWilliams, 1999 for an alternative approach.)

The dynamic perspective

One radical implication of Freud's vision of the unconscious is that all behaviour is purposeful and motivated; all human activity is meaningful, and has potential significance. Even the most obscure actions, experiences or behaviour can be understood in terms of the logic of the unconscious, through which we can interpret the hidden meaning. This 'latent' meaning can only be unravelled through a careful process of detective work that involves interpreting the surface material to arrive at the unconscious intentions underneath. Dynamic formulation is a process of discovering (or constructing) meaning in confusing and unclear areas of experience. It re-tells the client's story as intentional and meaningful.

The dynamic perspective views mental life as a shifting flow constantly influenced by interacting forces. Fundamentally, these forces concern psychic pain and the wish to avoid it through distorting or concealing our knowledge of its sources. Pain was initially thought of as the product of external trauma, and the memory of distressing events. A crucial theoretical move was made in seeing the source of pain as more fundamental, as having fundamentally internal roots: pain originates from inner conflict between parts of the self.

These conflicting internal forces can be conceptualised in various ways, including Freud's (1936) view about acceptable and unacceptable impulses. Probably the simplest way of representing these ideas is via the diagram in Figure 3.1, commonly known as the 'triangle of conflict' (Malan, 1995). (Alternative simplified 'formulae' of these key dynamic processes have been developed by Luborsky (1984) and Levenson (1995).) This portrays conflict as arising from a 'hidden feeling', which could be a wish or an impulse. Awareness of this feeling arouses anxiety, because its expression is in conflict with another perceived need, and thus is feared to have catastrophic consequences. For example, a feeling of anger or rage and an associated impulse to hurt is disturbing, perhaps unacceptable, in the context of a relationship in which you are dependent on the other person and need their love or good opinion for continued well-being. Expressed verbally, the conflict becomes: 'I hate you' *but* 'I am afraid that I will destroy our relationship, which I need and depend on'. In the case of Jack, there seems to be conflict between his intense desire for success and admiration, and an associated fear which appears to involve feelings of threat and shame.

However, conflicts are always unique and generally more complex than any simplified formulation can capture. Hinshelwood (1991), building on object relations theory (see below), proposes that the underlying conflict can be viewed as an ambivalent and anxiety-ridden personal relationship – but one operating internally between parts of the self (what has come to be called an 'object relationship' in psychodynamic theory). It can often be thought of (again in a simplified way) in terms of a parent and child trying to manage a conflicted situation. This kind of formulation allows us to visualise the internal situation in a familiar way. However, a crucial element of this perspective is that these relationships are subject to the rather different 'rules' of unconscious mental life (which will be outlined below).

The anxiety signals that there is an internal danger situation. Some action must be taken to avert the threat posed by the conflicting aspects of the self, the ambivalent state of mind. The 'solution' is to avoid conscious acknowledgement of the conflict. This is the third element in the triangle

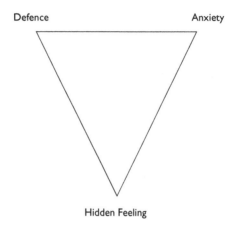

Figure 3.1 The triangle of conflict

– the process of defence. Where the person does not have the capacity to tolerate or cope consciously with the threat posed by an internal conflict, some aspects must be warded off, to avoid the threat to personal coherence and the fear of disintegration. This defensive alteration of experience is a kind of self-deception, in which some aspect of the self is disguised.

There are a myriad of ways in which this disguise can be achieved; almost any element of experience can be used defensively in some context or other. Jack, for example, initially turned to delinquent 'acting out' which substitutes dramatic and provocative behaviour for the uncomfortable experience of difficult feelings. His subsequent substance misuse also distracts from and dulls emotional pain. Hinshelwood (1991) suggests that these strategies can be thought of as the establishment of a different internal object relationship which 'evades' the anxiety-provoking situation. There will typically be more than one such diversionary route available, and different possible 'substitute' ways of relating.

A number of consequences follow from our tendency to distort awareness in order to sustain a sense of internal coherence. Crucial elements of our actions are taken out of conscious control and as a result we are poorly equipped to manage our true internal state and less able to adapt our behaviour to the external world. We are limited in our ability to anticipate damaging consequences of our actions and to learn from our experience. We may blindly repeat patterns of behaviour again and again.

When routine defences do not work well enough to manage the conflict, further measures may have to be resorted to as a 'second line of defence', which may take the form of a 'symptom'. This is understood as a solution to a conflict through the formation of a compromise in which both sides of the conflict find a means of expression. Both the need to keep a wish out of awareness and the force of the wish itself can be felt in these situations. For example, obsessional checking is often thought to be a way of managing unacceptable hostility. The damage which, it is feared, would result from the hostility requires the constant reassurance of the checking; meanwhile the hostile impulses push for expression via compulsive quality of the behaviour, and achieve some results by torturing the person, and those round them, with its frustrating repetitiveness. This kind of re-appearance of the underlying impulse in a distorted form has been called 'the return of the repressed'. In Jack's case, his delusional belief system has the same quality of a desperate further attempt to manage his unbearable experience after his initial defensive strategies failed him. Equally, it seems to reveal at every turn something of the underlying nature of his core wishes and anxieties.

In summary, from the dynamic point of view, personal difficulties are considered in terms of the meanings and motivations that individuals bring to them. These meanings are formulated as conflicted desires and relationships and the unmanageable anxiety which they generate. Such meanings always have to be sought behind the defensive surface presentation which serves to protect us from overwhelming anxiety. Psychological problems arise from the rigidities and restrictions in behaviour and experience created by these compulsive defences. The aim of therapy is to reduce their hold over us, to facilitate greater flexibility and increase the scope for choice by bringing about some resolution of conflict. By integrating the parts of the personality that have been defended against we can have a more full ownership of all aspects of the self.

Thus, a psychodynamic formulation must consider:

- What are the main underlying conflicts? What self-other relationships or wishes, impulses and fears make up these conflicts?
- What is the quality of the anxieties that arise from the core conflicts? How manageable do they seem to the individual?
- What defensive strategies and relationship patterns are deployed in order to manage these anxieties? How effective are they and what are their maladaptive impacts?
- How are the presenting problems or symptoms related to these defensive strategies and to the underlying conflicts?

The developmental perspective

In the developmental perspective we look to the past to understand the present. Early experiences are considered to be of fundamental significance in forming both dynamic and structural aspects of our mental life. This perspective, although commonly assumed by psychology, originated in and remains strongly associated with psychodynamic theory.

Perhaps the main element of this assumption is the idea of a sequence of developmental phases. This was originally conceived in terms of libidinal energies and erogenous zones – the well-known oral, anal and phallic stages. However, it became clear that these phases can be understood in a broader sense as characterising particular modes of relationship with caretakers. For example, the idea of an oral phase highlights issues of taking in sustenance, of dependence on others for life and the issues of what is inside the body and what is outside, of the boundaries of the self. Erikson (1950) elaborated Freud's work into a well-known sequence of eight psychosocial developmental stages, each with a relational dimension. The task of the individual is to achieve progressive degrees of separation and differentiation, starting from an early experience of unity and moving towards greater personal identity, and an integrated sense of self (Mahler et al., 1975).

The school of thought known as object relations has highlighted the crucial role of the parental relationship, particularly with the mother. However, it is the personal meaning of such experiences that is important in the psychodynamic view; the sense that the child made of any particular traumatic separation or personal abuse or conflicted family constellation. What were the unconscious meanings and fantasy elaborations of the situation and of the pain it caused? What were the defensive strategies that the child had available and resorted to manage the distress? The interplay of internal reactions and external events is regarded as forming the matrix out of which personality is created. The child manages early deficits and traumas as well as he or she can, and these adaptations become the foundation for later distortions in relating which may ameliorate, maintain or exacerbate the early failures. Jack's difficulties seem to emerge in mid-adolescence when the developmental pressures of sexuality, gender identity and achievement in the wider world start to make themselves felt. However, psychodynamically we would want to think also of the impact of earlier events and relationships – perhaps his father's successes and difficulties and the reactions of his mother both to those and to her growing son, and how Jack might wish and wished to be the same as and also different from his father.

A key idea in the developmental point of view is that dysfunction is closely associated with problems occurring at particular stages. Childhood problems, whatever their origin, are experienced in relation to, and have their subsequent impact through, the particular developmental issues that are 'active' in that phase of life. The effect may be to disrupt and hinder the developmental process.

A central feature of the psychodynamic perspective, unlike that of developmental psychology in general, is that the present is interpreted in terms of the developmental past; the past is 'alive' in the here and now. Dysfunction may be thought of as repetition. Patterns of feeling, thinking and acting which were established in previous developmental contexts are replayed in current, often very different, situations. These patterns are rigid and not readily open to correction through new experience; indeed present experience comes to be actively organised in terms of patterns that were current at some earlier time. Thus infantile modes of experience and behaviour persist but in a way that is sealed off from the influence of the present day. Early patterns of relating to the world, normal at their appropriate developmental phase, become a template for understanding the nature of current psychological dysfunction. We might think, for instance, of the grandiosity and 'omnipotence' of Jack's delusional stance as akin in some ways to how toddlers quite normally relate to the world about them.

Malan (1995) has summarised this in a diagram termed the Triangle of Person (see Figure 3.2), which shows how the past (particularly family) relationships are echoed in the present. But – and this is a distinctive feature of the psychodynamic therapeutic approach – they are replayed not just in the client's current relationships but also in the therapy room also. This brings in the idea of transference: that is, how certain aspects of the person's perception of and relationship to her therapist might be understood as reflecting some earlier significant relationship. How the client approaches and experiences the therapist is a clue to how they experience (and perhaps distort) other relationships. This also casts light on the past and the way the situations experienced in childhood and adolescence were understood and responded to. Jack's defensive distancing of the (female) therapist through his retreat into delusional ruminations might offer a clue to his experience of some unmanageable pressure (to perform? To achieve?) that he feels from others, particularly when they get close to him. The therapist's own response – at both an emotional and behavioural level – to

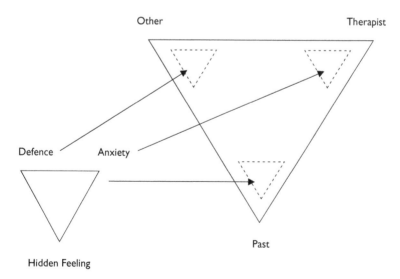

Figure 3.2 The triangle of person combined with the triangle of conflict (adapted from Molnos, 1984)

how the client presents in the therapy room is often a vital key to assessing the hidden emotional quality of these repetitions. These 'counter-transference' responses give a clue as to the interpersonal situations which are, at an unconscious level, being replicated in each relationship context, including the therapy. We seek to identify similar patterns of relating repeated across different contexts.

In summary, the developmental point of view looks to the past in order to cast light on what might be thought of as the personal context in which certain 'decisions' about how to survive were originally made. Patterns which are thus established often create self-perpetuating cycles. Individuals are seen as both the product and the author of their life history. Framing understanding in the light of development in this way can often enable people to acknowledge less acceptable aspects of their personality.

In considering a formulation, the developmental point of view directs our attention to such issues as:

- What were the nature and quality of family (and other social) relationships at various times during the person's life (in childhood, adolescence and subsequently)?
- What events and experiences appear to have been significant in the person's life?
- At what ages/developmental phases were these relationships or events experienced and what may have been the impact of these on psychological development?
- What has been the person's conscious experience/account of these experiences? Does this accord with what might be expected or is there the possibility of defensive distortion? What meaning may these have had?
- What relationship and coping patterns or themes appear to be repeated at different phases of development and across different relationship contexts?
- What developmental phase appears to be most associated with these thematic issues?
- How are these themes represented within the therapeutic relationship? What is the pattern of transference and counter-transference interaction and experience?

The structural perspective

The structural perspective focuses on the framework within which psychological functioning is understood and the ways in which individuals might differ in their psychological structures. In psychodynamic theory the principle feature of this psychological map is the different levels of organisation operating in the mind. In particular, we need to be aware of the very different ways that the unconscious, as opposed to the conscious, realm functions: mental life 'as we know it' structured by verbal syntax and logic is not all there is to us. In the world of the unconscious there are no opposites and no negation so that contradictory propositions co-exist without challenge; there are no ordered sequences and so no sense of time; there is no clear division between different things or between subject and object, and so one thing can stand for another (displacement) or for many things at once (condensation); meanings are absolute rather than conditional and there is no doubt or degrees of certainty. In this realm of internal rather than external reality, everything is at once single minded and fluid; mental phenomena have a similar character to dreams. This model is used as a framework for interpreting the presence of hidden meaning, transformed and disguised by the need to maintain repression.

In psychodynamic theory, the internal world is seen as the dominant force, structuring our perception of the world. By selection and manipulation, all the situations, people and relationships that we encounter can be made to conform to its assumptions and expectations. The structural perspective considers the characteristic forms of the relationship between these internal and external realities, and the degree to which our relationship with the world is either flexible and reality-based or dominated and distorted by unconscious needs. Freud made the famous division of the mind into the ego, id and superego. While the tri-partite model plays a much less significant part in modern psychodynamic thinking, it does point to this vital element in an overall formulation.

It is usual to think in terms of more or less 'healthy' kinds of defence, that is, degrees to which we need to alter our experience of reality. *Repression*, which involves keeping some impulse or emotion out of conscious awareness, is a relatively straightforward form of avoidance. It involves only the distortion of one element of our internal reality, although it often lays the foundation for further defensive transformations of it. *Dissociation* involves cutting off a whole area of self-experience with an associated complex of feelings, memories and aspects of the self: there is thus a more radical alteration to internal reality. *Denial* can be thought of as more serious still, involving the distortion of significant aspects of both internal and external reality. Jack's use of acting out and substance abuse would be regarded as a relatively serious deficit in his capacity to manage reality, involving significant levels of denial and associated 'primitive' defences such as projection (of feelings into others) and weak behavioural controls. These are the context for his further regression to psychotic levels of functioning, which suggests that he has what is termed poor 'ego strength', that is a fragility in his capacities for reality testing, emotional regulation and self-control. We all have our ways of defending ourselves, and the pervasiveness, rigidity and severity of these distortions distinguish personality style from 'personality disorder' (not as a 'diagnosis' but as a functional description). The seriousness of dysfunction depends on how early the developmental disruption occurred and how severe it was. Thus problems in the first year of life – Freud's 'oral stage' – such as a deficit in care-taking due to a mother being incapacitated by depression or absent through illness, could cause quite fundamental developmental damage, resulting in distortions to the basic sense of reality, and the capacity to relate to others and to regulate the self. Both Winnicott (1965) and Kohut (1977) suggest, for example, that an experience of 'good-enough' dependence provided by the mother's empathic attunement to the infant's needs and communications lays the foundation for future development. Deficits in these areas may have to be filled defensively with a 'false self' – an artificial persona and way of relating to others which conceals the internal lack arising from the unmet dependency needs.

In summary, formulation from a structural perspective is based on an understanding of the mental structures that enable the psyche to maintain some balance in the face of internal and external stresses. Therapeutic change consists of an increased capacity to take responsibility for our behaviour and to become more flexible, capable and aware. The 'structural theory' is clear too about the limits to change: we are always engaged in a balancing act between conflicting demands. However, if the ego is strengthened and the power of the primitive superego reduced, a more effective, satisfying and less self-defeating balance is achievable.

In considering a formulation from a structural point of view we might ask:

- What are the person's characteristic defences? What level of 'maturity' do these suggest, how effective are they and at what cost of personal restriction?
- What is the person's capacity for self-reflection? Can they think about their internal states and motivations in a 'psychological' way?
- What degree of 'ego strength' does the person display? Are they resilient or fragile, flexible or rigid? Can they utilise their adaptive strengths and abilities?
- How able is the person to regulate their emotions? Is there an ability to manage distress and anxiety and reasonable differentiation of response to different situations? Is there a capacity to sustain disappointment and loss?
- Is the person able to regulate and sustain their sense of self-functioning? Is there a sense of personal coherence, stability and self-esteem? susceptibility to shame or grandiosity? clear and stable ideals, goals and values?
- Does the person's mode of relating to others achieve a balance between the tensions of intimacy and autonomy, dominance and submission, neediness and nurturing?

The adaptive perspective

One of the many developments in psychodynamic theory has been an increased interest, influenced partly by systemic and behavioural thinking from the 1970s onwards, in the relationship of the internal to the external 'real' world, that is, how experience affects and interacts with our life situation and interpersonal relations. Strupp and Binder (1984), followed by Levenson (1995), for example, explicitly introduce this element into their system of formulation. Defensive responses to relational conflicts often end up as self-perpetuating because they tend to confirm the individual's worst fears. This happens through a variety of linked processes: the distortion and misinterpretation of other people's motives and actions; the selection of specific individuals and relationship contexts which are familiar and meet our expectations; and the subtle pressure which at unconscious levels invites others to respond in particular ways. For example, someone who tends to expect and fear rejection in close relationships may have a tendency to approach intimacy in a guarded and suspicious way (in spite of, indeed because of, the strong underlying sense of need), and so react strongly to any minor rift and interpret it as betrayal. This produces the feared result of a breakdown in the relationship which seems to confirm that people are untrustworthy and always disappoint you in the end, and the cyclical pattern is strengthened. Jack appears to be caught in a version of just this kind of trap, in which an oversensitivity to perceived slights or anticipated demands causes him to react suspiciously and rejectingly to people, depriving him in turn of the support and validation which he needs and longs for. However, from a psychodynamic perspective this can be a golden opportunity for both therapist and client to understand these patterns, to intervene with them directly as they are played out in the therapeutic relationship, and to discover the possibility of a new outcome. So, if Jack's therapist were to notice signs of this process as a response to something she said, it might be possible to explore how Jack had reacted there and then 'in the transference' and to clarify and correct the interaction, later linking this to other instances of how things go wrong for him in relationships.

Malan (1995) believes that this adaptive perspective is necessary to integrate the various psychodynamic issues during the process of assessment and formulation. The key to this is what he calls the 'Life Problem', the way in which the underlying dynamic and developmental issues intersect with the current situation in the person's life. Careful note must be taken of an individual's life-style, work circumstances and intimate relationships, but the main purpose of this is not simply to look at the surface rewards and stressors, but at how they reflect the key developmental and dynamic themes and issues which are crucial for that client. Events and relationships have an idiosyncratic meaning for that individual which gives them their particular force. It is especially important (as in so much psychological understanding) to take note of – perhaps to seek out – what may have changed in the life situation in order to understand what has created the perceived need for outside help. A dynamic compromise may have been working however unsatisfactorily until something occurred – what that was may lead to an exploration of what it meant and so to what the prior conflicts and compromise solutions might have been. For Jack, the emergence into manhood and the added element of abuse at this time take on their meaning for him in the context of the deep ambivalence about masculinity and fears concerning untrustworthiness and violence in men which have become part of his and his family's story.

However, this perspective should also encourage an interest in what is going well for an individual. While the psychodynamic tendency to see all living as a kind of 'compromise' between conflicting needs can seem pessimistic or even cynical, there is also a corrective and compassionate sense that we are all in the same boat! Clients are no different from therapists in the issues that we all struggle with. The charge that this language 'pathologises' people (which of course it can do if misused) has to be understood in this context. We should also look therefore at what is working in the person's life: what compromises are successful? how developmental traumas have been managed and what achievements have been won in the struggle? Jack clearly started life demonstrating various capabilities. However, perhaps the most troubling aspect of Jack's life has been the lack of any sign of capitalising on these strengths with any real achievement. This should give us pause in our natural wish for a transformative therapeutic outcome and may direct us to seek more limited stabilising goals.

The adaptive view thus sees psychopathology as a process of mismatch with the environment in which compromise solutions to conflict are limiting to the person's creative responses to life's challenges and self-confirming in their cyclical repetitive quality: they prevent learning from experience. Change is the process of opening up a wider range of creative options and breaking out of maladaptive cycles.

In the adaptive point of view on formulation we should ask:

- What pattern is being repeated in these life problems or symptoms and with what unconscious aim?
- Why has this arisen *now* or become intolerable and presented for help at this time?
- What maladaptive cycles are operating which maintain the management of the core conflicts? In what ways are the person's responses distorting or manipulating their experience of life to bring about these self-confirming repetitions?
- How do these stereotyped patterns of response limit the person's continued development and achievement in life?
- What ways of handling conflict have worked relatively well and how have these been a positive response to developmental problems?

An intrinsic part of the psychodynamic approach (and perhaps of the creation of any psychological narrative) is the search for themes and patterns appearing across these differing perspectives and contexts, which help to build a coherent formulation of an individual's experience of personal difficulty. The presence of similar themes in different arenas and from diverse points of view will tend to support a formulation's validity. This circularity – though potentially problematic 'scientifically' – is a key to how formulations are created in practice. The therapist must test out hypotheses with the client in the therapeutic context through interpretation and attention to the response it receives. The difference from other more cognitively based approaches to this task is that it is not the client's conscious assent to a 'formulation' (offered in the form of an interpretive intervention) that counts, but their unconscious reaction to and elaboration of it. This is a subtle process and certainly one with considerable room for error. This difficulty is greatly exaggerated when we only have rather abstract case material to work from, with no data about the therapist's experience or the client's response to his or her interpretations.

Jack: a psychodynamic formulation

A prince betrayed and disinherited

The main themes of Jack's developmental history as offered to us hinge around the success and then the failure of his father and its effect on the family – capturing the internal drama of this, we might think of Jack as a young 'prince' who feels 'disinherited and betrayed'. From nothing, the father builds a business 'empire' but then destroys it; his is initially a success story but there is a dark side of violence and drunken unreliability to it; he abuses then abandons his family and becomes (to the women) a denigrated figure. The heart of Jack's story might be read in his relationship to this: he is offered and responds to a vision of himself as the inheritor of the 'kingdom', he has a sense of himself as growing into a man entitled to power, seemingly secure and enabled to develop and use his talents and social position. However, the shadow elements of this emerge as his father's 'realm' disintegrates and a substitute father is found who replicates an abuse he already feels in a seduction and betrayal of his sexuality just as he is becoming heir to it as an adult. Jack's life starts to disintegrate in a mirror image of his father's before it has even started.

This somewhat dramatised narrative certainly makes various speculative assumptions, but it endeavours to capture something of the possible experiential quality of the young man's life. The impact of Jack's story (on me) is of an overwhelming feeling of devastation and loss together with the omnipresent sense of threat and betrayal. It also points towards key themes to be explored in dynamic terms in other parts of the case material. These themes are the nature of masculinity; its roots in the identification with both parents and their images of manhood as a foundation for self-esteem and entitlement to success in life and for sustaining work, creativity and personal relationships in the real world; and the relation of sexuality and aggression to these. How does one 'come into one's own'? This is the core conflictual area – 'narcissistic' strivings probably closely liked to masculine identity but involving ambition and pride and the desire for recognition against the fear of failure, shame and humiliation. Jack's identification with his father is highly ambivalent – as perhaps it would inevitably be in a family situation where this father, and hence perhaps men in general, are both idealised and denigrated. To be strong and in charge is also to be violent and untrustworthy; success leads to failure and failure is not sustainable and leads to collapse, abandonment of others and shame for oneself. This ambivalence is intense enough to lead to confusion over what is reliable and, indeed, what is real. It is experienced as a profound betrayal: Jack needs his father desperately but feels as though his birthright has been taken from him by some trick – but one in which by his need and his ambivalence he is complicit. The sexual abuse (presumably) has this quality in his mind. This leads to further guilt as well as shame – because sexuality appears to figure as dangerous and destructive, a kind of rape. Someone in this story is sexually dangerous and it is (presumably in part experienced as) Jack: he is himself a (fantasised) betrayer. He and the world are unsafe and fragile – collapse is always imminent.

These anxieties about the masculine are likely, of course, to be intimately linked with ideas of femininity: the world that Jack grows up in (though information is lacking) appears to be a very female environment and may be experienced as overwhelming and engulfing. The fear of women may be thought of as an aspect of his need for his father and of his lack of safety with his masculinity. It may also be related (though this is less clear) to the issue of a safe and secure sense of home, of a right to belong. This is obviously connected to the family's immigrant status: are they as a whole settled securely (psychologically) in their new homeland? It is the men who principally suffer this uncertainty, and the fragility of their world, their identity and entitlement to a place, is emphasised at this wider social level too. This insecurity and the aggression it gives rise to are projected and experienced in a paranoid and persecutory form.

Many of the clinical features of Jack's history may be thought of as defensive responses to these core anxieties and conflicts. Initially there is acting-out in delinquency, violence and substance misuse – all are, of course, identifications with the father but are also escapes from overwhelming affect and anxiety – and, one would guess, chiefly experienced in terms of shame and humiliation. This becomes more explicit in the hypomanic symptoms and the omnipotent and compensatory aspects of his fantasy system which are fragile efforts to triumph over these shame-filled experiences. It is likely that these break through again in the depressed phases of his symptoms where escape is into self-blame. These defences are not completely effective, and they deepen into the severely regressed state of psychotic delusion, blurred reality boundaries and transient hallucinations: primitive unconscious material emerges and massive projection and denial take over at points of stress, including when the therapist (a woman which may or may not be an added threat) attempts to make some meaningful emotional contact. The delusional system is a defensive retreat but at the same time, reveals in a rather obvious way the fantasies which structure Jack's anxieties: theft and betrayal, revenge and persecution, entitlement to stardom and 'royalty', sexual violence.

In summary then, Jack is a young man whose development has broken down in adolescence in the face of the demands of his developing sexuality and particularly of the need to forge a successful identity and capacity to achieve in the world. This has activated a core dynamic conflict around self-assertion and creativity that is associated with his sense of masculinity. Because of his ambivalent identification with his father these needs are associated with shame and fear of failure and probably also secondarily with anxieties about damage and sexual aggression. He has retreated into increasingly regressive defensive strategies and finally resorted to manic and paranoid psychotic delusional positions to which he is liable to return under stress. Adaptively, this has created a trap for him in heightening the sense of risk associated with efforts to build a life in the real world and of engaging in intimate personal relationships, especially sexual ones. The evidence suggests the presence of considerable structural ego weakness, in his difficulty sustaining his sense of self-coherence and reality and the dangers of severely regressive, particularly psychotic, strategies to deal with interpersonal or other life pressures.

Reflection on the formulation

It is difficult in such written case material to locate that vital element of psychodynamic thinking, the counter-transference (that is, the feelings that the client arouses in the therapist). However, a story may serve to fill some of this gap. I wished to reassure myself that I was not going to 'over-interpret' elements of the case material that were in fact put there as disguise, and asked to be alerted to any examples of this. I was not well informed about the details of Robbie Williams's career and image, so I looked him up on the internet, became duly excited by the correspondences to what I saw as the themes (omnipotence, sexualisation and sexual ambiguity, making good, betrayal and so on) – and only then realised I'd already been told this might be a disguise element! I duly felt ashamed (at my omnipotence and naivety), seduced and betrayed, and perhaps especially, confused, with my sense of what was real undermined: I had turned a blind eye to what I already 'knew' and blanked it out in favour of a fantasy! Unconscious material gets into us in the most surprising ways during the process of formulation itself: we have to stay alert and open in order to use it to deepen our capacity for empathic understanding of the subject and their relationships – including those with ourselves and with other professionals.

Towards intervention

Recent developments in psychology generally about new ways of working with psychosis together with the wish to offer the respect to clients which so often seems lacking in the mental health system might seduce us into being too tactful to mention that Jack is 'mad'! Of course, one has to take note of his abilities and popularity and to feel sympathy that his situation is 'understandable' in terms of the events of his life (as the nurses do in making the referral). However, we should not turn a blind eye to the utter lack of achievement from age fifteen, the very fragile ego capacities, the failure to find any place to 'lodge' in life and the resort to a delusional identity. These features, all indicating extremely serious structural deficits, should shape a therapeutic response as much as any understanding drawn from the dynamic and developmental features of the case material.

For these reasons, intensive exploratory therapy is not indicated as the choice of intervention. There is a considerable risk that Jack will feel too much emotional pressure in such a situation, and since he is unlikely to be able to utilise it to understand himself he will probably cut off emotionally, may act out in some way, and might have to resort to psychotic forms of coping. However this does not mean that the psychodynamic formulation has nothing to offer: it can and perhaps should inform the more social and life-building interventions and relationships which Jack needs in order to begin to establish a more coherent and well-founded identity and a positive life structure for himself. These might usefully include a supportive therapeutic relationship which responds to his delusions in an understanding, containing but non-pressurising way that is informed by psychodynamic appreciations of their significance (without 'pushing' interpretations of them). Such a form of therapeutic work would focus on clarifying Jack's relationships in the real world (not on their fantasy meanings), offering positive coping strategies and perhaps provide a positive and safe personal role model to relate to (the preferred therapist for this task would probably be a man). Many of these developmental functions are likely also to be made available in a good social care setting. However these positive relationships and social opportunities are all too commonly disrupted and undermined by difficulties in the way such care is provided. Psychodynamic theory understands this in terms of the counter-transference dynamics activated amongst the staff and within the service systems. While some of these are general responses to dealing with severely disturbed people, in Jack's case one might predict a wish to see him as rather special and make extra efforts to rescue him; he is likely to feel alarmed and pressurised by such opportunities and to retreat from them, which in turn may result in disappointment for the therapists, and rejection or abandonment which Jack will experience as a further betrayal. A dynamically informed care plan would offer consultation and containment to the care team to avoid this kind of replication of an old destructive pattern and enable them to hold Jack as he gradually (and probably falteringly) deals with his shame, self-doubt and fragile sense of safety. Through this process he might be helped to find a place in life in which he can start to establish his sense of himself as a man.

Janet: a psychodynamic formulation

A girl unheld

Perhaps what is most striking from a psychodynamic perspective about Janet and her situation is how it can seem as though we don't really know her in spite of a proliferation of detail: understanding feels elusive, information fragmentary, and she herself seems to slip through our hands. This is a consequence in part of the nature of the case material that is provided – it might be described as referral-level information and there are numerous gaps at the level of psychological data. However the fact that this is what has been offered as representing Janet's life story might be taken as in itself significant: we can 'read' the material counter-transferentially both in our own reactions as readers and (interpretively) in those of the professionals who provide it in this form! Janet, if not exactly missing, seems to be difficult to take in, to hold coherently in mind, and this can be felt as both enticing and frustrating; it may parallel the ambivalence (between merging and rejecting) that is there in others' reactions to her.

This kind of first impression can be useful as a clue to where to direct attention in assessment and how to integrate the overall story. In Janet's case it fits with and emphasises the evidence which suggests early attachment difficulties – Mary's depression in the post-natal period, problems 'bonding' and feelings of rejection towards Janet, the possible lack of care demonstrated by the attendances at the Accident and Emergency Department. Features of the current problems certainly lend themselves to being thought about in these terms – anxieties about sleeping in her own bed and transport difficulties. At the same time Mary's possible over-identification and confusion of her own anxieties with those of her daughter (around the issue of mobility problems for example) are also likely to contribute to difficulty in a developmentally appropriate resolution of the tension between secure attachment and necessary separation. Mary's health problems seem likely to mean that there is a limited amount of attention and emotional 'feeding' available.

These attachment issues within the mother–daughter relationship are set in a wider context. The relationship of both Janet and Mary to the father is crucial and the violence, drunkenness, deterioration and final breakdown of the marriage suggest themselves as major contributors to Mary's difficulties and to Janet's insecurities. There are darker hints about possible abuse of Janet but while this needs to be kept in mind during assessment it may be a red herring. The place of the grandchildren in Mary's affections and Janet's reactions (perhaps of displacement and jealousy) to them may be a very important factor, and may indeed be what has precipitated the current worsening of difficulties and the referral. Equally, such issues of insecure attachment are paralleled by some social and cultural aspects of the family's circumstances (the traveller background and the disruption to this culture, the social disintegration of the area and the anticipated but uncertain re-housing). Mary is unlikely to feel 'held' herself in these circumstances and so is less able to offer this to her daughter. On the other hand, Janet's close relationship with another adult (Cindy) may be an important protective factor and a potentially therapeutically helpful resource. In spite of her various problems, she is a girl with areas of achievement and good functioning.

While these features of the case can be pulled together to some degree under a general focus on attachment problems and the way that Janet is insecurely held in the relationship with her mother and her wider networks, this does not really constitute an adequate basis for a formulation, certainly not a fully articulated psychodynamic account. The details of the attachment anxieties, the fantasy elaborations and meanings that they have for Janet (or indeed the underlying quality of Mary's anxieties and coping responses or the meaning of her relationship with this 'late' child who has been associated with so much difficulty in her life) remain obscure. Some features of the case – including what may be the main presenting problem of refusal to eat – might be part of this mother–daughter attachment issue, but equally they might not. The meanings, both relational and dynamic, of Janet's various 'symptoms' require detailed exploration. The attachment issues and other areas are best regarded as lines of enquiry to follow up in a more detailed assessment process.

However, a psychodynamic approach to this assessment process would also have some features of an intervention, in that there would be an effort to understand some of the experience of both mother and daughter by offering tentative interpretive understandings as part of the enquiry. Further therapy could be with either Mary or Janet (or both) individually, or with both of them jointly, though individual assessment opportunities would be advisable. The aim would be to touch on and perhaps articulate for each their underlying needs and fears within the network of relationships and problem areas, and to differentiate their concerns at a developmentally appropriate level. Assessment and formulation would need to make an appraisal of the accessibility of each to being helped by such an exploratory relationship. But again (as for Jack) intensive individual therapy is not necessarily the only or even the preferred answer from a psychodynamic point of view. The strengths that Janet shows in the ways in which she continues to cope, plus the resources of her family and local community, might provide the means by which she can find the personal attention and security which she craves and needs. At the same time, a major component of the intervention must be to ensure that Mary receives sufficient support for herself and that Janet is not over-identified with her own needs.

Reflections

This clinical level of theory that we have articulated above has been developed to support the therapist in managing the many competing demands and pressures of her role. A dynamic formulation might help to select the therapeutic strategy and identify risks and aims. If exploratory therapy is indicated, there are other issues to be considered: the intensity of the therapeutic approach, the length of work, the specificity of the focus, the balance of supportiveness and challenge in the relationship and so on. Above all, each point of view can be thought of as a 'listening perspective': a way of hearing and understanding clinical material in a therapeutic session and hence using it to develop an empathic response (Hedges, 1983). The therapist might monitor the interventions and interpretations made against the overall case formulation to keep herself 'on track'. But there are risks in this too. Formulations might become a barrier to empathy through objectifying the client. This is one reason why it has not been the usual practice in dynamic therapy to explicitly share an overall formulation directly with the client. Such a move is thought likely to be experienced as an imposition which stands in the way of the client's autonomous self-exploration and discovery, a process which is in itself as important therapeutically as any explicit new understandings arrived at as its outcome. Understanding is found and offered only in the context of the therapeutic (transferential) relationship as it unfolds.

In this sense, from a psychodynamic perspective we would wish to ask what 'work' a formulation is doing (emotionally) for the therapist who is creating it. Often we formulate when we feel a 'need' to do so – but that need is formed by the therapeutic relationship itself: we never stand outside that transference/counter-transference matrix in such a way as to be objective. For instance, it is a common experience to feel that we have a good and clear understanding of a client at the beginning of therapy and then to lose that as the work proceeds. That sense of understanding is (hopefully) regained – we often have a feeling that this was something we knew all along – but is the meaning the same? In a modern psychodynamic practice, understanding is a mutually constituted process arising through the transformation of the relationship patterns. It is not an external, abstract or objective construction. Formulation in this sense is the therapist's continuing struggle to make meaningful – to symbolise or 'mentalise' – what is confused and unformed in experience. This depends, crucially, on the capacity not to know what is going on, to allow and tolerate the (often painful) experience of being lost, of disorganisation and confusion. Seeking an abstract formulation may be part of a wish to avoid this experience, to be defined, limited and in control: it can be defensive. A defensive need to understand makes us prone to oversimplify, to coerce meaning – and in doing so to coerce or seduce the client into a self-limiting version of themselves.

I suggested earlier that a psychodynamic view creates, in effect, a 'democracy of pathology' – we're all in it together, this painful and confusing mess of conflicting desires, hatreds and fears. This is why personal therapy is such a crucial part of psychodynamic practice, not so much, perhaps, to solve our own problems but to gain some familiarity with the workings of our own mind and emotions, and so, hopefully, to save ourselves from the worst traps that therapeutic work lays in its path. This appreciation of the shared pain and difficulty that being human involves for all of us is a basis for a profound empathy and respect for clients. But it does not appeal to everyone: psychodynamic theory is not, in this sense, a 'positive psychology' and it is, as it were, proud of the fact. Instead it takes a tragic and ironic view of existence. Psychodynamic formulation requires that we face the painful issues at the heart of life squarely and find hope for people, ourselves included, in honesty, humour and compassion for our common plight.

As therapists we need all the help we can get with the difficult and demanding task of therapy, and formulation must find its place in this, not as a refuge from the agonies of uncertainty but as an aid to tolerating the experience of not understanding, managing the sense of risk in relating therapeutically, promoting rather than stifling curiosity and encouraging the possibility of playfulness and aliveness. A formulation can function as a kind of 'transitional object' for the therapist in Winnicott's (1971) sense. Like a child's teddy, it is something that is both real and important but not entirely serious, something that we hold onto for security and that helps us think – but which can be discarded as wider fields of mutual understanding open up.

Over the past forty years psychodynamic clinicians have taken an increasingly relational view not only of therapeutic technique but also of the nature of the knowing that is established in psychotherapy: constantly shifting and highly contextualised understandings are constructed with the client in the process of interpreting and formulating clinical 'material'. However, there remains a substantial range of different theoretical approaches from the classical to the post-modern within the psychodynamic spectrum. This chapter has offered the outline of a 'clinical' approach to formulation which, to a degree at least, links these competing perspectives.

Key characteristics of a psychodynamic formulation

- Looks at symptoms and life problems as expressing an underlying order of meaning in the client's emotional life, arising from conflicting relationships, feelings, desires and fears.
- Identifies these key conflicts as ones which repeat across different contexts and which are being managed by characteristic defensive strategies giving rise to recurring cycles of dysfunctional and self-limiting solutions.
- Relates these conflicts and defences to the individual's developmental history, main past relationships and attachment patterns – finds meaning in the person's unique experience of their life course.
- Draws heavily on the notion of the unconscious and its workings – meanings are viewed as symbolised and purposefully concealed, as complex and multi-layered, fluid and shifting.

- Identifies what in the client's recent life situation has destabilised previous ways of resolving the core conflicts, in order to give meaning to the client's seeking help now.
- Validates these hypotheses by observing how they are played out within the therapeutic relationship (the transference) and the therapist's own experience of participating in it (the counter-transference), seeking parallel patterns and themes in these specific relational contexts.
- Uses the therapist's feelings/emotional resonances, not just thoughts and theories, as a guide to eliciting and understanding meanings.
- Does not explicitly share the whole formulation with the client, but validates it by observing how the client responds to the construction of specific meanings (interpretations) of his or her actions and experience based on that understanding.
- Looks for coherent responses and elaborations more than explicit agreement: the evidence being sought is hermeneutic (that is, it enriches meaning and understanding) and contextual rather than generalised.
- In considering such 'structural' issues as the degree of maturity, stability and flexibility or the stylistic regularities of typical defences in a person's psychological functioning, the psychodynamic approach can sometimes take on a broadly 'diagnostic' character – but its deeper thrust is intensely individualising and suspicious of general categorical statements about people.

References

Erikson, E. (1950) *Childhood and Society*, New York: Norton.

Freud, A. (1936) *The Ego and the Mechanisms of Defence*, London: Hogarth.

Hedges, L.E. (1983) *Listening Perspectives in Psychotherapy,* Northvale, NJ: Jason Aronson.

Hinshelwood, R.D. (1991) Psychodynamic formulation in assessment for psychotherapy, *British Journal of Psychotherapy*, 8(2) 166–174.

Kohut, H. (1977) *The Restoration of the Self,* New York: International Universities Press.

Leiper, R. and Maltby, M. (2004) *The Psychodynamic Approach to Therapeutic Change,* London: Sage.

Levenson, H. (1995) *Time-Limited Dynamic Psychotherapy,* New York: Basic Books.

Luborsky, L. (1984) *Principles of Psychoanalytic Psychotherapy: A Manual for Supportive-Expressive Treatment,* New York: Basic Books.

McWilliams, N. (1999) *Psychoanalytic Case Formulation,* New York: Guilford Press.

Mahler, M. S., Pine, F. and Bergman, A. (1975) *The Psychological Birth of the Human Infant: Symbiosis and Individuation,* New York: Basic Books.

Malan, D. H. (1995) *Individual Psychotherapy and the Science of Psychodynamics,* 2nd edn, London: Butterworths.

Molnos, A. (1984) The two triangles are four: a diagram to teach the process of dynamic brief psychotherapy, *British Journal of Psychotherapy,* 1(2), 112–125.

Rappaport, D. (1959) The structure of psychoanalytic theory: a systematizing attempt in S. Koch (ed.), *Psychology: The Study of a Science* (Vol. 3), New York: McGraw-Hill.

Strupp, H.H. and Binder, J.L. (1984) *Psychotherapy in a New Key: A Guide to Time-limited Dynamic Psychotherapy,* New York: Basic Books.

Wallerstein, R.S. (1988) One psychoanalysis or many? *International Journal of Psychoanalysis,* 69 (1), 5–21.

——(2002) The trajectory of psychoanalysis: a prognostication, *The International Journal of Psychoanalysis,* 83(6), 1247–1267.

Winnicott, D. (1971) *Playing and Reality,* London: Tavistock.

Winnicott, D.W. (1965) *The Maturational Processes and the Facilitating Environment: Studies in the Theory of Emotional Development,* London: Hogarth.

Chapter 4

Systemic formulation
Mapping the family dance

Rudi Dallos and Jacqui Stedmon

The systemic approach

In this chapter, a brief overview of systemic theory is offered within a historical perspective which describes how it has progressed through a number of phases from a relatively modernist and behavioural framework, emphasising patterns and sequences in family interactions, to frameworks which came to foreground shared meaning. The most recent developments focus on the centrality of language and the joint construction of understanding between family members. This has much in common with social constructionist approaches to therapy as described in chapter 5. A systemic approach to formulation is then illustrated through the two case studies of Jack and Janet.

Symptoms and family processes

Systemic family therapy is an approach which involves working with families or subsections of families. Originally there was a strong insistence on meeting with all of the relevant family members, though therapists nowadays may see part of a family system, and will sometimes even work with an individual member while keeping the dynamics of the wider family system in mind. The most formal version of family therapy is conducted by a team of therapists, most commonly with one person in the room with the family and the rest of the team observing live through an observation screen or video, or sometimes by being in the room with the family. However, practitioners use the ideas flexibly and may work alone, in pairs, carry out home visits and so on.

A characteristic feature of modern practice is that the therapist and the team will discuss their ideas with the family in the form of reflective conversations. For example, the observation team may come and join the family and the therapist and share their ideas or formulations with the family. Alternatively, when working as a pair, the two therapists may periodically turn to each other to have such a conversation in front of the family. Even working alone, family therapists may still engage in a conversation where they reflect their thoughts about the family back to them, followed by a discussion with the family members.

Core systemic concepts

Systemic theory and practice has evolved since its inception in the 1950s from a theory centred on a biological metaphor of families as homeostatic systems, to that of families as 'problem-saturated' linguistic systems. Nevertheless, an enduring concept is that problems apparently located in one individual can instead be seen as a product of the interactional dynamics in the family. In this way 'symptoms' are seen as problems in interaction and communication between people, rather than as residing within individuals. Central to systemic practice is the idea that cause and effect have a circular relationship whereby problems are maintained through vicious cycles of unhelpful feedback. This is most easily understood through thinking about quite widely held stereotypes of couple dynamics. Jane 'nags' John because he won't talk about his feelings, John feels blamed and 'withdraws', Jane feels unheard and angry and 'nags' more and so both feel trapped in a circle of anger/nagging and blame/withdrawal that has a natural tendency to escalate. The problem is not that John *is* emotionally illiterate or that Jane *has* a complaining personality, although each might construe the other's difficulties from this structural linear perspective. Systemic therapists view these narrow individualistic 'punctuations' of problems as unhelpful and actively seek instead to shed light on the relational interactions that maintain presenting 'problems' between people (Dallos, 1991; Dallos and Draper, 2010; and see chapter 7).

Another core concept adopted by family therapists is the importance of understanding triadic relationships, whereby conflictual processes between two people may recruit, or 'triangulate' to use technical jargon, a third person. For example, if we wind the clock forward, Jane and John may have a two-year-old child. They have given up resolving their difficulties as a couple and have stopped talking to one another about how they feel. However, their angry and blaming emotions towards one another find a new outlet in arguing about how to manage little Tom's temper tantrums; Jane wants to try a 'Naughty corner' while John thinks it best to ignore such outbursts altogether. Caught in the middle, Tom reacts anxiously to his parents' confusing messages and shows his frustration through further 'tantrums'. Hence the parents' unresolved conflict is 'detoured' through arguing over Tom. Alternatively, John and Jane may have escalated their arguments to a point where violence is threatened. In this context, Tom may feel aroused and frightened by his parents' arguments to the point that he throws a tantrum. This has the effect of bringing both parents together to calm him down and comfort him, momentarily diffusing the conflict between them. Later when Tom is settled, they find another source of dangerously escalating disagreement, triggering

Tom's distress once more. If this pattern between the three of them persists over time, Tom's behaviour may come to serve the function of regulating the marital distance and closeness between his parents (Byng-Hall, 1980).

Family therapists also recognise the importance of trans-generational processes for contextualising current difficulties and will often explore how parents' ideas about caregiving connect with their early childhood experiences of being parented. For example, John may have admired his father's apparent ability to remain unflustered during family arguments and may be attempting to replicate his style, while Jane may have been raised in a very liberal family with a brother who went 'off the rails' during his adolescence. She may want to do things differently by creating firm boundaries for Tom, thereby correcting perceived deficits in the parenting practices of her own family of origin.

One of the most influential early ideas in systemic family therapy was that families, like other social systems, can experience stress, anxiety and distress at points where significant and fundamental changes need to be made (Haley, 1973; Carter and McGoldrick, 1988). The onset of problems in families can be seen as connected to the emotionally destabilising aspects of family transitions, especially at family life cycle transition points, such as the birth of children and when young people leave home. We shall introduce some ideas for applying these systemic concepts when we return to the case scenarios for Jack and Janet.

Formulation in systemic practice

Importantly, systemic approaches have increasingly come to regard all aspects of therapy as an interactional and collaborative process. Formulation therefore is not seen as something that the therapist *does to* the family but as something that they *do with* the family. Thus therapy has been seen as a co-constructional process whereby the therapist, supervision team and the family members jointly come to develop new formulations of their problems. This is not as an objective process, but as a perturbation which starts to change the family system. How formulation is undertaken, the questions that are asked, when and how they are asked, are all seen as having the potential to bring about significant changes. This carefully crafted sequence of questioning, attending to moment-by-moment feedback and eliciting fresh information for family members to consider constitutes a style that Tomm (1987) refers to as 'interventive interviewing'. The way in which this process of formulation is undertaken starts to shape the relationship with the family. Thus, there is less of a distinction between the stages of assessment–formulation–intervention than in many therapies.

A cornerstone of early systemic thinking was that symptoms in families served a *function* of stabilising a family system. In many ways this appeared a counter-intuitive idea since the established view was that the symptoms were the very thing that was causing the distress and unhappiness. One of the most enduring and helpful ideas from the first phase is the model of formulation proposed by the Mental Research Institute team (Watzlawick et al., 1974). This consists of the elegantly simple idea that many problems arise from the failing solutions that are applied to difficulties (see Figure 4.1).

In this approach to formulation, the focus is on an identification of what is seen as the problem and how this is linked to difficulties which the family has attempted to overcome. The formulation consists of the following steps.

Exploration of the problem

- Deconstruction of the problem – how do family members define the problem, when did it start, who first noticed, what was first noticed?
- Linking the problem to ordinary difficulties.
- Exploration of what was attempted in order to solve the difficulties.
- Beliefs about the difficulties and what to do about them.
- Discussion/evaluation of what worked and what did not work.
- What decisions were made about whether to persist with the attempted solutions and which solutions to pursue.

With the growing influence of constructivist ideas about unique personal meanings as being central to human activity and experience, systemic family therapy came to view descriptions and formulations as having an 'as if' quality, in that they were held to be propositions rather than truths. As such, these propositions could be more or less useful in terms of the extent to which they facilitated positive change. Instead of assessment and formulation being seen as one-off scientific activities they came to be viewed as a continual and dynamic process of developing, testing and revising formulations (see also Dallos, 1991; Hoffman, 1993; and chapter 7).

PROBLEM

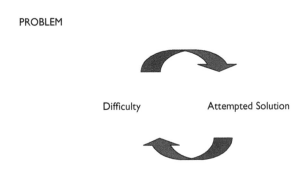

Difficulty   Attempted Solution

Figure 4.1 Attempted solutions

Progressive hypothesising

The Milan team of family therapists (Palazzoli et al., 1978) added the useful idea that therapy and formulation are inter-twined, and inevitably progress through a recursive process of hypothesising.

> By hypothesising we refer to the formulation by the therapist of a hypothesis based upon the information he possesses regarding the family that he is interviewing. The hypothesis establishes a starting point for his investigation as well as verification of the validity of that hypothesis based upon scientific methods and skill. If the hypothesis proves false, the therapist must form a second hypothesis based upon the information gathered during the testing of the first.
>
> (Palazzoli et al., 1980: 4)

They argued that there could be no objective truth about a family; the best that could be achieved was to formulate hypotheses (hunches) about what was going on which could be more or less helpful in our ways of working. Hence a hypothesis was to be judged in terms of how effective it was in facilitating positive change.

The Milan team argued that the process of developing hypotheses was not only fundamental to the process of formulation but also to the practice of clinical work. The beginning of therapy with a family can be an extremely confusing affair and it would be easy for a therapist to feel overwhelmed by the amount of information that a family presents. A hypothesis can help to cut through this potentially overwhelming complexity and organise the information into a meaningful and manageable structure. Holding a clear hypothesis can help the therapist to actively engage the family by pursuing issues and asking questions to explore and test the hypotheses. This gives a direction to the work and helps to avoid the risk of unwittingly getting caught up in, or even aggravating, the family's problems. It also helps to reduce the anxiety of the initial contact (which can be considerable for all concerned, not least the therapist).

Another key function of the hypothesis was to be elaborative; that is, to help to elicit new information. Cecchin (1987) questioned the notion of 'hypothesising' and argued that it implied an inappropriate idea of a 'scientific' testing for truth. In contrast, he went on to compare the process of formulation to a form of creative curiosity. The therapist is encouraged to maintain this position of curiosity in relation to the family.

The team went on to note a number of other important aspects of this process:

- explicitly forming and stating our hypotheses can help to reflect on our implicit assumptions which might otherwise impede therapeutic progress;

- articulation of hypotheses can help to reveal differences and agreements within the therapy team which again might hinder therapy if left unstated;
- this view of hypotheses puts less pressure on the therapist to 'get it right', and thus reduces anxiety especially in the early stages of therapy;
- as the engagement with the family is from less of an 'expert' position it may be easier for the therapist and the team to remain curious and interested as opposed to trying to develop a 'correct' formulation.

In practice there seemed to be times when the Milan team deviated from a constructivist position into making statements about their hypothesis being 'correct' or 'hitting the nail on the head'. There was also a sense that the hypotheses were not invariably formed in a collaborative way with families and might even convey implicit theories about how families function. For example, the Milan therapists assumed that all family members have benign intent, a position that has since been challenged by feminist family therapists working with domestic violence and abuse (Goldner, 1998). The 'correctness' of a hypothesis was seen in terms of whether it was accurate about the family's beliefs. For example, the team describe a case of an adolescent boy who was displaying delinquent problems. The boy was living alone with his 'attractive' divorced mother. Their first hypothesis was that his behaviour was intended to draw his father back into the family. However, this was rapidly disproved and it became clear that a more *accurate* hypothesis was that:

> The mother was an attractive and charming woman, and perhaps after these years of maternal dedication, she had met 'another man', and perhaps her son was jealous and angry, and was showing this through his behaviour ... Our second hypothesis hit the target. For the past two months the mother had been dating a friend.
>
> (Palazzoli et al., 1980: 2)

Family therapy and social constructionism

Contemporary systemic family practice has shown a significant move towards social constructionism. This extends constructivist ideas by emphasising the importance of language and culture. Language is seen not only as an attempt to describe the world but as helping us to actively make meaning and 'construct' it (see chapter 5). These constructions are shaped by the dominant ideas or discourses that a given culture holds as central. In turn these ideas have their own influence and may be reaffirmed and reproduced in local conversations. Dominant ideas such as that of 'mental health', 'satisfactory family life', 'good mother', 'appropriate behaviour' and so on will shape the expectations and actions of family members. Systemic therapy tries to bring these discourses into consciousness so that families can be freed up from the constraints imposed by everyday language use. This has also heralded a more collaborative approach to therapy in which the therapist and the team work alongside the family and attempt to work in a transparent and open way. Recent approaches thus put forward a view of formulation as a shared activity rather than as something predominantly conducted by the therapist (White and Epston, 1990; and see chapter 5).

Use of self-reflective formulation

Central to the developments described above was a recognition that the therapist brought both personal and professional experiences to the process of formulation. It was therefore necessary to explore these reflectively; for example, why am I so concerned and angry about Jack's father? Furthermore, systemic therapy started to regard the relationship between the therapist and the family, and also between the therapist and the consulting team, as essential aspects of the formulation. As an example, they started to observe that sometimes the consulting team could show similar ambivalences, splits and divisions in their formulation about parenting as the child was experiencing. In relation to Jack, part of the formulation might be that some members of the team would feel angry towards the father and very sympathetic towards the mother. In addition, formulation included the dynamics in the therapy room, such that for example the team might notice and comment on their observation of the therapist–family dynamics; perhaps that the therapist appeared to talk mostly to the mother and to ignore one of the sisters. The therapist could discuss with the family whether this was something that they had also observed happening in the room. Did anything like this happen at home? How did they communicate about feelings of not getting their fair share of attention and so on? This feature of systemic family therapy formulation is harder to illustrate since we do not have a transcript of a family therapy session with Jack or Janet. However, we will attempt to demonstrate a similar process in chapter 9 through a piece of imaginary dialogue between Jack and a therapist.

A proposed model of systemic formulation

Though systemic therapy has evolved from an emphasis on structure and pattern to one on meanings, we suggest that a number of common threads can be drawn out (see also Carr, 2006):

1   Deconstruction of the problem.
2   Problem-maintaining patterns and feedback loops.
3   Beliefs and explanations.
4   Transitions, emotions and attachments.
5   Contextual factors.

Contemporary systemic formulation has shown a shift from an emphasis on patterns and processes, to a focus on understandings and narratives, and most recently to an emphasis on language and cultural contexts (see Dallos and Draper, 2010). We suggest in addition that it is important to think about assessment and formulation in terms of two inter-connected processes: analysis and synthesis.

- *Analysis*: this entails exploration with the family about their patterns of interactions, understandings of each other, their explanations of problems and their attempts to solve them. This happens not just in the early sessions but throughout therapy.
- *Synthesis*: this may follow or run alongside the assessment and analysis. Here, we start to integrate the strands of information into preliminary hypotheses or formulations of the problem.

This suggested inter-dependence between analysis and synthesis is consistent with a constructivist view which regards observation and gathering of information as an active, selective and interpretative process. In starting to analyse the problem we are inevitably making assumptions and interpretations, for example about what evidence is relevant and what further material we need. We are selectively attending more to some factors and less to others. By adopting a reflexive stance we may be less vulnerable to being limited by our implicit assumptions (see Stedmon and Dallos, 2009, for an extended analysis of reflective processes in systemic practice). In addition, we emphasise formulation as a dynamic and collaborative process (see chapters 8 and 9) that is developing between us and the family. By sharing our ideas with them we move towards a co-constructed formulation.

Jack: a systemic formulation

Deconstructing the problem

The initial starting point from any therapeutic perspective is to explore the nature of the 'problem/s'. This involves an analytical process in which we search for clues about what may be causing and maintaining them. From a systemic perspective this typically involves a number of related questions:

- How is the problem defined? Is it framed predominantly as individual or interpersonal?
- Contexts – why does the problem occur *now*? Where does the problem occur and in what settings (home, school, work)? And where is it at its worst?
- How does the problem affect important relationships in the family and elsewhere? How do relationships affect the problem?

- For whom do the problems cause most difficulties and distress – the parents, siblings, people outside the family?
- What is the life history of the problem, when and how did it start, how has it altered over time, and what factors influenced its development?
- The development of the problem in relation to the financial resources, environmental factors, extended family, the role of professional agencies, and cultural discourses.

Exceptions

Alongside this exploration it is important to consider exceptions since these can offer a clue as to what the causal and maintaining processes might be, and can help to construct a more positive and hopeful framework with the family. Exceptions are times when the family has been successful in resolving the problems or can draw from other aspects of the wider family network to develop stories of competence, achievement and so on, such as:

- recent cases of success in overcoming the problem or times when it has been absent;
- exceptions that have occurred further back in time or in other contexts as above;
- exceptions in the wider family network;
- hypothetical exceptions – these are invitations to consider possible circumstances or developments where the problems might be reduced or absent.

Genograms

Systemic formulations often start with a visual depiction, or genogram, of the immediate family and its connections with external systems (see Figure 4.2).

The genogram gives a map of the family system and its relationships and sources of support, and helps to direct the gathering of further information. In Jack's case it might lead us to ask:

- How isolated is this family? What contact is there with other relatives? How much support has the family had since father left?
- Why is there no contact between Jack and his father?
- What is Jack's relationship with his sisters like? Have they visited him in hospital?
- Who knows about the sexual abuse? Did his parents support him in dealing with it?
- Is Jack the child who carries some allegiance to his father whereas his sisters may have given up on him? Has this led to conflicts between Jack and his mother and sisters? Is Jack's drinking a form of loyalty to his father – following in his footsteps in his use of alcohol?

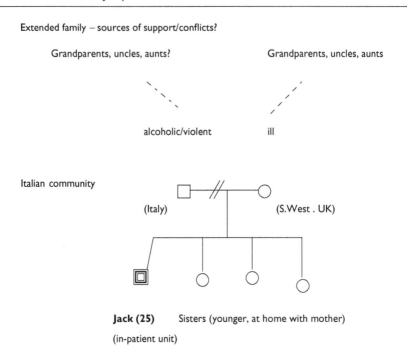

Figure 4.2 Genogram of Jack's family system

Problem-maintaining patterns and feedback loops

It is possible that Jack is caught between the women in the family, and his father. A cycle may be occurring whereby he has tried to be helpful, to be the 'man of the family', but feels he has failed, and is humiliated and displaced from his role as the caring big brother. Perhaps he is now seen by the family as a burden and a cause of problems, which may make them angry with him. This response may be intensified by their anger at his father for 'abandoning' them all to poverty and distress. Likewise, Jack may be worried about his mother's health but also angry with her for kicking him out, and perhaps for taking her feelings about father out on him. Again, Jack may feel caring and protective towards his sisters but feel humiliated and resentful about their 'good' role. This sense of resentment may in turn fuel a mixture of feelings such as defeat, confusion and retaliation (see Figure 4.3).

It may well be that this pattern bears some similarities to one that existed between Jack's father and his mother. It would be interesting to explore whether there have been similar marital dynamics on either or both sides of the parents' families.

Mixed feelings

Jack	Mother and sisters
Tries to help, fails, drinks,	Helpful, and concerned about
drugs, angry – feels rejected	the abuse… but then feel let down,
drink/drugs to feel better…	angry, rejecting…

Figure 4.3 Circularity indicating core pattern maintaining the problems

Beliefs and explanations

It is possible that Jack sees himself, and is seen in the family, as being like his father. He is said to miss his father and describes seeing his father's face in the mirror, which suggests pre-occupation with thoughts about him. Given the history of violence in the family, his mother and sisters may be frightened of Jack and worried that he will turn out the same. This perception, along with the fact that Jack does miss his father and may be angry at his mother for 'driving him away', could make it more likely that Jack will at times act like his father and subsequently hate himself for doing so.

It can be helpful to consider what some of the shared beliefs between the women in the family might be (Procter, 1981; Winter and Procter, this book; Dallos, 1996). Procter (1981) describes families as holding contrasting beliefs which encapsulate and maintain the patterns of relationships in the family. For example, seeing Jack as dangerous is likely to align the women in the family together in fear of him. In contrast, seeing him as 'ill' and needing care may mean he is less excluded. Thus, mother's and sisters' beliefs may include the following:

- Jack is abusive like his father, looks like him and acts like him – drinks, drugs and violence.
- Jack is a victim – he has been abused and cannot cope.
- Jack should be helping us, things are bad enough without him causing more problems.
- Mother is ill and cannot cope with all of this.
- The girls, in contrast to Jack, are helpful and good.
- Men are useless and dangerous.

Jack's beliefs may include:

- I am not like my dad who abandoned us.
- I am like my dad and I miss my dad and I don't know why he left – he doesn't care about me/us.
- Mum has made no attempt to get in contact with dad – she doesn't care about how I feel.
- My mother is ill and has been badly treated.
- Men, me included, are useless and dangerous.

Scaling questions

An effective way of exploring and clarifying family members' shared formulations is by the use of 'scaling' or 'least–most' questions. For example, seeing Jack as dangerous is likely to align the women in the family together in fear of him. In contrast, seeing him as 'ill' and needing care may mean that he is less excluded. They can be invited to consider some dimensions and to discuss where they think each member of the family might lie on the dimension: for example, sensitive–insensitive, similar to–different from dad (see Figure 4.4).

The questions invite the family members to consider differences in their views, to generate new information for the therapist and to arrive at shared viewpoints. For example, we might be surprised that they see Jack as the most sensitive, despite also being so frightened and wary of him. The questions also encourage the family to express their own understandings or formulations, whether agreed or not, and can help to promote more psychological formulations than for example, the dominant belief that Jack is 'ill'.

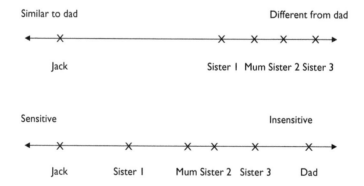

Figure 4.4 Scaling technique to explore family members' positions on core family dimensions

The role of illness

Both Jack and his mother are coming to share an illness identity, which can perform the function of helping to resolve some of the mixed feelings, thus:

- If Jack is ill then he is not responsible for his actions and we can forgive him and be sympathetic.
- Since mother is *ill* she cannot be expected to resolve Jack's feelings about his dad – she has enough on her plate.

The consequences, though, are that Jack has to remain ill and/or become increasingly incapacitated. This increases the burden on the family as well, and the longer he is ill the less possible it becomes to confront the underlying conflicts, which are concealed behind the 'illness' role.

Transitions, emotions, attachments

A helpful way of mapping transitions and changes is through the use of family sculpts. This can employ objects, such as coins, buttons or stones, to represent family members (and also can be elaborated by adding friends, professionals and so on) with distances between the objects representing emotional closeness and proximity. Rather than focusing on normative stages, such as leaving home, the sculpt can offer a more focused and idiosyncratic view of what transitions were important for the family. In Jack's case it might be possible to consider the patterning of their relationships while Jack's father was still living with them as opposed to during the stage of him leaving the family and afterwards, or when Jack was well and after he became 'ill'. Family members are asked to arrange the objects on a large piece of paper and explain their decisions as they do so. The discussion continues until they reach a consensus or agree to differ. Interestingly, families usually find it possible, despite initial differences of perspective, to agree on a shared position. In carrying out the sculpt the family members in effect reveal their own formulations along with being prompted to consider relational formulations – how the problems have influenced their relationships and vice versa (see Figure 4.5).

This initial sculpt might reveal graphically how Jack was caught in the middle in having split loyalties to his father and mother, as opposed to his sisters who had aligned themselves with their mother (see Figure 4.6).

It appeared that the family almost completely lost contact with Jack's father after he left. Despite this, his place on the edge of the sculpt shows that Jack was still pre-occupied with thinking about him. However, the splits became wider with Jack's sisters retreating even further from their father. It might also be apparent that Jack has become more distant from his sisters due to their fear of him. It also becomes evident that Jack's mother might feel in a very ambivalent position in being concerned about Jack but also angry and

While dad was at home:

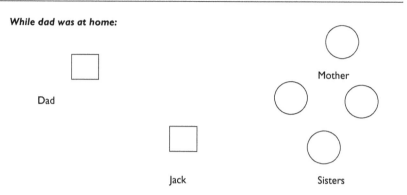

Figure 4.5 Sculpt with shapes indicating pattern of emotional relationships before dad left the family

After dad left

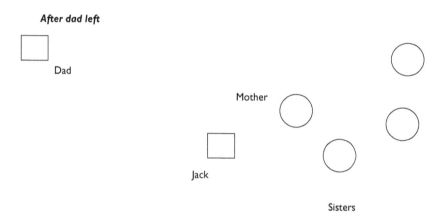

Figure 4.6 Sculpt with shapes indicating pattern of emotional relationships after dad left the family

frightened of his father. It may also be revealed that, for example one of his sisters had tried to help Jack but increasingly felt trapped in her ambivalent feelings about him as vulnerable but also frightening and similar to their father.

The process of conducting a sculpt can also assist in promoting re-formulations, or therapeutic changes. This integration of exploration/ formulation/intervention is central to systemic practice. The information gathered can also prompt different ideas, questions and formulations about the changes and causes of events in the family:

- Jack started drinking around the time that his father and mother divorced. Possibly this was to deal with the pain, or in the hope that they would recognise his distress and stay together?

- This divorce was also close to the time that Jack was sexually abused and in need of emotional support, but his parents may have been distracted by their own distress and anger surrounding their separation?
- The divorce also coincided with Jack taking on a job, presumably to help out because of the deteriorating family fortunes?
- Jack's leaving home appears to have occurred in a very negative and destructive way – did being thrown out contribute to his deterioration and admission to psychiatric services shortly afterwards?
- The next serious development in Jack's problems is associated with his mother developing serious health problems – is she now even less able to offer Jack support?

We may observe a pattern in the family whereby distress, illness and misfortune are accompanied by further problems. It seems extremely difficult for family members to meet each other's needs, and people appear to respond in a symmetrical way to each others' neediness by becoming more needy themselves. As a result, there may be so much distress at times of crises that there is no spare capacity to resolve the issues associated with the transitions, e.g. negotiating contact between the children and their father (see Figure 4.7).

We could also see the situation here in terms of the entrance of professional agencies – the 'comfort of strangers' entering the dynamics of this family so that, for example, the hospital takes on the role of the missing parent/s (see Figure 4.8).

The family may benefit by gaining some relief while Jack gets looked after, but at the expense of a transition to the hospital and Jack acquiring a chronic 'illness' identity. The support of the hospital system may depend on Jack being seen and seeing himself as 'ill'.

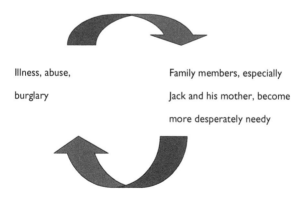

Illness, abuse, burglary

Family members, especially Jack and his mother, become more desperately needy

Figure 4.7 The transition to a family–hospital system

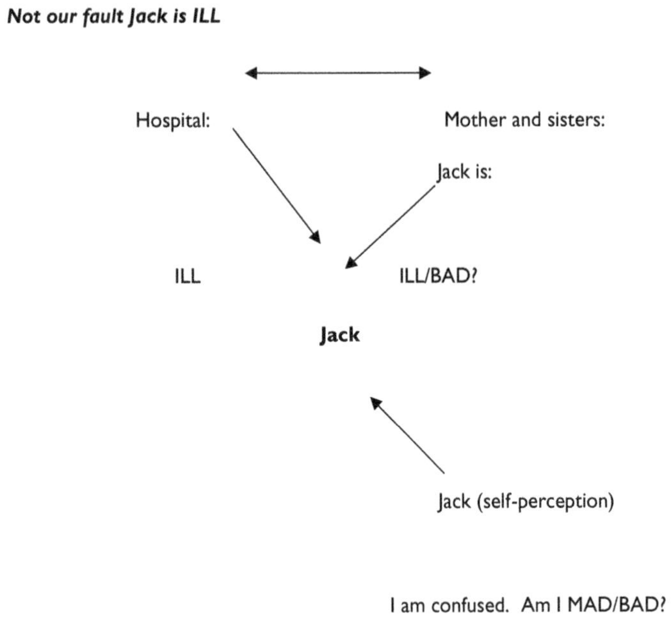

Not our fault Jack is ILL

Hospital: Mother and sisters:

Jack is:

ILL   ILL/BAD?

Jack

Jack (self-perception)

I am confused. Am I MAD/BAD?

Figure 4.8 Process maintaining the definition of Jack as 'ill'

Contextual factors

Systemic approaches emphasise that systems are profoundly influenced by contexts. In this they typically include the influence of cultural factors, the extended family, the community and different environmental situations. For Jack's family we would consider the following factors:

- The family has roots and connections to a different (Italian) culture which has a strong emphasis on religion, family loyalty and closeness.
- We do not know much about mother's background except that she seems to have come to accept and value her role in an Italian community.
- There appears to be a tradition of drinking on the male side of the family and it would be interesting to know whether there were other problems on either side of the family.
- There is a sense that this family is very socially isolated and that their only support comes from the psychiatric services.
- We do not know whether Jack's sisters have their own friends and supports.

Summary

The initial stages of formulation consist of the generation of a range of questions. In systemic therapy this is seen as a recursive and fluid process as captured in the notion of 'progressive hypothesising'. The search is not for a definitive formulation but one that helps to orient us in our search for further information and at the same time offers a guide towards possible areas of intervention. In turn, the initial attempts at interventions are seen as offering further information which serves to re-shape the formulation and the direction of interventions. What determines the usefulness of the formulation is the extent to which the family starts to derive benefits from the work that results from it.

One of the main ways that systemic therapists share their formulations with families is through the use of reflecting teams, where the team members supporting the therapist discuss their ideas in the presence of the family, and share their multiple formulations with them (see Figure 4.9).

Synthesis: a systemic formulation for Jack

So what might be a synthesis of our formulation about Jack and his family? There are a variety of ways we could combine the available information, and the direction we choose will also be shaped by our own clinical and personal experiences. One version that fits for us is the following, though we emphasise that this would only be held as tentative.

Our formulation is centred around a theme of multiple distress. Though Jack is the identified patient in this family there is sense of the whole family

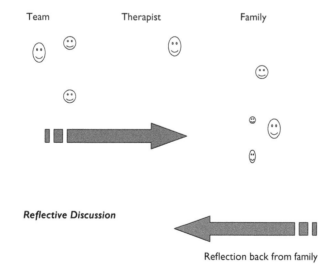

Figure 4.9 Family therapy and reflecting teams – sharing formulations

being 'under siege'. Certainly Jack and his mother are both weighed down by troubles and it seems likely that the sisters are also feeling exhausted. There is a strong sense that when painful, disastrous events happen this family has not been able to support each other in dealing with the resulting distress. It is as if their lives are taken up with just trying to survive. To feel happy, secure and reassured may seem like a luxury they never have been, and never will be, able to enjoy.

Tracing this back in time, Jack seems to have been very distressed by the loss of his father, especially since the breakdown of the marriage may have occurred in a violent and frightening way. This may have left the whole family feeling upset and vulnerable. Subsequently they have experienced multiple traumas, not least the abuse that Jack was subjected to by his boss. Since Jack's mother was herself emotionally exhausted it is unlikely that Jack felt he could or should turn to her for support – she had 'enough on her plate'. So Jack may have attempted to bury his anger and upset in an attempt to play the role of the 'strong man' in the family. However, this pressure may have been too much for him and he subsequently turned to drugs for comfort and showed his distress through outbursts of anger.

Unfortunately all of this may have led others to see Jack not as different from, kinder and more caring than his father, but more like his embodiment. Sons are often seen as similar to their fathers, especially if there is a physical resemblance, which can be taken to imply similarities in temperament and personality. Thus, it is possible that Jack has increasingly come to be seen as a threat – like his father. This sense of not being understood, being seen as dangerous despite his good intentions, may be extremely distressing for Jack, and his oscillation between anger, anguish and self-medication with drugs may have added to this perception of him. Because of their own experiences of poverty, burglary and residual pain from the divorce, the women in the family may have had very little 'spare emotional capacity' to be understanding towards Jack. However, as Jack's distress increased, his frightening actions may increasingly have come to validate the belief that he 'really' is just like his father. The women's fear and anger may have reached a point where they felt they had no option but to seek outside help and have Jack admitted to a psychiatric unit. This in turn may have compounded Jack's sense of rejection, hurt and anger. There can be a self-perpetuating cycle whereby the hospital becomes perceived as a source of support or a sort of benevolent 'father figure'. Unfortunately one of the costs of this is that Jack becomes to be seen, and increasingly sees himself, as 'mad'.

Family therapy might proceed in a number of ways. Central is the initial process of gaining a positive relationship with all members of the family. It might be the case that initially family sessions with Jack, his mother and sisters might be too emotionally explosive. The family therapist might first meet with Jack and utilise the systemic formulation in work with him, for example to discuss positive aspects of the role he has had in the family and how this has changed. The therapist could also meet with the rest of the family to start to explore their understandings and anxieties. Both Jack and his mother and his sisters can be prepared for the eventual joint sessions and the therapist can then utilise the positive relationships developed with all of them to help steer the family through the difficult feelings and dynamics that may arise. Techniques drawn from other models, such as an empty chair to represent Jack's father, can also be employed to explore what appears to be a central issue in this family which is the father's continuing emotional influence over them. Ideally, once trust and confidence with the family has developed it may be possible to organise some communication with him, or even his attendance at a session. This is potentially a dramatic move and would have to be considered in full collaboration with Jack and his family. Individual work with Jack might include a discussion about a hypothetical future family session of this kind. For example, the therapist might ask what he imagines might be said and felt by himself and his mother and sisters and father. Likewise, the sculpting and scaling activities can also usefully be incorporated into work with Jack to explore his perceptions of family relationships and how they relate to his problems and vice versa.

The family sessions usually take place at intervals of two weeks and in Jack's case might be expected to last for at least 10 sessions. A successful outcome might consist of Jack being able to meet with his mother and sisters outside of the family sessions in a constructive and calm way. Therapy might be concluded when the family had a shared confidence about being able to communicate calmly with Jack and with each other, and that they could work together to assist him. The decision about when to end is a reflective one in which the therapist also feels confident that the family can manage in the future and will be able to request further help if needed.

Janet: a systemic formulation

A large proportion of systemic work takes place in the context of work with children, not adults, as the identified clients. This is the genogram for Janet, a 9-year-old girl suffering with anxiety and developmental problems (see Figure 4.10).

Deconstructing the problems

The key features of the systemic formulation are indicated below:

- Mary has a number of concerns about Janet's behaviour and fears. She appears to be worried that Janet is not eating properly, and that she is becoming socially withdrawn and isolated as a result of her fear of transport and hence loss of contact with friends and family. It is also likely that Mary regards Janet's temper, especially when directed towards

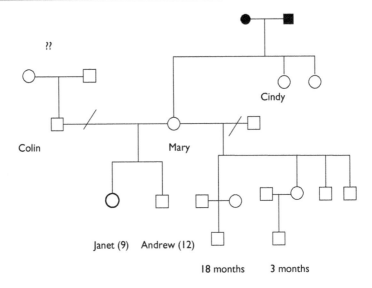

Figure 4.10 Janet's family tree

her, as a problem. In addition Mary has concerns about her own feelings about Janet, having found it difficult to bond with her. She links these feelings to the breakdown of her marriage and her fatigue. Given the concerns from social services and school, Mary may feel a failure as a mother and possibly that she is 'under the microscope' in relation to suspicions of abuse or neglect of the children.

- Janet appears to be angry with her mother, and may see the problems as mainly to do with home since she is able to go to school and has friends there. Perhaps she is frustrated by her mother's loss of mobility and ill health and is in a sense copying her.
- Social services appear to have had serious concerns that Janet might be suffering some abuse or physical neglect resulting in the hospital admissions. This concern has also been voiced by the school nurse, who was worried by Janet's weight loss.
- Mary's clairvoyant appears to have a supernatural belief that a vision of a 'white van' is connected to Janet's fear of transport.

Mary's father's views are not known, but he may feel rejected by Janet and under scrutiny from Mary and social services.

Exceptions and competencies

Janet has friends and is achieving adequately at school. Mary appears to have a close relationship with her sister who is said to be fond of Janet. Mary has also had success as a mother with the son who has become a schoolteacher, and Mary is apparently proud of this achievement.

Problem-maintaining patterns and feedback loops

There appears to be a pattern of both rejection and dependence between Mary and Janet. Certainly Janet displays both a need for her mother, such as sleeping in her bed, as well as venting her anger on her mother, setting the dog on her and refusing to eat her food. Not eating and being afraid of using transport keeps Janet ill and dependent. Mary also appears to have a mixture of positive and negative feelings towards Janet. This may reflect a dynamic in which Mary attempts to be patient, caring and considerate but becomes exhausted and then becomes angry and rejecting. Janet is the last of Mary's six children; she may have felt desperate exhaustion, but also protectiveness, after the arrival of this 'last straw' (see Figure 4.11).

Janet may have witnessed her father's violence towards her mother and be imitating it. Mary may find it hard to be consistent since she feels both angry about and responsible for the painful events that Janet has experienced, and guilt about her early feelings of wanting to reject her.

Beliefs and explanations

Mary appears to believe that Janet's problems are caused by the early difficulties in bonding. In effect, this is a belief that there may be something fundamentally wrong in their relationship and possibly also that she may be a 'bad mother'. She counters this with the view that lack of bonding was caused by the exhaustion and relationship breakdown. She is also likely to see Janet's father as partly to blame because of his violence, though she has tried to maintain contact between him and Janet. Since her children have such different levels of achievement, one a schoolteacher and the other with 'autistic' problems,

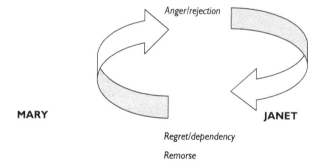

Figure 4.11 Problem-maintaining cycle between Janet and Mary

Mary may have a belief that there is something innately or medically wrong with Janet. She may also believe that Janet has inherited certain characteristics, such as a bad temper, from her father. It is also possible that Mary sees her problems in terms of being exhausted, living in a poor area, trying to keep contact with a violent ex-partner and coping with ill health.

Janet may believe that her mother does not care about her. She may be frustrated by her mother's ill health. She may be angry or anxious – perhaps feeling unsafe with her father and thus reluctant to stay with him overnight.

Extra-family beliefs

Social services may also hold a belief that family dysfunctions or even abuse are the cause of Janet's anxieties. This belief might be supported further by the fact that Janet seems to be calm at school in contrast to the problems that are presented at home.

Socio-cultural beliefs and discourses

The dominant discourses shaping the beliefs of the family members and professionals are likely to be either about neglect and abuse, or about some form of organically based problem suffered by Janet. Less dominant discourses might be about their social conditions, living in a socially deprived area and perhaps being marginalised due to their Romany origins. Another dominant discourse in play may be that of the 'naturalness of motherhood'; the idea that despite her circumstances Mary, as a good mother, ought to feel positive and loving towards her children rather than having 'bad' or 'unnatural' thoughts such as wanting to put Janet into care.

Ethnic/sub-cultural beliefs

Due to their Romany origins the family appear to hold beliefs about supernatural causes of problems, which although meaningful to them, place them outside dominant cultural norms.

Transitions, emotions and attachments

This refers to the nature of the emotional dynamics, especially the attachments and emotional dependencies between family members and across the generations. Depicting the changes through a sculpt may reveal, for example, that even before her father had left Janet was already feeling isolated and anxious (see Figure 4.12).

It seems clear that there were early problems in the attachment between Mary and Janet. Mary felt sad and depressed when Janet was born and consequently was less able to be emotionally warm, comforting and emotionally attentive to

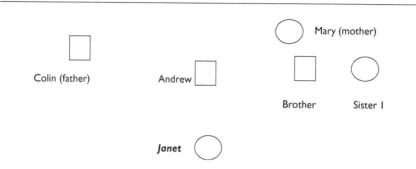

Figure 4.12 Sculpt: when Janet's father Colin was with the family

her. These responses may have led to an insecure attachment representation in Janet – a sense that she was not loved, wanted and worthy of affection. This could partly explain why Janet now behaves in ways which keep her anxiously tied to her mother and seeking her approval and affection. It also looks from the sculpt as if Janet may early on have started to see herself as not preferred or liked by her mother. Since her father was frightening and violent she might have been ambivalent towards him along with feeling increasingly isolated and unloved. Mary had the problematic task of trying to manage some connection between the children and their father whilst feeling intimidated by him.

The anxiety about transport may express Janet's fear of being taken away from her mother. We do not know about Mary's attachment history though she appears to have a close relationship with her sister. She has certainly had losses – her parents and her relationships with the fathers of her children. It is not clear when her parents died, but this may be linked to the attachment problems with Janet.

We do not know whether Mary's relationship with the father of her older children was abusive, but women who are abused in relationships have often had a history of insecure childhood relationships, witnessing and/or being a victim of violence. This often leads to a sense of inadequacy and low self-esteem which makes them vulnerable to entering into abusive relationships as adults on the basis of a belief that 'I don't deserve any better'.

Contextual factors

Mary and her family face many disadvantages: they live in a socially deprived area, Mary has poor health, she has no parents to support her and Janet's father has been violent, alcoholic and is possibly still abusive towards her. It is also quite likely that they have limited financial resources. In addition their Romany identity may contribute to their marginalisation. The professional agencies may have a high degree of suspicion about the family and about Mary's abilities as a parent. This may feed into her anxiety, distress and sense of failure and self-blame. Since the involvement with social services has extended over a considerable period of time, Mary may have become dependent on professionals to give her advice and direction. Equally, she may feel that her authority as a mother is being undermined, leaving her feeling depressed and incompetent (see Figure 4.13).

Synthesis: a systemic formulation for Janet

The above framework may help to direct our attention to the complex web of factors that have shaped and maintain the problem/s. However, it is easy to see that even the brief examples that we have offered regarding Mary and Janet can quickly turn into an overwhelming kaleidoscope of factors. Somehow this mass of information needs to be combined into a manageable formulation. This requires us to select the factors that we see as key to our understanding of the problem. We need to construct a narrative which links events, actions and contexts into a story or 'pattern that connects'.

We have drawn up two possible systemic formulations of this family. Neither claims to be exhaustive but both attempt to offer a view which fits with the available information. In practice this means that some features or details may be given more attention than others.

First formulation

Janet's and the family's difficulties may have arisen from Mary's early parenting experiences with Janet. Mary was experiencing abuse and the family were in difficult circumstances. Since Janet is the last of her six children, Mary may have been physically and emotionally exhausted, and felt she had no energy

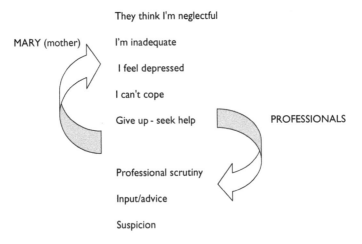

They think I'm neglectful

MARY (mother)   I'm inadequate

I feel depressed

I can't cope

Give up - seek help   PROFESSIONALS

Professional scrutiny

Input/advice

Suspicion

Figure 4.13 Professional–family dependency cycle

left for Janet. This was the second child by Janet's father, but because of the marital difficulties Mary may have lost the hope that she perhaps held earlier for the relationship when their first child, Andrew, was born. Not infrequently parents hope that a child will repair a failing relationship or bring about a change in a partner. If Janet's father did not respond positively to the birth of his daughter, Mary's feelings of being overwhelmed, abused and exhausted may have made it hard to bond with Janet. This may have set in motion a pattern of guilt which made Mary even less able to cope with Janet. For example, it may be hard for Mary to set clear rules about Janet sleeping with her because of her guilt about earlier feelings of rejection. In turn, Janet may respond to, and aggravate, this pattern by making greater demands for reassurance from her mother and finding ways of becoming dependent but also hostile towards her. Hence there may be a self-maintaining and escalating pattern of comfort/rejection between them. This pattern may also be fuelled by Mary's self-doubt about her abilities as a parent, and her general low self-esteem resulting from domestic abuse and her deprived living conditions.

Second formulation

The second formulation is concerned more with the relationships between Janet and her father, and between the professional systems and Mary. Janet has recently refused to stay overnight with her father, suggesting some anxieties about this situation. At home she is afraid of sleeping on her own, which might be connected to possible abusive events with her father. Refusal to eat can also be associated with sexual abuse, for example being forced to perform oral sexual acts. Mary may be reluctant to think about these possibilities since contact with the father has given her some occasional respite from Janet; also, as a responsible mother she appreciates that Janet needs to have a relationship with her father. Furthermore, Mary may be aware of social service suspicions, and be afraid that being more open about her worries may lead her to being blamed for not having drawn attention to possible abuse earlier. She may even fear that her children might be taken away from her. This lack of action might in turn engender anger in Janet towards her mother 'not protecting her'. The escalating pattern of mutual suspicion and concern is illustrated below (see Figure 4.14).

Comments

These two formulations are not exclusive and can be seen as additive. The second one may seem blaming in its suspicions about Janet's father. An alternative view is to see Janet's father as caught up in a process where he is stereotyped as an 'abuser', alcoholic, violent and irresponsible. Families who live in such deprived social contexts may tend to be seen in this way, but it is important to remember that this is not the only context in which abuse occurs,

They don't trust me

They may remove children

I can't reveal my concerns

I don't trust them

MARY

SOCIAL
SERVICES*

Mary doesn't show appropriate
concern about possible abuse

Not sure we can trust her

Child protection concerns

* Also other professionals

Figure 4.14 Escalating pattern of distrust between Mary and social services

and it can be discriminatory to assume that because a family is poor and live in a deprived area that abuse is occurring. However, in the context of a history of injuries such a hypothesis would at least need to be considered. Importantly, though, a systemic hypothesis attempts to consider how the family–professional system can escalate and make matters worse as well as better. Escalating cycles of suspicion can fuel a sense of failure and eventual hopeless passivity in mothers like Mary.

An important initial question is which parts of the family to convene for family sessions. Given the potential dangers and conflicts between Janet's mother and father, an initial meeting might be planned with just Janet and her mother's side of the family. Both in order to most effectively promote change but also to develop the formulations, it is important to see a range of family members. This might usefully include Janet, her mother, aunt Cindy, and Janet's brother Andrew and her half siblings. The initial work might focus on gaining everyone's perspectives on the problems and their ideas about the causes. The exploratory ideas already described, such as sculpts and scaling questions, also serve the function of promoting change in that they help to reveal each family member's thinking. The activities also require family members to interact in new less problematic ways and, with the therapist's and team's help, to be able to discuss potentially difficult and suppressed issues. It would also be important to try and arrange a session attended by Janet's parents. Children can benefit greatly by seeing their parents being able to move beyond their conflicts and talk in a constructive way about their welfare. Where the parents are still in considerable disagreement, some initial sessions for them as parents before a session which includes the child can be a helpful start.

The politics of formulation

It is tempting to try and produce assessment and formulation schemes which set out clear and detailed guidelines for clinicians to follow. While this may be helpful, not least in revealing the complexity of the task involved, we prefer to suggest that formulation contains within it the core conceptual, psychological and philosophical issues relating to all types of therapy. Most fundamentally we are compelled to consider what we understand to be a problem or symptom. Family therapy offers a social model of the causes and maintenance of problems. It has also become increasingly critical of medical and pathologising processes (White and Epston, 1990; Hoffman, 1993; Dallos and Draper, 2010). Within this framework, family therapy offers a critical position that endeavours to question the potentially oppressive assumptions that may be made about family members and that family members may even have been conscripted into holding about themselves:

> I sometimes think that 99 per cent of the suffering that comes in through my door has to do with how devalued people feel by the labels that have been applied to them or the derogatory opinions they hold about themselves
>
> (Hoffman, 1993: 79)

In essence this is the cornerstone of the social constructionist (post-modern) position that characterises contemporary family therapy practice. More broadly this places the clinician working with families in a variety of complex positions regarding formulation:

- as (usually) an employee of the state we may feel pressure to offer formulations which contain elements of social control, for example to enable a child in a family to become 'less disruptive' and return to school;
- it is important to consider how families may internalise dominant medical difficulties and come to apply diagnostic categories such as ADHD or Asperger's in their own formulations of the problems (Rapley et al., 2011);
- we need to pay attention in our formulations to patterns of inequalities and oppressions which have aggravated some of the distresses and conflicts in the family and which contribute to the development of problems;
- we may be aware of the competing definitions of what their problem is and whether there is a 'problem'. Differing views may be held by the individual, the family, members within the family, various agencies such as the police and social services, the school, the legal system, cultural systems and the therapist's professional system.

In effect, a primary aspect of formulation is the juggling of these competing definitions or constructions about family problems. A clinician engaged in family therapy needs to take account also of the legacy of their profession and the expectations that colleagues hold. For example, there may be an expectation that clinical psychologists are 'experts' at assessment and formulation and more specifically that they will be able to assess whether an individual in a family 'really' has an individual or a family problem.

Referring back to the quote from Lynn Hoffman, we can see that including a political dimension to systemic formulation permits a wider formulation of how self-punishing, negative and destructive views have arisen and are being maintained. Although systemic approaches take the family and other intimate relational systems as the primary focus for formulation, this is only the starting point. Systemic therapy recognises that families are connected to multiple systems and that we need to extend formulation to all of these. This is a profound shift from the early days of family therapy when there was a danger of the family becoming just the new site of the pathologising process – subject to formulations which in effect blamed families for making their members mad or bad. An approach which sees families and their members as influenced by powerful cultural forces, both structural and ideological, shares with others (Boyle, 1990; Johnstone, 2000) a strong emancipatory aim.

Key characteristics of a systemic formulation

- Problems are regarded as residing in relational processes as opposed to within individuals.
- Formulation is seen as centrally concerned with exploring the meanings, understandings and explanations that family members hold about the problems.
- Formulation is seen as an active, recursive, dynamic process (progressive hypothesising).
- Exploration and gathering information for formulation is seen as also promoting change. There is not considered to be a clear distinction between exploration–formulation–intervention.
- Formulation is seen as collaborative in that the therapist is jointly developing formulation with family members in order that new ways of understanding the problems can evolve.
- Family members may have different and conflicting formulations and therapists need to try and gain a picture of the range of different formulations held.

References

Boyle, M. (1990) *Schizophrenia: A Scientific Delusion?* 2nd edn. Hove, UK: Brunner-Routledge.

Byng-Hall, J. (1980) 'Symptom bearer as marital distance regulator: clinical implications', *Family Process,* 19, 4: 355–365.

Carr, A. (2006) *Family Therapy: Concepts, Process and Practice.* 2nd edn. Chichester: Wiley.

Carter, E. and McGoldrick, M. (1988) *The Changing Family Life Cycle: A Framework for Family Therapy.* 2nd edn. New York: Gardner.

Cecchin, G. (1987) 'Hypothesizing, circularity and neutrality revisited: an invitation to curiosity', *Family Process,* 26, 4: 405–413.

Dallos, R. (1991) *Family Belief Systems, Therapy and Change.* Milton Keynes: Open University Press.

——(1996) *Interacting Stories: Narratives, Family Beliefs and Therapy.* London: Karnac.

Dallos, R. and Draper, R. (2010) *Introduction to Family Therapy: Systemic Theory and Practice.* 3rd edn. Milton Keynes: Open University Press.

Goldner, V. (1998) 'The treatment of violence and victimisation in intimate relationship', *Family Process,* 37, 3: 263–286.

Haley, J. (1973) *Uncommon Therapy: The Psychiatric Techniques of M.H. Erickson.* New York: Norton.

Hoffman, L. (1993) *Exchanging Voices: A Collaborative Approach to Family Therapy.* London: Karnac.

Johnstone, L. (2000) *Users and Abusers of Psychiatry: A Critical Look at Psychiatric Practice.* 2nd edn. London, Philadelphia: Brunner-Routledge.

Palazzoli, M.S., Boscolo, L., Prata, G. and Cecchin, G. (1978) *Paradox and Counter-paradox: A New Model in the Therapy of the Family in Schizophrenic Transaction.* New York: Jason Aronson.

Palazzoli, M.S., Boscolo, L., Cecchin, G. and Prata, G. (1980) 'Hypothesising-circularity-neutrality: three guidelines for the conductor of the session', *Family Process,* 19: 3–12.

Proctor, H. (1981) 'Family construct psychology'. In S. Walrond-Skinner (ed.) *Family Therapy and Approaches.* London: Routledge.

Rapley, M., Montcrieff, J. and Dillon, J. (2011) *De-Medicalising Misery: Psychiatry, Psychology and the Human Condition.* Basingstoke: Palgrave.

Stedmon, J. and Dallos, R. (2009) *Reflective Practice in Psychotherapy and Counseling.* Maidenhead: McGraw Hill.

Tomm, K. (1987) 'Interventive interviewing, part II. Reflexive questioning as a means to developing self-healing', *Family Process* 26: 167–183.

Watzlawick, P., Weakland, J. and Fisch, R. (1974) *Change: Principles of Problem Formation and Problem Resolution.* New York: Norton.

White, M. and Epston, D. (1990) *Narrative Means to Therapeutic Ends.* London: Norton.

Chapter 5

Formulation and narrative therapy

Telling a different story

David Harper and Dave Spellman

Formulation and narrative therapy

In this chapter we discuss how formulation might be understood within a tradition of narrative therapy (White and Epston, 1990). In common with approaches like systemic family therapy and community psychology, it does not see problems as lying within the person. However, it is sometimes misunderstood as a liberal humanistic approach seeking to empower people. Yet narrative therapy makes quite different assumptions, adopting a questioning approach to concepts like 'strengths' and does provide straightforwardly causal formulations. As a result we will begin by outlining the assumptions of this approach before turning to the issue of formulation and then describing how we might formulate our work with Jack and Janet.

Theoretical influences on the development of narrative therapy

Michael White and David Epston were both social workers who later trained as family therapists. They developed a collaborative approach despite living in different countries (Australia and New Zealand, respectively). Their work could be seen as having three main influences. Firstly, they noted that although therapeutic conversations involved people sharing stories about themselves, psychotherapy traditions did not give much attention to the importance of narrative. They began to read the work of theorists for ideas – for example what makes one narrative richer than another? Secondly, they were influenced by the work of anthropologists like Clifford Geertz and Barbara Myerhoff. Anthropology is often seen as a way of helping us to stand back and question our taken-for-granted understandings of the world by making the familiar strange, and the strange familiar. They developed Geertz's (1973) notion of thin and thick description, noting that the latter offered a way of developing more richly textured narratives than the more superficial 'thin' descriptions afforded by, for example, psychiatric diagnostic labels. They found in anthropology a way of looking at the rituals of everyday life and drawing on that knowledge to develop new rituals which might help strengthen new stories. For example, from Myerhoff's (1982) study of groups of elders they developed the notion that our stories about ourselves are not a private matter of finding the 'true self' within; rather identities were public achievements with people telling stories about themselves and others which shaped the way those listening storied themselves and others.

A final influence was the work of the French philosopher and historian of thought, Michel Foucault. Foucault was one of a number of 'post-Structuralist' thinkers who questioned the influence of structuralist philosophies in the human sciences. We can see the influence of structuralism in therapeutic traditions where actions are seen as behaviours flowing from 'deeper' mechanisms like internal states, emotions, drives, thoughts and so on. Examples can be seen in cognitive therapy (with its cognitions and schemas), psychoanalysis (with its drives and defences) and structuralist family therapy (with its hierarchies and boundaries). In particular White and Epston were influenced by Foucault's focus on the link between power and knowledge and by how particular ways of viewing the world are embodied in certain institutions. They drew from Foucault a concern with how people are subtly – and often not so subtly – regulated by the normalising gaze of society.

Relating these ideas to social constructionism

Some of these theoretical currents had already been taken up within the discipline of psychology. Thus psychologists like Jerome Bruner, Theodore Sarbin and Miller Mair had sketched out the implications of viewing narrative as a fundamental metaphor in psychology. Psychologists like Ian Parker and Erica Burman had drawn on Foucault's work in social psychology. In addition, from the mid 1980s onwards a number of psychologists like Kenneth Gergen began to take these ideas forward under the broad banner of social constructionism[1] which can be seen as an incorporation into psychology of many of the ideas associated with post-structuralism (Burr, 2003).

There is no singular definition of social constructionism, since it is more of a conceptual framework than a clearly delineated theoretical model. Moreover, there is a very broad church of theorists within this tradition. Gergen (1985) has argued, however, that there are four assumptions implicit in most social constructionist work. Firstly, there is a radical doubt about our taken-for-granted knowledge. Thus social constructionists adopt a questioning approach towards psychological concepts. For example, as Burr (2003) notes, they do not seek explanations in terms of innate discoverable psychological properties or essences like 'personality' or 'cognitions'. Secondly, they view knowledge as historically, socially and culturally specific. Thirdly, they argue that social and cultural processes influence what is seen as 'true'. Finally, they argue that the ways we describe and explain phenomena are not 'neutral' but, rather, served to sustain certain viewpoints to the exclusion of others. In other words, by talking and writing about the world in particular ways, we bring into being – or construct – certain ways of seeing the world. However, it is only really within psychology and, to some degree sociology, that these ideas are labelled as social constructionist. Many authors, including White and Epston, have not used this label to describe their work, preferring the term post-Structuralist instead. Social constructionism does nevertheless provide a useful way of identifying a family resemblance amongst a group of therapists influenced by similar ideas (McNamee and Gergen 1992).[2] As social constructionism tends to be a more familiar framework for psychologists and psychotherapists, we will use this term throughout the chapter.

The assumptions of narrative therapy

Narrative therapy has been described by a range of practitioners (e.g. Freedman and Combs, 1996; Madigan, 2011; Morgan, 2000; Payne, 2006; White and Epston, 1990).[3] For this reason we will not provide a detailed account here, but essentially, it sees problems in living as occurring when the stories people have available about themselves do not accord with their lived experience. There is a link here with the social constructionist concern to take a questioning approach to our taken-for-granted knowledge and to see it as historically and culturally specific. Thus diagnostic constructs, which are often portrayed as real scientific entities – part of nature – are, for example, seen as only one story available to people. In their work White and Epston sought to 'de-naturalise' these taken-for-granted notions. When people seek professional help, often their lives have become single storied, limiting, limited and superficial rather than richly textured and multi-storied. If people have experienced their difficulties for a long time and have received mental health intervention these stories are often problem-saturated and pathologising and they will have acquired individualising and internalised problem labels. White and Epston aimed to have different kinds of conversations which might open up alternative meanings of distress. For example, they were interested in the history of the problem and of the dominant narrative but they also sought to plot a history of new, previously hidden alternative stories. However, because they saw stories building on internal state or trait concepts as inherently limiting, they drew on Bruner's notion of intentional narratives, encouraging people to develop stories which featured 'purposes, values, beliefs, hopes, dreams, visions and commitments to ways of living' (White, 2004: 86) rather than on internal states like 'strengths' (a concept which is dependent on the notion of weakness in order to have any meaning). Moreover, they continually invited people to stand back from these stories and to make choices about whether they enhanced and enriched their lives or else limited and diminished them. Often people came to see that they had options and choices of which they were previously unaware, and by developing criteria by which to judge these stories, clients became more aware of their values (i.e. what was important for them).

White and Epston sought to have conversations which might identify the traces of more marginalised or subordinated stories, stories which broke with the dominant narrative and which would be experienced by clients as enhancing the way they saw themselves and increasing the options available to them in their lives. They showed how knowledge is sustained by social processes by drawing attention to the cultural rituals which currently support certain dominant narratives – thus the process of diagnosis sustains the stories (e.g. chronicity) and identities (e.g. 'schizophrenic') provided by diagnostic categorisations whilst also serving to obscure the influence of other factors (e.g. stigma, discrimination or the side effects of psychiatric medications). However, they also saw here the possibility of creating new rituals which could sustain more subordinated narratives.

It is easy to lose the traces of alternative stories and they can become edited out of the dominant narrative of our lives; important people and connections with them can be lost and forgotten. One way of elaborating these stories is, during therapeutic conversations, to engage in a process of scaffolding – a notion developed by theorists following Vygotsky's (1978) concept of the zone of proximal development. Here particular questions are asked in order to support (or 'scaffold') the development of emerging stories. White and Epston also engaged in *externalising conversations* whereby clients were invited to consider their problems not as signs of internalised and individualised deficit or pathology – something that was their fault – but, rather as lying outside themselves. The therapist, client and others were thus united in a struggle against a problem which was seen as external – 'the problem, not the person, is the problem' became a key motto – and this could help to undermine the sense of failure which is often a consequence of the dominant narrative. Later, White noted how stories became richer when they were responded to by others. Thus when we are telling someone a story about ourselves and they respond with another story, or an emotional response or a joke, these shape our telling of the story. Seeing identity as a public achievement it became important to include others' responses to a client's story. The people who were an audience to a person's story were seen as 'outsider witnesses' and, in therapy sessions, Michael White would often interview one member of the family and then interview other family members or members of an outsider witness group (similar to Tom Andersen's Reflecting Team approach) about their response to this story (e.g. how it resonated with something they experienced). He would then return to the person and interview them about how they responded to these responses, leading to a greater elaboration of these stories.

Finally, White and Epston were acutely aware of the influence of power and how the normalising gaze of society supported more dominant stories. For example, we cannot understand young women's concerns about their bodies and eating without understanding the way in which they view their bodies through a societal prism – a prism sustained by the advertising, fashion and publishing industries for profit – which equates thinness with beauty and moral good and which sets different standards of beauty for women than for men. There is a relationship between dominant narratives and power in society (see chapter 6). For example, they obscure and mystify the effects of power relations by inviting people to compare themselves unfavourably to unattainable and idealised images of what is normal. As a result people begin to elaborate problem-saturated descriptions of themselves – for example as a 'chronic schizophrenic' or as a 'child with ADHD'. White and Epston sought to make a positive use of their understanding of power by interviewing people so that they became aware of the tactics which their problems used to get the upper hand in their lives.

Narrative therapy represents a move away from a linear cause and effect paradigm where the role of the expert is to find out and fix, and for this reason, like solution-focused therapy, it has no position on the aetiology or cause of problems (White in Stewart, 1995). Narrative therapists prefer rich, multi-storied and intentional narratives to causal explanations framed in terms of 'factors' like internalised psychological processes which would be seen as thin descriptions and single storied narratives. As a result, causal formulations of problems are not a part of this approach. The assumptions of narrative therapy pose a challenge for efficacy research since this is traditionally based on quite different epistemological assumptions (Harper et al., 2013), yet there is an emerging and promising evidence base (Chenail et al., 2012).

Stretching the notion of formulation

A formulation is usually interpreted as an explanation of the causes (e.g. precipitants and maintaining factors) of problems which indicates priorities for therapeutic intervention. Such a definition, which positions the therapist as a technical expert, poses a particular challenge for social constructionism (Harper and Moss, 2003). But do formulations only have to be about problems? How might this fit with theoretical traditions which are not based on theories of aetiology and pathology? Moreover, who gets to define what the 'problem' is (Boyle, 2001; see also chapters 4 and 12)? Do formulations have to be causal and historical?

One solution to these dilemmas has been proposed by Alan Carr (2012) who has suggested that, as well as formulations of problems, it is also possible to construct an analogous formulation from a solution-focused perspective of exceptions to those problems, identifying the interactional processes which sustain them. Another proposal by one of us (DH) in collaboration with Duncan Moss is that therapists could see their work as a process of on-going collaborative sense-making rather than one of developing objective or semi-objective descriptions of the causes of a problem. This is similar to the notion of progressive hypothesising found in other family therapy traditions (see chapter 4). Formulations, then, are situated in particular contexts and oriented to particular purposes. In other words, they are perspectives: a view from somewhere, rather than the scientific notion of a view from nowhere. To express this in more narrative terms: if clinical work is seen as a series of dialogues or conversations, then a therapist's formulation is one person's story (their story, though authored in collaboration with the client) and account of that conversation (Harper and Moss, 2003). From this viewpoint, a formulation is a structured story for therapists and clients which gives one account of why things are the way they are and what might need to happen for things to change, and which orients therapist and client towards ways forward (Bob, 1999; Corrie and Lane, 2010; Parry and Doan, 1994). Formulations are stories which are constructed rather than discovered and so it is their usefulness and fit for the client which is most important. But does this mean that formulations are fictions? Family therapist Bebe Speed offers an interesting perspective on this question:

> I can tell many stories about myself, who I am and the different selves or parts of me which are called forth in my interactions with others [but how] I behave and feel in any context is not random, but patterned. My life is not a fiction ... Clients and I construct together some account of what's going on. It won't be the only one possible, the *truth* about the situation ... There will be other versions of their situation that I (not to mention other therapists) and they together could have constructed that would also have had some fit and been relatively adequate to their situation.
>
> (Speed, 1999: 136)

Our definition of formulation may seem vague, but the notion of formulation needs to be stretched somewhat if it is to cover a range of approaches from the more conventional conceptualisation of biographical and historical causes of problems to non-causal and non-pathological understandings.

Preamble to the case examples

As the other contributors to this volume have noted, it is challenging to offer formulations in relation to clients whom we have not met, especially since one of the foundations of narrative therapy is the emphasis it places on listening to clients' actual words and asking the kinds of questions which may not be asked in other approaches. However, we are persuaded of the pedagogical value of trying to attempt a formulation, with the proviso that readers bear in mind that we have not met these clients or their families and that these case examples, like all vignettes in the literature, are particular narrative constructions based on interviews conducted by therapists from a different theoretical orientation.

Systemic and community psychology traditions see formulations as dynamic and ongoing, and a narrative therapy perspective takes this further in that therapy and formulation are mutually inter-woven activities. Since narrative therapy may be relatively unfamiliar to many readers, in the examples that follow we will develop a more descriptive kind of formulation, focusing both on how we might have proceeded in the sessions (e.g. what questions we might have asked and why) and on what narratives might have emerged from these sessions. The latter will be necessarily more speculative as the directions in which the therapeutic conversations went from there would very much depend on how the people in the room responded.

Jack: a narrative therapy formulation

The narrative therapist would come to the session with Jack with some knowledge of alternative ways of conceptualising and working with people reporting experiences which others would see as symptoms of psychosis or of 'schizophrenia' (Brigitte et al., 1996; Dulwich Centre, 1995; O'Neill and Stockell, 1991; Parker et al., 1995; Stewart, 1995; White, 1987). There has been a great deal of recent interest in more hopeful narratives about experiences seen as psychotic (Dillon, 2011).

In the section that follows, we have followed Morgan's (2000) introductory guide to narrative therapy to provide a structure for thinking about how conversations with Jack might proceed. Obviously, therapy is a dynamic and recursive process and so these elements would not necessarily follow each other in a linear fashion and the order in which areas would be explored would depend on both Jack and the therapist. One approach here might be for the therapist to reflect on the assumptions within the referral letter, considering both the implicit dominant narratives at work (as expressed by Jack; by his family; by professionals; and in the wider culture) as well as possible subordinate narratives (e.g. Jack's competence and the impact of traumas on him). In Jack's case, the therapist had little referral information before he was first seen, which limits the opportunity to give these issues some thought.

Externalising conversations: naming the problem

As we have noted earlier, narrative therapists use a variety of practices in order to try to make previously invisible options visible by helping clients elaborate more hopeful but *subordinate narratives*. Externalising conversations can be useful here as many people who seek help feel they are to blame in some way for their problems. From a narrative therapy viewpoint, we might see this discourse as an effect of the normalising gaze of society.

Morgan (2000) suggests that a number of things can be externalised: feelings; problems between people; cultural and social practices; and the metaphors people use in talking about their problems. From the account of Jack's difficulties there seem to be a number of candidates for externalisation. It is important to bear in mind the question of whether there is a problem and, if so, who gets to define it. As a result the therapist would very much focus on how Jack saw the problem, if he saw one at all.

The therapist would listen out for opportunities to externalise using Jack's own words and phrases, rather than professional jargon – for example Jack might talk of 'fear' rather than 'anxiety'. A well-known example of this is that Winston Churchill often referred to his depressed feelings as his 'black dog'. Indeed, many clients spontaneously talk about an issue in an externalising way, which the therapist can then extend.

From the information about Jack we surmise that he might talk about the problem of fear. Fear impacts on Jack's life in a number of ways. He is afraid of Robbie Williams and his minders. He is fearful about leaving his accommodation in case he is attacked. He is also afraid of seeing his father's face reflected back at him in the mirror, possibly suggesting 'fear' might persuade him that he was like his father (especially given that he has developed similar difficulties in relation to alcohol). He is also afraid for his mother and sisters, especially the sister who, he believed, had been raped (although there was no evidence that this had really happened).

Another thing which might be externalised is guilt. One might be interested in how 'guilt' affected Jack. He might talk here about guilt about sex, particularly given that he had been sexually victimised by the male manager at his Saturday job. He might also talk about guilt at feeling he had brought trouble on the family and about the events which led up to his mother asking him to leave the house. Given dominant cultural discourses about men being the breadwinners, 'guilt' may make him feel that he has been a 'failure' according to these dominant stories. Guilt might also have persuaded him that he might be to blame for his parents separating.

Although anger might present itself as ideal for externalising, this would need careful thought. For example, externalising 'anger' here might invite Jack to move away from a sense of responsibility for the effects of his actions. Carey and Russell (2002) discuss some of the issues involved in considering whether, when and what to externalise. Alan Jenkins (2009) has outlined some other alternatives were Jack to want to focus on his anger. However, one might be able to explore what impact the anger has had on Jack and those close to him, for example anger about Robbie Williams; his father's behaviour; and his own abuse. Similarly, Jack might wish to talk about the effect that drink, drugs, theft and homelessness have had on his life and on the lives of others.

Our main point is that there are many things which could be externalised, but which ones are taken up depends on Jack and the therapist working together. Interestingly, from his own account Jack did not identify his *beliefs* about Robbie Williams, the royalty cheque, or the alleged rape of his sister *per se* as problems and so we have not included them here as targets for intervention. Were they to prove a focus for Jack, the narrative therapist might note how beliefs not shared by others become constructed as socially devalued by more powerful others like professionals (Boyle, 2002; Georgaca, 2000; Harper,

2011; Heise, 1988). However, they often provide dramatic narratives for those who believe them (de Rivera and Sarbin, 1998). This suggests that it may be less important to focus on the veracity of the beliefs than on the person's relationship with them; for example, the extent to which the beliefs disrupt the life they wish to lead (Harper, 2011; Knight, 2009). Narrative therapy and social constructionist thinking about 'paranoia', for example, readily links it to experiences of victimisation, surveillance and discrimination (e.g. racial discrimination) in Western culture (Cromby and Harper, 2009; Hardy, 2001; Harper, 2011).

Morgan (2000) suggests that narrative therapists ask the client to give the problem a name. Then begins a thorough exploration and personification of the problem in order to continue the process of helping the person to separate their identity from that of the problem/s. Questions here might focus on the tricks and tactics which the problem uses to gain the upper hand in Jack's life (for an example of this kind of discussion see Brigitte et al., 1996). What are its purposes for Jack? Who are the problem's allies? For example, Jack might say that throughout his life he had had jokes aimed at him as a British Italian man or had experienced discrimination because of mental health problems, and thus, racism and injustice might be seen as an ally of the problem (see Patel and Fatimilehin, 1999).

Following this kind of conversation, the therapist would ask Jack how he described his relationship with the problem. Was he happy with how it was or would he like it to change? The purpose of such questions is to engage Jack in a conversation in revising his relationship with the problem (e.g. to resist it or to live with it in a different manner) opening up choices where Jack may have seen none previously. Jack might say he was unhappy with how the problems dominated him and that he wanted things to change, to be more hopeful for the future.

Tracing the history of the problem

Although narrative therapy is sometimes misrepresented as a 'here-and-now' therapy not interested in the past, narrative therapists spend a lot of time asking questions which track forwards and backwards in time between the present, past and future, and so the therapist might next turn to examining the history of the problems in Jack's life, and his relationship to them. For ease of reading we will refer here to one problem, though in cases where clients discuss a number of problems, Morgan (2000) suggests asking them to prioritise them.

One might ask Jack when he first noticed the influence of the problem. How has it changed over time? Conversations like this can help people to feel that the problem is not necessarily static and unchanging. Allen (1994) quotes an example from Michael White about how he might approach a client diagnosed as 'paranoid':

If a person is totalised as 'paranoid', I might ask them a series of questions like: How did you get recruited into the sense that you are under surveillance? In response to this question, persons speak of their experience more politically.

(Allen, 1994: 31)

So one might ask Jack when 'fear' began persuading him that he might be attacked. He might say that this began around the time his mother became physically ill and when finances were stretched. We might also ask what things or people might have been in league with the fear (for example the manager who sexually abused Jack).

Exploring the effects of the problem

Problems often leave a legacy of negative effects on people's lives and it is important, indeed essential, to gain a full appreciation of the problem's legacy. In narrative therapy the focus is on doing this in a way which allows the client to separate their identity from that of the problem. One way to achieve this is to map the effects of the problem on the person's life. Thus, one might ask Jack how the problem has affected his view of himself and his future. How does it interfere with his life? For example, what does 'fear' stop him doing? Jack might say that it has stopped him going out and that he has begun to lose significant relationships with others like family members. He might talk about how he has begun to lose his interest in music. One could also ask him about how 'guilt' has changed the way he views himself. How has 'anger' changed his relationships with those close to him?

The therapist also asks the client to evaluate these effects. In his later work Michael White drew on a reading of the work of Jacques Derrida to develop the notion of the 'absent but implicit' (Carey et al., 2009), in other words, how implicit values can be detected in clients' accounts of their experiences. For example, when a client tells us about the negative effects of a problem they are simultaneously also telling us about the values, people and activities which are important to them and which can provide the basis for a new story. Thus one might ask Jack what these effects are like for him and his family. If he saw these in negative terms, one could ask him why, and he might then talk about how these problems get in the way of him showing his love for others; developing friendships outside his family; allowing him to be as close to his family as he would like; and/or doing good to others as he would like.

Situating the problem in context: deconstruction

Morgan (2000: 45) argues that from a narrative therapy perspective, 'problems only survive and thrive when they are supported and backed up by particular ideas, beliefs and principles'. As a result of a normalising societal gaze, people often feel as if they are failing when judging themselves according to an idealised norm or standard. Narrative therapists are interested in making these assumptions available for exploration. Morgan refers to this as a deconstruction. Dallos and Stedmon (chapter 4) have discussed how systemic therapists also use this practice.

One might be interested, for example, in taken-for-granted cultural ideas which may be related to the problems. For a British-Italian man, particular Roman Catholic ideas about guilt, the role of men and the place of the family might play a role in the story. As a man, there might be culturally available stories about alcohol, violence and the expression of some emotions (e.g. anger) but not others (e.g. fear, sadness, loneliness, etc.). There might also be beliefs about who should be the breadwinner in a family and the role of fathers and sons (such as carrying on the family business) in relation to mothers and sisters.

Others (e.g. family members) present in a session could be interviewed about these cultural ideas. These kinds of conversations can be particularly powerful in the context of group or community meetings, revealing that problems are political, not simply private and personal (Brigitte et al., 1996; Denborough, 2008; Freedman and Combs, 2009; O'Neill and Stockell, 1991). One option is to encourage group members to look through magazines and newspapers or videotapes of TV programmes and films to see what dominant stories are culturally available – in the case of Jack this might include stories about mental health, about Italians or about young men. Such conversations can help people to begin to stand back from these dominant stories, seeing them as culturally and historically specific rather than as universal truths.

So far, the therapist has focused on the problem, its effects and the implicit assumptions which sustain it. However, in order to begin the process of tracing out alternative stories the therapist needs to seek out examples of times when the problem has not been totally successful in achieving dominance in Jack's life. In narrative therapy these are called *unique outcomes* (similar to the idea of exceptions in solution-focused therapy). They can provide the building blocks for the new stories we seek to scaffold with clients.

Unique outcomes

The therapist shows particular interest in times when the person has, even in a small way, managed to challenge, resist or in some other way develop a more hopeful relationship with the problem.[4] He or she will listen for any times when the problem appears to have had less of an influence on the client or even no influence at all. These provide an opportunity to start to plot an alternative story to the dominant problem-saturated one. Unique outcomes could include a plan; an action; a feeling; a dream; a commitment; a thought and so on (Morgan, 2000). If the client is unable to think of such episodes, the therapist might ask something like 'How have you managed to stop the problem from getting even worse?'

Thus, one might ask Jack in what ways he has resisted the power of 'fear'. He might describe how he had overcome 'fear' in order to come along to the session or to accompany his mother to the corner shop. The therapist might ask how Jack had managed to deal with the fear that, at other times, appears to paralyse him. One could also ask whether the influence of 'guilt' on his life has ever changed or whether there have been any times when he has been able to resist the urges of 'anger'. Further questions will help to richly elaborate the emerging story.

From what we know of Jack, there are a number of avenues which might lead us to unique outcomes. One might ask about how he had managed to survive on the streets when he was homeless, or develop new relationships in the homeless project. How did he manage to stick at jobs even for a short time? The therapist might also ask how Jack had coped with his own sexual abuse and his father's violence. Wade (1997: 23) has argued that whenever people are badly treated, they find some way to resist. Thus 'alongside each history of violence and oppression, there runs a parallel history of prudent, creative and determined resistance'. Similarly, Warner (2009) has pointed out how activities like drinking alcohol or using legal and illegal drugs to excess, which may be viewed as problems by professionals, can also be seen as creative ways of coping with the legacy of abuse, even if they are subsequently experienced by people as getting in the way of the life they now want to lead.

These unique outcomes and the responses of the person (or anyone in an outsider witness position or from Jack's life outside the therapy room), become the building blocks of the subordinate narratives of the person's life. As a result of rich descriptions of these unique outcomes or 'sparkling events', Jack might develop new stories of his life. For example, he might begin to see himself less as a passive observer of his life and more as an active agent. These new stories are often very fragile and considerable effort and skill goes into helping the person elaborate them by rooting them in their history.

Tracing the history and meaning of the unique outcomes and naming an alternative story

The therapist attempts to trace the history of the unique outcomes in order to 'firmly ground them, make them more visible, and link them in some way with an emerging new story' (Morgan, 2000: 59). This takes a lot of effort: the therapist is interested in the particularities of each unique outcome. Who? What? Where? When? Two particular categories of enquiry are 'landscape of action' questions, and 'landscape of identity' questions.

Landscape of action questions might include, 'How did you manage to look after yourself whilst you were homeless? When did it happen? Who else was there? How long did it last? What happened just before or after? How did you prepare yourself?' Landscape of identity questions focus on the person's desires, intentions, preferences, beliefs, hopes, personal qualities, values, commitments, plans and so on. For example, one might ask Jack whether his survival on the street led him to revise his opinion of himself as a 'failure', and he might be able to see that he drew on his ability to be streetwise to keep himself safe at times. Thus, Jack might begin to reconnect with his own knowledges and agency.

After tracing and elaborating an alternative story, the client might then be invited to name it. Jack might name this as a story of strength and survival in the face of 'failure' and 'fear'. However, it is important to go further and to thicken these alternative stories, rooting these new discoveries.

Re-membering conversations

As Morgan (2000) notes, people can often feel isolated and disconnected from relationships when faced with problems. 'Re-membering' conversations are attempts to help clients reconnect with these significant relationships or 'memberships' – what Michael White referred to as a person's 'club of life' (Payne, 2006). Such memberships can include people alive or dead (e.g. friends, family members, teachers, neighbours, family friends, etc), real or imaginary and may also include animals, toys, pets, places, symbols or objects. So one might ask Jack, 'Who else would know that you stand up to fear?' or 'Can you think of someone who could tell a story about your commitment to fight injustice?' These kinds of conversation help to solidify the new emerging – yet fragile – alternative story. As it becomes inhabited with people and memories from the person's past and, as the therapist asks questions which track from the past to the present to possible futures, the new story becomes more firmly woven into the fabric of a person's life.

Therapeutic documents

Morgan notes that therapeutic documents are often written 'when people make important commitments or when people are ready to celebrate important achievements' (2000: 85), and Fox (2003) has reviewed a number of types. They are written collaboratively with the client and can act as 'counter-documents' to the more usual pathologising and problem-saturated descriptions that clients find in their case notes or discharge letters. They should, as much as possible, draw on the actual words, phrases and metaphors used by the client – indeed in his therapeutic work Michael White would write notes consisting entirely of verbatim phrases used by clients. Something that might help Jack is a 'document of identity' which records new stories about the person. This has been found to be useful in helping people cope with victimising voice-hearing (Brigitte et al., 1996; Stewart, 1995).

Therapeutic letters

One form of therapeutic document is a letter. Various types of letter can be used in narrative therapy (Fox, 2003; Morgan, 2000; White and Epston, 1990). For example, Jack might find it helpful to have a letter written after each session to summarise the new stories which had been heard in them (and perhaps pose questions to consider before the next session); and a letter of reference addressed 'To whom it may concern' which records accounts of a person's developing identity and aims to counter negative reputations. There are also *rituals and celebrations* which can be constructed to celebrate particular steps away from the dominant problem story. These might draw on particular family or cultural traditions.

Expanding the conversation: leagues and teams

Those who have experienced problems and escaped from their influence have considerable knowledge, skills and expertise. Narrative therapists have helped facilitate the setting up of a number of networks – for example, anti-Anorexia and anti-Bulimia Leagues (Grieves, 1997), some of which have engaged in letter-writing campaigns to protest about the use of 'waif' models in magazines for young women. Epston (2008) describes this in more detail and there is the *Archive of Resistance: anti-Anorexia/anti-Bulimia*.[5] In Jack's case we might consider how to draw on the knowledge of other young men who had struggled with fear, or lived with the legacy of physical or sexual abuse, or managed to revise their relationship with drugs or alcohol. A more recent development of the 'club of life' metaphor is Ncazelo Ncube's practice of the 'Tree of Life' – a creative way of exploring and documenting significant relationships developed in collaboration with children and young people living with the legacy of AIDS in southern Africa. The Tree of Life has also been used elsewhere – for example the Trailblazer project in Hackney in London with African Caribbean men involved with mental health services (Byrne et al., 2011). The Tree of Life and an associated sports-based metaphor, the Team of Life, is discussed in more detail in Denborough (2008).

O'Neill and Stockell (1991) have described work with a group of marginalised young men with a diagnosis of 'schizophrenia', who had attracted negative reputations amongst professionals – such an approach might be very useful in helping Jack to feel less isolated. Michael White facilitated a group for people who heard negative voices (Brigitte et al., 1996). Narrative work can also be conducted in large community gatherings (ACT Mental Health Users Network and Dulwich Centre, 2003; Byrne et al., 2011; Denborough, 2008; Dulwich Centre, 1995; Freedman and Combs, 2009; White, 2003). Finally, some of this work could potentially be done through others (e.g. nursing staff, the community psychiatric nurse and so on).

Outsider-witness groups and definitional ceremonies

As we noted earlier, in narrative therapy anyone present in a therapy session could be invited to adopt an 'outsider witness' position. However, sometimes a group of outsider witnesses might be used. These kinds of processes come under the category of definitional ceremonies. In Jack's case the 'audience' might include family members, professionals involved in his care, or other people who have struggled with similar issues (e.g. a group of young men: O'Neill and Stockell, 1991). These meetings follow a particular structure of a conversation between the therapist and Jack (a 'telling') followed by the therapist interviewing those in the 'audience' position about what they have heard and exploring what new ways of seeing Jack this leads to (a 're-telling'). The therapist would then interview Jack about what he heard and what new stories about himself these led to (a 're-telling of the re-telling'). Conversations can move between tellings and re-tellings and often prove to be enormously enriching and profoundly moving, particularly for people from marginalised groups.

Of course, it is important that these new stories are rooted in action. As Jack begins to develop an account of his hopes for the future, he can be enabled to make choices about what he wants to do next in his life. This might lead into conversations about where he wants to live – with his family? On his own? With others? How would he like to spend his time? Would he like to use his creative and musical talents in some way? – undertake further education? – or make other choices?

To formulate or not to formulate?

Given that narrative therapists do not aim to produce causal stories about problems, we do not feel it would be appropriate to shoe-horn the approach into the traditional formulation structure. A more theoretically consistent narrative therapy analogue of a formulation would be a therapeutic document such as a post-session summary letter, detailing the effects of the problem and outlining the emerging traces of an alternative story. Normally, as we have already noted, this would be done in collaboration with Jack, using his own language and preferences and with actual examples of unique outcomes. As a result, what follows is quite speculative. The content of the letter might be influenced by whether the letter was for Jack alone or intended to be read by others, such as his family, or other professionals, as well. As we are presenting this letter for pedagogical purposes, it is a little longer and more detailed than the letters that we would normally send.

Dear Jack,

You'll remember that when we met recently we said that we would write to you to put on record some of the important things we have been talking about recently.

You told us about the ways in which Fear had entered your life soon after your mum became physically ill and money at home was short. It seemed it had crept up on you and was stopping you doing the things you wanted to do and living the life you wanted to lead. The Fear tried to convince you of many frightening things. However, as we talked, it seemed to us that you were now onto what this Fear wanted to do to your life. We were very moved by the many small ways you stood up to it, for example in actually managing to get out of the house at some points and in attending our meetings. You said that you thought your medication had a part to play in this, but when we asked you how you had joined forces with the medication to bring change, it seemed you had taken a number of initiatives. You recognised that what the Fear wanted with your life and what you wanted were two very different things, and you started to tell us about some of the hopes you had for the future, which we found very inspiring.

Another problem which you identified was the way that Guilt was trying to wreck your life by making you feel that you were to blame for many of the difficulties you faced. It seemed that Guilt was in league with some of the people who had abused their positions of trust in your life in the past. However, it could not cope with hearing of how your family loved you, or you talking about the times when you accepted yourself or you expressing your hopes for the future.

We got wise to some of Guilt's tactics: it tended to pick on you when you were feeling low and also sensationalised any little setbacks which cropped up in your life, as they do in all of our lives at some point. Throughout all this, you began to rely on your wish to do good in the world and wanting the best for your family. These values seemed to give you strength in your attempts to win your life back from Guilt.

You have really been through the mill recently with these problems and the challenges you have faced in dealing with your anger, the drink and drugs and homelessness. Many people do not realise how hard it can be to survive on the streets and how much it takes when facing problems like these to manage to go to work. However, in our meetings with you we heard how creative you had been in surviving from day to day on the street and were amazed at how long you had stuck at the jobs you'd had, and how, after a setback, you had picked yourself up and gone for another job. These did not sound to us like a story of 'failure', more a story of hope and overcoming.

We very much look forward to meeting you again in the near future. We wondered, in the meantime, whether there might be other small ways in which you were managing to get your life back from the control of Guilt and Fear. Perhaps you could keep an eye out for these so that we can hear more about them when we meet?

Best wishes,
Dave Harper and Dave Spellman

Janet: a narrative therapy formulation

The practitioner working from a narrative perspective would be familiar with some of the literature pertinent to adopting this approach with children and their families (e.g. Freeman et al., 1997; Morgan, 1999; Smith and Nylund, 1997; Vetere and Dowling, 2005; White and Epston, 1990; White and Morgan, 2006). Having outlined this perspective in some detail in relation to Jack we will illustrate some possible approaches to Janet and her family more briefly.

The context of the referral

Finding a starting point that is likely to be helpful can be difficult. A useful question to ask oneself at this point is: 'What is being asked of me and by whom?' Long lists of 'concerns' are often provided by referrers with little indication as to why they are a concern and to whom. It is important to explore such assumptions and not be automatically organised by them. As in the case of Jack, then, one might already be deconstructing the dominant and subordinate stories in the referral letter and initial conversations (e.g. with referrers and with the clients).

Although adults often play little part in their referral to mental health services, this is even more true of children, who may be unaware of the referral, let alone consulted about it. Their views are rarely included in such decisions, and the social convention is that adults speak first and convey what they see as the truth of the problem.

It is very important to begin the first session with a friendly introduction and a simple but open description of the aims of the session. It is also important to get to know a family aside from the problem, if that is possible, by finding out a little about them and hearing from everyone rather than launching straight into what solution-focused therapists refer to as 'problem talk'.

Collaboration

After some general conversation oriented to getting to know the family, it is helpful to hear from members about what has brought them to the service.

Questions might be asked about what they would like to change and whether they agree with the referrer's ideas about the nature and priority of particular worries. Narrative therapists tend to place an emphasis on describing in detail how everyone would prefer things to be. After this the therapist sets about interviewing with an eye to helping the family colour the picture in. In this way the scene is set for a more collaborative way of working with and relating to family members.

If we treat the case description as a referral, then we can attempt to delineate some key themes. From our reading, these seem to include concern about Janet eating enough; Janet losing her temper; the effects of potential social exclusion; and some difficult aspects of the family history. With such a range of issues it can be difficult to know whether to try and find a central theme or deal with each separately. Checking out such dilemmas with the family directly would be common practice for us.

Our preference is to consider themes which connect with relationships rather than those which seem more individualised. Referrals tend to be focused on individual 'pathology' and request 'anger management' or 'parent training'. We would draw on systemic ideas (see chapter 4) and invite family members to map the effects of events upon relationships (e.g. 'How does the Temper affect the way you both get along?' 'To what extent does arguing about how much Janet eats stop the two of you having fun together?'). This can be blended with externalising conversations where the therapist interviews the family to plot the influence of a problem and disentangle it from people.

As we noted earlier, throughout such an interview clients are asked to make evaluations, even when it may seem pretty obvious how they might respond. For example one might ask, 'When you managed to count to ten and not lose your temper that time, how did that turn out for you and your Mum?' If the reply was, 'Oh it was much better when I did that', this would be followed by an invitation to justify the evaluation, by asking, for example: 'How was that a good thing for you?' 'What good effects did you notice? 'Good in what kind of way?' A sensitivity to the clients' responses is required here. What kind of questions do they prefer? How do they like to talk? What images or metaphors do they respond to?

Conversations with Janet and family members might focus on who expresses a preference for change and what kind of change they prefer. Professionals commonly hold quite clear views about what 'needs' to change and refer with this in mind, sometimes without much regard for the wishes or preferences of parents and children, whose views may be quite different. Narrative practitioners would aim at developing stories that do not blame anyone in the family or professional system.

The next step in these therapeutic conversations might be an exploration of unique outcomes – for example, how close the family have come to seeing their preferences enacted. These might include times when the arguing did not have such a negative effect on their relationships; or when Janet was able to give herself more nourishment; or when, despite their alleged history of 'lack of bonding', they had a good time together. We would explore these unique outcomes and consider in detail how they happened.

In work with parents it is often important to identify common unhelpful dominant cultural stories such as 'child-blaming', or 'mother-blaming' and 'parent-blaming', some of which may originate from the 'psy' disciplines (see also chapter 6), and to develop stories that counter these viewpoints.

Externalisation

Possibilities for externalising something which both Mary and Janet could join forces against, include the Fears; the Temper; the Arguing; the Not Eating, the Conflicts which get between Mary and Janet, and so on. Finding imaginative names for problems to be externalised can be fun for all family members.

In a narrative approach it is not just one person's job to tackle a problem; a team of 'co-workers' (e.g. family members, other significant relationships in the family's 'club of life') needs to be recruited. The family can be asked about the best ways of working together, communicating, staying focused and developing common tactics. This can be an antidote to the fragmentation seen when the problem can appear to get in between people and their relationships. It can also enable the separation of person from problem. So, one option is to invite the family to consider themselves as a team fighting an external problem together. The therapist can discuss with the family what might be achieved if it was possible for everyone to agree on some goals and work together, harnessing everyone's strengths. This can help them develop ideas about alternative possibilities for themselves.

Since an aim of narrative therapy is to shift the balance of power away from the problem, individuals can be helped to find the resources to move in the direction of their choosing. One potential resource here might be Mary's strong interest in spiritualism and clairvoyance. We could invite the family to say something about how these notions influence their lives in positive ways. It may be that they are rooted in the rich history of Romany tradition and that there are significant people alive or dead who could be talked about in re-membering conversations.

There are obviously countless ways in which therapeutic conversations may develop, but for the purposes of this chapter we have put together a letter that might be written to Janet and her mother as part of a narrative approach. Since letters are not always helpful, it is essential to discuss with families how they might feel about being sent one and, afterwards, what it was like to receive it.

Dear Mary and Janet,

When we met today we agreed to write to you to record some of the things we talked about and wanted to remember. It would be great if you could tell us what it was like getting this letter.

We both admire the commitment the two of you are showing, trying to work out some of the difficulties. You have demonstrated that you are not willing to let your relationship slip away from you and that you are determined to win it back.

We wondered what it was that made you both feel the relationship meant so much to you. You had told us what a difficult start in life you had together. It would be hard to list all the set-backs you had, but there were many. You, Mary, felt very guilty at how the sadness and depression got in the way of you being with Janet in the way that you wanted to be when she was very young. Guilt made you feel that the violence which you experienced at the hands of Colin was your fault, rather than *his* responsibility. Despite this, you have not lost sight of how you would like things to be. Some people would have given up and lost hope by now, but something seems to have kept the hope alive for you. We were really curious about that and wondered what that could be.

It was also quite striking to see how you, Janet, had made a decision to stay in touch with your dad but not to stay overnight anymore. We wondered how you found the courage to make such a big decision to take care of yourself. This also questions the idea (which you had heard from others) that you weren't able to look after yourself, wouldn't you say? We have talked quite a lot about how the arguments seem to overshadow everything in the house sometimes. You said it was like a big fat rain cloud, didn't you, Janet?

You both said very clearly that that's *not* how you want it to be. You, Mary, said you'd like to see the sunshine again and you agreed with that, Janet. We were delighted to see some sunshine in our meeting when you were able to hold hands at the point when you were both feeling upset. Did you notice that? Is that a sign of the sunshine you'd like to see more of?

When we started to look closely at your lives we thought there were quite a few shafts of sunlight that crept in, like the way you laugh together when you watch your favourite TV programmes and how you enjoyed your day trip to the seaside a few weeks ago. You both seemed to start noticing the sunshine in your lives more than the rain cloud by the end of our meeting. Was that a good thing, do you think? We can't ignore the rain cloud but we wonder what the effects would be if you were able to team up together and notice the sunshine more?

If you thought it was a good idea, you could both try to do that and we could talk about how you got along at our next meeting. We'd be interested to hear what your lives would be like if you were able to bring in more sunshine.

Best wishes

Dave Spellman and Dave Harper

Key characteristics of a narrative therapy approach to formulation

- Formulations are seen as a story developed collaboratively by therapist and client/s using their own words, phrases and metaphors as much as possible.
- These stories are seen as local and provisional and are not intended to be causal explanations.
- Psychiatric diagnoses and other professional classifications would be seen as 'thin' descriptions in need of elaboration. The aim is to encourage the development of richly textured, 'thick' and multi-storied narratives of people's lives.
- A formulation might include:
  - a description of an externalised problem, identifying the tactics by which it exerts its power, including how it is sustained by dominant societal discourses;
  - the identification of new maps and knowledges – for example ways in which the person has resisted or found a way of living alongside the problem – to scaffold the emergence of new stories;
  - the identification of more subordinate narratives framed in terms of intentions (rather than internal states) so the person can live a richer, more multi-storied life;
  - the responses of others (e.g. 'outsider witnesses');
  - reconnections with significant relationships from the client's past which may be drawn on to help sustain these alternative previously 'hidden' stories;
  - a record of the choices the client has made in relation to the place of these stories and relationships in their life;
  - creativity in its presentation (e.g. a variety of different kinds of documents and rituals) as well as some (sensitive and appropriate) humour!

Acknowledgements

Dave Harper would like to thank past and current UEL trainee clinical psychologists, past and present members of the Narrative East peer supervision group (Heleni Andreadi, Angela Byrne, Grace Heaphy, Gillian Hughes, Georgia Iliopoulou, Philip Messent and Heather Qualtrough), Duncan Moss, Jane Herlihy, Tania Thorn and the contributors to the workshop on formulation at Bristol in 2002 for interesting conversations on social constructionism, narrative therapy and formulation. Jonathan Buhagiar provided helpful comments on a previous draft of this chapter. This chapter is dedicated to Michael White (1948–2008).

Notes

1 One important confusion to clear up is the difference between constructivism and social constructionism as, unfortunately, many authors use these terms interchangeably. Constructivist approaches to therapy pre-date narrative therapy and therapists following Kelly's (1955) Personal Construct Theory would most accurately be termed constructivist. Constructivists acknowledge that individuals construct their own views of the world. However, social constructionists go one step further, arguing that those individual constructions are developed in a social world where, moreover, different constructions have different social power.

2 Since the publication of McNamee and Gergen (1992) a number of other approaches consistent with a social constructionist perspective have appeared, for example Ekdawi et al. (2000), Sam Warner's Visible Therapy approach to working with sexual abuse (Warner, 2009) and the contributors to Parker (1999).

3 For those interested in learning more about narrative therapy, many books, resources and freely downloadable articles can be found at: http://www. dulwichcentre.com.au/

4 In early narrative therapy work therapists drew liberally on protest metaphors in talking about problems (e.g. fighting, resisting, etc) but in later narrative work a much fuller range of metaphor is used (Stacey and Hills, 2001).

5 See   http://www.narrativeapproaches.com/antianorexia%20folder/anti_anorexia_ index.htm (accessed 20 August 2012).

References

ACT Mental Health Consumers Network and Dulwich Centre (2003) These are not ordinary lives: the report of a mental health community gathering, *International Journal of Narrative Therapy and Community Work*, 3: 29–49.

Allen, L. (1994) The politics of therapy: Michael White in conversation with Lesley Allen, *Context: A News Magazine of Family Therapy and Systemic Practice*, 18: 28–34.

Bob, S.R. (1999) Narrative approaches to supervision and case formulation, *Psychotherapy*, 36: 146–153.

Boyle, M. (2001) Abandoning diagnosis and (cautiously) adopting formulation, paper presented at symposium on *Recent Advances in Psychological Understanding of Psychotic Experiences*, British Psychological Society Centenary Conference, Glasgow.

——(2002) *Schizophrenia: A Scientific Delusion?* 2nd edn. London: Routledge.

Brigitte, Sue, Mem and Veronika (1996) Power to our journeys, *American Family Therapy Academy Newsletter*, Summer: 11–16.

Burr, V. (2003) *Social Constructionism.* 2nd edn, London: Routledge.

Byrne, A., Warren, A., Joof, B., Johnson, D., Casimir, L., Hinds, C., Mittee, S., Johnson, J., Afilaka, A. and Griffiths, S. (2011) 'A powerful piece of work': African Caribbean men talking about the 'tree of life', *Context: A Magazine for Family Therapy and Systemic Practice*: 117: 40–45.

Carey, M. and Russell, S. (2002) Externalising: commonly asked questions, *International Journal of Narrative Therapy and Community Work*, 2: 76–84. (Also available at www.dulwichcentre.com.au accessed 20 August 2012).

Carey, M., Walther, S. and Russell, S. (2009) The absent but implicit: a map to support therapeutic enquiry, *Family Process* 48: 319–331.

Carr, A. (2012) *Family Therapy: Concepts, Process and Practice*, 3rd edn. Chichester: Wiley-Blackwell.

Chenail, R.J., DiVincentis, M., Kiviat, H.E. and Somers, C. (2012) A systematic narrative review of discursive therapies research: considering the value of circumstantial evidence. In A. Lock and T. Strong (eds) *Discursive Perspectives in Therapeutic Practice*. Oxford: Oxford University Press, pp. 224–244.

Corrie, S. and Lane, D.A. (2010) *Constructing Stories, Telling Tales: A Guide to Formulation in Applied Psychology*. London: Karnac.

Cromby, J. and Harper, D. (2009) Paranoia: a social account. *Theory and Psychology*, 19: 335–361.

De Rivera, J. and Sarbin, T. (eds) (1998) *Believed-In Imaginings: The Narrative Construction of Reality*. Washington DC: American Psychological Association.

Denborough, D. (2008) *Collective Narrative Practice: Responding to Individuals, Groups and Communities Who Have Experienced Trauma*. Adelaide: Dulwich Centre.

Dillon, J. (2011) The personal *is* the political. In M. Rapley, J. Moncrieff and J. Dillon (eds) *De-Medicalizing Misery: Psychiatry, Psychology and the Human Condition*. Basingstoke: Palgrave MacMillan, pp. 141–157.

Dulwich Centre (1995) *Speaking Out and Being Heard*. Special issue of *Dulwich Centre Newsletter*, 4.

Ekdawi, I., Gibbons, S., Bennett, E. and Hughes, G. (2000) *Whose Reality is it Anyway? Putting Social Constructionist Philosophy into Everyday Clinical Practice*. Brighton: Pavilion Publishing.

Epston, D. (2008) Anti-anorexia/anti-bulimia: Bearing witness. In D. Epston and B. Bowen (eds) *Down Under and Up Over: Travels with Narrative Therapy*. Warrington: AFT publishing, pp. 169–191.

Fox, H. (2003) Using therapeutic documents: a review, *International Journal of Narrative Therapy and Community Work*, 4: 26–36.

Freedman, J. and Combs, G. (1996) *Narrative Therapy: The Social Construction of Preferred Realities*. London: Norton.

——(2009) Narrative ideas for consulting with communities and organizations: Ripples from the gatherings, *Family Process*, 48: 347–362.

Freeman, J., Epston, D. and Lobovits, D. (1997) *Playful Approaches to Serious Problems*. London: Norton.

Geertz, C. (1973). Thick description: Toward an interpretive theory of culture. In *The Interpretation of Cultures: Selected Essays*. New York: Basic Books, pp. 3–30.

Georgaca, E. (2000) Reality and discourse: a critical analysis of the category of 'delusion', *British Journal of Medical Psychology*, 73: 227–242.

Gergen, K.J. (1985) The social constructionist movement in modern psychology, *American Psychologist*, 40: 266–275.

Grieves, L. (1997) From beginning to start: the Vancouver Anti-Anorexia Anti-Bulimia League, *Gecko* 2: 78–88.

Hardy, K.V. (2001) African-American experience and the healing of relationships. An interview with Kenneth V. Hardy. In D. Denborough (ed.) *Family Therapy: Exploring the Field's Past, Present and Possible Future*. Adelaide: Dulwich Centre Publications, pp. 47–56.

Harper, D. (2011) The social context of 'paranoia'. In M. Rapley, J. Dillon and J. Moncrieff (eds) *De-Medicalizing Misery*. Basingstoke: Palgrave Macmillan, pp. 53–65.

Harper, D. and Moss, D. (2003) A different kind of chemistry? Reformulating 'formulation', *Clinical Psychology*, 25: 6–10.

Harper, D., Gannon, K.N. and Robinson, M. (2013) Beyond evidence-based practice: rethinking the relationship between research, theory and practice. In R. Bayne and G. Jinks (eds), *Applied Psychology: Practice, Training and New Directions*, 2nd edn. London: Sage, pp. 32–46.

Heise, D. R. (1988) Delusions and the construction of reality. In T. F. Oltmanns and B.A. Maher (eds) *Delusional Beliefs*. New York: Wiley, pp. 259–272.

Jenkins, A. (2009) *Becoming Ethical: A Parallel, Political Journey With Men Who Have Abused*. Dorset: Russell House Publishing.

Kelly, G. (1955) *The Psychology of Personal Constructs*. New York: W.W. Norton.

Knight, T. (2009) *Beyond Belief: Alternative Ways of Working with Delusions, Obsessions and Unusual Experiences*. Berlin: Peter Lehmann Publishing. Available for free download from: http://www.peter-lehmann-publishing.com/beyond-belief.htm, accessed 20 August 2012.

Madigan, S. (2011) *Narrative Therapy*. Washington, DC, US: American Psychological Association.

McNamee, S. and Gergen, K. (1992) *Therapy as Social Construction*. London: Sage.

Morgan, A. (ed.) (1999) *Once Upon a Time: Narrative Therapy with Children and their Families*. Adelaide: Dulwich Centre Publications.

——(2000) *What is Narrative Therapy? An Easy to Read Introduction*. Adelaide: Dulwich Centre Publications.

Myerhoff, B. (1982) Life history among the elderly: performance, visibility and re-membering. In J. Ruby (ed.) *A Crack in the Mirror: Reflexive Perspectives in Anthropology*. Philadelphia: University of Pennsylvania Press, pp. 231–247.

O'Neill, M. and Stockell, G. (1991) Worthy of discussion: collaborative group therapy, *Australian and New Zealand Journal of Family Therapy*, 12: 201–206.

Parker, I. (ed.) (1999) *Deconstructing Psychotherapy*. London: Sage.

Parker, I., Georgaca, E., Harper, D., McLaughlin, T. and Stowell-Smith, M. (1995) *Deconstructing Psychopathology*. London: Sage.

Parry, A. and Doan, R.E. (1994) The re-vision of therapists' stories in training and supervision. In A. Parry and R.E. Doan, *Story Re-Visions: Narrative Therapy in the Postmodern World.* New York: Guilford Press, pp. 187–205.

Patel, N. and Fatimilehin, I. (1999) Racism and mental health. In C. Newnes, G. Holmes and C. Dunn (eds), *This is Madness: A Critical Look at Psychiatry and the Future of Mental Health Services.* Ross-on-Wye: PCCS Books, pp. 51–74.

Payne, M. (2006) *Narrative Therapy: An Introduction for Counsellors.* 2nd edn. London: Sage.

Smith, C. and Nylund, D. (1997) *Narrative Therapies with Children and Adolescents.* New York: Guilford Press.

Speed, B. (1999) Individuals in context and contexts in individuals, *Australian and New Zealand Journal of Family Therapy*, 20: 131–138.

Stacey, K. and Hills, D. (2001) More than protest: Further explorations of alternative metaphors in narrative therapy, *Australian and New Zealand Journal of Family Therapy*, 22: 120–128.

Stewart, K. (1995) On pathologising discourse and psychiatric illness: an interview within an interview. In M. White, *Re-Authoring Lives: Interviews and Essays.* Adelaide: Dulwich Centre Publications, pp. 112–154.

Vetere, A. and Dowling, E. (eds) (2005) *Narrative Therapies with Children and their Families: A Practitioner's Guide to Concepts and Approaches.* Abingdon, Oxford: Taylor & Francis.

Vygotsky, L.S. (1978) *Mind and Society: The Development of Higher Psychological Processes.* Cambridge, MA: Harvard University Press.

Wade, A. (1997) Small acts of living: everyday resistance to violence and other forms of oppression, *Contemporary Family Therapy*, 19: 23–39.

Warner, S. (2009) *Understanding the Effects of Child Sexual Abuse: Feminist Revolutions in Theory, Research and Practice.* London: Routledge.

White, M. (1987) Family therapy and schizophrenia: addressing the 'in-the-corner' lifestyle, reprinted in M. White (1989) *Selected Papers.* Adelaide: Dulwich Centre Publications, pp. 47–57.

——(2003) Narrative practice and community assignments, *International Journal of Narrative Therapy and Community Work*, 2: 17–55.

——(2004) Folk psychology and narrative practice. In M. White, *Narrative Practice and Exotic Lives: Resurrecting Diversity in Everyday Life.* Adelaide: Dulwich Centre Publications, pp. 59–118.

White, M and Epston, D. (1990) *Narrative Means to Therapeutic Ends.* London: Norton.

White, M. and Morgan, A. (2006) *Narrative Therapy with Children and their Families.* Adelaide, South Australia: Dulwich Centre Publications.

Chapter 6

Reformulating the impact of social inequalities

Power and social justice

Lynn McClelland

What is a social inequalities approach?

The central feature of a social inequalities approach to formulation is that it goes beyond the traditional boundaries of psychology in emphasising the role of social and cultural contexts in shaping problems. This is shown in two main ways: structural features of society are seen as systematically marginalising and disempowering some people and not others; and psychology itself is viewed as part of an ideological dimension which shapes how we think and feel about ourselves. Importantly, this includes what is regarded as acceptable or deviant behaviour, such as what is seen as mental 'ill health'. In fact the very notion of psychological experience as indicative of a state of 'health' is a pervasive and questionable assumption.

Most psychological and social practitioners are unable to avoid awareness of the very real forms of suffering that many people experience: lack of access to basic material goods, shelter or healthcare; lack of safety and exposure to violence or abuse; environmental degradation; the impact of war, genocide or terrorism; migration and displacement; and the influence of toxic work environments. Their work often directly addresses the emotional and practical consequences of broader scale trauma and 'disruptive globalisation' on the local and personal level. Yet most therapeutic 'solutions' tend to be focused on the intra-psychic or inter-personal level.

In contrast, a social inequalities perspective suggests that there are structured differences or hierarchies of power that limit and constrain some people, and privilege and empower others, thereby creating and revealing conflicts of interest, and drawing attention to social relations, power and context. It is an approach which is influenced by the Frankfurt School of thought and the 'critical theory' of late capitalist society and culture that emerged from it (Kagan et al., 2011).

This theory of human and social reality, which incorporates ideas from psychoanalysis, philosophy and sociology, looks at the contradictions and conflicts of interest between economic and social processes within capitalism, and whether progressive change is possible. Such an account of human behaviour differs from the more traditional individualised accounts of drives, motives, intentions or internal conflicts that are dominant within psychology and psychotherapy. A social inequalities approach questions the concept of an atomistic free-floating individual as the central unit of analysis in psychology, and its preoccupation with intra-psychic processes and individual behaviour. Instead it sees the psychological as both emerging from, and dependent on, social relations – not only inter-personal ones, but also collective and social-systemic relations. This approach also suggests that a key aspect of reflexive practice is to ask the question: if psychology as a body of knowledge and practices had developed in a different society or culture, would it have looked different? In this way it highlights the fact that our current forms of theory and practice are not inevitable.

Formulation needs to reflect a complex picture where the ambivalences and inconsistencies of inner thoughts and feelings are not simply individually driven, or inherent faults of the person needing to be 'fixed', but part of a social world which is shaped by contradictory and conflicting expectations. As Kagan et al. (2011) point out, this need not deny the bodily reality of being human, but it does try to articulate how social phenomena beyond the level of the inter-personal shape the construction of human actors – their ideas, desires, prejudices, feelings, preferences, habits, customs and culture.

What are social inequalities?

Social inequality exists when an ascribed characteristic such as sex, race, ethnicity, class, and disability determines access to socially valued resources. These resources include access to money, status and power, especially the power to define societal rules, rights and privileges.

(Williams and Watson, 1988: 292)

We can use this definition to develop a working map of the impact of social inequalities on mental health which may help us articulate the processes through which people experience and resist the operation of inequality in their lives. This draws attention to the presentation of mental health problems as 'signs and symptoms' of inequality in a deliberate attempt to make conceptual links and to disrupt the common use of these terms to define distress within a medical model.

An example of the model that has informed our approach to formulation is given in Figure 6.1.

Social inequalities and mental health

The unequal distribution of economic and social resources in society is central to explaining why some groups are more likely than others to seek help from psychological services (Fryer, 1998). Unfortunately, as has been documented

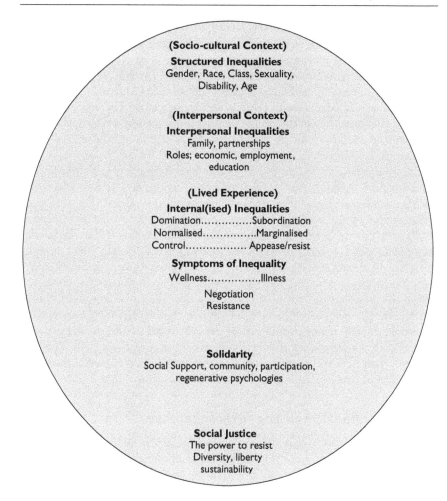

(Socio-cultural Context)

Structured Inequalities
Gender, Race, Class, Sexuality,
Disability, Age

(Interpersonal Context)

Interpersonal Inequalities
Family, partnerships
Roles; economic, employment,
education

(Lived Experience)

Internal(ised) Inequalities
Domination...............Subordination
Normalised...............Marginalised
Control................. Appease/resist

Symptoms of Inequality
Wellness................Illness

Negotiation
Resistance

Solidarity
Social Support, community, participation,
regenerative psychologies

Social Justice
The power to resist
Diversity, liberty
sustainability

Figure 6.1 Map of social inequalities

many times, it is 'low status' groups who also experience the most negative and disempowering contact with services (Morgan et al., 2001; British Psychological Society, 2008, 2012).

There are many different possible definitions of inequality and a number of psychological perspectives that attempt to address the intersection between the person and oppression. My main approach here is best described as *critical community psychology* (Kagan et al., 2011; Fryer, 2008). All these approaches are 'critical' of mainstream Western psychological theories and practices that tend to decontextualise individuals and obscure social, political and material realities, and argue for a community or societal-level formulation and community-level or a broader systems-level intervention.

Orford (2008), in his major review of community psychologies, describes an 'emerging consensus' in theory and practice organised around core values of *liberation, empowerment* and *social justice*. Kagan et al. (2011) have added *'stewardship'* to their model of critical community psychology, which links with the emergence of Ecopsychology (Rust and Totton, 2012) as a psychological response to our current ecological crisis. The importance of building sustainable environments and of recognising our fundamental interconnectedness within the human system is increasingly seen as vital to psychological wellbeing.

So, at present we are seeing a potential revisioning of psychology and psychotherapy through the infusion of a wide range of international social justice perspectives related to personal, community and societal wellbeing (Prilleltensky et al., 2007). Liberation psychologies (Watkins and Shulman, 2008) and critical race and postcolonial theories (Dalal, 2002; Fernando, 2010; Hook, 2011) contribute to what Aldorondo (2007) calls 'the reformist spirit' in the mental health professions. These views are part of an emergent tradition of critique which includes critical and community psychologists, radical psychotherapists, sociologists, philosophers and policy-makers. It also includes the perspectives of the survivor, service user and disability movements, feminists, LGBT groups and critical race activists – all of whom have contributed to a growing weight of evidence, theories and practices. The best emerging practices and services are often characterised by partnerships across these different professional and non-professional groups.

Critical evaluation of the 'evidence base'

> It was through attempts to diagnose, conceptualise and regulate pathologies of conduct that psychological knowledge and expertise first began to establish its claims for scientific credibility, professional status and social importance.
>
> (Rose, 1985: 226)

A social inequalities perspective takes a particular perspective on the current emphasis on evidence-based practice within clinical psychology, medicine and other disciplines. This involves a recovery of ideas about the human condition which tend to become marginalised or excluded in mainstream practice, reaching out to the 'evidence' that lies within sociology and feminist theory, and taking a 'critical' approach to the widespread adoption of a 'metaphorical medical model' or the 'bio-bio-bio model masquerading as the biopsychsocial' (Boyle, 2002; Read et al., 2009). This perspective disrupts the notion of an objective, socially neutral investigation which is inherent in the scientist–practitioner model and takes a critical view of the focus on individual 'cognitions' and behaviour rather than, for instance, toxic environments, as mediating distress.

This perspective also questions the validity of research designs, vested stakeholder interests, and publication bias involved in the presentation of evidence in, for instance, the NICE guidelines. It recognises instead that the presentation of 'data' and 'facts' can serve an ideological function as Jones (2011) demonstrates in his analysis of prejudice and stereotyping within the UK media, in which 'chavs' and 'welfare scroungers' appear as a demonised underclass. He argues that this formulation obscures a more complex picture of poverty and exclusion of people abandoned by the aspirational society-fragmenting policies of both Tories and New Labour, and illustrates the clash in versions of the 'truth' through a series of interviews with people living at the sharp end of disenfranchisement. A woman voices a challenging alternative version:

> We died! … Once all the mines closed, all the community had gone. It's just been a big depression ever since … just struggling to survive, that's all … loads of men over 45 never worked again.
>
> (Jones, 2011: 185)

This study is reminiscent of Pierre Bourdieu's (2000) analysis of the weight of social suffering as described in interviews across several generations of ethnic groups in working-class communities in France. The resulting 'data' was used to illustrate his theories of social capital, habitus and symbolic violence – ideas which have become closely linked to individual and collective wellbeing in critical community psychology.

The relationship between social inequalities, health and mental health has been extensively documented in national and international health and social care policy reports (BPS, 2008; Department of Health, 2010, 2009; Marmot, 2012; Institute of Health Equalities (IHE), 2012; World Health Organisation, 2009; UNICEF, 2011) and in service user consultations (Bates, 2002; Sashidharan, 2003; Morgan et al., 2001). The Marmot Review argues that reducing health inequalities is a matter of fairness and social justice, and demonstrates that there is a marked social gradient in health and mental health. Collective and personal wellbeing are intimately connected with action to reduce social inequalities (Wilkinson and Pickett, 2009). The present economic situation presents a direct threat to our mental health and psychological wellbeing with pressures on communities increasing during economic recession – particularly if social and financial inequalities are permitted to increase and people with mental health problems becoming more vulnerable. They may also become more so, via threats from cuts in public spending on health and social services.

The IHE Report (2012) on the likely impact of economic downturn on policy change summarises a number of factors that increase social inequality, including rising unemployment, poorer working conditions, depressed incomes, inability to pay for basic needs, lack of decent and affordable housing, and child poverty. They predict a decline in mental and physical health (e.g. more suicides and depression, homicides and domestic violence) with possible long-term effects (p.7).

This research suggests that particular groups may be differentially affected by these changes, especially young people (under 25 years), and men with lower level skills and education, or those in insecure jobs. Previous research into economic downturns suggests that the psychological impact of deteriorating work conditions for those in work, including job and financial insecurity, higher debt levels and less sense of control in face of increasing demands, will lead to much higher rates of anxiety and depression, and will have a knock-on effect on families and community cohesion (another indicator of wellbeing). It is therefore crucial that psychological practitioners ask the right questions about these powerful 'distal' forces (Smail, 1993) in people's lives and psyches.

These processes potentially affect those 'being helped' and those 'helping', as well as the relationship between them, and are likely to become part of a 'polarisation of disadvantage', placing particular stress on public services in the most deprived areas (Marmot, 2012; Hoggett, 2006). Despite a number of attempts to call attention to these links within clinical psychology (Bostock, 2003, 2004; Fryer, 1998, 2008; Orford, 2008; Smail, 2011; Rapley et al., 2011), this perspective remains peripheral to clinical psychology theory and practice (Boyle, 2011; Miller and McClelland, 2006). Disturbingly, social inequalities and their oppressive psychological effects may be on the rise.

Power and inequality

> Power derives more from the routine application of effectively unchallenged assumptions than from the manifest dominance of one group over others in open conflict ... simply the routine operation of social institutions.
>
> (Ng, 1980: 14)

A further aspect of a critical-social approach is the attention to the presence of ideologies or dominant discourses within traditional formulation practice. These tend to mask and legitimise inequalities, misdirect our attention (Newnes, 2012) and work to sustain established power balances (Williams, 1999). Mental health professions and disciplines such as medicine and psychology are seen as key sites for the production of such discourses, and also of contesting them (Foucault, 1980; Rose, 1989).

The institutional context of clinical discourses is the 'clinic' in its broadest sense, which is part of a historical process of the development of ideas about madness/normality, and a co-dependency between mental health professions and marginalised groups (who treats/who is treated). From this perspective, it can be argued that in formulating we are located within a process of social control which has shifted away from overt forms of extended incarceration and the more brutal physical treatments towards subtler forms of control such as the processes and technologies of diagnosis, medication and therapy, which nevertheless serve the same ends.

As Hoggett (2006) argues, mental health services are situated within complex public organisations characterised by continuous questions and debates about values and policies. These are played out and intensified at the point of delivery where clients and practitioners meet. It is therefore crucial that we extend our gaze beyond the world of the clinic. He formulates the role of the mental health services themselves as to act as receptacles for social anxieties about disorder and madness, performing the explicit and implicit function of containing much of what is disowned by the society in which they are situated.

This approach is wary of the current tendency to adopt managerialist and neo-liberal language within mental health settings as indicated by talk about the 'delivery of goods and services' to 'clients' and 'consumers' who are able to make empowered choices about this or that 'treatment'. It draws attention to the potential commodification of relationships, and the consequential stripping of ethics and meaning inherent in this version of practice. In contrast, in a recent review of medical and health professionals' role in addressing health inequalities, Allen, Allen, Hogarth and Marmot (2013) propose that they are well-placed to take action on the social determinants of health (including mental health) as committed and potentially powerful advocates.

Miller and McClelland (2006: 132) recommended the use of reflective questions about how power is operating in the lives of people we work with (Bostock, 2003; Prilleltensky and Nelson, 2002) as part of a critical approach to formulation which recognises the contested nature of values and interests involved. For example, what ideas of a 'good life' and 'good society' are promoted by our formulations (self-interest or cooperation? based on pursuit of equality or at the expense of others?)? How have people gained power/ agency in any domain?

These questions create a challenge to individualistic explanations of the origins of mental health problems and relocate responsibility for oppression and change. They also highlight issues of ownership of the problem; in other words, we need to ask: whose problem is this?

Reflecting real-life diversity and recognising difference

Third-wave feminist theories (Gillis et al., 2007) have also influenced the understanding of gendered experiences, giving a voice to those outside the ethnic, sexual and sociological mainstream (Boyle, 1997). Critical race, post colonial and multi-cultural approaches (Dalal, 2002, 2012; Hook, 2011; Ryde, 2009; Sewell, 2009; Fernando and Keating, 2008) have flourished and influenced the development of individual, systemic and group therapies.

Many of the best models consider the impact of *multiple sources of inequality*, a common element in service user accounts as an accumulative 'risk factor' for mental health and trauma (White, 2004; McGoldrick and Hardy, 2008). An early example of this was the study of the impact of 'everyday' racial micro-aggressions – the subtle, common-place, often non-verbal indignities experienced particularly by marginalised groups, even in those exchanges considered to be fair and non-discriminatory (Sue et al., 2007). Another example is Almeida's Cultural Context Model (CCM) (Almeida et al., 2007) which combines social justice principles, post colonial analysis and multi-level intervention to explore multi-generational histories of cultural resistance and survival. This offers a 'reformulation' of both the structure of services and the process of therapy in an effort to make therapy a journey of liberation and healing instead of renewed compliance and acquiescence to society's everyday oppressive expectations (p. 179). Some of these ideas are reflected in the accounts of Jack and Janet below.

Making Jack more visible: critical formulation

Before we even begin to understand Jack, it is important to recognise how little we can do without his personal involvement and participation. The 'cases' are already decontextualised and have been subjected to the clinical gaze. It isn't Jack telling us about himself. It isn't Jack who appears to be directly involved in the process of making sense of his predicament. It should be Jack who is at the heart of his own story, and Jack who is the expert on his own life. This cautions us not to complicate Jack's already tenuous feeling (one supposes) of ownership over his own life with well-meaning but potentially oppressive narratives. We are uneasy about having this conversation about Jack, without Jack.

Furthermore, it is likely that as a mental health service user Jack will already have been subjected to the dominant models inherent in Western cultures regarding distress – namely, medicalised, pathologising accounts about his difficulties, in which his own account of his experiences will have been ignored except as an indicator of various symptoms. One need only look through the often voluminous notes documenting the treatment of mental health service users to confirm the detachment of the 'person' from the 'story'. The psychiatrising or psychologising of distress (Dillon et al., 2012; Smail, 2011; Fryer, 1998) can achieve this separation very easily with people already made vulnerable by distress, confusion and hopelessness. Clinical formulation runs the risk of simply being another 'expert' monologue which, in the attempt to obtain clinical coherence, locates the centre for recovery at arm's length from the person, adding to their experience of objectification and alienation, and complicating genuine therapeutic engagement. Clinical formulation must therefore demonstrate its credentials in terms of how the service user experiences it. In particular we would ask: how participatory is the process? How well is it rooted in the person's own experience and beliefs?

Collaborative formulation: situating Jack's experiences

In 2006 we took this problem to a 'reference group' of young men whose life experiences seemed to us (and them) to provide some basis for informed 'witnessing' of some of the themes identified in the account about Jack. These young men had all encountered mental health services, had all experienced alienation and had all been subjected to abuse in one form or another. They all had many other kinds of experiences too, not to mention a diverse range of talents, interests and hopes for their lives. In this respect our methodology has links with Almeida and colleagues' (2007) 'Cultural Circles' and 'coalition groups' (Friere, 1970), using mixed groups of professionals and non-professionals to challenge oppressive norms, create solidarity and develop more accountability. We can only hope that Jack would have shared in this sense of commonality. This approach is connected but different to the narrative therapy technique of a 'reflecting team' (White, 1995) in terms of its membership being non-professional, although in this case a summary was provided by a male clinical psychologist. The conversation that unfolded, summarised below, helped us to identify some key issues and themes.

Dialogue: 'A few lines about a world of trouble'

Paragraph 1, page x

The descriptions of Jack in paragraph 1 drew interest. Several of the young men shared their experience of having their emotions 'measured' against some invisible norm. A medicalised context allows this, and reserves the right to determine 'appropriateness' against a template of signs and symptoms. The quantifying and objectifying of expressed feeling can obscure the simpler question of why? Why is Jack feeling what he is feeling?

Paragraph 2

Several young men identified with the theme of social and familial expectation in paragraph 2. This led into an interesting discussion about the privileges and burden of being 'favoured'. People spoke about the costs of compliance in terms of giving up your own ambitions, and the costs of resisting, such as rejection or censure or further pressure. One young man said that as the only son he had felt this pressure of expectation as a 'heavy hand on my shoulder' and that, looking back, the only means of resistance was to fail. Several in the group also enjoy music and wondered if this put Jack in conflict with the expectation of running the family business.

Paragraph 3

This paragraph provoked considerable discussion amongst the group. One man commented: 'A few lines about a world of trouble'. Does this reflect the tendency of mental health services and 'case formulation' to minimise the impact of either witnessing or experiencing violence, or being subjected to sexual abuse as a child? The group identified similar experiences of power abuse in their own lives and the often ruinous consequences for them.

Paragraph 4

In paragraph 4, the group quickly noted the chronological proximity between sexual abuse and the emergence of alcohol use. Many of our young men identified with the use of alcohol and drugs as a seductive means of 'self-medicating' distress. Other significant life events were identified, including:

- Stresses associated with GCSEs.
- The fact that Jack also has to contend with the breaking up of the family, his parents and the disappearance of his father back to Italy. Perhaps it was his gender as a man that made his father's departure more difficult for Jack than for his sisters.
- The group speculated about the period leading up to the separation. How emotionally available would Jack's parents have been to Jack and his two sisters? Several, perhaps like Jack, had not felt able to disclose their abuse because they felt they wouldn't or couldn't be heard.

Paragraph 5

After reading this paragraph, one or two of the young men spoke about having lived through similar periods of alienation and disruption in their own lives. They described these times as like being 'lost to the world', feeling uncared for and not caring for anything or anyone, least of all themselves. One said, 'Someone should have seen that being depressed isn't just about your head, but your life; they didn't for me and they didn't for him'. Many, though not all, described their first contacts with mental health services as like 'confirming all the worst things you thought about yourself'. There was a strong feeling of solidarity with Jack in the group.

Paragraph 6

The whole family now appeared to be struggling. Our group thought that Jack was sounding in desperate straits at this stage. The diagnoses Jack was attracting are more serious, with more power to label him negatively, and yet, our group felt, were still missing the point of what may have been going on for him. Some observations were:

> 'He wants out of his life.' 'He sounds like he's really lost it, he just doesn't want his life anymore, he wants Robbie's life.' 'Is he worrying about his family? His sisters? Does he feel bad because he hasn't helped them?' 'He is really haunted by his father.' 'He'd rather be Robbie than his father, maybe? Well, he needs to be someone! But who?'

We will now consider in more detail the themes that emerged from this discussion.

Critical reflections on the discussion

Masculinity as problematic

Masculinity, the experience of being born male, of trying to learn how to relate to himself and the world as a male, seems to play a significant role in several key areas of Jack's life. In relation to his father: 'He described the frightening experience of looking in the mirror and seeing his father's face reflected back at him.' Jack is exposed to his father's alcoholism and his violence towards his family and towards Jack himself. Jack was also expected to carry on the family business, literally, to follow in his father's footsteps. These experiences form part of Jack's socialisation and introduction to masculinity.

More specifically, we wondered if Jack has learned the male-typical strategies for managing distress. Miller and Bell (1996) argue that the privileged male role imposes expectations about masculinity that may have a serious detrimental effect on the mental health of men and the women and children in their families. They argue that one of the most pernicious consequences of male socialisation is that it requires men to be silent and strong, leaving individuals little scope to acknowledge and deal constructively with feelings of vulnerability or powerlessness. Instead men are offered safety through dominance and control of the external world, and survival through the sanctioned means of violence. Does Jack learn that this is how men manage their distress – through objectifying others and through violence and alcohol abuse? Does Jack feel 'caught' between his family and his father? Does Jack identify with his disempowered, female, victimised family? And does he also crave acceptance and inclusion from his father? We might speculate as to whether Jack experiences himself as alienated from both, a member of neither.

He may experience his father as powerful, but it seems that Jack experiences himself as powerless. Jack is left to somehow reconcile the disparity between the expectation of dominance and the actualities of his life. In this sense our formulation is not that Jack has ambivalences and inconsistent inner thoughts and feelings, but that his inner world is shaped by the inconsistent and contradictory expectations in his culture.

This dilemma is dramatically and seriously compounded by Jack's sexual abuse by another male in a position of power in relation to him. That Jack was silent about this is unremarkable. In a review, Watkins and Bentovim (1992) suggest that the under-reporting of sexual abuse is consistent and universal. Within the terms of masculinity the consequences of assault are compounded by a form of psychological emasculation, literally implying a loss of power, gender and the failure to be a man (McMullen, 1990). For Jack this occurs at a highly critical and vulnerable period in his life. The man in question could have made a huge difference to Jack, by taking a fatherly interest in a vulnerable boy. Instead, his vulnerability was exploited. Jack, as we know, did not disclose this to his parents at the time, and is barely able to mention it subsequently. Jack's story points to a 'failure of recognition' (Fraser and Honneth, 2003).

Formulating power

We tried to focus on experience, not symptoms, using 'thick' not 'thin' descriptions of people's lives (White, 1995; and see chapter 5). Whether we succeeded in avoiding reductionism can, perhaps, only be judged by Jack himself. Our formulation sought to avoid 'vocabularies of deficit' (Gergen, 1999). Jack has been diagnosed as, not is, a 'delusional schizophrenic', so we don't imply a consensus or objective reality that is in fact highly debated (Boyle, 2002; Johnstone, 2000; Harper, 2011; Knight, 2012). This approach recognises that diagnosis and formulation are relational processes involving power imbalances. A response that renders his behaviour insane/psychotic, or 'beyond the pale', would confirm his process of alienation, and contribute to the 'loss of myself' already set off by the experience of multiple trauma and social inequalities (White, 2004).

The initial and primary focus is not on the removal of delusions. Rather, the beliefs Jack holds are accepted and meaning is co-constructed. The 'delusions' are re-framed as a positive, active coping strategy that works to keep him safe at the moment. The confusion over reality in Jack's case relates more to the feeling that there has been a 'cover-up' on many levels in his life, than to an organic disease process. There have been many times when he had to lose himself to survive and contort himself to fit with others' actions. Real threats and persecutions to abused children, and consequent fears of dying, are common tactics of abusers. When compounded by secrecy and the sanctioning of emotional expression due to social stigma and taboo, this creates still further potential confusion. So a belief that 'I mustn't go out – I might get attacked', is embedded within a real experience of lack of protection and exploitation in the world. It is not a figment of Jack's imagination, nor a dysfunctional belief, but rather an attempted solution to real-life conditions.

If we don't assume the discontinuity between normality/abnormality that so much of mental health practice seems to rely on (Dillon et al., 2012), we minimise the development of 'otherness' or 'them-and-us' thinking (May, 2000; Dalal, 2002) that is characteristic of so many practitioner–client relationships. In positioning Jack as 'delusional' and 'paranoid' we position ourselves, in contrast, as sane, balanced and informed. Jack is then forced into a false choice between 'I am wrong' or 'The world is wrong' that mirrors and exacerbates these dynamics.

Social justice and empowerment potentials

In contrast to most mental health practice, we were more interested in making sense of Jack's so-called 'delusions' in terms of his local inter-personal and cultural context than in categorising his experiences in terms of particular diagnoses. We don't have to look far to see the potential for empowerment and recovery in an alliance between Jack and Robbie Williams, a powerful collective cultural icon of contemporary masculinity representing success, a rags-to-riches journey (a working-class hero who has proved the existence of social mobility), potent sexuality and musical creativity. Jack's choice of 'delusion' is not random or meaningless, and provides a positive contrast to other male role models in his life. Nor is Robbie such an idealised image that Jack is unable to relate to him – Robbie is known for his own struggles with substance abuse, sexuality and pressure. Similarly Jack's preoccupation with 'stolen money' and 'money owed' has deep resonances with a sense of social justice and the profound impact that socioeconomic decline has had on his life. He is owed something, a lot has already been taken away from him. The world needs to give him back something he has lost, and in this sense he is presenting a 'complaint' (Bentall, 2009).

In common with many other victims of abuse and domestic violence, Jack can be seen as having been socialised into a hierarchical victim–perpetrator model of social relations. He anticipates the possibility of causing sexual harm and appears stuck in a traumagenic process commonly seen in abuse victims (Baker and Duncan, 1985) where the potential for abuse and revenge, and ultimately a repeat of the violence he experienced, can become a paralysing preoccupation. Jack may be influenced by a dominant discourse that is widely held both outside and within mental health services, despite research that shows that victims are at least as likely not to abuse as become abusers themselves (Hester et al., 2000). In dwelling on these fears he inadvertently draws attention to the denial of social inequalities and power processes that are so central to abuse.

Sources of resistances for Jack are to be found within the survivor and service user movement, or clinical approaches that encourage the 'transformative' (where emphasis is placed on meaningfulness and creativity, e.g. Mad Pride, the Hearing Voices movement, the Survivor movement, Experts by Experience groups), rather than on the 'accommodative' (where the emphasis is on resignation and disability). Jack's passion for music appears to us to be a major resource and a possible source of creativity and resistance, part of his self that feels OK, pre-disempowerment, free, able and whole. This may contain potential for a redefinition of a positive male role. Significantly, when we created a local space for young men experiencing psychosis in our collaboration with MIND (Young Voices Project), their chosen means of connection was music rather than talk. MAC-UK is an excellent example here (www.mac-uk.org.uk).

Making Janet more visible: critical formulation

Space and time did not permit us to describe a reference group for Janet and Mary, but we were able to draw on Appleton et al.'s (2003) example of power-mapping (Hagan and Smail, 1997b) with a group of Gypsy and Traveller women. This study, and our experience of working alongside Community Development Workers, suggests that a history of marginalisation and fear, loss of perceived status, lack of job opportunities and difficulties in accessing education is likely to be relevant. My experience on training courses and in mental health teams, is that recent media portrayals of this community have had a largely negative influence.

These themes are now explored in relation to Janet and her family.

Femininity as problematic

Firstly, there is a fundamental 'risk of being' for women presenting to services with experience of oppression (Williams, 1999; Chesler, 1994; Beckwith, 1993; Ussher, 1991) where their thoughts, feelings and behaviour are highly likely to be interpreted as 'madness' or 'badness' depending on whether they encounter psychiatric or social care institutions. Secondly, as Walkerdine (1996) asserts following her analysis of dominant discourses within sociological and psychological literature, women are present in discussions of disadvantaged or 'working class' women in Britain primarily as a 'mother':

> a mother who must be watched and monitored at all times through the available medical, educational, social work and legal apparatuses because she is seen as the relay point in the production of the democratic citizen. It is she, above all others, who will obey the moral and political order and not rebel.

> (Walkerdine, 1996: 146)

This, she argues, has led to a mode of regulation through psychology which targets groups of women and particularly mothers, and ascribes them the role of 'transmitters' of social pathology (e.g. through faulty or damaging child-rearing practices, or failure to bond). At the same time, any attempt to engage seriously in the psychological effects of their oppression is avoided. This dynamic is even more likely to be present when mothers have lived experience of other kinds of difference – mothers from minority groups, lesbian mothers, teenage mothers, older mothers, mothers of sexually abused children, etc. These 'soft forms of regulation' are in operation in a wide variety of institutional settings (e.g. social services), and particularly within mental health services (e.g. child and adolescence mental health teams), where subjectivity and development are only understood in terms of normality or pathology, as applied to children or mothers (e.g. the ADHD discourse; Timimi, 2011).

Formulating power

In the case of Mary and Janet we would want to recognise the ideological function of much research and practice which claims expertise about motherhood, often from a white, male, middle-class vantage point. Instead we would be searching for grounded, contextualised evidence where attempts are made to consult and put mothers themselves in a central position. One complication that arises from this suggestion is that 'the anxieties and projections onto them, which are entailed in their regulation, will be present in their views of themselves and their own insecurities' (Walkerdine, 1996: 152). For example, the women may have internalised views of themselves as stupid, sexually damaged or inadequate mothers. This does not need to be conceptualised as a straightforward process of internalisation by a passive subject, but can be seen as the outcome of a long historical practice of survival in minority groups within deprived material conditions and in defence of the myths and fantasies of dominant oppressive groups.

Formulation would benefit from approaches that use critical consciousness-raising (Almeida et al., 2007; Dalal, 2002; Prilleltensky et al., 2007; Ryde 2009; Friere, 1978). This would attempt to deconstruct diagnoses and pathologised accounts of motherhood (Woollett and Phoenix, 1997; Van Scoyoc, 2000) thus raising awareness of a number of power processes that may be operating in Janet and Mary's case. Firstly, Mary is 'captured' by medical diagnoses, a traditional way of concealing social inequalities by pathologising and medicalising women's distress (Ussher, 1991; Woollett and Phoenix, 1997). Secondly, there is the obscuring of the impact of domestic violence on both Mary and Janet, which is perhaps being played out in Janet's night terrors, aggression towards her mother and eating problems.

We might hypothesise that the formulation of Mary and Janet so far is likely to be influenced by mother-blaming discourses (Woollett and Phoenix, 1997), the double-bind of traditional motherhood roles within heterosexual relationships (lack of power and access to resources combined with full responsibility for childcare; exposure to violence; lack of childcare support; the psychological and emotional costs of caring), along with the absence of accounts of fathers' influences on relationships and children's development. As is typical of many referrals to CAMHS services, this gendered nature of clinical discourses about families remains unquestioned (Almeida et al., 2007). We might ask why there is ongoing unsupervised contact with an abusive father when there are many personal accounts as well as much research pointing to the risk of further harassment for Mary and abuse for Janet (Hester et al., 2000).

Janet's hidden and internalised distress is characteristic not only of being a girl, but also of being a child witness to domestic violence. Boys' needs, although no less complex, may tend to be more evident in mental health services, schools and society as a whole, due to their tendency to act out distress in highly visible ways such as behavioural problems, youth offending and so on. Similarly, the interdependence of mothers and daughters as a survival strategy in adverse conditions is unlikely to be valued, but will tend to be pathologised and measured against socially constructed Western, gendered norms of separation and autonomy. In extreme cases there may even be a diagnosis of factitious disorder by proxy (formerly 'Munchausen's by proxy') syndrome. The relational needs of women in services are recognised in the Women's Mental Health Strategy (Department of Health, 2003). This might suggest the possibility of Cindy as a potential non-abusive co-parent, and the involvement of 'outsider witnesses' (White, 1995: 26; and see chapter 5) within the Romany or local community. Mary could therefore be reframed as a 'surviving mother' and grandmother instead of a 'failing mother' as she appears to be in the referral. Mary's experience as a mother of older children, one of whom has special needs/disabilities (autism), would be an important part of her story, her sense of self and the skills that she could bring to an encounter with services.

Restoring meaning through making socio-cultural context visible

There is growing interest in family interventions which emphasise broader social and cultural contexts. Korbin (2003), for example, highlights the contextual and multi-dimensional factors in child maltreatment, especially the influence of social networks, neighbourhood ties, and community connectedness. In Gracia and Musitu's (2003) comparison of families in two different cultural contexts, families where abuse had occurred were less involved in local activities and held more negative attitudes towards the wider community. Abusing parents had smaller peer groups, less contact with families of origin, received less help from family relations and felt more isolated in their communities. The existence and meaning of these kinds of sub-cultures is not necessarily picked up by mainstream services. Gracia and Musitu (2003) described a process of 'social impoverishment': an isolation from formal and informal sources of support so that some families do not use services even when they are available. There is potential for this kind of marginalisation in Mary and Janet's case.

Sheppard's (1998) study in the UK has shown the influence of disadvantage, low income and lack of social support on the 'progression' of families towards social service caseness, and the link between disadvantage, abuse and depression amongst mothers on social service and health visitor caseloads, independent of pathways into care. Where social support and involvement of services was lowest, there was an increased risk of injury and neglect of children.

Fatimilehin, Raval and Banks (2000) have also made some important points about the cultural context of formulation. As applied to Janet, these may include:

- The combination of factors in this case because of minority group status: multiple disadvantage in relation to the power and dominance of mainstream cultural values, racism, harassment, alienation from professional discourses.
- Generational impact of acculturation through assimilation, and the consequent dilution or disconnection from cultural history and heritage. Use of cultural genograms (cultural family trees) may be helpful (Hardy and Laszloffy, 1995).
- Normative theories of child development: independence, separation, child-rearing practices.
- Formation of self-identity and racial/ethnic identity may be problematic.
- Ethnic definitions of distress differing from mainstream: child abuse, bereavement, impact of racism, harassment denied.
- Interaction with education system: language, aspirations, stigma, achievement.
- Lack of specific provision for black and minority ethnic family support for parents with mental health problems.

We would also want to make a note of the many resiliences Janet shows, for example her enthusiasm for school, her sociability and the family's spiritualism as a potential connection to the past.

Practitioners should be able to work with difference (Sewell, 2009), and the cultural competence of services is increasingly becoming important. We would therefore want to develop an understanding of the institutional inequalities (myths, explanations, racism) that are present. We would focus on qualitative assessments and seek the involvement of cultural consultants, outsider witnesses, community groups or representatives to assist with the issues of cultural accountability (Tamasese and Waldegrave, 1993). We could also explore the possibility of alternative spiritual and holistic interventions and a community base for delivering them.

Reflexive practice

A social inequalities approach implies a reclaiming of the *reflexive* practitioner (Bleakley, 2000). This demands personal and collective reflection on both the content and context of formulation. It highlights the vulnerability of formulation to the idiosyncratic as well as the normative, and the importance of creating a context for it that shapes its accountability. Are we, in this, speaking for the other? Are we attending closely to the client's story or indulging our own intellectual interests and predilections?

We also need to adopt the position of the critical practitioner who recognises the wider social processes, the organisational and institutional context, and their own, value-based practice as much as possible. This particular account, for instance, is situated in, and constrained by, my own position as a white, female, heterosexual mental health professional. A supervision process that takes power and privilege into account and develops awareness of social inequalities (Aitken and Dennis, 2004; Patel, 2004; Ryde, 2009) is of enormous help in developing and sustaining this.

It is never easy to hold a position that is almost inevitably counter-cultural and often sits in painful contrast with the dominant discourses and ideologies, attracting defensive responses (Boyle, 2011). These ethical dilemmas can be played out on a daily basis, and at every level. 'Do I challenge a colleague?' 'Do I attend a ward round?' 'Do I challenge diagnosis x or treatment plan y?' 'Do I participate in a flawed service development plan?' These questions can seem endless and difficult to answer. Similarly, the challenge of working in these ways brings complexity rather than simplification. The answer to the question 'What do I do?' is unlikely to be simple or straight-forward. Perhaps most of all, it places a requirement on us to subject our values and practices, and our own life experiences with oppression and victimisation, to critical reflection and debate. What helps with many of these challenges is to look to our own social contexts, and to actively seek connection with like-mindedness wherever it is to be found. For me, this has included involvement with user groups as well as professional networks. These are hugely important sources of support and sanity. Nor should we be scared of passionate commitments and embodied reactions as energisers of social and political action (Crociani-Windland and Hoggett, 2012; Shohet, 2008), as an appropriate response to the 'cognitivised and over-civilised' talk of 'emotions' and 'formulation' with which we are so familiar.

Key characteristics of formulation from a social inequalities perspective

- Providing opportunities for recognition and respect.
- Making material realities and relevant social contexts visible (domains of life, structures, relationships, resources, processes).
- Critical consciousness-raising about the presence of ideology and dominant discourses that lead to obscuring of social inequalities.
- Mapping significant events and reactions across time; acknowledging resources, abilities; mapping resistances and survival strategies alongside oppressions and misuses of power.
- Paying attention to language, differences of positioning and sense-making.
- Recognising difference but avoiding 'othering'.
- Situating personal accounts within the wider socio-political narratives.
- Recognition of embodiment as a psychosocial process where oppressive practices become internalised and interact with identity formation.
- Centrality of the client. De-centredness of the therapist, who offers non-expert 'solidarity' with the person, the emerging accounts of victimisation and the social plights that underpin these.
- Naming of power processes and abuses. Creating of further opportunities for disclosure of abuse or other inequalities. Embargos on the expression of distress are acknowledged and explored in terms of culture, gender, and personal narratives.
- Deconstruction of symptoms/diagnosis: jettisoning of burdens, useless or disempowering concepts (abnormality, medical model) – reclaiming of ownership, power to resist, challenge, contesting and talking back to the ascribed diagnoses. Constructions of alternative models of distress.
- Collaborative or participatory formulation. Does it promote peaceful, respectful and equitable processes whereby people have meaningful input into decisions affecting their lives? Is the client constructed as active/passive in this formulation? What does the formulation act upon? Does it promote respect for diversity (identities, meanings, actions)? Does it address issues of social justice?

Acknowledgements

I would like to thank Joe Miller for his helpful comments on this reformulation.

References

Aitken, G. and Dennis, M (2004) Gender in supervision. In Steen, L. and Fleming, I. (eds) *Supervision and Clinical Psychology: Theory, Practice and Perspectives*. London: Brunner-Routledge.

Aldorondo, E. (ed.) (2007) *Advancing Social Justice through Clinical Practice.* New Jersey: Lawrence Erlbaum Associates.

Allen, M., Allen, J., Hogarth, S. and Marmot, M. (2013) *Working for Health Equity: The Role of Medical and Health Professionals.* London: IHE UCL.

Almeida, R., Dolan-Del Vecchio, K. and Parker, L. (2007) Foundation concepts for social justice-based therapy. In E. Aldorondo (ed.) *Advancing Social Justice through Clinical Practice.* New Jersey: Lawrence Erlbaum Associates.

Appleton, L., Hagan, T., Goward, P., Repper, J. and Wilson, R. (2003) Smail's contribution to understanding the needs of the socially excluded: the case of Gypsy and Traveller women, *Clinical Psychology*, 24, 40–46.

Baker, A. and Duncan, S. (1985) Child sexual abuse: a study of prevalence in Great Britain, *Child Abuse and Neglect*, 9, 457–467.

Bates, P. (2002) *Working for Inclusion: Making Social Inclusion a Reality for People with Severe Mental Health Problems.* London: Sainsbury Centre for Mental Health.

Beckwith, J.B. (1993) Gender stereotypes and mental health revisited, *Social Behaviour and Personality* 21 (1), 85–88.

Bentall, R. (2009) *Doctoring the Mind: Why Psychiatric Treatments Fail.* London, New York: Allen Lane.

Bleakley, A. (2000) Adrift without a life belt: reflective self-assessment in a post-modern age, *Teaching in Higher Education,* 5, 4, 405–418.

Bostock, J. (2003) Addressing power, *Clinical Psychology* 24, 36–39.

——(2004) Addressing poverty and exploitation: challenges for psychology, *Clinical Psychology* 38, 23–26.

Bourdieu, P. (2000) *The Weight of The World: Social Suffering in Contemporary Society.* Palo Alto, CA: Stanford University Press.

Boyle, M. (1997) Clinical psychology theory: making gender visible in clinical psychology, *Feminism and Psychology* 7 (2), 231–238.

——(2002) *Schizophrenia: A Scientific Delusion?* (2nd edn) London: Routledge.

——(2011) Making the world go away, and how psychiatry and psychology benefit. In Rapley, M., Moncrieff, J. and Dillon, J. (eds) *De-Medicalizing Misery: Psychiatry, Psychology and the Human Condition.* London: Palgrave Macmillan, pp. 27–43.

British Psychological Society (2008) *Socially Inclusive Practice. Discussion Paper.* Leicester: British Psychological Society.

——(2012) *Guidelines and Literature Review for Psychologists Working Therapeutically with Sexual and Gender Minority Clients.* Leicester: British Psychological Society.

Chesler, P. (1994) Heroism is our only alternative. Cited in Women and madness: a reappraisal, *Feminism and Psychology,* 4 (2), 298–305.

Crociani-Windland, L. and Hoggett, P. (2012) Politics and affect, *Subjectivity* 5, 161–179.

Dalal, F. (2002) *Race, Colour and the Processes of Racialisation.* London: Routledge.

——(2012) *Thought Paralysis.* London: Karnac.

Department of Health (2003) *Women's Mental Health Strategy: Into the Mainstream.* London: Department of Health.

——(2009) *Tackling Health Inequalities: 10 years on.* London: Department of Health.

——(2010) *Equity and Excellence: Liberating the NHS*. London: Department of Health.

Dillon. J., Johnstone, L. and Longden, E. (2012) Trauma, dissociation, attachment and neuroscience: a new paradigm for understanding severe mental distress, *Journal of Critical Psychology, Counselling and Psychotherapy*, 12 (3), 145–155.

Fatimilehin, I.., Raval, H. and Banks, N. (2000) Child, adolescent and family. In N. Patel, E. Bennett, M. Dennis, N. Dosanjh, A. Mahtani, A. Miller and N. Nadirshaw (eds) *Clinical Psychology, 'Race' and Culture: A Training Manual*. London: BPS Books.

Fernando, S. (2010) *Mental Health, Race and Culture*. London: Routledge.

Fernando, S. and Keating, F. (2008) *Mental Health in a Multi-Ethnic Society: A Multi-disciplinary Handbook*. London: Routledge.

Foucault, M. (1980) *Power/knowledge: Selected Interviews and Other Writings*. London: Harvester Wheatsheaf.

Fraser, N. and Honneth, A. (2003) *Redistribution or Recognition: A Political-Philosophical Exchange*. London: Verso.

Friere, P. (1970) *Pedagogy of the Oppressed*. New York: Continuum.

——(1978) *Education for a Critical Consciousness*. New York: Seabury Press.

Fryer, D. (1998) Mental health consequences of economic insecurity, relative poverty and social exclusion, *Journal of Community and Applied Social Psychology* 8, 75–80.

——(2008) Community psychologies: what are they? What could they be? What does it matter? *The Australian Community Psychologist*, 20 (3), 7–15.

Gergen, M. (1999) *An Invitation to Social Constructionism*. London: Sage.

Gillis, S., Howie, G. and Munford, R. (2007) (2nd edn) *Third Wave Feminism: A Critical Exploration*. London: Palgrave Macmillan.

Gracia, E. and Musitu, E. (2003) Social isolation from communities and child maltreatment: a cross-cultural perspective, *Child Abuse and Neglect* 27, 2, 153–168.

Hagan, T. and Smail, D. (1997a) Power-mapping I. Background and basic methology, *Journal of Community and Applied Social Psychology*, 7, 4, 257–284.

——(1997b) Power-mapping II. Practical application: the example of child sexual abuse, *Journal of Community and Applied Social Psychology* 7, 269–284.

Hardy, K. and Laszloffy, T. (1995) The cultural genogram key to training culturally competent family therapists. *Journal of Marital and Family Therapy* 3, 227–237.

Harper, D.J. (2011) The social context of paranoia. In Rapley, M., Moncrieff, J. and Dillon, J. (eds) *De-medicalizing Misery. Psychiatry, Psychology and the Human Condition*. Basingstoke and New York: Palgrave Macmillan.

Hester, M., Pearson, C. and Harwin, N. (2000) *Making an Impact: Children and Domestic Violence: A Reader*. London: Jessica Kingsley.

Hoggett, P. (2006) Conflict, ambivalence, and the contested purpose of public organizations. *Human Relations* 59 (2): 175-194.

Hook, D. (2011) *A Critical Psychology of the Post Colonial: The Mind of Apartheid*. London: Routledge.

Institute of Health Inequalities (2012) *The Impact of Economic Downturn on Policy Changes on Health Inequalities*. London: UCL.

Johnstone, L. (2000) *Users and Abusers of Psychiatry: A Critical Look at Psychiatric Practice*, (2nd edn) London, Philadelphia: Brunner-Routledge.

Jones, O. (2011) *Chavs: The Demonisation of the Working Class.* London: Verso.

Kagan, C., Burton, M., Duckett, P., Lawthom, R. and Siddiquee, A. (2011) *Critical Community Psychology: Critical Action and Social Change.* BPS Blackwell for John Wiley and Sons.

Knight, T. (2012) Can the mental health system cause paranoia? *Asylum Magazine,* Spring.

Korbin, J. (2003) Neighbourhood and community connectedness in child maltreatment research, *Child Abuse and Neglect* 27, 2, 137–140.

Marmot, M. (2012) Executive summary in: *Fair Society, Health Lives: The Marmot review Strategic review of Health Inequalities in England post-2010.* London: UCL.

May, R. (2000) Routes to recovery from psychosis: the roots of a clinical psychologist, *Clinical Psychology Forum* 146, 6–10.

McGoldrick, M. and Hardy, K.V. (2008) (2nd edn) *Revisioning Family Therapy: Race, Culture and Gender in Clinical Practice.* New York: The Guilford Press.

McMullen, R. (1990) *Male Rape: Breaking the Silence of the Last Taboo.* London: Gay Men's Press.

Miller, J. and Bell, C. (1996) Mapping men's mental health concerns, *Journal of Community and Applied Social Psychology* 6, 317–327.

Miller, J. and McClelland, L. (2006) Social inequalities formulation. In L. Johnstone and R. Dallos (eds) *Formulation in Psychology and Psychotherapy: Making Sense of People's Problems.* London: Routledge, pp. 26–153.

Morgan, E., Bird, L., Burnard, K., Clark, B., Graham, V., Lawton-Smith, S. and Ofari, J. (2001) *An Uphill Struggle: A Survey of People who use Mental Health Services and are on a Low Income.* London: Mental Health Foundation.

Newnes, C. (2012) Introduction to the Special Issue: *The Journal of Critical Psychology, Counselling and Psychotherapy,* 12 (3), 145–155.

Ng, S.H. (1980) *The Social Psychology of Power.* San Diego: Academic Press.

Orford, J. (2008) *Community Psychology: Challenges, Controversies and Emerging Consensus.* Chichester: Wiley.

Patel, N. (2004) Power in supervision. In Steen, L. and Fleming, I. (eds) *Supervision and Clinical Psychology: Theory, Practice and Perspectives.* London: Brunner-Routledge.

Prilleltensky, I. and Nelson, G. (2002) *Doing Psychology Critically: Making a Difference in Diverse Settings.* Basingstoke and New York: Palgrave Macmillan.

Prilleltensky, I., Dokecki, P., Frieden,G. and Ota-Wang, V. (2007) Counselling for wellness and justice: foundations and ethical dilemmas. In E. Aldorondo (ed.) *Advancing Social Justice through Clinical Practice.* New Jersey: Lawrence Erlbaum Associates.

Rapley, M., Moncrieff, J. and Dillon, J. (eds) (2011) *De-Medicalizing Misery: Psychiatry, Psychology and the Human Condition.* London: Palgrave Macmillan.

Read, J., Bentall, R. and Fosse, R. (2009) Time to abandon the bio-bio-bio model of psychosis, *Epidemiologia e Psichiatria Sociale* 18, 299–310.

Rose, N. (1985) *The Psychological Complex.* London: Routledge.

———(1989) *Governing the Soul: The Shaping of the Private Self.* London: Routledge.

Rust, M-J. and Totton, N. (2012) *Vital Signs: Psychological Responses to Ecological Crises.* London: Karnac.

Ryde, J. (2009) *Being White in the Helping Professions: Developing Effective Intercultural Awareness.* London, Philadelphia: Jessica Kingsley Publishers.

Sashidharan, S. P. (2003) *Inside Outside: Improving Mental Health Services for Black and Minority Ethnic Communities in England.* Maryland, US: National Institute for Mental Health.

Sewell, H. (2009) *Working with Ethnicity, Race and Culture in Mental Health.* London: Jessica Kingsley Publishers.

Sheppard, M. (1998) Social profile, maternal depression and welfare concerns in clients of health visitors and social workers: a comparative study, *Children and Society* 12, 125–135.

Shohet, R. (ed.) (2008) *Passionate Supervision.* London: Jessica Kingsley Publishers.

Smail, D. (1993) *The Origins of Unhappiness: A New Understanding of Personal Distress,* London: Secker and Warburg.

——(2011) Psychotherapy: illusion with no future? In Rapley, M., Moncrieff, J. and Dillon, J. (eds) *De-medicalizing Misery. Psychiatry, Psychology and the Human Condition.* Basingstoke and New York: Palgrave Macmillan, pp. 226–238.

Sue, D.W., Capodilupo, C.M., Torino, G.C., Buceri, J.M., Holder, A.M.B., Nadal, K.L. and Esquilin, M. (2007) Racial micro-aggressions in everyday life: implications for clinical practice, *American Psychologist*, 62(4), 271–286.

Tamasese, K. and Waldegrave, C. (1993) Cultural and gender accountability in the 'Just Therapy' approach, *Journal of Feminist Family Therapy*, 5, 229–245.

Timini, S. (2011) Medicalizing masculinity. In Rapley, M., Moncrieff, J. and Dillon, J. (eds) *De-medicalizing Misery. Psychiatry, Psychology and the Human Condition.* Basingstoke and New York: Palgrave Macmillan, pp. 86–97.

UNICEF (2011) *State of the World's Children Report: Adolescence: An Age of Opportunity.* New York: UNICEF.

Ussher, J. (1991) *Women's Madness: Misogyny or Mental Illness?* Amherst, MA: University of Massachusetts Press.

Van Scoyoc, S. (2000) *Perfect Mothers, Invisible Women.* London: Constable and Robinson.

Walkerdine, V. (1996) Working-class women: psychological and social aspects of survival. In Wilkinson, S. (ed.) *Feminist Social Psychologies.* Philadelphia: OUP.

Watkins, B. and Bentovim, A. (1992) The sexual abuse of male children and adolescents: a review of current research, *Journal of Child Psychology and Psychiatry and Allied Disciplines*, 33, 197–248.

Watkins, M. and Shulman, H. (2008) *Towards Psychologies of Liberation.* London: Palgrave Macmillan.

White, M. (1995) Reflecting teamwork as definitional ceremony. In M. White (ed.) *Re-Authoring Lives: Interviews and Essays.* Adelaide: Dulwich Centre Publications.

——(2004) Working with multiple trauma, *International Journal of Narrative Therapy and Community Work*, 1.

Wilkinson, S. (ed.) *Feminist Social Psychologies.* Philadelphia: OUP.

Wilkinson, R. and Pickett, K. (2009) *The Spirit Level: Why More Equal Societies Almost Always Do Better*. London: Allen Lane.

Williams, J. (1999) Social inequalities and mental health. In C. Newnes, G. Holmes, and C. Dunn, (eds) *This is Madness: A Critical Look at Psychiatry and the Future of Mental Health Services*. Ross-on-Wye: PCCS Books.

Williams, J. and Watson, G. (1988) Sexual inequality, family life and family therapy. In Street, E. and Dryden, W. (eds) *Family Therapy in Britain*. Milton Keynes: OUP.

Woollett, A. and Phoenix, A. (1997) Deconstructing developmental psychology accounts of mothering, *Feminism and Psychology*, 7 (2) 275–282

World Health Organisation (2009) *Mental Health, Resilience and Inequalities*. Copenhagen: WHO Regional Office for Europe.

Chapter 7

Formulation in personal and relational construct psychology

Seeing the world through clients' eyes

David Winter and Harry Procter

Personal Construct Psychology

Personal Construct Psychology (PCP) was originated by the American psychologist George A. Kelly. His two-volume magnum opus appeared in 1955 and further writings were collected posthumously by Maher (1969). The approach has continued to be elaborated in a rich literature to this day (e.g. Fransella, 2003; Neimeyer, 2009; Walker and Winter, 2007; Winter and Viney, 2005). PCP developed out of the pragmatist philosophy of Peirce and Dewey, in which people are seen as involved in a process of *inquiry*, of making hypotheses and developing an understanding of the world through discovery and experiment. A person is thus like a scientist. Central to Kelly's approach, therefore, is the notion that the person is constantly responding to the validation or invalidation of his or her hypotheses. Just like scientists in 'real life', the experience of invalidation of, and having to change, our ideas is a highly passionate affair. Scientists do not operate on the basis of bland, unemotional progression of testing and refutation but become attached to their theories and can experience joy, anger, distress, despair, and even a sense of annihilation when their theories, perhaps encompassing a lifetime of work, are refuted. So it is with our world views, or 'core constructs'.

In therapy this means that both client and therapist are already involved in *formulation*, making sense of things and making choices in accordance with how they construe the situations in which they find themselves. PCP is often classified under the larger category of *constructivism*, which typically includes the work of Piaget, the radical constructivists, Von Glasersfeld and Maturana, and others. Social constructionism (see chapter 5) is also sometimes included in this wider category (Raskin, 2002). Constructivism could be defined as 'the study and application of how human beings create systems of meaning in making sense of and acting in the world'.

One of the main distinguishing features of PCP is its contention that we function by developing and utilising a unique set of *bipolar* constructs. Giving meaning to an experience involves seeing similarities as well as differences. If a person sees him or herself as *reserved*, a comparison is being made to another particular state s/he has in mind such as *happy, active* or *sociable.* To understand a person's judgement involves knowing what specific distinction s/he is making as well as the similarities that are being drawn. Constructs thus have two poles. They govern a person's unique experience as well as structuring his or her actions, as s/he makes choices between two alternatives. Psychological change involves either moving along the dimension of the construct from one pole to the other, or revising the meaning of the construct, or replacing it with a different construct dimension. The construct is a rich psychological notion that allows us to unite many different areas of human functioning which are usually seen as distinct, for example cognition, emotion, action and relational interaction (Procter, 2009a). As mental health workers, we need to be very aware of the professional and diagnostic as well as personal constructs we may be applying as we conduct the business of formulation (Procter, 2009b).

The origin of a person's construing will be in the culture, belief systems and discourses in which s/he grows up (Procter and Parry, 1978) but within this each one of us develops our own way of construing the world as we negotiate the unique events of our biography. Even common problems and complaints are made sense of by each person in idiosyncratic ways (Wright, 1970), and so PCP is wary of standardised ways of explaining difficulties and manualised ways of addressing them. The process of formulation must therefore be conducted afresh with every new client and situation, taking account of the particular construings of the person him/herself and those of the people who surround him/her, especially families, friends, colleagues, and the professionals involved.

PCP can therefore operate at two levels. It is a theory about how clients make sense of their worlds, and at the same time it can be used reflexively as an overarching perspective in which the construing involved in different psychological or therapeutic approaches can be compared and utilised (Procter, 2009b). Each therapeutic model, such as those presented in this book, involves applying particular sets of constructs. 'Negative automatic thoughts', 'projective identification' and 'symmetrical escalation', for example, are all professional constructs used within cognitive-behavioural, psychoanalytic and systemic models respectively. PCP thus becomes an excellent meta-therapeutic framework as we organise and integrate different ways of understanding the client's predicament. In the spirit of Kelly's *constructive alternativism*, we are not limited to looking at things in one way. PCP provides its own methods and language but we are free to note the construing used by other models and frameworks, bearing in mind that these may not always be philosophically compatible with PCP. The spirit of the approach is one of experiment and playfulness: 'Let's try this new way of looking at this!' Therapy often involves re-construing a situation in an entirely new way that opens up new choices and possibilities for a way forward.

Personal construct formulation

Although the concept of formulation has often been regarded as deriving from the cognitive-behavioural tradition (Bruch, 1998), in fact it was central to Kelly's approach. He distinguished between two types of formulation, which he termed *structuralisation* and *construction* (Kelly, 1955: 454). The former is more tentative, and essentially involves the clinician roughly structuring the clinical information for future reference. In doing so, the clinician will construe the client's behaviours, both from the normative viewpoint of society, and from the viewpoint of what the client considers, and believes that others consider, to be the problem. For example, after an initial meeting with Jack the clinician might note how, from a normative viewpoint, his construing is deviant and 'delusional', but would also note Jack's own view of his problems, not only the themes expressed in his 'delusions' but also his concerns about his family. In addition, the clinician would compare Jack's view with what Jack regards as his family's view of his problems, which had led them to request his hospital admission. In a structuralisation, some attention is also likely to be given to the client's validational fortunes, namely the extent to which he or she has been able to anticipate events successfully.

Kelly's second type of formulation, construction, involves organising the client's behaviours in terms of the client's inferred personal constructs, and then construing, or 'subsuming', these constructs. Subsuming involves bringing another person's construct into one's own construct system with as little as possible interference from one's own personal construing and values – "stepping into their shoes", as it were. For this purpose, Kelly developed a 'subsuming construction system' consisting of professional, diagnostic constructs, described in the next section, which the clinician could use in order to construe the client's construing. For example, when we come to consider Jack, we shall see that the clinician will not only be concerned to identify some of his major constructs but also, by applying what Kelly called 'diagnostic constructs', to consider how Jack's constructs are structured, used and revised.

Kelly's system constitutes a radical alternative to Kraepelin's nosological approach which is the foundation of psychiatric diagnosis. He was at pains to point out that his system of diagnostic constructs was 'not a nomenclature of diseases', in that these constructs could be applied to the construing of any individual (including, reflexively, that of the clinician), whether or not he or she is regarded as presenting a psychological disorder. As he said, 'In themselves, they are neither good nor bad, healthy nor unhealthy, adaptive nor maladaptive' (Kelly, 1955: 453), and they are therefore very different from psychiatric classifications. Rather than pigeonholing the client in a fixed diagnostic category, the personal construct approach is to formulate a 'transitive diagnosis', which highlights the avenues of movement open to the client. Before outlining Kelly's diagnostic constructs, we shall consider more generally the personal construct theory perspective on psychological disorder.

As we have seen, Kelly viewed the person as, like a scientist, forming hypotheses (or constructions) about the world, testing these out, and revising them if they are invalidated or consolidating them if they are validated. He referred to this cyclical process as the Experience Cycle (Kelly, 1970), and indeed formulation can be seen to involve just such a cycle, in which the clinician formulates, tests, and refines his or her constructions of a client. The optimal process of construing described in the Experience Cycle can be contrasted with that involved in a psychological disorder, which Kelly (1955: 831) defined as 'any personal construction which is used repeatedly in spite of consistent invalidation'. In effect, the construing process in the person with a psychological disorder has become blocked, and it has been argued that the earlier in the Experience Cycle the blockage occurs, the more severe the disorder (Neimeyer, 1985). Thus, from this perspective, the inability to frame any coherent anticipations about the world would be regarded as indicative of a more severe disorder than the failure to revise construing following its invalidation. In both these cases, though, the person is essentially not adequately testing out his or her construing, or is in what Walker (2002) has termed a state of non-validation. He or she thereby avoids having their constructs invalidated, which, as Leitner (1988) has argued, may be a terrifying experience if the constructs involved are central to the person's view of the self in relation to others.

Diagnostic constructs

For Kelly, the essence of all interpersonal relationships is what he termed sociality, the attempt to construe the other person's construction processes, or see the world through his or her eyes. The clinician's diagnostic constructs are essentially a means of facilitating sociality with the client, providing goggles through which various aspects of the client's construing can be viewed.

Covert construing

Although Kelly did not use the concept of the unconscious, he did acknowledge that some of a person's construing may be at a low 'level of cognitive awareness'. For example, *preverbal constructs* are those which have no consistent verbal symbols, perhaps having been developed before the person had the use of words. For some constructs, one pole may be relatively inaccessible, or *submerged*, and this may prevent it from being tested. Occasionally, constructions may be *suspended*, or held in abeyance, if their 'implications are intolerable' (Kelly, 1955: 474) in that they are incompatible with the rest of the person's construct system.

Some aspects of the client's predicament may therefore be explained in terms of such features of covert construing, and one focus of therapy may then be to raise the client's level of awareness of his or her construing.

Structure of construing

A person's constructs differ in their importance to the individual. Kelly considered that construct systems are hierarchically organised, with *superordinate* constructs, those at the top of the hierarchy, subsuming other, more *subordinate*, constructs. A personal construct formulation is therefore likely to include some indications of what the client's superordinate constructs might be. The importance of identifying these constructs is indicated by research findings that they are resistant to change (Hinkle, 1965). The clinician would therefore do well to avoid challenging such constructs, at least in the early stages of therapy. The same applies to *core* constructs, those which, in contrast to *peripheral* constructs, are central to the client's maintenance of his or her 'identity and existence' (Kelly, 1955: 482).

Strategies of construing

People employ various strategies in an attempt to make better sense of their world or avoid invalidation of their construing. As might be expected in a theory which emphasises the bipolarity of constructs, Kelly (1995) presented some of these strategies as polar opposites, namely dilation and constriction; and loose and tight construing. In *dilation*, the person who is faced with incompatible constructions extends his or her perceptual field in an attempt to reorganise the construct system at a more comprehensive level. In Kelly's words (1955: 477), the person 'jumps around more from topic to topic, he lumps his childhood with his future, he sees vast ranges of events as possibly related, he participates in a wider range of activities, and, if he is a client undergoing psychotherapy, he tends to see everything that happens to him as potentially related to his problem'. In disorders involving dilation (such as in people who might be labelled 'manic' or 'paranoid'), 'the person's exploration has outrun his organization' (Kelly, 1955: 846). The converse strategy, *constriction*, involves delimiting the perceptual field to minimise apparent incompatibilities in construing. However, this runs the risk that 'it may let issues accumulate which will eventually threaten a person with insurmountable anxiety' (Kelly, 1955: 908). Disorders involving constriction may be particularly apparent in people who are regarded as 'phobic' or 'depressed'.

In *loose construing*, a person's constructions are vague and variable. Their imprecision makes them very difficult to invalidate, and therefore an individual may loosen his or her construing in an attempt to avoid repeated invalidation. Bannister (1960, 1962) provided evidence that this is the case in clients diagnosed as thought-disordered schizophrenics. *Tight construing*, by contrast, involves very precise predictions and a construct system with 'no loose fits which might let anxiety seep in' (Kelly, 1955: 849). However, such a system is very vulnerable to invalidation and therefore brittle.

Most of us at times show constriction and at other times dilation; or oscillate between loose and tight construing, a cyclical process which Kelly regarded as being necessary for creativity. It is the exclusive use of a particular strategy, without use of the converse strategy, which may be found in psychological disorders. In such cases, therapy may usefully involve attempts to balance the client's use of strategies, for example by attempting to tighten some of the constructions of the habitually loose construer.

Control

A further cycle described by Kelly (1955) is the *Circumspection–Preemption–Control (C-P-C) Cycle*, which is involved in decision making. In the circumspection phase of this cycle, the person considers the issues involved in a decision; in the pre-emption stage, the most superordinate issue, or construct, is selected; and in the control phase, the choice is made of applying a particular pole of this construct to an event. Again, it is failure to complete the cycle, for example by excessive rumination in the circumspection phase or foreshortening this phase and acting impulsively, that may characterise a disorder. Indeed, in Kelly's (1955: 927) view, 'all disorders of construction are disorders which involve faulty control'.

'Emotions'

As we have seen, Kelly (1955) took a holistic view of the person and did not make traditional distinctions between cognition, emotion, and motivation. A construct involves emotion and feeling just as much as it does cognition and action (Procter, 2009a). As Kelly says, 'Human discrimination may take place also at levels which have been called "physiological" or "emotional." Nor is discrimination necessarily a verbalized process. Man discriminates even at a very primitive and behavioral level' (Kelly, 1969: 219).

For Kelly, what would normally be regarded as emotions involve awareness of transitions in construing. These may be experienced as embodied states, which of course are themselves construed. Some of these transitions will be the result of invalidation, and the emotions concerned characterise particular types of disorder. For example, *threat* occurs when one becomes aware of an imminent comprehensive change in core structures. *Anxiety* occurs when one finds one's world unconstruable, and therefore attempts to avoid invalidation of construing in effect to aim to reduce anxiety by ensuring that the world remains predictable. *Guilt* is experienced when one perceives a dislodgement from one's core role, one's characteristic way of interacting with others. *Aggression* is the active elaboration of one's perceptual field, and may be problematic when, for example, it occurs with scant regard for the construing of other people. *Hostility* is the attempt, when faced with invalidation, to make the social world fit with one's constructions rather than vice versa. For example, a belief that one is unlovable may lead someone to behave in such a way that makes sure that anyone who does show love for them will eventually be rejecting.

Dependency

Kelly (1955) viewed optimal functioning as involving a variety of different types of dependency relationships, whereas in psychological disorder there may be *undispersed dependency*. The person may either depend on only one person, or very few people; or, conversely, be undiscriminating and turn to a large number of people for every need. Although dependency was not a principal axis of Kelly's system of diagnostic constructs, it may be an important aspect of the formulation of a client's difficulties, and of the consequent focus of therapy.

Content of construing

Kelly's diagnostic constructs primarily concern the process and structure of construing, but he did indicate that disorders may arise out of 'the content rather than the form of personal constructs' (Kelly, 1955: 935). Since, unlike rationalist cognitive approaches, his theory does not assume that there is a correct way of viewing the world, it is not surprising that he paid relatively little attention to such disorders. Nevertheless, a personal construct formulation will consider the predominant content of the client's constructs as this will indicate the pathways open to, and thereby help to explain the choices made by, him or her. In particular, it may identify the dilemmas posed by logical inconsistencies in the client's construing, as when the preferred pole of one construct is associated with the non-preferred pole of another (e.g. 'I do not want to be depressed; I want to be sensitive; but depressed people are sensitive').

Developments in the personal construct view of disorder

Although the writing in Kelly's (1955) two-volume exposition of the psychology of personal constructs is generally very systematic, this is less so in the two chapters presenting his taxonomy of psychological disorders (Winter, 2009). He prefaced this section with the statement that 'It is not practical to attempt to catalogue all the typical psychological disorders – even if he could, who would have the stomach for writing that kind of cook book?' (Kelly, 1955: 836). These chapters in some respects reflect his lack of enthusiasm for the task. Even the term disorder itself appears too mechanistic to be consistent with Kelly's theory, and a possible alternative (reflecting, for example, the predominant use of one of a contrasting pair of strategies) might be 'imbalance' (Walker and Winter, 2005; Winter, 2003a). Kelly's diagnostic constructs have, nevertheless, provided the basis for personal construct formulations of a wide range of different clinical problems, many of them supported by research findings and leading to evidence-based personal construct therapeutic approaches for the problems concerned (Winter, 1992; Winter and Viney, 2005).

Sociality is a major component of an alternative personal construct view of disorder proposed by Leitner and his colleagues, as is the individual's developmental history (Leitner et al., 2000). They consider that childhood traumas may cause 'developmental/structural arrests' in construing of the self and others, which effectively becomes 'frozen'. This then impacts upon the person's attachment style, and particularly on interpersonal styles concerning dependencies and distancing of self from others. Central to this view of disorder is retreat from role relationships, or in other words, those relationships that involve construing the other's construction processes. Intimate relationships such as these, in which people attempt to construe the most central aspects of each other's experience, and act accordingly, pose a risk of invalidation of one's core role, or 'deepest understanding of being maintained as a social being' (Kelly, 1955: 502). Difficulties with sociality, or the related concepts of theory of mind or mentalisation, may also be central to the difficulties presented by people diagnosed with autistic spectrum or other psychiatric disorders (Bateman and Fonagy, 2012; Procter, 2001). Kelly's concept of sociality in comparison with theory of mind and mentalisation is discussed in Procter (in press). Fonagy's mentalisation consists more of reflection on one's own inner mental states as opposed to the mental states of others. This was anticipated by Kelly and Procter has extended this by recognising that there is also an awareness of the sharing and interaction of people's mental states (see below).

Relational extension of PCP

An area of development in personal construct theory and formulation is its extension to interpersonal construing (Dallos, 1991; Procter, 1981, 1985). Kelly's constructs apply not only to the construct systems of individuals but also to those of families or broader social systems (Procter, 1981). A personal construct formulation will therefore also generally consider the patterns of interaction between different members' construing within their family and social system and the position(s) that he or she takes up within this wider system. This allows us to see how relational patterns and discourses constrain, structure, and facilitate the development of individual construing and experience. We could even argue that these constructs do not 'exist' in a preordained manner but are created continuously as we anticipate, act, and interact with each other. This is compatible with the spirit of Kelly's original theorising. These developments give more equal weight to relationships and persons, allowing us to re-title the approach as 'personal and relational construct psychology' (Procter, 2009b). This allows us to recognise that many human difficulties are relational, and involve, for example, loss, conflict, invalidation, neglect, abusive power relationships or individual dysfunction (for example, alcohol abuse or dementia) in another family member.

Relationality and levels of interpersonal construing

Part of this programme of development involves an extension of Kelly's idea of sociality to include not just one person's construing of another's construing but their construing of the relationships between people, including their own relationship with others. For example, a person construes the relationship between two people (dyadic construing) as being very *similar* or *different*, as *agreeing with each other* or not, as being *close* or *misunderstanding each other*. We can thus consider the *levels of interpersonal construing* involved (Procter, in press; Ugazio et al., 2008). Thus, the monadic level involves one person's construing of another person and their constructions, the dyadic level is as above, and the triadic level concerns the relationship between three people. An example of the latter might be to construe a situation where two people are seen as excluding and disempowering a third, or a situation of rivalry between two people for the attentions of a third. The higher levels of construing will include construing at the lower levels, dyadic containing monadic sociality and triadic containing the dyadic and monadic levels (Procter, 2011). This method of analysis is exemplified in the formulation provided below in the case of Janet.

Personal construct assessment methods

In arriving at a personal construct formulation, the clinician may draw upon a range of methods of assessment of construing (Caputi et al., 2011), and we shall briefly describe some of these.

Interviews

A fundamental component of any such assessment is to seek the client's view of his or her problem, as well as of what others believe the problem or complaint to be. As Kelly (1955: 797) indicated, 'From the standpoint of the psychology of personal constructs the statement of the client is, by definition, a true formulation of the problem'. This is a 'credulous approach', in which the client's view is respected and taken at face value, whether or not the clinician may also entertain an alternative formulation of the problem. Such an approach is neatly expressed in Kelly's so-called 'first principle': '*If you don't know what's wrong with a client, ask him; he may tell you*' (Kelly, 1955: 201). The primary focus of an initial interview is therefore likely to be the complaint: 'the layman's formulation of the clinical issues' (Kelly, 1955: 789). The elaboration of the complaint may be aided by various interview questions suggested by Kelly (1955: 963), which as well as seeking the client's view of his or her problems, attempt to enable the client to see these on 'a time line' and 'as fluid and transient'. Examples of these questions are 'Under what conditions did these problems first appear?' and 'What changes have come with treatment or the passing of time?' (Kelly, 1955: 962). The interview is then likely to go on to explore other aspects of the client's construing. Particular forms of questioning have been proposed for the elicitation of core constructs (Leitner, 1985a), or for use if the client is a child (Procter, 2007; Ravenette, 1980) or family (Procter, 2005).

Self-characterisation

The client's self-construing may be explored further by asking him or her to write a character sketch, which in Kelly's original method would be written in the third person as if by someone who knows the client very well and sympathetically.

Repertory grid technique

Repertory grid technique is the principal assessment method derived from personal construct psychology (Fransella et al., 2004). It generally commences with the elicitation of a series of elements, usually aspects of the self (e.g. current self; ideal self; future self) and significant other people, from the client. In our hypothetical example of Jack's grid, we have used the elements of self now, ideal self, self as a child, self in the future, father, mother, his three sisters, Robbie Williams, and his ex-boss. The client's personal constructs are then elicited, usually by presenting the client with successive triads of the elements and asking, for each triad, how two of the elements are alike and thereby different from the third. The client's own words are then used for the constructs. In Jack's case, we are hypothesising that constructs such as 'successful – hopeless mess' and 'abusive – abused' emerged from this process. Finally, the client sorts the elements in terms of the constructs, usually by rating or ranking each element on each construct. Thus, Jack might be asked: 'How successful do you think 'yourself now' is, on a scale from 1 to 7?'

The content of the client's constructs may be analysed, and the grid can also be subjected to various methods of quantitative analysis by software packages. Such analyses provide, amongst others, measures of the degree of similarity in the client's construing of different elements; relationships between their constructs; structural properties of construing, such as tightness; and conflicts and dilemmas in construing. The use of principal component analysis allows a graphical representation of the client's construing to be produced. This may be shared with the client, providing a focus for therapy, and completion of another grid at the end of therapy can allow an individualised assessment of therapeutic outcome in terms of changes in the client's construing (Winter, 2003b).

Qualitative grids and the 'bowtie'

Several variations on repertory grid technique have been developed, including qualitative grids. Amongst the latter is the perceiver element grid (Procter, 2005), in which each member of a family, or other group, indicates how s/he sees him/herself and each of the others, and these views are entered into a grid in which the columns refer to the family members as perceived (or as elements) and the rows refer to these individuals as perceivers. This method, as well as the perceiver dyad grid (Procter, 2002), in which construing of relationships is explored, are exemplified in the formulation of Janet, below. This case also illustrates the 'bowtie' diagram (Procter, 1985), a method for examining the construing and actions of people caught in self-perpetuating patterns of interaction. These methods are useful in the therapy process itself, where the construing of different figures in the client's life are displayed side by side, facilitating a more dispassionate reflection and understanding of situations.

Tracing of construct implications

Superordinate constructs may be identified by laddering (Hinkle, 1965), a procedure in which the client is successively asked which pole of a construct s/he would prefer to be described by and why. Each construct thus elicited is considered to be more superordinate than the last.

The ABC technique (Tschudi and Winter, 2011) involves elicitation from the client of the positive and negative implications of each pole of a construct, often one relating to the client's symptom.

Jack and Janet

The task that we have been set, of providing formulations of clients' situations on the basis of brief vignettes, although challenging, is similar to one that Kelly (1961) himself undertook when he was invited to contribute to a book in which clinicians from different theoretical perspectives considered the case of a suicidal client. Kelly (1961: 259) noted that this challenge involved making 'precarious inferences from the slimmest available evidence'. This will also be the case for our formulations of Jack and Janet, in which we fully acknowledge that the clients are open to alternative constructions, as indicated in the other chapters in this book.

Jack

Validational history

The shared construct system of Jack's family, itself perhaps rooted in shared ways of construing family life and relationships in the Italian community, seems to have provided a fairly firm basis for predicting events for the first ten years of his life. The way in which Jack developed during this time, as reflected in his progress at school and in his interpersonal relationships, must only have served to validate the construction of him as destined to lead a successful and rewarding life. However, it is clear that his and his family's construct system then suffered a series of major invalidations. Not only did these involve his view of his father, but also his and his family's views of himself and of the future. His first experience of employment, and of another male authority figure, must also have been profoundly invalidating. With the loss of his father, his mother may well have become a particularly important validating agent of his constructions, and it is likely that his arguments with her, culminating with his being thrown out of the house, will have been experienced as yet further significant invalidations, as may his admission to psychiatric hospital at his family's request.

Jack's invalidating experiences over the last 15 years may be viewed as having involved a series of losses. He has not only lost his father but also his visions of himself and of the future. As contemporary constructivists might describe this, his self-narrative has suffered profound disruption (Neimeyer, 2004). Just as in many people who have been bereaved, he has had to search for meaning, which he has perhaps found in his 'delusional beliefs'.

Jack's constructs

With no access to Jack's own account of his situation it is difficult, if not impossible, to infer the constructs that he may be employing in an attempt to anticipate his world. However, the problem areas that he identified do indicate some of the superordinate issues for him, such as being deprived of what is due to him; fear; physical and sexual abuse; concern for his family; missing his father; and confusion. A further superordinate construct for him appears to concern being a hopeless mess, in contrast to the success and prosperity that had been anticipated for him as a child and that he continued to anticipate would be the case when he received the royalties that were owing to him.

Given his experiences of powerful men in his life as being abusive, and less powerful figures such as his mother and sisters as being abused, it is possible that he construed abusiveness as being associated with power and success. This would also seem to be reflected in his construing of Robbie Williams. Such a dilemma would make it difficult for him to move towards seeing himself as successful as to do so would imply that he would also be likely to have to see himself as abusive.

Structure and process of construing

The switches in Jack's constructions and behaviour are indicative of what Kelly (1955: 38) referred to as 'slot rattling', in which an individual's construing of a person or event moves from one pole of a construct to the other. Thus, Jack switches from being 'high' to feeling hopeless, and from loving to hating his father, and his history has involved a pattern of oscillation between the relative stability of holding down a job and 'going off the rails'. Such inconsistencies, and his feelings of confusion, suggest that his construct system may be generally loosely structured. It may be that this is a response to the invalidation of his construing that he experienced, for example by being exposed to his father's violence and the abuse by his ex-boss. As we have seen, loosening one's construing makes it less vulnerable to further invalidation. However, it may be that his 'delusions' about Robbie Williams serve the purpose of providing an island of tight structure in an otherwise loose system. The persistence of his 'delusional disorder' is therefore comprehensible as the delusions do at least provide him with a means of making sense of his world. His 'tendency to escape into fantasy' may reflect a constrictive process in which Jack attempts to delimit his world to those areas where his construing is relatively well elaborated rather than, for example, facing the chaos of the 'real world' issues that his psychologist would prefer to discuss. However, within the sphere of his 'delusions' it is likely that his construing is dilated, with more and more events being explained in terms of his persecutory themes.

Constructs of transition

Jack's history indicates that his foundations were severely shaken as a child, and these will have been threatening times as he became increasingly aware of fundamental changes in his core construing. His current confusion, for example concerning his feelings for his father, would appear to indicate an area of anxiety in which his constructs do not allow him to make sense of his experiences. It may be that he has suspended some constructions about his father because their implications are intolerable, and because of the threat that they pose. This may also be the case for his experience of sexual abuse, and it is possible that, as Sewell (1997) describes in regard to post-traumatic stress, he has been in a state of 'constructive bankruptcy' concerning this experience. His reluctance to discuss it will have denied him an opportunity to elaborate his construing of the abuse.

There is also evidence of guilt in his departure from his early core role as a popular, sociable person who was likely to succeed. It is possible that, as with many other survivors of sexual abuse (Erbes and Harter, 2005; Freshwater et al., 2001), he now sees himself not as sociable but as very different from others. Paradoxically, although the role that had been cast for him in his family was essentially to follow in his father's footsteps, he is now, in effect, doing so not as head of the family business but as the failing heavy drinker that his father became. Small wonder that he experiences fear and self-loathing when he looks in the mirror and sees his father's face looking back at him.

Kelly (1955: 512) considered that 'one may keep his face away from the dark empty void of guilt by taking a hostile attitude towards people'. Jack's hostility may well have been manifested in fabricating evidence for his beliefs about Robbie Williams. These allowed him to retain a view of himself as someone who was at least potentially successful, and who was only denied current success by injustice.

Jack's retreat into his 'delusional' world may also have served the purpose of allowing him to escape from role relationships, those in which a person attempts to understand another's construing. Such understanding on Jack's part is likely to have been very limited in his significant relationships, and the inconsistency in his own behaviour will probably also have meant that significant others found it difficult to show sociality with him. His experience of role relationships is therefore likely to have largely been one of invalidation of his core role, and the conglomeration of associated 'negative' emotions that Leitner (1985b) refers to as terror. He will therefore probably have approached future significant relationships with profound distrust, 'the expectation of invalidation of one's core construing' (Rossotti et al., 2006: 165).

Towards intervention

Fundamental to a therapeutic relationship with Jack, as with many survivors of sexual abuse (Cummins, 1992), will be the establishment of some degree of trust by such means as the therapist taking care not to provide further major invalidation of his construing. As with any other client, the personal construct psychotherapist would adopt a credulous attitude with Jack, taking seriously his view of the world, even though this might appear delusional. As Bannister (1985) has described, this would involve considering the superordinate themes of his beliefs, their metaphorical aspects, rather than their specific content. Thus, issues such as his being denied what is due to him and his fear of abuse can be discussed without consideration of the particular evildoings for which he considered Robbie Williams to be responsible. Subsequent interventions with him, as with other people who have experienced losses, may be regarded as attempting to further a process of meaning reconstruction (Neimeyer, 2001), perhaps with the elaboration of a more viable means of anticipating his world than is provided by his 'delusions'.

As we have indicated, his construing might usefully be explored further by means of personal construct assessment methods such as the repertory grid. Figure 7.1 is the plot derived from principal component analysis of a grid that Jack might hypothetically have produced. The relative proximity of elements and constructs in this plot indicates that he contrasts himself with Robbie Williams on such constructs as 'deprived of their dues – privileged', 'confused – certain', 'hopeless mess – successful', 'afraid – fearless', and 'abused – abusive'. He views himself now as much further from his ideal self than he was as a child. The grid also reveals that he is, indeed, faced with dilemmas concerning success, which for him is, for example, associated with being abusive and uncaring. If this was the case, techniques described by Feixas and Saúl (2005) might be used to resolve these dilemmas by, for example, elaborating ways in which it is possible to be both successful and caring. This might include the use of what Kelly (1955: 1075) termed time binding, acknowledging that his dilemmatic constructions (e.g. 'successful people are abusive') served a purpose in helping him to make sense of events in his early life, but limiting their application to these events and thereby freeing him to develop alternative ways of construing present and future events.

Therapeutic elaboration of a new role for Jack might usefully draw upon his interest and skills in music. At the very least, music might be used as a fairly non-threatening means of exploring his identity (Button, 2006; Scheer, 2006), provided that this could be done without further elaborating his 'delusions'. Music might also enable him to begin to find a way of expressing constructions, for example, of traumatic past events, that are at a low level of awareness and to which he may not have attached verbal labels.

Finally, it may be that, as with other survivors of sexual abuse (Harter and Neimeyer, 1995), joining a group of people who have had similar experiences might provide for Jack an experience of 'universality' (Yalom, 1970) in which he is enabled to view himself as less different from other people. Group therapy might also provide a means of developing his capacity for sociality. Another means of achieving this might be by family therapy, perhaps including the use of techniques such as the perceiver element grid (Procter, 2005) to facilitate family members' understanding of each other's construing.

Given Jack's history, therapeutic gains will not be expected to come quickly or easily. Nevertheless, as with every client, the personal construct psychotherapist would approach Jack with the attitude that, since 'there are always some alternative constructions available to choose among in dealing with the world ... no one needs to be the victim of his biography' (Kelly, 1955: 15).

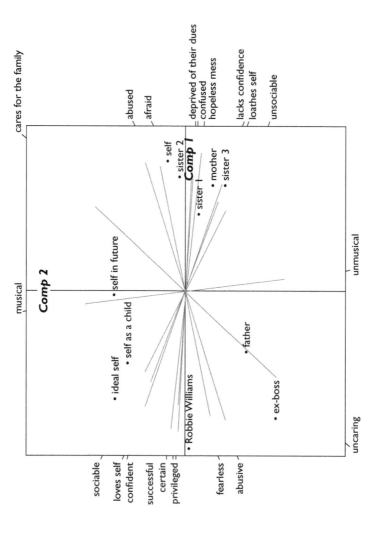

Figure 7.1 Hypothetical repertory grid analysis for Jack

Janet

In personal and relational construct psychology, we only understand human problems to the extent that we understand the construing of the people involved in a situation and how the different positions that they take relate to each other in the present and over time. The protocol provided for Janet contains very little about the family members' construing, which makes formulation within this approach very challenging. However, it is very typical of a referral letter to child services (let's call it the 'referral') and the lack of information allows us to elaborate the kind of thinking that our approach involves. We shall organise the discussion in accordance with the *levels of interpersonal construing* (Procter, in press) described above.

For Kelly (1955: 687–700), it is vital to understand a person's cultural background. We are not merely a product of it: each person builds a construing system anew using its materials, but it provides a lot of validational evidence about what we see as 'true'. Janet's Romany culture is likely to have much bearing on our formulation. Romany or Gypsy travelling communities are subject to enormous hostility and abuse from the 'settled community' or 'Gorgios' in the UK. They feel their way of life is under threat and in an attempt to protect it many feel great ambivalence to education and literacy, as involving 'brainwashing', and yet are aware these are means of empowering their children (Levinson and Silk, 2007; Silk, 2011). Thus, in interacting with 'Gorgio' services they may hide their construing and use strategies to get help for their children amidst a strongly held fear of the child being taken into care. This may throw light on Mary's use of the accident and emergency department as opposed to 'settled' services such as the GP. Medical construing of problems may be one of the few areas of overlap and communication in the contact between the cultures (Silk, 2011). We need to establish how central or peripheral Mary is in her own Romany group. Have Mary's partners also been Gypsies? Her pride in her older teacher son may indicate a more peripheral membership but Andrew's wish to join the police may still be seen as a capitulation to the dominant culture. The children are likely to have experienced significant ethnic abuse, for example being called 'pikeys', etc., especially given the area in which they live.

Monadic construing

It is useful to start by drawing up a type of qualitative grid, a perceiver element grid or PEG (see Figure 7.2). The arrow clarifies that perceivers on the left construe the people or 'elements' listed along the top. With more space, more perceivers could be added, for example the Romany view, school friends, etc. The elements here are all people, but other elements could include, for example, *the services, school, Gorgios, how I would like things to be, the family* or particular relationships, as we shall see later. Selecting individuals as

FAMILY MEMBERS

→	Janet	Mother	Father	Brother	Cindy
Referrer	A&E 'no abuse' Developmental worries: no physical probs. Fears transport Walks to school Low appetite School: friends, joins in enthusiastically, achieving adequately	4 older children Proud of older son & grand-children Poor bond with Janet: guilt Close to Cindy Heart op. due Limited mobility Romany beliefs	Lives nearby Recent overnight contact stopped Still sees Janet Heavy drinker Violent to Mother *Sexual abuser?*	Doing well at school Wants to join police when older	Special relationship with Janet Takes an interest in her
Janet	*?Romany*	*?Don't like mother's food* *?Poisoning me* *?Worry she might die*	Don't want to stay with him overnight *?Scary behaviour*	*?Approves of wish to join police*	
Mother	Concern re her weight loss, behaviour at home, refusal to use transport Needs wheelchair Prisoner in own home	Sad, depressed long time after Janet's birth I wish she could be taken away Feel guilt at my bonding with Janet – don't understand this Heart/mobility problems Clairvoyance	Violent Heavy drinker *?He is responsible for Janet's problems* *?Positive view of him when first together*		*?Helpful*
Father					

Figure 7.2 Perceiver element grid: Janet's family (hypotheses in italics)

elements teases out construing at a monadic level. The method can be drawn up and shared with the client or family, or used mainly as a guide to the professional in formulation or supervision.

The first row looks at the *referrer's construing* as summarised from the referral. Putting this into the grid emphasises that it is *construing* – it is easy for case material to be presented impersonally, 'objectively' as 'facts', but actually any description always 'belongs to someone', in this case a doctor, social worker, or school nurse. Ignoring this can lead us to overlook the fact that any observers have personal and ideological positions based in their culture, agency and profession which carry enormous implications and power issues; for example, attitudes about gender, the Romany culture, class, medical, social and religious constructions. The material in this row is likely to be construed with suspicion by the family as 'Gorgio'.

The gaps or blank squares in a PEG are often as useful as those that are filled out. Frequently in this work we tend to attend to what we do know and forget whole areas of which we are unaware. In this case, it may be the source of data that is inadequate, but gaps may also indicate subjugated voices, secrecy, or inability or unwillingness to articulate or be aware of their own construing by the members themselves. We can overlook the construing of certain figures, particularly children and young people, people with special needs, absent parents such as Colin, siblings, grandparents, etc. We must keep in mind the construing of all the members, even if we are not going to work with them directly.

Concentrating first on Janet, even though we have no information about her construing (the items in italics are our hypotheses or questions), we may speculate about some aspects of her world. Reading down the first column of the PEG, we see that we don't know anything about how she, her father, Cindy, Andrew, or her friends construe her, but the referrer and her mother make her the subject of a great deal of quite elaborated *medical construing.* In spite of some reassurance that there is no evidence of physical problems or abuse, we hear about visits to accident and emergency, paediatric involvement, low weight and appetite, mobility problems requiring a wheelchair, and concerns for her overall development. She has been seen as ill and disabled, possibly for much of her life. Such experience may be associated with high levels of *invalidation* affecting her own attempts to construe the world with a confidence in her own resources and personal development and a positive sense of self-worth, health, agency, and power. This may be offset by her walking to school, having friends there, joining in enthusiastically, knowledge that she is achieving 'adequately', and a positive view of her by Cindy and her friends.

This may be where to start a first interview with her, to draw out and elaborate her interests and spontaneous choices, to hear something of what she enjoys and is good at in school, who she likes and who likes her, and the constructions of self that she holds in these situations (Procter, 2005, 2007).

This will be done ideally with other members of the family present, maybe Mary, Andrew and Cindy, which will begin already to boost her status in the family's construing of her and counter the current elaborated problematic identity placed upon her. In a session with Andrew, can we find some good and enjoyable times that the children can remember? We are aiming to elicit some of her constructs in various ways, particularly *superordinate constructs* (see the laddering method, above) allowing us to understand what governs her choices and to enhance her feeling of being understood and valued. This will function to elaborate her and the others' construing of her as a person instead of only in terms of medical problems and disabilities. And is Janet already developing her own views as regards a Romany identity and aspirations? This could be underlying the conflict between her and her mother and be regarded as disloyalty.

At the level of psychological construing there is also much construing of her as anxious, fearful and phobic. In spite of her walking, she is seen as avoiding the outside world, a 'prisoner in her own home', wishing to end overnight stays with her father, and terrified of public transport, including something about a white van. As noted earlier, in PCP terms *anxiety* is seen as an awareness that events lie outside the range of convenience of one's construing – a fear of the unpredictable or uncontrollable. This may apply, or possibly *threat* is more here at stake – an awareness of comprehensive change in core construing of self. She seems to be dealing with events through *constriction*, narrowing her range of construing by avoiding the outside world and public transport, and trying to cut her father out of her life, at least in terms of overnight stays. The white van invokes various hypotheses – has she had bad experiences, for example bullying or ethnic abuse on a school bus? Has she had some kind of threat of abduction or witnessed criminal activity involving a white van? Is it more about an ambulance that may come and take her mother away, with Janet terrified about a heart operation and that her mother might die? It resonates with her mother having feelings that she wishes Janet could be taken away. It is also noteworthy that, coming from a Romany culture, her mother or ancestors lived in trailers as a way of life. Construing around abduction, removal, abandonment, being thrust into an unpredictable and terrifying world, and no longer 'being my mother's girl' could be at stake. Added to this are issues around her father (see below). All this will need to be explored sensitively in a session in which Janet has invested enough trust and safety with the therapist.

Dyadic construing

We could continue looking at Mary, Colin and others at a monadic level, but let us now look at how we and the members themselves could construe the various key dyadic relationships.

DYADS

→	Mother/ Janet	Father/ Janet	Mother/ Father	Andrew/ Janet	Cindy/ Janet
Referrer	Poor Bonding Sleeping together Janet refuses mother's food ?'Munchausen by Proxy' S	Overnight contact stopped at Janet's request ?Abuse	Couple split when Janet was 3 Conflict and Violence		Special Relationship Cindy takes a close interest in Janet
Janet	?Don't like mother's food ?Harming me ?Worry she might die ?Cares more about others than me ?Furious with Mum	Don't want to stay with Dad ?His scary behaviour ?Dilemma	?Observed conflict and violence		?Does Janet return these feelings
Mother	Hard to love her from the start Clingy We fight Dog incident		Conflict Violent to me		
Father					

Figure 7.3 Perceiver dyad grid: Janet's family (hypotheses in italics)

We can again use a qualitative grid to organise our formulation at this level, a perceiver dyad grid (PDG) as in Figure 7.3. Again there is really almost no detail of how the members construe their relationships, an understanding of which is of key significance in formulation in personal and relational construct psychology. However, the dyad grid is useful in focussing on the relational aspects of the case. Constructions of relationships tend to vary much more than those of individual traits, and are therefore a source of therapeutic optimism and realisation that changes can take place.

The Mother/Janet relationship will be central to the difficulties and seems to have got off to a difficult start. We may wonder if she found it hard to love little Janet because she didn't want a sixth baby, because the baby was a girl and seemed to have developmental difficulties, or because her own relationship with Colin was falling apart. She may feel guilt at her own feelings and find them hard to understand. To not want a child is likely to be a particular anathema in a Romany culture (Silk, 2011). Currently they may be caught in a vicious circle in which their constructions of each other are maintained by the evidence of the other's actions. This is illustrated in the so called 'bowtie' diagram (Procter, 1985), shown in Figure 7.4, in which each person's construing of the other is maintained in a cycle of tension and conflict. Mary is exhausted with her own heart problem and feels overwhelmed by Janet's behaviour, temper, fears and clinginess. Expressions of this construing confirm to Janet that her mother doesn't love her (especially in contrast to her siblings and nephews). She therefore feels major insecurity, fear and anger and behaves in a challenging way, which validates her mother's construing.

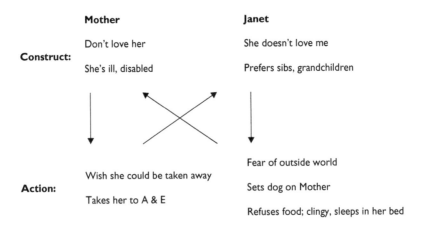

Figure 7.4 Hypothetical 'bowtie' diagram of construing between Mother and Janet

The fact that Janet had been going to stay with her father regularly for several years may indicate acceptance and love between them. However, this seems to have been overwhelmed by his heavy drinking, which could be an issue particularly in the evenings. The possibility of less satisfactory relating must be questioned, and statistics indicate that drinking and violence to a partner can be associated with physical and sexual abuse towards children as well (Hester et al., 1998). For Janet this could create an intense dilemma, in which her love and loyalty to her father conflict with construing based on frightening or inappropriate contact. She may have totally rejected him, with further invalidating feelings of loss and abandonment. We shall want to understand the construing of other dyads too; for example, her relationship with Andrew and particularly Cindy, which are likely to involve more satisfactory experiences and sources of positive construction of self.

Triadic construing

At the triadic level (Procter, in press; Ugazio et al, 2008), there are likely to be issues around Janet comparing her mother's relationship with her to the much more positive relating between her mother and her other children and grandchildren. Mary may even say to Janet, 'Why can't you be more like the others?' compounding the issues of Figure 7.4. The mother/father/Janet triad is likely to be the source of much trouble, which may well involve intense 'fragmentation' or incompatible construing as she struggles to reconcile loyalties to two parents who have fallen out, and who probably blame each other and argue to the extent of physical violence. She is likely to have witnessed this violence and this could go further in helping us understand her phobic reactions and lack of eating, which may well also entail a 'hostile' attempt to force her parents together, hoping for a shared parental concern for her needs.

We may speculate that her mother is concerned about Janet's relationship with her father. This is a common feature of many divorced/separated families. Likewise, Janet is likely to be very concerned about her mother and father's relationship. Many children experience considerable ambivalence since they want their parents to re-unite but are also scared by memories of their conflicts and fights. Hence, at dyadic or triadic levels, their construing may contain in PCP terms 'implicative dilemmas' (Feixas et al., 2009): "I want them to be together but that reminds me of fights/I don't want them together because that makes me sad that my Mum and Dad hate each other".

Discussion

Formulations, especially based on referral information, very often turn out to be way off the mark. PCP emphasises how each of us is unique, even when from identical backgrounds. We are exploring the 'uniqueness of common complaints' (Wright, 1970) in which even very similar experiences arise out of very different construings. For these reasons, PCP is very cautious about elaborating tight formulations at this stage. Their purpose must always be paradoxically to open the therapist's mind to the client's unique construing and situation. However, a consciously constructed formulation may be easier to revise or dispose of by raising the level of cognitive awareness of the therapist's presuppositions and prejudices.

It is important that a formulation makes sense to the particular therapist involved. He or she should not automatically take a formulation wholesale from a supervisor, although this obviously depends on the experience level of the therapist. To quote Kelly (1961: 277), discussing the man who attempted suicide: 'If his therapist is a psychoanalyst, it would be best to lay out the therapeutic plans in analytic terms rather than to risk the confusion of trying to follow personal construct plans seen through analytic spectacles'. This underlines the flexibility and openness to different ways of construing psychological situations that characterises the personal construct approach both as a meta-therapeutic frame and as an approach to psychological therapy in its own right.

Key characteristics of Personal Construct Psychology formulation

- PCP assumes that people constantly formulate constructions about their world, which are open to replacement by alternative constructions.
- Formulation involves recognising that people's behaviour, experience and difficulties are shaped and structured by the way they construe them, which they do by utilising a unique set of personal constructs which are bipolar in nature.
- Formulation must be based on a good understanding of the way the client construes his or her situation as well as the construing of other key figures in his or her life.
- The therapist is encouraged to take a *credulous* and accepting approach towards clients' views and beliefs, attempting to see the world through their eyes.
- PCP provides a set of professional or diagnostic constructs and assessment methods to aid the process of formulation.
- Formulations may consider not only individual, but also broader family and social constructions, and not only monadic but also dyadic and triadic construing.
- A formulation should be loosely held, allowing maximum openness to the unique situation and construing of the client's predicament.
- PCP's inherent reflexivity, or ability to account for itself as a psychological theory, makes it ideally suited to reflective practice through clinicians' continual awareness and examination of their own constructs and actions as they work with a client.

- Formulations may be developed and discussed with clients, and personal construct assessment methods such as the ABC technique, laddering, the bowtie, repertory grids or qualitative grids may be used to aid this process.
- A formulation should be designed and structured to anticipate and facilitate the process of psychological movement and therapeutic change. It may remain in the therapist's mind as a guide but more likely it will be shared in an appropriate way with the client in discussion or in letters written to the client or family between sessions.

Acknowledgements

Thanks to Patricia Stewart, Avril Silk, Bernadette O'Sullivan and of course Rudi Dallos and Lucy Johnstone for their valuable suggestions.

References

Bannister, D. (1960) Conceptual structure in thought-disordered schizophrenics, *Journal of Mental Science*, 106, 1230–49.

——(1962) The nature and measurement of schizophrenic thought disorder, *Journal of Mental Science*, 108, 825–42.

——(1985) The psychotic disguise in W. Dryden (ed.), *Therapists' Dilemmas*, London: Harper and Row.

Bateman, A.W. and Fonagy, P. (2012) *Handbook of Mentalizing in Mental Health Practice*, Washington: American Psychiatric Association.

Bruch, M. (1998) The development of case formulation approaches, in M. Bruch and F.W. Bond (eds.), *Beyond Diagnosis: Case Formulation Approaches in Cognitive-Behavioural Therapy*, Chichester: Wiley.

Button, E. (2006) Music and the person in J.W. Scheer and K.W. Sewell (eds.), *Creative Construing: Personal Constructions in the Arts*, Giessen: Psychosozial-Verlag.

Caputi, P., Viney, L.L., Walker, B.M. and Crittenden, N. (2011) *Personal Construct Methodology*, Chichester: Wiley-Blackwell.

Cummins, P. (1992) Reconstruing the experience of sexual abuse, *International Journal of Personal Construct Psychology*, 5, 355–65.

Dallos, R. (1991) *Family Belief Systems, Therapy and Change*, Milton Keynes: Open University Press.

Erbes, C.R. and Harter, S.L. (2005) Personal constructions in therapy with child sexual abuse survivors in D.A. Winter and L.L. Viney (eds.), *Personal Construct Psychotherapy: Advances in Theory, Practice and Research*, London: Whurr.

Feixas, G. and Saúl, L.A. (2005) Resolution of dilemmas by personal construct psychotherapy in D.A. Winter and L.L. Viney (eds.), *Personal Construct Psychotherapy: Advances in Theory, Practice and Research*, London: Whurr.

Feixas, G., Saúl, L.A. and Avila, A. (2009) Viewing cognitive conflicts as dilemmas: implications for mental health, *Journal of Constructivist Psychology*, 22, 141–169.

Fransella, F. (2003) *International Handbook of Personal Construct Psychology*, Chichester: Wiley.

Fransella, F., Bell, R. and Bannister, D. (2004) *A Manual for Repertory Grid Technique* (2nd Edition), Chichester: Wiley.

Freshwater, K., Leach, C. and Aldridge, J. (2001) Personal constructs, childhood sexual abuse and revictimization, *British Journal of Medical Psychology*, 74, 379–397.

Harter, S.L. and Neimeyer, R.A. (1995) Long term effects of child sexual abuse: towards a constructivist theory of trauma and its treatment in R.A. Neimeyer and G.J. Neimeyer (eds.), *Advances in Personal Construct Psychology*, Vol. 3, Greenwich, CT: JAI.

Hester, M., Pearson, C. and Harwin, N. (1998) *Making an Impact: Children and Domestic Violence*, Barnardo's; School for Policy Studies; University of Bristol; NSPCC; Department of Health.

Hinkle, D. (1965) *The Change of Personal Constructs from the Viewpoint of a Theory of Construct Implications*, unpublished PhD thesis, Ohio State University.

Kelly, G.A. (1955) *The Psychology of Personal Constructs*, Vols 1 & 2, New York: Norton. (2nd edn, London: Routledge, 1991)

——(1961) Suicide: The personal construct point of view in E. Schneidman and N. Farberow (eds.), *The Cry for Help*, New York: McGraw-Hill.

——(1969) The psychotherapeutic relationship in B.A. Maher (ed.), *Clinical Psychology and Personality: The Selected Papers of George Kelly* (pp. 216–223), New York: Wiley. (Original work written 1965.)

——(1970) A brief introduction to personal construct theory in D. Bannister (ed.), *Perspectives in Personal Construct Theory*, London: Academic Press.

Leitner, L.M. (1985a) Interview methodologies for construct elicitation: searching for the core in F. Epting and A.W. Landfield (eds.), *Anticipating Personal Construct Psychology*, Lincoln: University of Nebraska Press.

——(1985b) The terrors of cognition: on the experiential validity of personal construct theory, in D. Bannister (ed.), *Issues and Approaches in Personal Construct Theory*, London: Academic Press.

——(1988) Terror, risk and reverence: experiential personal construct psychotherapy, *International Journal of Personal Construct Psychology*, 1, 299–310.

Leitner, L.M., Faidley, A.J. and Celentana, M.A. (2000) Diagnosing human meaning making: an experiential constructivist approach in R.A. Neimeyer and J.D. Raskin (eds.), *Constructions of Disorder: Meaning-Making Frameworks for Psychotherapy*, Washington, DC: American Psychological Association.

Levinson, M. and Silk, A. (2007) *Dreams of the Road: Gypsy Life in the West Country*, Edinburgh: Berlinn.

Maher, B. (1969) *Clinical Psychology and Personality: The Selected Papers of George Kelly*, New York: Wiley.

Neimeyer, R.A. (1985) Personal constructs in clinical practice in P.C. Kendall (ed.), *Advances in Cognitive-Behavioral Research and Therapy*, Vol. 4, New York: Academic Press.

———(2001) *Meaning Reconstruction and the Experience of Loss*, Washington, DC: American Psychological Association.

———(2004) Fostering posttraumatic growth: A narrative contribution, *Psychological Inquiry*, 15, 53–59.

———(2009) *Constructivist Psychotherapy: Distinctive Features*, London: Routledge.

Procter, H.G. (1981) Family construct psychology: An approach to understanding and treating families, in S. Walrond-Skinner (ed.), *Developments in Family Therapy*. London: Routledge and Kegan Paul.

———(1985) A construct approach to family therapy and systems intervention, in E. Button (ed.), *Personal Construct Theory and Mental Health*, Beckenham: Croom Helm.

———(2001) Personal Construct Psychology and Autism, *Journal of Constructivist Psychology*, 14, 105–124.

———(2002) Constructs of individuals and relationships, *Context, 59*, 11–12.

———(2005) Techniques of personal construct family therapy in D.A. Winter and L.L. Viney (eds.), *Personal Construct Psychotherapy: Advances in Theory, Practice and Research.* London: Whurr.

———(2007) Construing within the family in R. Butler and D. Green, *The Child Within: Taking the Young Person's Perspective by Applying Personal Construct Theory*, 2nd Edition, London: Wiley.

———(2009a) The construct in R.J. Butler (ed.), *Reflections in Personal Construct Theory*, Chichester: Wiley-Blackwell.

———(2009b) Reflexivity and reflective practice in personal and relational construct Psychotherapy in J. Stedmon and R. Dallos (eds.), *Reflective Practice in Psychotherapy and Counselling,* Milton Keynes: Open University Press.

———(2011) The roots of Kellian notions in philosophy: The categorial philosophers Kant, Hegel and Peirce in D. Stojnov, V. Džinović, J. Pavlović and M. Frances (eds.), *Personal Construct Psychology in an Accelerating World*, Belgrade: Serbian Constructivist Association/EPCA.

———(in press) Qualitative Grids, the Relationality Corollary and the Levels of Interpersonal Construing, *Journal of Constructivist Psychology.*

Procter, H.G. and Parry, G. (1978) Constraint and freedom: The social origin of personal constructs in F. Fransella (ed.) *Personal Construct Psychology 1977*, London: Academic Press.

Raskin, J.D. (2002) Constructivism in psychology: personal construct psychology, radical constructivism, and social constructionism, *American Communication Journal*, 5, 3.

Ravenette, A.T. (1980) The exploration of consciousness: personal construct intervention with children in A.W. Landfield and L.M. Leitner (eds.), *Personal Construct Psychology: Psychotherapy and Personality*, Chichester: Wiley.

Rossotti, N.G., Winter, D.A. and Watts, M.H. (2006) Trust and dependency in younger and older people in P. Caputi, H. Foster and L.L. Viney (eds.), *Personal Construct Psychology: New Ideas,* Chichester: London.

Scheer, J. (2006) Living with jazz: Construing cultural identity in J.W. Scheer and K.W. Sewell (eds.), *Creative Construing: Personal Constructions in the Arts*, Giessen: Psychosozial-Verlag.

Sewell, K. (1997) Posttraumatic stress: towards a constructivist model of psychotherapy in R.A. Neimeyer and G.J. Neimeyer (eds.), *Advances in Personal Construct Psychology*, Vol. 4, Greenwich, CT: JAI.

Silk, A. (2011) Personal communication.

Tschudi, F. and Winter, D. (2011) The ABC model revisited in P. Caputi, L.L. Viney, B.M. Walker and N. Crittenden (eds.), *Personal Construct Methodology*, Chichester: Wiley-Blackwell.

Ugazio, V., Fellin, L., Colcagio, F., Pennachio, R. and Negri, A. (2008) 1 to 3: From the monad to the triad. A unitizing and coding system for the inference fields of causal explanations, TPM. *Testing, Psychometrics, Methodology in Applied Psychology*, 15: 171–192.

Walker, B.M. (2002) Nonvalidation vs. (In)validation: implications for theory and practice in J.D. Raskin and S. Bridges (eds.), *Studies in Meaning: Exploring Constructivist Psychology*, New York: Pace University Press.

Walker, B.M. and Winter, D.A. (2005) 'Psychological disorder and reconstruction' in D.A. Winter and L.L. Viney (eds.), *Personal Construct Psychotherapy: Advances in Theory, Practice and Research*, London: Whurr.

——(2007) The elaboration of personal construct psychology, *Annual Review of Psychology*, 58, 453–477.

Winter, D.A. (1992) *Personal Construct Psychology in Clinical Practice: Theory, Research and Applications*, London: Routledge.

Winter, D.A. (2003a) Psychological disorder as imbalance, in F. Fransella (ed.), *International Handbook of Personal Construct Psychology*, Chichester: Wiley.

Winter, D.A. (2003b) 'Repertory grid technique as a psychotherapy research measure', *Psychotherapy Research*, 13, 25–42.

Winter, D.A. (2009) The personal construct psychology view of disorder: did Kelly get it wrong?, in L.M. Leitner and J.C. Thomas (eds.), *Personal Constructivism: Theory and Applications*, New York: Pace University Press.

Winter, D.A. and Viney, L.L. (2005) *Personal Construct Psychotherapy: Advances in Theory, Practice and Research*, London: Whurr.

Wright, K.J.T. (1970) Exploring the uniqueness of common complaints, *British Journal of Medical Psychology*, 43, 221–32.

Yalom, I. (1970) *The Theory and Practice of Group Psychotherapy*, New York: Basic Books.

Chapter 8

Integrative formulation in theory

Rudi Dallos, Jacqui Stedmon and Lucy Johnstone

Integrative formulations

In the preceding chapters we have presented an overview of how formulation is conceptualised and developed within a range of therapeutic models of intervention. This includes ideas about the *content* of formulation: what the ingredients are, and also the *process*: how it is done. An important question, though, is whether and how we can combine or integrate the various models in ways that are most helpful for guiding our clinical work. We believe that one way forward is through a change of focus from formulation, or *formulation-as-an-event*, to formulating, or *formulating-as-a-process*. In this chapter we will discuss the strengths and limitations of some current approaches to integrative formulation and then attempt to move towards a more complex and dynamic model of integration which draws on the therapeutic relationship, personal meaning, personal development, and the idea of formulating as a fluid collaborative process.

Professional guidelines generally specify that clinicians should be able to draw from a number of different models in their therapeutic work, and hence presumably in their formulations as well. For example, Health Professions Council (2009: 3a.1) criteria for clinical psychologists require them to 'Understand psychological models related to how biological, sociological and circumstantial or life-event-related factors impinge on psychological processes to affect psychological well-being'. Surveys consistently show that some kind of eclecticism is the single most popular approach for psychotherapists and counsellors (McLeod, 2009). Curiously though, there is little consensus about how to construct an integrative formulation, although a number of different frameworks have been suggested (Lapworth and Sills, 2009; Gardner, 2005; Eells, 1997; Ingram, 2006; Weerasekera, 1995; *Journal of Psychotherapy* 1996, 6, 2; Corrie and Lane, 2010). Attempts to solve the problem as discussed in the related literature on integrative therapy are also only partially successful. This is not surprising if we consider that even within so-called 'single model' perspectives such as CBT, psychodynamic, or systemic, psychological therapy and formulation is bedevilled by divisions and splits (Norcross and Goldfried,

2005; Palmer and Woolfe, 2000; Lapworth and Sills, 2009). These include differences about person-specific versus problem-specific formulations, about emphasising the individual versus the social context, and about the 'truth' versus the 'usefulness' of the resulting product (see Divison of Clinical Psychology (DCP), 2011 for further discussion). Furthermore, models have different philosophical roots which make varying assumptions about the nature of human beings and their relationship to the world (Howard, 2000). For example, the models we have explored so far differ in the following set of implicit assumptions (among others):

Origin of the problem. Is the 'problem' primarily located in our biology/body/ brain chemistry (psychiatry); in our minds (cognitive therapy, psychology in general); in our family and relationships (relational/systemic); or in wider society (feminist, community psychology)?

Agency. Are we in control of our lives and actions (humanistic therapies); or simply responding to our environments (behaviourism); or our internal drives (psychoanalysis); or biochemical imbalances (psychiatry)?

Ethics. Are we essentially loving and well intentioned (humanistic); or in a constant battle to keep instinctual drives under control (psychoanalysis); or do we react to our environment in a morally neutral way (strict behaviourism)?

The immediate response – that all of these perspectives have an element of truth – fails to address the fundamental question, which in integrative therapy and integrative formulation is: can we combine these elements in a conceptually coherent way? Do we simply throw all our chosen components into a common pot as in *eclecticism?* Or do we instead attempt to tease out what the underlying conceptual connections are, by way of a *conceptual synthesis/integration?* This choice goes further than the pragmatics of any given piece of clinical work since arguably, conceptual synthesis can pave the way to developments in clinical theory and models of aetiology, and stimulate new approaches to intervention. Integrative formulation which attempts a *conceptual synthesis* aims to identify and combine the core features of different models in order to create a fresh, vibrant and effective new model of formulation and intervention.

This is an important point, since in a context of financial uncertainty, restricted budgets and long waiting lists, new developments typically have to compete with more established practices for these limited resources by claiming to be more cost-effective and more effective with difficult cases. As a result, proponents of new integrative developments may feel pressure to make strong claims about effectiveness to justify themselves to purchasers. Perhaps this is also why many so-called integrative models are pragmatically driven and do little more than combine models, or aspects of models, based on strategies that appear to be supported by the evidence and/or seem to work in practice.

We will now take a closer look at both these main approaches to integration in psychotherapy, eclecticism and conceptual synthesis. Some, but not all, have outlined the kind of formulation that might result from this.

Eclecticism

In an eclectic approach we are not particularly concerned about reconciling and integrating the conceptual features of different models. Instead, the combination is a pragmatically driven one, combining models or aspects of models and based on strategies that are supported by the evidence, and/or seem to work in practice (Wachtel, 1991). Eclecticism is implied by professional guidelines which, while requiring counsellors, clinical psychologists and others to incorporate a wide range of *factors* into their practice, do not specify how these are to be synthesised.

The various versions of simple eclecticism may not have an official name as such. However they are likely to derive from one of the following positions:

1   *The matching of 'diagnosis' or 'symptoms' to the type of therapy.* This can involve considering, for example, the clinical utility of exploratory (brief psychodynamic) versus prescriptive (e.g. CBT) therapies for a given problem such as depression. This approach has also been described as drawing on a medical or 'drug metaphor' (Stiles and Shapiro, 1994; Green and Latchford, 2012), whereby we reach for the appropriate drug or treatment for a particular diagnosis. It often claims to be guided by a research 'evidence-base' which points towards integration. This assumes that we know and can identify the active ingredients of a helpful therapy for clinical conditions; for example, a combination of CBT and systemic therapy has been said to be an effective treatment for adolescents with eating disorders (Dare et al., 1990). It also assumes the validity of the notoriously unreliable psychiatric diagnostic system in order to match intervention to 'illness'. In fact there is very little support for this medically based model of how therapies work, as extensively discussed elsewhere (e.g. Green and Latchford, 2012).

2   *Developmental stages.* These approaches are based on the finding that different therapeutic approaches may be suitable for the same client at different stages in therapy. Two of the best known include the Assimilation Model (Stiles and Shapiro, 1994) and Stages of Change Model (Prochaska and DiClemente, 1982). These suggest that clients may be at different stages of preparedness for therapeutic intervention. For example, at a 'pre-contemplation' stage they have not yet become aware of or started to contemplate the fact that they have problems which may benefit from help. It is suggested that exploratory approaches may be helpful at this stage in order to raise awareness and start to generate motivation for change. At the 'contemplation' stage there is some awareness and recognition of the problems, and cognitive approaches may be helpful in starting to reveal the underlying beliefs and thoughts. It is suggested that this may lead to awareness of contradictory thoughts and feelings which are holding back the next

stage of contemplating and 'enacting change'. A psychodynamic approach may also be employed to help expose defences which are preventing change.

3   *Collections of techniques and strategies.* This is sometimes known as 'technical eclecticism'. One example is the multimodal approach developed by Lazarus (2005) for therapists who employ 'effective techniques from many orientations without subscribing to the theories that spawned them' (p. 103). He uses the acronym BASIC ID to prompt therapists to consider interventions in relation to the areas of behaviour, affect, sensation, imagery, cognition, interpersonal and drugs/biology. Another example is Gerard Egan's *The Skilled Helper* (2009), which guides the trainee therapist through a very comprehensive set of communication and problem-solving skills and strategies suitable for various stages and tasks within therapy. While it is made clear that all the work has to happen within an empathic helping relationship, there is no explicit attempt to integrate the skills at a conceptual level.

4   *Collections of clinical hypotheses.* Two of the best-known examples of integrative formulation fall into this category. Ingram (2006) provides an ambitious list of 28 core clinical hypotheses which are claimed to embrace all theories and orientations. The headings include loss, biological causes, faulty information processes, lack of social support, and so on. She explicitly describes this framework as summarising core ideas from all models, rather than attempting conceptual synthesis. Arguably, Weerasekera (1995) also fits into this category, as discussed below.

Conceptual synthesis

As described above, these are attempts to do more than simply combine approaches; the aim is to achieve theoretical integration in order to develop new, more effective and comprehensive models. It has been argued that therapies that develop within the same broad tradition (humanistic, behavioural and psychodynamic) are more likely to be compatible; indeed, each named therapy is likely to contain elements of concepts from its related family of therapies anyway (Lapworth and Sills, 2009).

Attempts at conceptual synthesis are likely to fall into one of the following categories:

1   *Off-the-shelf integrative models.* These use standardised integrative formats for all formulations. A good example is Cognitive Analytic Therapy (Ryle, 1995) which combines a number of other models such as Personal Construct Theory (chapter 7) and Object Relations Theory (see chapter 3). Lapworth and Sills (2009, chapter 9) also outline a detailed integrative framework that can be used as the basis for an integrative formulation and

intervention. These approaches probably represent the most sophisticated attempt at conceptual integration to date. A recent addition to this category is Attachment Narrative Therapy (Dallos, 2006) which will be explored in detail in the next chapter. It aims to integrate different levels of ideas about the origins of the problem, namely relational (systemic) and individual (attachment and narrative).

2   *Common factors integration.* The search for more conceptually coherent integrations has in part been fuelled by a wider interest in the idea that it may be possible to identify common active ingredients across different psychotherapies – the 'Holy Grail' of psychotherapy researchers. The most consistent and useful findings are related to what is called the 'therapeutic alliance', which encompasses the relationship between client and therapist, and the degree of agreement on the aims of the therapy and on how to achieve change (Toukmanian and Rennie, 1992; Paley and Lawton, 2001; Wampold, 2001; Luborsky et al., 2002; Green and Latchford, 2012). There is also the finding that effective therapy involves a 'transformation of meanings' (Sluzki, 1992), that is, a fundamental shift in how the problems are seen and in the person's view of themselves.

Examples of approaches which use the therapist–client relationship as an integrating factor are outlined by Michael Kahn in *Between Therapist and Client* (1996) and by Petruska Clarkson in *The Therapeutic Relationship* (2003). Kahn argues that 'the relationship *is* the therapy' (1996: 1), and believes it can be most effective through a synthesis of the warmth and openness of the humanistic therapists and insights into transference and counter-transference derived from the psychoanalysts. Clarkson takes a slightly different angle. She explicitly distances herself from the task of conceptual integration, arguing that 'all stories are true at certain times and from certain perspectives' (2003: xxiii). Instead, she proposes a meta-theoretical framework which encompasses the five different aspects of the relationship that may be present at any one time: the working alliance, the transference/counter-transference, the developmentally needed relationship, the person-to-person or 'real' relationship, and the trans-personal relationship. We will look at the therapeutic relationship as an integrating factor in more detail later.

3   *Idiosyncratic integration.* Finally, we acknowledge that experienced clinicians have generally, over a period of years, evolved their own personal approach to therapy and formulation, drawing on the models, concepts and strategies which make most sense to them and appear to achieve the best outcomes. The extent to which this represents true integration, as opposed to simple eclecticism, is of course hard to judge in any particular case. At the end of the chapter, we will suggest some general principles which help to support the former rather than the latter position.

Some reflections: implicit integration in practice

An interesting wider question concerns the extent to which all models (and hence to an extent all formulations, at least in their formulating-as-a-process sense) necessarily involve integration in actual practice. We have witnessed many conversations where therapists from different schools have levelled criticisms of each others' approach; for example, CBT is sometimes accused of emphasising techniques for changing dysfunctional cognitions at the expense of ignoring the therapeutic relationship. In defence, CBT practitioners typically reply that they are very sensitive to the need to build a therapeutic relationship and that clients will not undertake the laborious homework tasks involved in CBT unless they have faith in and trust the therapist. Interestingly, this is borne out by a qualitative study by Borrill and Foreman (1996) of CBT therapy for clients who had a fear of flying. The clients reported that the most important factor for them was establishing a good relationship with the therapist. This was poignantly illustrated by one of the core themes which was expressed as 'being able to borrow belief' from the therapist that they would be able to overcome their fear. In a similar vein, psychoanalytic therapists are often criticised for being too concerned with predisposing intra-psychic processes and not paying adequate attention to the current interpersonal dynamics that may be maintaining problems. In defence they typically argue that in practice there will be considerable discussion about current circumstances and how to work with these dynamics in order for progress to be possible.

Part of this discussion turns around the question of whether what therapists say they do in terms of their theory corresponds with what they do in practice. A classic investigation of this is Truax's (1966) study, which showed that Rogerian (Rogers, 1955) non-directive counselling could be conceptualised not so much in existential terms of acceptance and trust, but in terms of subtle changes in reward contingencies during the process of therapy. Thus, the therapist was seen as differentially encouraging types of behaviours such as self-disclosure, insight and self-acceptance in clients by nods and smiles, by vocalisations such as 'Yes I see' and 'That's interesting', by paralinguistic messages ('ahhmms'), and by non-verbal communication by posture and so on. It is also true that as the basic models have developed and become more sophisticated, they have increasingly borrowed ideas from each other, though often without acknowledgement. For example, CBT has incorporated a concept very like the unconscious in its recent focus on 'schemas', which are deeply rooted core beliefs of which the client may not be aware. Similarly, Bertrando (2007) describes how systemic therapists such as the Milan team drew on their previous psychoanalytic training in calibrating their interventions to the emotional tones of the family members.

It is highly likely that therapists are influenced by other models in their formulating and their practice even if this is not overtly stated in their work.

To take an obvious example, it would be hard for any therapist not to be aware of ideas about the therapeutic relationship originating from psychodynamic theory even if they disagreed with many of the tenets of the underlying model. Such an awareness is likely to influence the therapy even if it is expressed in terms of patterns of reinforcement and rewards. Moreover, it is well established by research that experienced therapists from different theoretical orientations resemble each other more closely than novices trained within particular approaches (Luborsky et al., 2002; Wampold, 2001.) This suggests, in line with the point made above, that over time all clinicians develop their own synthesis, and furthermore that it is likely to be implicitly based on certain core relational factors. Research indicates that so-called 'supershrinks', whose outcomes are as much as 10 times better than average, are 'hypersensitive to threats to the alliance with the client' and work extremely hard to maintain the therapeutic relationship (Okiishi et al., 2003).

Finally, returning to the topic of formulation, we should note, along with the DCP Guidelines, that formulations are designed for particular situations and purposes. A simple, single-model CBT diagram illustrating the link between anxious thoughts, panicky feelings and avoidance behaviours may be the most appropriate starting point with a client at a given point in time. 'Clearly, most formulations in day-to-day practice will not cover the whole range of possible contexts and causal factors'; a fully integrated formulation is not always necessary or helpful. However, 'a narrower or single-model formulation needs to be a conscious and justifiable choice from a wider field of possible models and causal influences' (DCP, 2011: 15). In other words, the clinician always needs to be able to hold a sophisticated, multi-model formulation in mind.

Weerasekera's framework

We will now take a more detailed look at an approach to integrative formulation which illustrates both the benefits and the challenges of attempting this task. It uses the 4 Ps framework (Predisposing, Precipitating, Perpetuating, Protective) as a starting point. The inclusion of 'Presenting issues' as a first step, that is, a summary of the difficulties that a client brings to therapy, means that it is sometimes described as 5 Ps (see chapter 2 for a more detailed outline).

Weerasekera's (1995) model has two axes. The first axis comprises the *origins of the problems* (individual and systemic/relational) and the second uses the PPPP framework. The first axis also includes different therapeutic approaches, such as CBT, psychodynamic approaches and behavioural interventions at the individual level (see Figure 8.1).

These two axes are an over-arching framework for deciding on the intervention package. The model also considers coping styles – characteristic aspects of clients' ways of dealing with problems in their various different

	Individual Factors: 1. Biological – e.g. temperament, physical disabilities, genetic factors 2. Behavioural – e.g. learning, modelling 3. Cognitive – e.g. NATs, schemas, core schemas 4. Psychodynamic – e.g. defences, attachments	Systemic Factors: 1. Couple – communication, intimacy, support 2. Family – family dynamics, traditions 3. Occupational/ school – employment, school 4. Social – race, gender, class, community resources
Predisposing: factors that make the person or the system vulnerable to experiencing difficulties		
Precipitating: events that are close in time to the development of the problem		
Perpetuating: factors that are involved in maintaining the problem.		
Protective: factors that contribute to resilience		

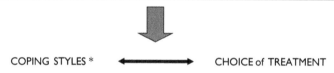

COPING STYLES * ⟷ CHOICE of TREATMENT

* characteristic ways of reacting to stress and distress:

1.   dispositional – enduring personal styles
2.   episodic – varying from situation to situation
3.   individual – biological, behavioural, cognitive, psychodynamic
4.   systemic – couple, family, occupational or social

Figure 8.1 Weerasekera's grid

contexts, such as home, work, leisure and so on. Family relationship patterns of coping are also included; this corresponds to the systemic family therapy concept of 'attempted solutions'.

Jack: formulation using Weerasekera's framework

Assessment

The first stage is to carry out an assessment using the 4 Ps as an initial guide. This involves thinking about each of the Ps in relation to both the individual and systemic factors. The information required for this is drawn widely from case notes, referral information and the assessment interviews with the client and their family, perhaps supplemented by diaries of behaviours and thoughts, and observation of and reflections on family interactions. As this assessment proceeds, ideas about characteristic family coping styles are developed. The grid also serves to highlight gaps in our knowledge and information.

Once the grid is filled in, consideration is given to which of the therapeutic models may be utilised to address the 4 Ps at either the individual or systemic levels. This decision is further guided by the client/s' preferred coping style. For example, if the client/s express a preference for an action-oriented approach, a behavioural strategy may be the best starting point.

The grid can also indicate consecutive as opposed to simultaneous combinations of models. As therapy progresses, there may be a shift from a behavioural to a psychodynamic perspective in order to explore underlying defences and feelings. In some cases the grid may suggest that two or more models may be employed at the same time: for example child-focused CBT work alongside systemic therapy to address issues in the family relationships (see Figure 8.2).

Individual coping styles

It appears that Jack is currently most accepting of a biological perspective in taking medication and finding it 'useful'. There is a sense that action-orientated techniques might be more acceptable to him as a first step towards engagement. He appears not to have been able to tell his family about some very upsetting experiences, such as abuse. Perhaps he has tried to keep things to himself in order to protect them. However, this coping style means that unresolved problems may escalate until they explode.

Systemic coping styles

Like Jack, his family appears to value a medical input at this point. Given their traumatic experiences it seems likely that their coping style is also action-orientated, for example needing to feel safe and to have strategies to manage Jack and get help when they need it.

Advantages and limitations of the Weerasekera framework and the 4 Ps

The Weerasekera framework has some advantages, which also apply to the 4 Ps when used on their own. For example, they encourage a thorough assessment and analysis which alert us to look for factors that we might miss or ignore. In its full version, the Weerasekera framework also offers some guidance about the timing and ordering of intervention, and also considers coping styles. Matching the intervention to client/family styles of coping can promote a collaborative stance and strengthen the therapeutic alliance.

	Individual Factors	Systemic Factors
Predisposing: factors that the person or the system vulnerable to experiencing difficulties	Individual: Jack has experienced sexual abuse and family disintegration. He has witnessed family violence and possibly been a victim of it, his father became alcoholic, the family business failed, and there was loss of contact with his father and the family's cultural base. He has had a broad experience of loss and failure in this transition from a bright, capable student to abandoning his studies.	A similar pattern of stress and distress appears to have resulted in the family feeling overwhelmed, threatened and inadequate. There has also been a severing of their connections with the Italian community.
Precipitating: events that are close in time to the development of the problem	Jack's 'paranoid' symptoms appear to coincide with his mother developing 'serious' health problems and the family finances becoming 'even more stretched'.	Family rows may have played a part in triggering Jack's problems.
Perpetuating: factors that are involved in maintaining the problem	Jack's problems are likely to be maintained by his low self-esteem, negative beliefs about himself, insecure attachments and his many fears. He may continue to identify with his father but experience great ambivalence about this. His identity as inadequate, failed and 'ill' is now likely to be maintained by his position as a 'psychiatric patient'. In addition, the medication he is taking may further reinforce the idea that there is something wrong with him and may make it harder to engage in therapeutic activities due to lethargy and so on.	The family may feel that they are failing, and may also feel anxious about and afraid of Jack. This cycle of a sense of rejection and fear may be serving to maintain Jack as excluded from the family. The family's anxiety may mean that they continue to require psychiatric support and hence Jack is maintained in an 'ill' identity. In effect, the psychiatric system can be seen as co-parenting Jack. This can establish a self-perpetuating dependency.
Protective: factors that contribute to resilience	Jack is reported to have been an intelligent, sociable and creative child. He is also described as 'compliant' which perhaps indicates a potential for forming a good therapeutic alliance. Despite his difficulties, he displays care and concern about his family, for example worrying about his sister's safety.	Despite adversities the family appears to remain connected and have survived financially. We do not know much about Jack's sisters but it is possible that they have strengths and successes on which the family could draw.

Figure 8.2 Illustration of the use of Weerasekera's grid for Jack and his family

The framework also has some clear limitations from the perspective of the themes of this book, and these may also apply to the 4 Ps when used on its own. These limitations fall into the following areas:

Colloborative versus expert-based. There appears to be an assumption that the formulation is largely carried out by the therapist from an expert position as opposed to a more collaborative, co-constructed process of meaning-making.

Reflexivity. This, for example a consideration of the therapist's own assumptions, values and beliefs, is absent from both frameworks.

Compatibility of different models. Individual and systemic therapies imply different kinds of causation and responsibility for the problems. Weerasekera appears to assume that an 'illness' model can be unproblematically combined with the psychological one, and similarly that a systemic model can simply be added to an individual focus (see chapters 10 and 12 for further discussion of this issue).

Compatibility of interventions. Similarly, there is no debate about whether the interventions that may flow from the models are compatible with each other; for example whether medication can simply be added onto family therapy without undermining it, either by reducing the ability to feel or by conveying a message about the origin of the problem.

Certainty and pattern matching. As noted earlier, there is little support for the assumption that particular therapies can be matched to particular types of problems in an 'off-the-shelf' way.

Cultural and other contexts. There is no consideration of power and the ideological dominance of some of the models, such as the biomedical model, or of cultural issues that may shape the emergence and presentation of difficulties.

Impractical. An obvious practical point is that busy clinicians may not have the time to undertake assessment in such detail, and it is even less likely that the whole list of resources and interventions indicated by the assessment will be available.

But perhaps the most serious limitations from the perspective adopted by this book are in the following areas:

Conceptual integration. The Weerasekera framework does not clarify how the different models might be used together. In other words it is essentially eclectic and not conceptually synthesised. This is also true of the 4 Ps. Either could be used as an initial step towards this goal, but neither on their own attempts to do this, or indicates how it could be done.

The therapeutic relationship. As discussed earlier, the most widely supported common feature in effective therapy of all orientations is the therapeutic alliance. This is not acknowledged in either the Weerasekera or the 4 Ps framework, apart from some discussion about increasing client co-operation by matching models of therapy to the client's coping style.

Personal meaning. There is a risk in both the 4 Ps and the Weerasekera framework that the numerous possible influences on a client's life will simply be listed in an additive fashion without reference to their personal meaning. In this respect the end result may be similar to the axes, or additional dimensions, of psychiatric diagnosis in the Diagnostic and Statistical Manual (DSM). We might thus end up with what has been referred to as a 'list-of-factors' formulation: for example, 'Jack's parents separated following arguments and domestic violence. His father was alcoholic. He was sexually abused by his boss. He misses his father. His family have faced many social stresses. He has developed depression'. This list of Ps can only be developed into a formulation by the inclusion of personal meaning, elicited through sensitive collaborative discussion, which shows how these factors are linked by their impact on Jack's identity, self-confidence and feelings and views about himself and others.

In summary, the Weerasekera and the 4 Ps frameworks are perhaps best understood as assessment methods, tools for gathering information systematically, and as such, a useful first step in developing a formulation. They do not, however, fulfil the criteria of a best practice formulation, and have not achieved, or even attempted, the conceptual synthesis that is essential for a fully integrated formulation. Moreover, by focusing on formulation-as-an-event rather than formulating-as-a-process, they do not allow for the large body of research showing the primacy of the quality of the therapeutic relationship.

Integrative formulating: towards some principles in practice

To summarise the arguments so far:

Historically there has been an excessive focus on outcome research that purports to demonstrate the superior effectiveness of some models of therapy over others, with 'head-to-head' comparisons of different treatments. Despite the inappropriateness of 'attempting to fit the round peg of psychotherapy into the square hole of medicine', this approach 'remains attractive for several reasons, including the general acceptance of the medico-scientific view in Western society and harsh economic realities of our healthcare system' (Miller, et al., 2004: 4).

One danger is that the most heavily researched therapies, which tend to be those like CBT that fit this paradigm most easily, assume an unwarranted dominance based on their apparently stronger claims for effectiveness. Paradoxically, the extensive literature on evidence-based practice in therapy generally ignores the fact that 'one of the most consistent findings in over 30 years of psychotherapy research is that despite different philosophical emphases and applications, models of therapy tend to achieve broadly similar outcomes' (Paley and Lawton, 2001:13; see also Wampold, 2001; Luborsky et al., 2002). This can be explained by the well-supported finding that it is the quality of the relationship that is the most important factor within the therapy room in achieving change – for example, warmth, attention, understanding and encouragement. In fact the therapeutic alliance has been found to account for between 30–60 per cent of the variability in outcome, whereas models and techniques only account for 5–10 per cent (Miller, 2006). This leads Paley and Lawton (2001) to argue for 'empirically supported relationships' over 'empirically supported treatments', with profound implications for research, practice and training. They also argue that:

> It is too early to argue for either the supposed superiority of any approaches or to define adequately an eclectic or integrative model of therapy. In our current state of not knowing, all approaches will have to be respected as valid methods of travelling the therapeutic route ... The challenge to researchers, trainers and practitioners is to embrace this diversity as different manifestations leading to the primacy of the therapeutic relationship.
>
> (Paley and Lawton, 2001: 16)

In recent elaborations of these findings, it has been shown that therapy outcomes can be significantly enhanced if the therapist works closely alongside what is known as 'the client's theory of change'. In other words, 'rather than the client having to accommodate the *therapist's theory* of how change occurs ... the views of the *client* are central and therapy is tailored to *their* views about what is helpful or unhelpful' (Robinson, 2009: 60; italics in the original). This is consistent with the requirement, in best practice formulation, for collaboration and respect for the client's perspective, and on our emphasis on formulating-as-a-process rather than formulation-as-an-event. In Duncan and Sparks' (2004: 31) words: 'The client's theory of change is not an anatomical structure in the client's head to be discovered by your expert questioning. Rather, it is a plan that co-evolves via the conversational unfolding of the client's experience, fuelled by your caring curiosity'. Responses (and, by implication, formulations) that fit with the client's world of subjective meanings are experienced as helpful and, moreover, are significantly more likely to achieve good outcomes over the course of therapy. So-called 'supershrinks' are flexible enough to employ almost any therapeutic means to achieve the client's ends.

In summary, all models, and hence all formulations based on those models, have their own, often complementary, strengths and limitations. This is one of the reasons for offering a wide range of approaches to formulation in this book. Recognition of this, rather than a partisan allegiance to a particular model and hostility towards others, allows us to draw from different approaches as needed. We will thus be more able to offer clients the kind of intervention that fits with their theory of change. 'While remaining respectful to each approach, integrative psychotherapy draws from many sources in the belief that no one approach has all the truth' (Humanistic and Integrative Psychotherapy Section of the UK Council for Psychotherapy 1999: xiv quoted in Lapworth and Sills, 2009: 9).

Conceptually integrated formulation, like conceptually integrated therapy, is a goal that has yet to be reached. However, there are some useful signposts along the way. The most relevant clues, in our view, lie in the recognition that formulation is best understood as a verb not a noun, a process not an event. This suggests that the most clinically useful type of integration needs to happen through *formulating-as-a-process*, which is an activity inseparable from the therapeutic relationship itself. There are of course different theories about the nature of the therapeutic relationship and how to foster it. Nevertheless, the emphasis on formulation as a flexible, fluid activity with a strong focus on the therapeutic relationship is characteristic of experienced clinicians from a variety of theoretical backgrounds. They are likely to have developed an idiosyncratic set of preferred concepts and strategies which make up their own personal style, but will also be drawing on qualities such as intuition, capacity to listen and to synthesise disparate information, and to hold a tentative position which includes a number of different perspectives. This position, sometimes described as 'both/and', can be seen as the end result of many years of working in therapeutic settings, and is primarily reached by starting at the clinical and relational end rather than being top-down and theory-driven. The implication is that in the real world of clinical practice, 'there will be as many integrative psychotherapies as there are integrative psychotherapists' (Lapworth and Sills, 2009: 15). By extension, the same applies to integrative formulation.

Integration through formulating in the therapeutic relationship

If we accept this as a guiding principle, the following emphases will inform our integrative formulating.

Formulating as an active process

Formulating is an interactive and vibrant activity. It is not simply an intellectual pursuit but a subjective and interpersonal one, as we interact with our clients within a dynamic social context. Nor is it simply about collecting facts in a rational 'objective' manner, but rather takes place within the context of an evolving therapeutic relationship. Thus, the process implies *reflexivity, collaboration* and a constant willingness to *re-formulate* at its heart. This emphasis on formulation as a dynamic, recursive process is a central theme of this book and the subsequent chapter.

Personal meaning as the central integrating factor in formulation

As discussed in relation to Weerasekera's framework, there is a risk that the numerous possible influences on a client's life will simply be listed in an additive fashion. A strong focus on *personal meaning* as a central integrating thread will help to avoid this. This is consistent with the DCP Guidelines (2011:15): '*Personal meaning* is the integrating factor in a psychological formulation' (italics in the original).

Personal development and integration

It has long been established that the clinician's selection of preferred therapeutic approaches is not random or strictly evidence-based; rather, personality and value systems play a part in the choice of orientation (Horton, 2000). As an extension of this argument, Fear and Woolfe (2000) suggest that it is our job as therapists to use our primary preferred model as a basis for extending our therapeutic repertoire in the service of our clients. Thus, 'The counsellor's journey towards integration mirrors the client's central if unconscious task in therapy: to join up the discontinuities of one's life so that ... "cut off" parts (are) reintegrated and accepted ... It is the task of the counsellor to ... achieve a personal integration' (p. 328). This fits with the finding that the success of treatment is much more closely related to the characteristics of the therapist than to the type of treatment (Miller, et al., 2007). We may all need to notice which models and approaches we prefer, to ask what this says about us, and to make a conscious attempt to balance our choices with knowledge and awareness of the strengths of other perspectives.

Checklist of best practice integrative formulation

Finally, it may be helpful to refer to a best practice checklist in order to help assess an integrative formulation's quality and completeness. The DCP Guidelines audit tool (2011: 29–30) lists the essential characteristics of both formulation and formulating, and includes the issues discussed in this chapter.

Summary

Integrative formulation raises a variety of complex issues. We have outlined some of the difficulties in achieving a conceptually integrated, as opposed to eclectic, formulation model and have looked at the characteristics, strengths and limitations of some current attempts at this task. We have also outlined some general principles of an effective and clinically useful integrative approach to formulation based on the following principles:

- Formulating as a process, and as an intrinsic aspect of the therapeutic relationship.
- Formulating and re-formulating sensitively, collaboratively and reflexively.
- Using personal meaning as the central integrating factor.
- Linking professional to personal development.

In this way, our formulating will most closely fit the definition in the first chapter of a process of fluid, dynamic, collaborative shaping of meaning.

In the next chapter, these integrating principles will be illustrated through the use of Attachment Narrative Therapy. We will attempt to show not only what a formulation from this perspective might look like, but also how we might work collaboratively with Jack to develop one. In other words, we will consider integration both in formulation and in formulating.

References

Bertrando, P. (2007) *The Dialogic Therapist,* London: Karnac.

Borrill, J. and Foreman, E.I. (1996) Understanding cognitive change: a qualitative study of the impact of cognitive-behaviour therapy on fear of flying, *Clinical Psychology and Psychotherapy* 3(1): 62–74.

Clarkson, P. (2003) *The Therapeutic Relationship* (2nd edn), London, Philadephia: Whurr.

Corrie, S. and Lane, D. (eds) (2010) *Constructing Stories, Telling Tales: A Guide to Formulation in Applied Psychology,* London: Karnac Books.

Dallos, R. (2006) *Attachment Narrative Therapy,* Maidenhead: Open University Press.

Dare, C., Eisler, I., Russell, G.F. and Szmukler, G.I. (1990) The clinical and theoretical impact of a controlled trial of family therapy in anorexia nervosa, *Journal of Marital and Family Therapy,* 16: 39–57.

Division of Clinical Psychology (2011) *Good Practice Guidelines on the Use of Psychological Formulation,* Leicester: British Psychological Society.

Duncan, B.L. and Sparks, J.A. (2004) *Heroic Clients, Heroic Agencies: Partners for Change. A Manual for Client-Directed Outcome-Informed Therapy and Effective, Accountable, and Just Services,* E-Book: ISTC Press.

Eells, T.D. (ed.) (1997) *Handbook of Psychotherapy Case Formulation,* New York: Guilford Press.

Egan, G. (2009) *The Skilled Helper* (9th edn), Belmont, CA: Brooks/Cole.

Fear, R. and Woolfe, R. (2000) In S. Palmer and R. Woolfe (eds) *Integrative and Eclectic Counselling and Psychotherapy*, London: Sage, pp. 329–340.

Gardner, D. (2005) Getting it together: integrative approaches to formulation, *Clinical Psychology Forum* 151, 10–15.

Green, D. and Latchford, G. (2012) *Maximising the Benefits of Psychotherapy: A Practice-Based Evidence Approach,* Chichester: John Wiley and Sons.

Health Professions Council (2009) *Standards of Proficiency: Practitioner Psychologists,* London: Health Professions Council.

Horton, I. (2000) Principles and practice of a personal integration. In S. Palmer and R. Woolfe (eds) *Integrative and Eclectic Counselling and Psychotherapy,* London: Sage, pp. 315–328.

Howard, A. (2000) *Philosophy for Counselling and Psychotherapy: Pythagoras to Post-Modernism,* Basingstoke: Palgrave MacMillan.

Ingram, B.L. (2006) *Clinical Case Formulations: Matching the Integrative Treatment Plan to the Client,* New Jersey: John Wiley and Sons.

Kahn, M. (1996) *Between Therapist and Client: The New Relationship* (2nd edn), New York: W.H. Freeman/Owl Books.

Lapworth, P. and Sills, C. (2009) *Integration in Counselling and Psychotherapy* (2nd edn), London: Sage.

Lazarus, A.A. (2005) Multimodal therapy. In J.C. Norcross and M.R. Goldfried (eds) *Handbook of Psychotherapy Integration,* New York: Basic Books, pp. 105–120.

Luborsky, L., Rosenthal, R., Diguer, L., Andrusyna, T.P. et al. (2002) The Dodo bird effect is alive and well – mostly, *Clinical Psychology: Science and Practice,* 9, 1, 2–12.

McLeod, J. (2009) *An Introduction to Counselling* (4th edn), Buckingham: Open University Press.

Miller, S. (2006) ShrinkRapRadio no.66, Dec 14. Available at: www.ShrinkRapRadio.com (accessed 18 September 2012).

Miller, S.D., Duncan, B.L. and Hubble, M.A. (2004) Beyond integration: the triumph of outcome over process in clinical practice, *Psychotherapy in Australia,* 10, 2, 2–19.

Miller, S.D., Hubble, M. and Duncan, B. (2007) Supershrinks: what is the secret of their success? *Psychotherapy in Australia,* 14 (4), 14–22.

Norcross, J.C. and Goldfried, M.R. (eds) (2005) *Handbook of Psychotherapy Integration,* New York: Basic Books.

Okiishi, J., Lambert, M.J., Neilson, S.L. and Ogles, B.M. (2003) Waiting for supershrink: an empirical analysis of therapist effects, *Clinical Psychology and Psychotherapy,* 10, 6, 361–373.

Paley, G. and Lawton, D. (2001) Evidence-based practice: accounting for the importance of the therapeutic relationship in UK National Health Service therapy provision, *Counselling and Psychotherapy Research,* 1, 1, 12–17.

Palmer, S. and Woolfe, R. (2000) *Integrative and Eclectic Counselling and Psychotherapy,* London: Sage.

Prochaska, J.O. and DiClemente, C.C. (1982) Transtheoretical therapy: towards a more integrative model of change, *Psychotherapy, Theory, Research and Practice* 20, 161–173.

Robinson, B. (2009) When therapist variables and the client's theory of change meet, *Psychotherapy in Australia,* 15, 4, 60–65.

Rogers, C. (1955) *Client-Centred Therapy,* New York: Houghton Mifflin.

Ryle, A. (1995) *Cognitive Analytic Therapy,* Chichester: Wiley.

Sluzki, C.E. (1992) Transformations: a blueprint for narrative changes in therapy, *Family Process,* 31, 217–230.

Stiles, W.B. and Shapiro, D.A. (1994) Abuse of the drug metaphor in psychotherapy process-outcome research, *Clinical Psychology Review,* 9, 521–543.

Toukmanian, S.G. and Rennie, D. (eds) (1992) *Psychotherapy Process Research: Paradigmatic and Narrative Approaches,* London: Sage.

Truax, C. (1966) Reinforcement and non-reinforcement in Rogerian psychotherapy, *Journal of Abnormal Psychology* 71(1), 1–9.

Wachtel, P.L. (1991) From eclecticism to synthesis: towards a more seamless psychotherapy integration, *Journal of Psychotherapy Integration* 45, 709–720.

Wampold, B.E. (2001) *The Great Psychotherapy Debate: Models, Methods and Findings,* Hillside, NJ: Erlbaum.

Weerasekera, P. (1995) *Multiperspective Case Formulation,* Florida: Krieger.

Chapter 9

Integrative formulation in practice

A dynamic, multi-level approach

Rudi Dallos and Jacqui Stedmon

Formulating and the therapeutic relationship

We concluded in the last chapter that formulating is an active process in clinical work. It is an interactive, vibrant and fluid activity during which we start to get to know and engage with the uniqueness of our clients. In this chapter we will suggest that this view offers a basis for conceptualising the process of integrative formulation, and that the formation, maintenance and development of the therapeutic relationship is at the core of this dynamic process. Formulation can thus be seen as occurring through a number of central processes.

1 Focusing on the beliefs, feelings and stories of the client.
2 Attending to the nature of the interactions between the client/s and therapist.
3 Considering the external factors influencing our client/s, for example their family context.
4 The therapist processing personal beliefs and feelings as the interview unfolds.

The different therapeutic models arguably make relative contributions to each of these components, allowing for various integrative combinations. For example, CBT, psychodynamic, narrative, PCP and attachment perspectives can all contribute to 1; systemic, attachment and psychodynamic perspectives particularly contribute to 2; narrative and systemic models are particularly weighted toward 3; and psychodynamic, attachment, PCP and systemic perspectives toward 4.

We shall employ a piece of transcript to illustrate the process of formulating 'in action' as a therapeutic interview progresses. Using this we hope to show how different models can be woven into a moment-by-moment dynamic process of formulating 'in the moment' as well as building up over-arching formulations. We shall then exemplify how integrative formulating happens in this process by describing our attempt at developing an integrative model which combines attachment, systemic and narrative perspectives. Of course it is equally possible to consider our extract through the lens of different integrative combinations of models.

As already pointed out, formulating is not simply an intellectual activity but a subjective and interpersonal one, as we interact with our clients within a dynamic social context. It is not merely about collecting facts in a rational 'objective' manner, but rather takes place within the context of an *evolving therapeutic relationship.* The therapist must stay attuned to clients' levels of engagement, pacing the flow of communication to scaffold new meanings, avoiding ruptures to the working alliance and responding sensitively to signs of distress. The act of formulating therefore requires 'use of self' and has considerable overlap with reflective practice (Stedmon and Dallos, 2009); formulating then is not a dispassionate process, but a passionate one!

Another important link with reflective practice is that formulating, in the sense of formulation-as-a-process, occurs *in the moment* as well as offering meanings *about the moment.* Indeed therapeutic work, by its very nature, requires us to formulate in the heat of the moment, making spontaneous clinical decisions as we respond in the here and now to the client's feedback during the flow of our interactions. For example, the questions we ask, the topics that we decide to pursue, and conversely what we choose not to ask or deliberately avoid, our hesitations, pauses and emotional reactions can all be seen to constitute micro-formulations which may be part of a wider over-arching formulation. This process can also be described as 'assessment', but we suggest that the questions we ask, and the paths we choose to explore with clients, are in fact guided by such micro-formulations unless we attempt to stick extremely rigidly to a pre-determined assessment protocol.

As we proceed, our conversations and interactions with a client, family or team may be peppered with bursts of feelings, or momentary intrusions of thoughts, memories and visual images that connect with our own experiences. Indeed the process of formulating is a multi-sensory activity and we access information at the verbal–semantic levels of representation as well as the non-verbal, *procedural* and embodied, emotional levels. In short, when we work therapeutically we are not only listening but also employing all our senses; visual, olfactory, emotional and empathetic mentalisation, and reflection. Arguably, it is perhaps only later, for example during supervision, when we can reflect in a calm manner, that it is possible to develop a more theoretically informed map of formulation which forms the basis of 'the formulation-as-an-object or event', which is written up in notes, communicated to other professionals, and guides the therapist's preparation for the next clinical session. This distinction is similar to Schon's (1983) distinction between reflection 'in' action and 'on' action.

Hypothetical conversation with Jack

Since it is difficult to illustrate these experiential and dynamic features of formulating by talking *about* cases, we invite you to consider this hypothetical extract of a therapeutic/clinical interview with Jack that demonstrates how the on-going process of building a therapeutic alliance between the client and therapist is central to evolving formulations that are guided by reflexive practice (see Stedmon and Dallos, 2009). This extract is based on an edited version of a real client who had similar difficulties to Jack. We have incorporated some details of the interview with this 'real' client to indicate how in the process of formulating new information may emerge; for example, that both of Jack's parents had had problems with alcohol, contributing to the escalating patterns of violence that Jack describes.

We have not systematically offered indications of how Jack might also be formulating in this interview to produce co-constructed meanings and shared formulations. However, we do suggest some important points where he appears to be doing this.

Activity: Try to read this transcript first without looking at our commentary and notice some of your emerging ideas, explanations and feelings. What formulations begin to come to mind for you? What questions might you have added, developed or possibly excluded in order to pursue your own process of formulating? What formulations appear to be in the mind of the therapist/ interviewer?

Therapist (in bold)	Commentary: Reflections and emerging formulations
Jack, can you remember some of the times when things were difficult between your parents?	In this first question the therapist appears to be exploring the possibility (shaped by a systemic relational framework) that there were problems *between* the parents. This is adding a different slant to the dominant formulation that Jack's father was 'abusive'. He is also exploring whether Jack is able to remember some of these events or whether they have become dissociated and somatised.
Hmmm, (long pause), I mean when they were having an argument and I was quite young and erm, me and, I always tried to split them up even when I was a little kid you know, shout or whatever but it just never took effect, ever. Yeah and getting violent, that is what I call distracted and stressed really.	It is also significant here that Jack remembers trying to intervene, which could have been physically and emotionally dangerous for him.

Therapist (in bold)	Commentary: Reflections and emerging formulations
So were there violent arguments?	
Yeah quite a lot (nodding), yeah.	This reinforces a formulation that his exposure to violence associated with repeated traumatic states underlies the development of his 'psychotic' symptoms.
You mentioned that your father had been drinking quite a bit? How do you understand that?	This appears to be an attempt to explore a formulation about Jack's beliefs and his narrative about why his father was drinking heavily. Perhaps drinking was not simply due to problems in the marriage. Implicit here in the therapist's mind is the idea from an attachment perspective that drinking may be a form of self-soothing.
Well yeah just the same kind of thing really with arguing and erm drinking and I didn't really register that drinking was kind of, like a, er you know, a tool for burying your head or that I just thought it was normal but then I kind of put two and two together in my later years.	Here Jack appears to offer a formulation that drinking may have served the function of helping his father to manage his emotions. *Next the therapist might explore through further questions a formulation (jointly developing with Jack) about the role that alcohol plays in offering emotional comfort or avoidance of distressing feelings. This hypothesis draws on an attachment model linking how feelings are managed through different attachment strategies – (see ANT final section). However, going down such a potentially emotional pathway for Jack may require a judgement about the safety and trust provided by the therapeutic relationship. Is it too early to take this risk?*
Was it always your father who drank or did anyone else drink as well, your mother?	This starts to explore a formulation that there may be some systemic processes in the family around drinking, introducing the possibility that his father is not simply to blame for all the problems; another formulation may be that drinking was a form of coping with painful feelings shared by the parents.
Yes, she did quite a bit as well. Drinking is always, when she drinks there's always normally an argument (hand gestures) two and two must be connected.	Here Jack starts to consider a connection between his mother's drinking and the onset of arguments. In moving his hands he may be unconsciously remembering the physical violence, in a relatively unprocessed form, stored perhaps as embodied memories. The therapist may register these gestures as a sign that Jack is emotionally aroused in this process of recall. *A rapid clinical decision must now be made by the therapist. The next sequence could move onto encouraging Jack to make semantic, reflective connections contributing to the emerging process of collaborative formulating but this may be harder if he is in an emotionally aroused state. Possibly at this point the therapist instead responded to non-verbal emotional communication and decided (perhaps intuitively) to explore Jack's feelings instead.*

Therapist (in bold)	Commentary: Reflections and emerging formulations
Can you remember a specific time when that happened?	The therapist here is possibly attempting to focus on a specific situation in order to assist Jack in teasing out what the sequence of events were that triggered violence between his parents. Attachment theory also attends in detail to individual recall of traumatic episodic events, so this question draws on the therapist's conceptual knowledge base.
Yeah when they were just fighting quite a few of them and it was always in the kitchen, or the living room, always downstairs (sigh ... pause) Yeah just the same thing, arguing, fighting, drunk, drink fuelled violence.	Jack locates the time and place and as he gives the details his language shows a rhythmic, depressed-sounding repetitive listing. The same thing, arguing, fighting, drunk. He has also moved into the present, possibly indicating his emotional pre-occupation and the bubbling up of traumatic memories.
How old were you at the time?	This factual question may reflect the therapist attuning to Jack's emotional state and taking care to monitor the pace of further exploration. This straightforward question allows space for Jack to decide whether he is ready to talk more about these memories. However, the question simultaneously implies a formulation about the impact that witnessing these events might have had on Jack at a potentially vulnerable age. *The therapist might have reflected on the moment, explicitly inquiring how Jack is feeling and reassuring him that he need not continue if this felt too difficult for now. This here-and-now processing in therapy helps to maintain a collaborative framework and may guard against rupturing the working alliance.*
Er, I can only remember it when I was, from when I was 5 or 6, yeah I can't remember being any younger than that. Yeah I wouldn't have been able to shout loud enough.	Jack clarifies and interestingly uses a little humour, 'not being able to shout loud enough' at his parents, in order perhaps to distance himself a little from the emotional intensity of these memories. *This levity may have prompted the therapist next to pursue the violence a little further, but arguably Jack's vulnerability could also have been explored by asking about what the experience might have felt like and whether he still feels so helpless now.*

Therapist (in bold)	Commentary: Reflections and emerging formulations
So can you tell me a bit more about what happened next? How often would drinking lead to violence? Was it physical? Like hitting out? Was it both of them?	Jack has already made a connection that when his mother drank it often led to violence. However, it is not clear yet what the violence was like and whether this constituted systematic abuse by his father or whether his mother was also violent. This is also a sensitive area of exploration in terms of cultural contexts, inequality between the genders and male oppression. In the process of therapy the therapist may be aware of a core dilemma for Jack. Already he has indicated that he might have felt frightened and one possible formulation is that he feared that his father would hurt his mother. This certainly seems to be Jack's and the family's dominant formulation about his father's behaviour. However, this leaves Jack potentially confused and conflicted if he feels some loyalty to his father, or even thinks that maybe his mother was jointly responsible for the violence. The therapist must tread a delicate balance, neither wishing to indirectly support or condone 'abusive' behaviour through a systemic formulation of the relationship being out of control nor assuming the contrasting formulation of abusive behaviour by his father.
I can't exactly remember how often they would fight but it became like normal, it wasn't a surprise if there was an argument. At least two times a week. Yeah I'm sure it was that regular, I could be wrong but it wasn't once a month and it wasn't once every two weeks. When it did become violent it was, yeah it was really quite upsetting. My mum would normally, it varied, my mum would sometimes hit my dad when she's drunk and then obviously then (sigh) I dunno then my dad would hit her back, and I kind of thought, that's bad. I don't know, her hitting him is bad but I don't know because she was drunk, so I didn't really know or kind of blame him because she's you know hitting him in face, doing this, doing that, and you know it kind of reaches a point where it can't go any further or it's going to get really out of	Jack starts to suggest that the fighting assumed 'normality' in his life. Jack appears to be formulating the violence in different ways, including provocation by his mother and the unjustifiability of male to female violence. He also appears to struggle with attributing responsibility and blame, oscillating between seeing the violence as wrong and upsetting and developing a competing formulation in which violence is minimised as 'making mistakes' and 'not really beating'.

Therapist (in bold)	Commentary: Reflections and emerging formulations

hand and then sometimes my dad would. (pause) People make mistakes. Sometimes he would be hit, and then he would hit mum, it would never be like really beating it wouldn't be beating, it would be a slap in the face, or a slap on the back, it wouldn't be punching or headlock, pushing yeah a lot of pushing, grabbing hold. It would start from pushing; sometimes like out of the blue a slap in the face, or something like that.

Where were you when this was happening ? How did it make you feel? Can you remember what you did?

In asking this question the therapist is exploring a formulation that Jack was distressed by these events, perhaps formulating that this may have influenced his later behaviours. Witnessing these events may have led him to develop an insecure attachment representation. Jack's sense of insecurity and anxiety may have contributed to his later 'problematic' behaviours. *The therapist notices that Jack has shared a lot of information now, implying that he is experiencing their relationship to be both trusting and safe, so it seems timely to explore feelings in more depth.*

Yeah I mean we (him and his sisters) wouldn't be in the same room but obviously I couldn't help myself I can't sit and watch TV and hear my mum and dad shouting their heads off and then someone go 'argh' you know and hear slapping and stuff like that. Hilary (older sister) I think she kind of tried to stop it as well, we would normally start to cry because you're seeing your mum and dad do that and that's normal to cry.

Interestingly Jack starts to talk again in the present tense: 'I can't sit and watch …' and he uses different representational systems, for example he makes the sound of violence 'Argh', slapping, makes a vivid visual reference – 'shouting their heads off'. This again suggests that he is becoming emotionally aroused by these memories but then goes on to distance himself from these memories by eventually referring to himself and his mum and dad in the third person … 'you're seeing your mum and dad do that' and then normalising this as a common reaction and 'that's normal to cry'. The therapist is formulating that this pattern of discourse indicates an avoidant attachment strategy.

So sometimes you and your sister tried to intervene to stop it? Can you remember how you felt when you did that?

In asking this question the therapist appears to be further exploring the developing formulation that being caught up in the violence between his parents has had a significant impact on Jack's current mental state.

Therapist (in bold)	Commentary: Reflections and emerging formulations
I think I was pretty upset and bit scared, sometimes I was crying like Carla. I said 'Please stop, don't shout at each other' but often I was so scared we just sat there and cried ...	Jack seems to again show arousal as he remembers. He goes into dialogue as if re-living the experience. *Some of the finer details such as Jack's use of the present tense may not have been consciously noted by the therapist at the time, though might have been registered at a semi-conscious level through monitoring Jack's higher level of arousal.*
Do you see any connection here between what you're describing and what you said earlier about how you were being abused but you never told your parents about it?	The therapist's question now suggests he is developing a formulation that Jack's parents may have been distracted by their own conflicts and unavailable to respond to the abuse that he subsequently experienced. *It is possible that this question was a little too ambitious at this point and Jack needs some more time to regain his calmness after talking about these distressing events.*
There could be a connection but I've never kind of thought of it. It's never come to me to think that. Could be, but ...	Jack here appears to be indicating that he has not considered this formulation previously but is willing to contemplate it. This exchange is an attempt to link the therapist's formulation with Jack's and thus test it out. It starts to indicate how a collaborative framework and formulation is gradually built up, though Jack's dominant discourse that he is 'mentally ill' might still be more influential in his thinking. The therapist must now take care gradually to co-construct alternative meanings with Jack so as not to impose his own formulation.

How different were your interpretations at various points to those suggested here? What models did you bring to looking at this transcript?

Firstly, we will make some general points about the dynamic and shifting nature of clinical work and formulating in action. In the commentary we can see some evidence of the therapist's use of conscious formulations guiding the conversation with Jack. Secondly, we can see how, perhaps in later supervision, we might reflect on some other possible formulations and consider what the therapist might have been formulating implicitly or semi-consciously. The commentary in practice was influenced by a combination of systemic, narrative and attachment perspectives, but arguably represents shared concepts from a range of models. There are likely to be some fundamental commonalities in how we think '*in action*' in therapy. Also, ideas drawn from these three models have gained a wide utilisation in the psychological map that most experienced therapists employ (see previous chapter).

In the analysis of this hypothetical conversation between Jack and his therapist we have attempted to indicate the fluid, dynamic and evolving nature of formulating 'in action'. In the moment-by-moment analysis of this conversation the therapist is continually engaged in formulating, moving between systemic/relational and individual hypotheses in an elaborate dance, caught between the emotional valence of Jack's reactions to key questions and the underlying theories that guide the following questions. Though the analysis above has focused on the therapist's formulating Jack is also actively engaged in meaning-making, each of them receiving reciprocal feedback, prompting further understanding, emotional reactions and formulations to emerge. In effect what appears to be a challenging division between individual and systemic levels of analysis conceptually, melts away as the conversation about Jack's life unfolds. This raises the question of whether the therapist here is engaged in an eclectic or conceptual form of integration. This distinction becomes blurred in practice because the responses between Jack and the therapist occur at various levels of conscious awareness. At times the therapist appears to ask questions that are consciously informed by explicit knowledge of psychological models, yet other responses feel much more empathic and attuned to Jack's emotional tone. There is movement between drawing on explicit declarative knowledge to inform questions and intuitively relying on implicit procedural knowledge to regulate and maintain the therapeutic relationship. For any approach outlined in this book it would be important to ensure that Jack is both emotionally safe and that he has sufficient cognitive resources to process any new information that particular questions elicit to build on our shared and evolving collaborative narrative. Arguably employing a psychodynamic or attachment-focused model might allow us to be more sensitive to these dual processes of communication. As therapists we need to monitor how Jack is feeling, how we are resonating with the emotional climate of our developing relationship and how this builds the potential to establish collaborative and co-constructed meaning. Subsequently we may bring our theories together to formulate 'on' what has occurred in the session and what avenues we think may be worth exploring next time.

In this chapter we set out an approach to formulation that offers a dynamic and collaborative framework, built upon a platform of established security and safety within the therapeutic relationship, and which supports clients to take risks and explore difficult memories and experiences. The Attachment Narrative Therapy Approach described below moves towards a conceptual synthesis that utilises the core psychological features of three models, systemic, narrative and attachment, retaining at its heart a recognition of the therapeutic relationship as central to both the content of formulation and the process of formulating.

Attachment Narrative Therapy (ANT) formulation

In the 'live' transcript with Jack we have illustrated how a therapist attends to the level of safety and security she is providing for her client and this creates a relational context that mirrors Bowlby's idea of a secure base. Bowlby (1973) described therapy as the process of creating a sensitive and emotionally attuned 'secure base' across the age range:

> For not only young children, it is now clear, but human beings of all ages are found to be at their happiest and to be able to deploy their talents to best advantage when they are confident that standing behind them are one or more trusted persons who will come to their aid should difficulties arise. The person trusted provides a secure base from which his (or her) companion can operate.
>
> (Bowlby, 1973: 359)

ANT builds on Bowlby's broad approach and provides a synthesis with systemic, narrative and individual models of therapy that is compatible at both a theoretical and pragmatic level. Dallos and Vetere (2009) have developed this approach into a common framework for understanding complex problems as diverse as ADHD, eating disorders, trauma and domestic violence. Importantly this model attempts a conceptual integration that is also sympathetic to the idiosyncratic attempts made by many practising clinicians to blend different approaches. Attachment Narrative Therapy (ANT) brings together models which operate at different levels: systemic (inter-personal); individual (attachment theory); and societal (narrative theory).

Integration based on a conceptual synthesis of complementary models

The starting point for ANT (Attachment Narrative Therapy) was an awareness of the conceptual overlaps between attachment, systemic and narrative models in the context of our work in the field of eating disorders and bereavement. Further to this was an awareness that in itself each model had deficiencies which could be complemented by the other. The attempted integration of the three approaches was therefore a conceptual one in that it is not merely a juxtaposing of the models but a synthesis of their central conceptualisations. The core of this synthesis relates to Bowlby's view of therapy as akin to the creation and maintenance of a secure base. We suggest further that the concept of the secure base and how this is created forms an embracing conceptualisation of these three models. Furthermore, attachment theory is in itself an integrative model in that Bowlby drew on systems theory to explain how the child and parent achieve a homeostatic emotional balance in their relationship. Subsequently, Main et al. (1985) extended attachment theory to focus on how these early experiences shape the structure and content of our individual narratives. In turn the other models extend attachment theory; systems theory moves beyond a dyadic to a triadic analysis and narrative therapies take account of the wider culturally shared narratives that shape family relationships and attachments.

Connections and differences between systemic, attachment and narrative therapeutic models

Systemic therapy

As we saw in chapter 4, systemic formulations emphasise the inter-personal nature of problems. Specifically, the formulation assumes that 'problems' serve a function in terms of the family dynamics. In addition, systemic formulations emphasise the 'here and now' current family processes that are maintaining the symptoms. Though there is an acknowledgement that problems may have been precipitated by historical events such as life cycle changes, the main focus is on current problems in achieving change. This leaves the single application of systemic models with central weaknesses.

1 It is not clear why a particular type of problem, for example, anorexia as opposed to depression or substance abuse, develops; nor why different members of the family develop their individual problems and ways of coping.
2 It is not clear how the family dynamics shape each individual family member's internal world, their feelings and beliefs.
3 Systemic formulation has less to say about the wider socio-cultural context, for example, how ideas of gender, family roles and morality shape the family processes.
4 There is a long-standing concern that systemic models, while explicitly less blaming of the individual, have in effect moved blame up one level to the family. Usually this means locating blame in the parents of the identified client.
5 Systemic models pay scant attention to the individual emotions of different family members and fail to integrate a theory of feelings alongside the predominance given to accounts of beliefs and actions.

Narrative therapies

Narrative therapies have many similarities to systemic therapies, especially in their emphasis on the importance of communication processes in therapeutic change (White and Epston 1990; Sluzki 1992; Tomm, 1988; chapters 4 and 5 this volume). Above all, they highlight the centrality of meaning in human experience, suggesting that the meanings we give to events shape our feelings and actions. Correspondingly if meanings shift, if we can see things in a 'new light', changes in feelings and behaviour will follow. Drawing on social constructionist ideas (see chapter 5), they emphasise that meanings are co-constructed in relationships and that language is the means whereby this occurs. In contrast to systemic approaches, the emphasis is on patterns of meanings, especially stories, rather than patterns of actions or behaviours in families. Vygotsky (1978) has proposed that the child learns by internalising the speech of adults around her. The child's inner world is said to be made up of conversations which later become internalised, and can include both supportive and punitive voices. In addition, through constructing narratives events are given meanings and connected over time. Bruner (1990) and Vygotsky (1978) further argued that parents provide 'scaffolding' to help their child make sense of his or her experiences. We might speculate that this process parallels the therapeutic relationships in so far as the therapist provides a scaffolding to help the client to reach new understandings. Narrative approaches stress that we strive to form coherent stories which enable us to connect events both negative and positive, to consider alternative possibilities, and to allow reflection on and integration of the events in our lives. Importantly, narrative therapy often makes use of writing as a natural medium to enable clients to organise and clarify their stories.

These aspects of narrative therapy complement systemic approaches but also share similar deficits. For example, there is very little explanation about how particular narratives develop nor of differences between stories held by the various family members. Rather, as in the systemic model, the emphasis in formulation is on describing dominant narratives that appear to actively maintain problems and to offer practical ways of altering these. One of the important ways that narrative approaches combine with systemic perspectives is in drawing attention to the wider socio-cultural contexts. Language is understood as conveying and perpetuating a range of beliefs and practices that can serve to subjugate and oppress. For example, many families are influenced by diagnostic terminology (e.g. 'ADHD' and 'depression'). Rapley et al. (2011) have developed social constructionist arguments that challenge the dominant 'medicalisation of misery' in Western cultures. Indeed these wider culturally shared ideas or discourses about mental illness and organic causes of problems are taken on by the family and individual family members and can profoundly influence and shape its dynamics. Narrative therapy also addresses how these same discourses may shape the treatment and provision of services, such as specialist ADHD clinics or running compassionate mind groups for people with 'borderline personality disorder'. One of its key aims is to help clients to resist the negative aspects of such labels which they often accept for themselves. In effect, narrative therapy aims to assist individuals and families to 're-formulate' their problems in less self-denigrating ways.

People vary in the extent to which they can link their experiences in detailed and coherent narratives. This has been termed *'narrative skill'*; a complex ability which is fostered and built by the ways that parents talk with their children (McAdams, 1993; Habermas and Bluck, 2000). Clinically this is an important issue since it is evident that narrative therapy requires a skill and sophistication with language that some people do not possess. The formulation needs to take this into account and to consider an educative or skill-acquisition component to the therapy; or else other forms of therapy may be indicated until these abilities become more established.

Attachment theory

John Bowlby's (1988) attachment theory consists of an integration of theories in that it incorporates a mixture of ideas from psychodynamic (object relations) theory, systems theory, cognitive neuro-science (representational systems – working models) and the naturalistic observations of animal behaviours. He argued that like other species, young human beings have an evolutionarily based instinct to seek safety and comfort from their parents when confronted with danger. Parents are said to respond to their child's need for comfort in a variety of ways which shape important aspects of the child's internal world. Specifically, where parents respond in a predictable and reassuring way the child develops a sense of the world as secure and of themselves as worthy of love and comfort. Where the parents respond reluctantly or inconsistently, make the situation less safe or are themselves a source of danger, infants are likely to develop a view of the world as unsafe and of themselves as unworthy and not good enough.

Attachment theory was initially based on natural observation of children who had been separated from their parents, and later on the systematic observation of structured parent–child separations in the 'Strange situation' research paradigm (Ainsworth, 1989). This led to the classification of attachment behaviours displayed by children into three patterns: secure, avoidant, and anxious/ambivalent. Bowlby (1969) proposed that the child's experiences become held as a 'working model', a set of beliefs or stories about fear, comfort, their parents and themselves (Main et al., 1985; Crittenden, 1998). This was developed to reveal that defensive processes are indicated in 'how' people speak about their early and current family experiences. Broadly differences in defensive processes employed are summarised as follows:

Secure – able to use both emotional and cognitive information to make sense of past experiences, and able to access memories of both negative and positive events with an ability to reflect on these experiences and integrate them.

Dismissive – this corresponds to the avoidant patterns with infants and is characterised by accounts in which feelings are minimised, and the style deployed is overly rational and semantic. There is little access to early memories; painful memories and rejections from parents are particularly shut down and there may be an idealising of the parents along with a dismissing of the self, 'I am not good enough'.

Preoccupied – this corresponds to the anxious/ambivalent pattern found with infants. The transcripts show an over-concern with feelings, little ability to connect events in a coherent way, blaming of others for problems, with a pre-occupation with the self.

Mixed/disorganised – Many people who, like Jack, have experienced abuse and traumatic events exhibit a complex mixture of both the insecure strategies. This can sometimes involve a rapid switching from one to the other, often accompanied by powerful bursts of feelings. Although these might seem like chaotic or dysfunctional strategies, they are frequently attempts to manage confusing emotional dilemmas in their lives.

Attachment theory therefore fills some of the key deficits in systemic and narrative approaches in that it offers a developmental account of the emergence of family patterns, the shaping of the child's internal world, and the development of narrative skills. However, like systemic approaches, it does not centrally focus on the wider socio-cultural contexts. To take an example; the development of girls and boys may differ in families due to cultural expectations of how they 'should' learn to deal with danger. Likewise, there may be broader cultural differences in what are seen as appropriate ways of expressing distress and expectations of comfort (Crittenden, 1998). Attachment theory places emphasis on historical rather than current interactional processes. Arguably, patterns of attachments are maintained not just by the internalisation of past experiences with parents but also by adult, ongoing relationships with them and other intimate partnerships.

ANT formulation for Jack

This consists of weaving together the three models presented above by taking account of their contributions to the individual, inter-personal and socio-cultural levels of analysis. Though the models operate at different levels of analysis regarding the view of the origins of the problems, these different perspectives can be considered to provide an overall integrative framework. This rests on the conceptualisation that individual experience (Jack's as an example) is influenced by the nature of the family dynamics and these in turn are influenced by wider cultural factors. Also family dynamics are shaped by the individual features of each member of the family. The ANT approach attempts to offer an explanation of how features of the different models, operating at different levels can be inter-woven:

- *Individual.* This includes the ways in which early experiences in the family serve to shape emotionally valenced beliefs about the availability of others to offer support, and feelings of self-worth. Importantly this includes an emphasis on the form and structure of the stories that people hold about these experiences.
- *Inter-personal.* This includes an analysis of both historical and current patterns of relating in families which shape the child's or adult's beliefs and feelings, and those of his or her parents. The shaping and maintaining of current patterns of actions and the attempts that families make to solve their difficulties will also be considered.

- *Socio-cultural.* This consists of an exploration of wider culturally shared beliefs and expectations and the ways in which they influence the ideas that family members hold about 'appropriate' ways of relating and dealing with distress and conflicts.

Jack

ANT formulation attempts to connect all three levels of analysis. However, the guiding focus is on the narratives, in the broader sense of stories which constitute both meanings and emotional states, and which shape our choices about actions.

In practice the ANT formulation of Jack revolves around these three core concepts:

- That his past and current attachment experiences shape how he manages distress, including his ability to place these experiences into narratives.
- That the meanings he holds about these experiences are crucial, and that re-storying these can help him to think about the past, himself, and the future in different ways.
- That the narratives that Jack and his family hold take place within a wider social-cultural context, which can include ideas about attachment and gender expectations and cultural differences about emotional expressiveness.

Centrally, it might be possible to help Jack and his family to think about his father in a less negative way. It often turns out in such cases that the abuser has himself experienced abuse. This might help Jack to see his father's actions as less personally motivated towards him. A revision of his story about these events could help him to develop some different attachment narratives which might free him from his overwhelming sense of inadequacy and rejection. ANT, in short, gives a greater weight in formulation to meaning-making and our power to 're-story' the past than is typically the case either in attachment theory alone or early systemic formulations.

Central to an attachment analysis is a consideration of the patterns of actions in families, particularly how they deal with danger, threat and anxiety. Jack has clearly faced many dangers, both within and outside the family. He had both witnessed and also been the victim of domestic violence. It is extremely confusing and distressing for a young child when the people who are supposed to offer comfort and support are instead sources of danger. This is likely to generate very ambivalent feelings, especially in regard to seeking protection and comfort. It is likely that Jack came to understand that his father was dangerous and his mother not available because she too was distressed and frightened. Although he might have understood his mother's situation, he would also have felt angry and resentful at not being looked after and comforted as he needed.

A typical attachment strategy in such situations is for a child to attempt to become a 'carer', to sacrifice his own needs and try to look after his parents instead. This strategy could also have helped to alleviate the guilt he felt for feeling resentful and angry towards his mother for not looking after him, even though intellectually he knew why she was unable to do this. The fact that he was such a 'good' boy at school, well-liked, talented and sociable suggests that he was superficially quite successful in covering up, to the outside world at least, the distress and fear experienced at home. This pattern of pleasing is described as 'false affect' and is a typical component of a role-reversal, 'compulsive care-giving' (Crittenden, 1998). It is likely that this pattern became more deeply entrenched when Jack's father left as he would have become the 'man of the house'. Jack, his mother and sisters would likely have been deeply worried about how they would cope emotionally and financially. In this situation the need to be a 'good' and helpful boy who did not worry his mother with his own problems might have become ever more important.

Attachment theory suggests that the nature of the internal model (set of core beliefs and emotions) that is likely to develop from such family experiences might include the following:

- My family is not safe.
- I cannot rely on my parents to protect and comfort me.
- One of my parents (if not both) is a source of danger.
- I need to try to please and look after my parents, and perhaps they might argue less if I do.
- The only person I can rely on is myself.
- Talking is dangerous and leads to violence.
- I should try not to think about my parents' actions or my own needs.

These thoughts are not necessarily conscious but are likely to be manifest in how Jack behaves, including his style of talking about himself and events in his family. To categorise Jack's attachment 'style' runs the danger of over-simplification, but on the other hand it can provide us with a starting point for our thinking about his potential needs and ways of emotional coping. A formulation which includes reference to some features of attachment styles may be helpful as long as we hold these as propositions or hypotheses rather than absolutes. For example, we can see some aspects of an 'avoidant' pattern of shutting down feelings and not talking, as well as signs of compulsive care-giving and self-reliance in the transcript. However, this may have changed as Jack became older and experienced extreme forms of distress and abuse. Furthermore, although this strategy may have been effective earlier, it did not seem to work so well later on since it did not halt the violence, the divorce or the abuse that Jack experienced. Taking the Saturday delivery job may have been Jack's attempt to 'care for' and help his family; but this action in itself led to further abuse. Subsequently, Jack may have adopted an increasingly anxious/ambivalent approach. At its extreme this leads to a sense of deep distrust in others which might come to be labelled as a 'paranoid' style of relating, characterised by a pre-occupation with the past, current and future potential dangers. It is possible that Jack has developed a mixed strategy of oscillating from one insecure attachment pattern to the other, neither of which is effective, so that he eventually abandons both strategies and becomes 'ill'. This may help to resolve his attachment dilemma of trying to please and be 'good' while also being pre-occupied with feelings of anger, hurt and resentment.

An ANT approach takes this basic attachment formulation further by considering how the family constellation shapes the ways that Jack made sense of, or processed, events in his life. Specifically, Jack's 'narrative skills' may have been under-developed. It is quite likely that he had little experience of his parents discussing difficult feelings, problems and dangers in a calm and contained manner. Rather, he appears to have witnessed escalating interactions, possibly with angry shouting, accusations and threats leading to physical violence. Most likely, Jack would have developed a sense of language and communication as untrustworthy and dangerous, particularly where intense feelings are involved, rather than a safe vehicle for conveying comfort and resolving problems. Jack would therefore be less likely to communicate about such matters and also less able to make sense of events internally to develop a reflective and coherent story about his life. During relatively safe periods of their life youngsters may be able to function reasonably adequately with this pattern, but for Jack a series of life events continued to be very dangerous and unsafe. Jack's vulnerability would leave him swept around by emotional currents with little opportunity to integrate and resolve conflicting feelings and events. He might stay locked in his current ways of attempting to solve his emotional problems, for example, through denial of his needs, self-destruction, paranoia and anger.

This pattern may also have made Jack vulnerable to people who appeared to show him affection and care, possibly contributing to him becoming the victim of sexual abuse, since Jack may have learned to minimise signs of danger as a way of trying to cope within his family. Subsequently it seems that he was unable to confide in his mother. Keeping this to himself may have increased his sense of shame and distress to the point where he resorted to managing his feelings with drugs and alcohol. In Jack's case, this was more about self-medication than thrill-seeking.

It is interesting to note that alcohol and barbiturates have the effect of shutting down cognitive, analytical and semantic processing and leave the person, initially at least, in a kind of warm emotional glow. However, such a state is unlikely to lead to insight. For a young man like Jack without the education and drive to engage in productive, integrative activities, drugs would leave him increasingly emotionally numb and could also prompt psychotic or paranoid reactions. An ANT formulation would suggest that this may be because drugs strip away the defensive strategy of actively avoiding painful thoughts of danger, abandonment, lack of comfort and rejection. Without practice in experiencing and integrating such thoughts and images these can become overwhelming, leading to feelings of terror and paranoia. While experimenting with drugs it is unlikely that Jack was able to access comforting and reassuring conversations with his parents to make the bad images, feelings and thoughts he was having more manageable.

Attachments and systemic processes

Attachment theory and systemic theory share an emphasis on examining patterns of interactions in families and considering how presenting problems may be 'functional' responses to the dynamics. We suggest that there are family attachment styles as well as individual ones. This fits with systemic theory; for example the structural family therapy concepts of enmeshed and disengaged families corresponds to ambivalent/pre-occupied and avoidant/dismissive attachment styles (Hillburn-Cobb, 1996). Systemic approaches, though, emphasise current maintaining patterns as well as historical ones. Jack's emotional pain and patterns of reaction were not just historical; he was in the care of mental health agencies and had been 'rejected' by his family on the grounds that he was now a source of danger to them. From being a child *in* danger he was now perceived as a *dangerous person by his* family. His worries that his sister might be raped by Robbie Williams were seen not as an indication of concern but a sign of madness. His use of medication to deal with uncontrollable feelings and his inability to communicate about problems, however, are almost certainly not just *his* tendency but fit with an ongoing family pattern. It would be interesting to know more about how his sisters and mother coped with distress; perhaps his mother's solution was also to use medication. Thus, the family pattern of avoiding difficult issues and feelings had arguably escalated to the point where Jack, like his father before him, had to leave. Difficult feelings in the family appear to be solved either by the use of medication or exiting. A summary of some key features in the family patterns is suggested opposite (see Figure 9.1).

This analysis suggests that it remains difficult for the members of Jack's family to look after each other. It is not clear how his sisters are coping; they may have been able to find sources of support outside of the family. This may be more difficult for Jack because his fear of danger has extended from his family to the outside world. However, most likely his sisters may also be vulnerable and prone to cope in similar ways to Jack in the face of major threats, losses or abandonments. In fact part of the family's anger towards Jack may be because he is raising painful and difficult memories which in effect

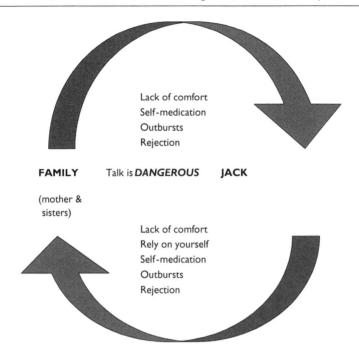

Lack of comfort
Self-medication
Outbursts
Rejection

FAMILY   Talk is *DANGEROUS*   **JACK**

(mother &
sisters)

Lack of comfort
Rely on yourself
Self-medication
Outbursts
Rejection

Figure 9.1 Family patterns, attachments and narratives

challenge the family style of forgetting, denying and dismissing distressing events and feelings.

Cultural contexts and narratives

Jack's case is clearly coloured by a number of important socio-cultural factors. To start with, his family may share a common discourse about the appropriate ways for men and women to express distress and receive comfort. These expectations are often less gender differentiated for infants but become increasingly so with approaching adolescence. Typically, boys may be expected to restrain their displays of fear and distress and to become more emotionally independent (Crawford and Unger, 2004). For many young men the process is complicated by the absence of a father from whom they can learn masculine ways of expressing feelings. In Jack's case his father was not only absent but had himself been a source of distress and danger. Jack may have become increasingly confused about how to express his feelings in a female household; in this way the cultural imperatives may have aggravated the existing reluctance to discuss feelings and needs in the family. Jack's family would no doubt also be influenced by Italian cultural norms, for example a greater acceptance of emotional expression but within the context of a 'macho' culture.

Consequently, Jack's feelings find an outlet indirectly through, for example, seeing his father's face in the mirror.

Psychiatric care may feed into these family patterns by offering management mainly through medication, thereby reinforcing the family's avoidance of feelings and locating the cause of the problems in a medical/ organic discourse; Jack is suffering from an 'illness' or 'psychotic disorder'. Jack is said to be relatively uncommunicative with his carers and is not engaging in therapy. However, he does comply with his medication which may indicate that he has accepted the powerful and prevalent discourse of a mental illness. This in turn will serve to reinforce the attachment problems that he and his family are experiencing.

Integration

One of the key features of an ANT approach is that the formulation is based both on the *content* and the *process* of the interactional dynamics and conversations in Jack's family. This requires that the therapist is able to observe and participate in interactions in Jack's family. Individual meetings with family members may offer some indication of the family dynamics but a meeting with the family is also central to the mechanisms of change. This would facilitate gaining information on which to base a systemic formulation regarding their dynamics. The interaction between the family and therapist importantly establishes a secure and safe emotional base from which both the therapist and family members can collaboratively engage in reformulating, supporting shift and change in their co-constructed narratives. Systemic family therapy emphasises a distinction between the content and process (relational patterns) in the family which is paralleled in ANT which attends to the content and process of their problematic narratives.

Interpreting transcripts of sessions serves as an aid to an integrative formulation. If other models in this book had similar opportunity to access the process of therapy some common interpretations might be revealed. However, even without transcripts it is possible to attend to the indicators of defensive processes in therapeutic conversations.

The hypothetical conversation between Jack and his therapist reveals some patterns in his narratives. For example, Jack slips into the present tense: 'I couldn't help myself, I *can't sit* and watch', indicating that he has become aroused and is re-living the abuse (a marker of a pre-occupied strategy). In contrast in describing the violence he says, 'We would normally start to cry because *you're* seeing *your* mum and dad do that and that's *normal* to cry'. Here he uses distancing language ('you, your') and says crying is 'normal' to disconnect himself from the painful feelings being aroused (dismissive strategy). It is interesting to note that he has the potential for using both these strategies in a more constructive manner if he were able to integrate them by becoming more aware of how he switches from one to the other since securely attached individuals are typically able to utilise both strategies in balance. In effect he has access to both his cognitions and feelings, and this can become a potential for growth. Perhaps Jack also has some resilient qualities; staff 'like' Jack because he is able both to show an interest in topics like music and at times also shows his feelings and vulnerability. In Jack's case both his cognitions about music and his feelings were at extremes some of the time on the unit.

Familiarity with the techniques for interpreting discourse markers indicating attachment style as summarised earlier, including some training in AAI analysis, would be a helpful future development for therapists using an ANT approach. We do not know how Jack talks about his experiences and current situation but it is possible that he has, as suggested earlier, tried to cope by shutting down his feelings and trying to look after other people's feelings. In attachment terms Jack is showing a mixed strategy whereby his avoidant-dismissive style of coping is breaking down and frightening, paranoid thoughts are intruding into his consciousness. Possibly, for Jack to talk about his feelings and experiences rather than shutting them down, will require considerable reassurance and learning. In fact it may be that the pain of his intrusive thoughts and feelings persuades him to even more extreme avoidance through obliterating his feelings with drugs as his only available solution.

Implications for interventions

ANT therapy has many similarities to systemic therapy. It can be conducted with the family and involve live supervision. In Jack's case this might be difficult initially since the family may be anxious or resistant to meeting together. A starting point might be to meet with the women in the family and to explore their views of the problems and attachment issues, including their relationship with Jack and with his father. This might be complemented by individual work with Jack, as illustrated in the earlier transcript. It would be helpful if these two strands of therapy could be integrated. In our experience it can be very helpful if the client's individual worker joins some of the family meetings (obviously with the client's permission) and this can pave the way to the whole family being seen together. The therapy is not time-limited and follows a similar path to systemic family therapy in holding family meetings at intervals of two to three weeks. Typically trans-generation processes would be explored, for example the nature of mother's own relationships with her parents, the patterns of parenting, attachments and comfort, and how these might impact on current family relationships.

There may, of course be cases where family meetings are not possible. An ANT approach could also be used in individual work with Jack, although it would be important to keep the family context in mind and discuss this during the sessions. It may also be feasible to have some contact with family members, for example by phone or e-mail, even when they are physically separate. ANT encourages us to reflect on the attachments that Jack might be making with the professionals with whom he is involved. Often young people like Jack are involved with a succession of different professionals with little recognition of how this prevents positive attachments from developing. Secure relationships are essential for Jack to be able to experiment with different ways of managing his attachment needs through talking and sharing his feelings to help him face up to the demons in his life.

The context in which we practise

A central consideration of the ANT approach, and arguably for all models, is the idea that formulation necessarily happens within social contexts (see Figure 9.2). This shapes the process in two important ways. Firstly, formulation is grounded in a variety of discourses or ideologies in terms of how psychological problems are defined (e.g. as individual deficits or symptoms of an illness). More generally the cultural context regulates what is seen as 'normal', 'legitimate' and 'appropriate' forms of thoughts, feelings and actions in contrast to what is deviant and not acceptable. These cultural frames inevitably influence the activities of therapists and counsellors since we are subject to laws and ethics of the society in which we work, irrespective of whether we agree with them.

Secondly there are structural realities about which services are available and how they are organised. In reality formulation must take account of wider structural constraints, such as funding restrictions on the types of treatments and number of sessions provided. For example, child services typically have an upper age limit of 18 years before young people are transitioned to adult services. In formulating about young people we would be foolish not to take the implications of this arbitrary cut-off into account.

Figure 9.2 also helps to summarise the process of *formulating* illustrated in the extract from the conversation with Jack. In particular we can see the recursive dynamic process whereby the therapist pays attention to the relationship in order to pace and time the questions, gauging when Jack might be ready to hear a new perspective or tolerate a submerged feeling to surface. We could also consider how Jack might himself be formulating through this process. Perhaps a pertinent example is Jack's response to the simple question:

THERAPIST: How old were you at the time?
JACK: Er, I can only remember it when I was, from when I was 5 or 6, yeah I can't remember being any younger than that. *Yeah I wouldn't have been able to shout loud enough.*

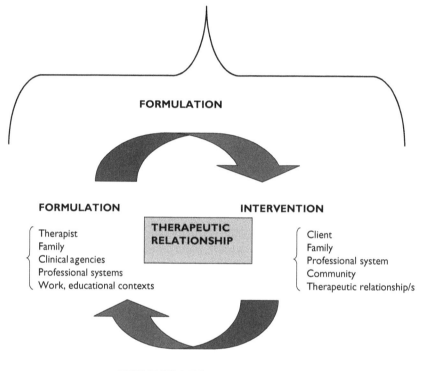

CULTURAL CONTEXT

Discourse: beliefs, expectations, social norms, views of problems

Structure: finance, available service, status, inequalities

FORMULATION

FORMULATION	**THERAPEUTIC RELATIONSHIP**	**INTERVENTION**
Therapist		Client
Family		Family
Clinical agencies		Professional system
Professional systems		Community
Work, educational contexts		Therapeutic relationship/s

REFORMULATION

Feedback: **As the relationship develops, client/s may trust the therapist more, reveal more, feel better understood → increased collaborative, reflective formulation**

Figure 9.2 A contextual dynamic view of integrative formulation

This allusion to his own vulnerability might lead us to consider that Jack believes his therapist is interested in him, is asking relevant questions and can be trusted with his feelings. This captures the essence of the idea that therapy develops through providing a secure base from which new ideas can be explored. Formulating in practice guides the therapist to ask questions that provide a safe scaffold for further information to be revealed so that a more meaningful narrative can be co-constructed with Jack. The emotional tone in Jack's response also suggests that he is ready to trust the therapist with his feelings of vulnerability and is perhaps asking both for acknowledgement and some comfort around the distress he felt as a child and may be re-experiencing in the present conversation.

Summary

In this chapter we have emphasised the idea of formulation-as-a-process, *formulating*, and seeing how it is inextricably linked in practice to the construction and maintenance of the therapeutic relationship. We have illustrated what a dynamic view of formulating looks like and the process of formulating 'in' action with the client as well as 'on' action. Is this sufficient to offer a framework for an integrative model? Our suggestion is that potentially this is an important step in the direction of generating an overarching integrative framework. By exploring the transcript of Jack and his therapist in conversation we have suggested that the collaborative process of therapy 'in' action necessary involves an integrative stance that emphasises beliefs, feelings and meanings of the clients, a focus on the nature of the interactions between the client/s and therapist and consideration of the external factors influencing our client'/s, for example their family context. It also emphasises a reflexive approach with the therapist attending to her own beliefs, feelings and meanings as the interview unfolds.

We suggest that therapeutic formulation is inevitably integrative in that all models draw to some extent on other models in order to include these common factors. However, we can take a further step in specifying how the different models can be linked together to offer an integrative framework. This integration, as discussed in the previous chapter, may be eclectic or a conceptual synthesis. We have described ANT, an attempt at a conceptual integration, and have emphasised that a significant contribution of this model is to indicate how formulation at the relational/systemic level can be combined with a more individually focused narrative and attachment framework.

ANT is just one example. Arguably different combinations of models can be considered though we do argue that there is an important conceptual difference between models which locate problems within, as opposed to between, individuals. To be specific, we suggest that integrative models need to contain systemic/relational components combined with a choice of different intra-psychic approaches.

Key characteristics of integrative formulation

- Formulation can be regarded as a fluid dynamic process which is best conceptualised as a verb – *formulating*.
- At the centre of this dynamic process is the co-construction of the therapeutic relationship.
- Formulating is a collaborative process and client/s and therapist construct formulations jointly.
- Different therapeutic models can be seen as contributing to this dynamic and collaborative process.

- An approach which draws on attachment, narrative and systemic models (ANT) provides one possible model of how different approaches can contribute to this over-arching integrative framework.

References

Ainsworth, M.D.S. (1989) Attachment beyond infancy, *American Psychologist*, 44: 709–716.
Bowlby, J. (1969) *Attachment and Loss, vol. 1*, London: Hogarth Press.
——(1973) *Attachment and Loss, vol. 2: separation, anxiety and anger*, London: Hogarth Press.
——(1988) *A Secure Base*, London: Routledge.
Bruner, J.S. (1990) *Acts of Meaning*, Cambridge MA: Harvard University Press.
Crawford, M. and Unger, R. (2004) *Women and Gender*, New York: McGraw Hill.
Crittenden, P. (1998) 'Truth, error, omission, distortion, and deception: the application of attachment theory to the assessment and treatment of psychological disorder' in M.C. Dollinger and L.F. DiLalla (eds) *Assessment and Intervention Across the Life Span*, London: Lawrence Erlbaum.
Dallos, R. and Vetere, A. (2009) *Systemic Therapy and Attachment Narratives: Applications across Diverse Settings*, London: Routledge.
Habermas, T. and Bluck, S. (2000) 'Getting a life: the emergence of the life story in adolescence', *Psychological Bulletin*, 126(5): 748–769.
Hillburn-Cobb, C. (1998) 'Adolescent-parent attachments and family problem-solving styles', *Family Process* 35: 57–82.
Main, M., Kaplan, N. and Cassidy, J. (1985) 'Security in infancy, childhood and adulthood: a move to the level of representation' in I. Bretherton and E. Waters (eds) *Growing Points of Attachment Theory and Research*, Monographs of the Society for Research in Child Development, 50: (1–2) Serial No. 209.
McAdams, D.P. (1993) *The Stories We Live By: Personal Myths and the Making of the Self*, New York: William Morrow.
Rapley, M., Moncrieff, J. and Dillon, J. (eds) (2011) *De-medicalizing Misery*, Basingstoke: Palgrave Macmillan.
Schon, D.A. (1983) *The Reflective Practitioner, How Professionals Think in Action*, New York: Basic Books.
Sluzki, C.S. (1992) 'Transformations: a blueprint for narrative changes in therapy', *Family Process*, 31, 217–230.
Stedmon, J. and Dallos, R. (eds) (2009) *Reflective Practice in Psychotherapy and Counselling*, Maidenhead: Open University Press.
Tomm, K. (1988) 'Interventive interviewing: Part 3. Intending to ask circular, strategic or reflexive questions', *Family Process*, 27, 1: 1–17.
Vygotsky, L.S. (1978) *Mind in Society*, Cambridge, MA: Harvard University Press.
White, M. and Epston, D. (1990) *Narrative Means to Therapeutic Ends*, London: Norton.

Chapter 10

Using formulation in teams

Lucy Johnstone

The literature on formulation generally assumes that it is a process carried out in collaboration with individuals or families, and this is how it is described and taught in textbooks and on training programmes. However, recent years have seen a growing literature on the use of formulation at a team level. Team formulation is the process of facilitating a group or team of professionals to construct a shared understanding of a service user's difficulties. Using formulation in teamwork is recommended by a number of clinical psychology professional documents such as the Health and Care Professions Council criteria (Health Professions Council, 2009), the Clinical Psychology Leadership Framework (Skinner and Toogood, 2010), the Accreditation through Partnership handbook criteria for training courses (British Psychological Society, 2010), and others. Team formulation is also discussed in the Division of Clinical Psychology (DCP) 'Good practice guidelines on the use of psychological formulation' (DCP, 2011).

In this chapter, I will summarise the current position in relation to practice and research on team formulation, and illustrate this through a hypothetical team formulation for Jack. I will then describe and discuss some of the strategies, benefits and challenges of the team formulation approach, based on my own experience of facilitating this kind of work in a range of Adult Mental Health settings. I strongly believe that such work needs to draw on a range of models in order to formulate at a sufficiently sophisticated level. As such, team formulation can be a powerful example of integrative formulation in practice (see chapters 8 and 9).

This kind of approach is more familiar in Child and Adolescent services, where systemic work is common. A version of team formulation is a central feature of systemic practice (see chapter 4). In this, family therapy teams discuss and develop formulations together and use reflecting team conversations to share them with families. In addition, some services hold regular network meetings in order to develop shared formulations with other agencies. Where appropriate, I will indicate some of the differences that may apply to team formulation work with a child like Janet.

Defining the team formulation approach

In one of the few studies looking at the practice of team formulation, Christofides et al. (2011) found that clinical psychologists in a range of Adult Mental Health settings reported a number of ways in which they attempted to introduce formulation into their day-to-day work in multi-disciplinary teams. They mainly described informal strategies such as using formulation-based thinking to make suggestions in a variety of contexts including team meetings, case presentations, ward rounds and staff training days; joint working with clients; informal conversations about clients; staff discussion groups about complex clients (often called 'reflective' or 'support' groups); supervision of team members; and in summary, generally encouraging curiosity and reflectiveness and 'chipping in' (the title of the paper) whenever they could. The term 'formulation' was not always explicitly used, but this process was seen as a first step towards introducing more structured formulation-based work: 'And we've actually got to the point now, where it's become identified as "formulation" and we are doing a team day in early September in a few weeks' time, where they are actually saying "you do us a session on formulation" ... stuff I've been doing very, very gently sort of round the edges, now it's actually got a name' (p. 2).

There are a few descriptions in the literature of more formal and explicit ways of using the team formulation approach, mainly implemented by clinical psychologists and psychiatrists. They can be broadly divided as follows.

Co-constructing a team formulation in response to a particular request

Offering to help the team to think about someone who is presenting challenges or seems 'stuck' can be valuable in its own right, and can also serve as a way of familiarising staff with the approach as a first step towards introducing regular formulation meetings for the whole team. The facilitator (psychologist or other professional) might proceed as follows:

- review the notes;
- meet with key staff in order to get a feel for the current difficulties and the staff feelings and reactions;
- draw up a tentative formulation;
- set up a meeting with the staff in order to get feedback on the formulation;
- revise the formulation into an agreed version;
- use the formulation to develop a shared intervention plan with the staff;
- share an appropriately worded version of the formulation with the service user, and incorporate his/her feedback into the plan.

Variations on this theme are described by Meaden and Van Marle (2008) in Assertive Outreach; Walton (2011) in Adult services; Ingham (2011) in Learning Disability; Dunn and Parry (1997) in CMHTs; Hewitt (2008) in a rehabilitation service; Clarke (2008) on an adult inpatient unit; and Wainwright and Bergin (2010) on an older adult inpatient ward.

Facilitating regular formulation meetings for the whole team

Models for facilitating formulation meetings for the whole team, usually weekly, have been developed by Lake (2008) with community mental health teams; Whomsley (2009) in Assertive Outreach; Down (Down 2010; Davies 2010) in a residential children's home; Kennedy (Kennedy et al., 2003; Kennedy, 2008) in an inpatient unit; Davenport (2002), Summers (2006) and Berry et al. (2009) in rehabilitation services; and Martindale (2007) in an early intervention team. In some cases where the approach was well embedded within the service, the aim was to provide a formulation for every client (e.g. Kennedy et al., 2003; Whomsley, 2009; Down, 2010).

Most of these projects used designated timeslots of up to 90 minutes. A typical format would be: review background information and reasons for referral; develop the formulation in discussion with the team; outline possible interventions; write up and disseminate the report afterwards. The facilitator's role is to reflect, summarise, clarify, encourage creativity and free-thinking and ask questions, not provide 'solutions'.

Some of the clinicians drew from a core model, often CBT (Kennedy, 2008; Ingham, 2011; Berry et al., 2009; Clarke, 2008) but sometimes psychodynamic (e.g. Davenport 2002; Martindale 2007). Others used a more integrative approach (e.g. Lake, 2008; Meaden and van Marle, 2008). This is particularly likely to be the preferred approach in work with young people, families and carers where attachment, developmental and systemic issues are foremost in clinicians' thinking (Down, 2010). Whomsley (2009) described the use of different versions of the formulation for different aspects of clients' care: engagement, risk, resources, moving on. Simple templates were often used to guide the work (e.g. Lake, 2008; Clarke, 2008; Whomsley, 2009; Davies, 2010) and were reported to help embed a shared understanding about formulation within a diverse staff group.

Integrating formulation into the work of the team and the service at every level

Although this might be seen as the ultimate aim from a formulation perspective, to date only one example exists: an ambitious project in an older people's service in Tees Esk and Wear Valleys NHS Foundation Trust (Dexter-Smith, 2010). Two hundred and sixty-five members of staff across five CMHTs, plus a young onset dementia team, care home liaison team, and four inpatient units (functional and organic) serving a population in the region of 107,600 people over 65 years of age, have been trained to implement formulation at all stages of the care pathway. Formulations are constructed with the help of a CBT-based diagram, supported by a range of materials such as crib sheets for staff, accessible documents for staff to complete with clients and families, a template to transfer the formulation to the electronic record system, and so on. Family and carers are sometimes invited to attend the formulation meetings – a decision that needs careful consideration of the pros and cons (Shirley, 2010). Psychology staff provide ongoing supervision to the teams. Craven-Staines et al.'s evaluation (2010) makes it clear that although the formulation training was received very positively, it has not been easy to implement such a large-scale culture change.

What do we know about the benefits of team formulation?

As is the case with individual formulation, this is an under-researched area. However, a small number of clinical reports, audits and qualitative studies suggest that the team approach can have benefits in addition to those attributed to the more traditional use of formulation with individuals such as clarifying hypotheses, informing the intervention, predicting difficulties and so on (see chapter 1). These benefits are (DCP, 2011):

- achieving a consistent team approach to intervention;
- helping team, service user and carers to work together;
- gathering key information in one place;
- generating new ways of thinking;
- dealing with core issues (not just crisis management);
- understanding attachment styles in relation to the service as a whole;
- supporting each other with service users who are perceived as complex and challenging;
- drawing on and valuing the expertise of all team members;
- challenging unfounded 'myths' or beliefs about service users;
- reducing negative staff perceptions of service users;
- processing staff counter-transference reactions;
- helping staff to manage risk;
- minimising disagreement and blame within the team;
- increasing team understanding, empathy and reflectiveness;
- raising staff morale;
- conveying meta-messages to staff about hope for positive change;
- facilitating culture change in teams and organisations.

(This list is based on Summers, 2006; Clarke, 2008; Lake, 2008; Kennedy et al., 2003; Onyett, 2007; Hewitt, 2008; Kennedy, 2009; Whomsley, 2009; Berry et al., 2009; Craven-Staines et al., 2010; Wainwright and Bergin, 2010; Walton, 2011; Christofides et al., 2011.) Similar benefits in terms of clarifying team communications and assumptions and revealing personal positions and prejudices have been noted by systemic family therapists (Palazzoli et al., 1980).

The clinical psychologists who were interviewed in Christofides et al. (2011) qualitative study were very enthusiastic about their use of team formulation, describing it as 'One of the most powerful tools we have.' They felt that without it, teams were 'fumbling in the dark ... because if there's no theory or structure to hang an understanding on then they're floundering with an intervention, not really knowing why it's not working' (2011: 7). Hood et al. (2013) carried out a follow-up study in which the non-psychologist staff members in these teams were interviewed, and found that they fully shared such views: '[Formulation] really, really was useful and I think just to have the head space to really think about what was happening'; 'It really should be a bit more about formulation, formulation, formulation' (2009: 9–10).

Similarly appreciative responses were made in audits and service evaluations: 'One of the most productive things on the ward'; 'Makes me more tolerant, more patient, increases empathy'; 'Afterwards the problems seemed understandable, something we could start to address' (Summers 2006: 342). Wainwright and Bergin's (2010) evaluation also suggested that staff empathy, understanding and tolerance were increased. Kennedy, Smalley and Harris's audit found 'entirely positive outcomes on all questions asked of all stakeholder groups' (2003: 23), including clients. Formulation-based consultations in a residential home for adolescents were associated with a reduction in staff sickness and overall number of significant incidents, including fewer calls to the police and charges of criminal damage. Staff comments included: 'Has enabled a greater understanding of the past experiences of the children's lives and how these experiences affect their behaviour and emotional well being' (Down, 2010: 3).

Promising qualitative results are also emerging from the project in Tees Esk and Wear (above). Staff describe a sense of emotional containment from having a framework that helps them make sense of the most distressing and challenging client presentations. A close look at individual outcomes has identified a number of complex situations where staff and managers were caught up in very emotive, resource-draining situations which changed once the formulation helped to introduce understanding and a potential way forward (Dexter-Smith, 2012, personal communication).

The list of proposed benefits in the DCP Guidelines receives some additional validation from an audit of the team formulation work of 3 psychologists based in adult mental health inpatient and CMHT settings (Hollingworth and Johnstone, 2013). The researcher re-phrased the suggested benefits into questions and asked MDT members to rate their experience of team formulation meetings in relation to each item. Using a scale of 1 (very unhelpful) to 7 (very helpful), staff rated team formulation as helpful or very helpful across all areas assessed. All of the 22 participants felt that the meetings had helped to develop a shared team understanding of a client's problems, strengths and difficulties; draw on the knowledge and skills from different professional backgrounds; generate new ideas about working with the client; develop an intervention plan; and improve risk management. They made comments such as 'Useful in planning a way forward which has given the client and professionals a sense of hope for future recovery'.

Since the DCP list of benefits overlaps with the general characteristics of good teamwork, which include having clear objectives, involving all members in team activities, reviewing performance regularly, and supporting creativity and innovation (Borrill and West, 2002), it might reasonably be assumed that formulation meetings contribute to more effective teamwork across the board.

The existing studies have also identified challenges to the team formulation approach. Psychologists described the informal team formulation role as one which was hard to define or document (Christofides et al., 2011). Non-psychologist staff often lacked the confidence to develop their own formulation work, even after training (Craven-Staines et al., 2010) implying the need for ongoing facilitation and supervision. Charlesworth (2010) reported that facing the full and often very distressing reality of clients' circumstances can leave staff feeling helpless and overwhelmed. There is a risk that the implications of the formulation meeting will not be followed through in the intervention (Wainwright and Bergin, 2010); a considerable amount of further input may be necessary to ensure that plans for complex clients remain consistent in the face of ongoing daily pressures. There is also the ever-present danger that formulation time will be eroded by other apparently more urgent crises and demands. Achieving high enough attendance to make the discussions representative and meaningful is particularly hard with shiftwork patterns in residential or inpatient settings (Down, 2010). Facilitating a formulation meeting can be challenging; the facilitator will need to draw on a wide range of skills, deal with complex group dynamics, and do a lot of 'thinking on your feet' (Shirley, 2010). The approach may be resisted by staff unless introduced with sensitivity (Christofides et al., 2011; Craven-Staines et al., 2010), and to be effective 'it must be supported by influential members of the team' (Lake, 2008: 23). In summary, 'Formulation may have most to offer if embedded as the core business of the unit, with robust links to patient care planning and to staff training' (Summers, 2006: 343).

Conflict with the predominant medical model is another potential area of difficulty. This issue will be discussed in more detail below.

Clearly, this is a promising approach which deserves further investigation. For clinicians such as clinical psychologists with a limited amount of input into teams, it seems to be an effective way of using a scarce resource to contribute to the care of service users with complex needs and to enhance the psychological thinking of the whole team (Christofides et al., 2011; Berry, 2007).

If the team formulation approach is to be adopted more widely, it is obviously important to document specific outcomes in terms such as reduction in medication use, shorter admissions, lower staff sickness rates, increased service user recovery rates, better identification and management of risks and so on. This is a gap that urgently needs filling.

A tentative team formulation for Jack can serve as a practical illustration of the implementation of this approach.

Jack: a tentative team formulation

The same caveats apply here as in the other chapters; we do not know much about how mental health professionals experienced their work with Jack. For this reason, the example of a team formulation below is very hypothetical. I have assumed that the formulation meeting on the ward included two members of the community mental health team in order to achieve consistency of approach across both settings. These are Jack's care co-ordinator, a psychiatric nurse, plus a support worker who knows Jack well. I have also assumed that all the staff are familiar with Jack's history, and that with facilitation from his psychologist, they have jointly drawn up this under-standing of his difficulties:

Jack's difficulties can be understood in the light of the fragmentation and decline of his family following his parents' divorce, coupled with his experience of violence and abuse. He witnessed and was a victim of his father's violence to the whole family, and was sexually abused as a teenager. All of these experiences will have been extremely traumatic, and are made worse by the fact that such high expectations were placed on Jack as a gifted and popular child and the inheritor of the family business. It seems that he has not been able to work through his mixed feelings about his father – someone he both misses and hates – and what this means for his own development as a man. Nor has he yet been able to disclose any details about the sexual abuse. He seems to be caught in a cycle where he is either abused or abusive, as demonstrated in the family arguments. He may use drink as both an escape and a means of self-punishment, and in this way is in danger of repeating the more damaging aspects of his father's life.

Jack's current presentation is perhaps a consequence of the overwhelming nature of these life events and the feelings of fear, betrayal, anger, guilt, shame and humiliation that they are likely to have evoked. His 'high' moods perhaps represent an escape from his difficulties, although at times he lapses back into despair. His unusual beliefs about Robbie Williams and the royalties owing to him may represent his longing for success and the regaining of everything that life has unjustly taken from him.

Jack appears to have mixed feelings about his status as a 'mental patient'. On the one hand, this devalued role is an even bigger decline from the bright future that was predicted for him, and perhaps for this reason he angrily rejects his various diagnoses. Instead of providing for his family in his father's absence, Jack is now in the position of needing care himself, something he finds hard to accept – which may explain the difficulty in engaging with him. Admission to hospital is a further step in a process that is likely to reinforce his feelings of being a flawed and hopeless failure. On the other hand, he is compliant with medication and has settled on the ward. There is a risk that the alternative 'career' and escape from the challenges of the outside world offered by the psychiatric services may come to seem like a solution to his difficulties. We should not underestimate the very real financial and employment challenges that face him and the impact these may have on his self-esteem and sense of identity.

Staff find Jack likeable but also frustrating. It is hard to get past his constant talk about music and royalties, and he has not really been able to make use of sessions with the clinical psychologist. It is easy to be sympathetic to his problems, but there is a feeling that we are not really helping him to move on, which has led to some differences of opinion about whether and when he should be discharged. In addition, staff have found it difficult to deal with the constant anxious phone calls from his sisters and mother. It is possible that some of the staff feelings reflect Jack's own dilemmas – stuck between the community and the hospital, unable either to work on the underlying traumas or to put them behind him, and torn between his own struggles and the needs of the family for whom he feels so responsible. It is important that we plan his discharge in a way that does not feel to him like a repeat of the rejection by his family, when his mother kicked him out.

On the positive side, Jack is a young man with many strengths and abilities. He enjoys the weekly music group on the ward, where he has been able to contribute constructively and make some friends. He relates well to Shabnam, his CPN, and Tony, his support worker, who has been investigating activities and accommodation options. He may feel that Tony's role makes him less of a threat, in contrast to staff who, like other powerful adults in his life, may have the means to hurt or control him. At times it is possible to distract him from his pre-occupation with Robbie Williams and encourage him to make short outings to local parks and cafes. He is lively, intelligent and full of ideas, even if they are not always realistic, and he can be very good company.

Comment on the team formulation

It can be seen that the team formulation draws from a number of models that have been presented in this book. These include core beliefs (CBT); family relationships and repeated cycles of rejection (systemic); symbolic meanings and transference/counter-transference (psychodynamic); and the social position and messages of the 'mental patient' role (narrative and social inequalities.) It also draws heavily on two bodies of knowledge that inform much current practice: attachment theory and trauma models. The formulation attempts to integrate these various models and theories *through their personal meaning to Jack* (see chapters 8 and 9.)

Intervention plan based on the team formulation

Sufficient time needs to be reserved during the meeting and/or in subsequent meetings to draw out the implications for intervention. This is a possible plan that the team might draw up based on the above team formulation:

- Write a letter to Jack summarising our thoughts and get his feedback. Reinforce the message that he needs to work actively alongside us in order to recover.
- The service needs to try to provide the consistent secure attachments that are currently missing in Jack's life. At present the ward is his main base and it is important that he withdraws in planned stages. Dr Aziz will meet Jack to negotiate a discharge date in 2–3 weeks with increasing periods of leave leading up to it. Shabnam will visit him on the ward weekly during this period.
- Jack will need a consistent core group to work with him and create a sense of trust and safety in his chaotic life. This will consist of Dr Robinson (community team consultant) in liaison with Dr Aziz (inpatient consultant), Shabnam (CPN), and Tony (support worker). Caroline (clinical psychologist) has ended her sessions with Jack by mutual agreement, but will arrange and facilitate regular formulation meetings with the core staff group.
- Tony has an important part to play as an older man who can provide a caring role model, in contrast to Jack's father and boss. Jack seems able to use this kind of low-key supportive relationship very well. Tony is helping Jack to find ways in which he can build on his interest in music, structure his days and so on. Jack may be interested in joining a self-help support group of service users who have had similar experiences.
- In preparation for discharge, Dr Robinson and Shabnam will invite Jack's family to a meeting to hear their views, try and contain their anxieties, and if possible re-build their relationship with Jack. This will need to be done very slowly and carefully, given the high degree of tension in the family. Rosie (social worker) will advise as to whether they are receiving the full range of benefits. Any help that can be offered with their finances is likely to relieve the stress on Jack.
- Shabnam will support Jack by focusing on his goals and strengths and building his self-confidence.

- Medication does not appear to be reducing Jack's unusual beliefs, but he says it calms him down and so he will continue on the same low dose.
- Jack is adamant that he does not suffer from 'paranoia' or 'delusional disorder', and his strong feelings about this are creating a barrier to working with the team. The formulation suggests that we can understand his difficulties and beliefs as a response to trauma, which may be more acceptable to him. Dr Aziz will discuss this with him.
- The general approach to Jack's unusual beliefs will be to avoid challenging them directly, although we will be open about the fact that we do not share them. Instead, we will discuss the possible meanings behind the beliefs – for example, does he feel that the world is an unsafe place? How can we make it feel safer for him? What would the royalties enable him to do, and how can he take small steps towards those goals rather than just waiting for a cheque to arrive? And so on.
- We recognise that Jack is not yet ready to work on his trauma and abuse memories, but we hope that this may change once he feels more stable and secure and has built up some self-confidence and structure in his life. At that time we will ask him whether he wishes to be referred back to Caroline. NB Shabnam will check that Jack is aware that if he discloses identifying information about his abuser, we will need to inform the child protection team.

Team formulation letter to Jack

In team formulations the main client is often, in effect, the team, who are asking for support with their own feelings and 'stuckness'. As in supervision, staff need to be able to be honest and open about their feelings but it will not necessarily be helpful or professional to share the entirety of the resulting formulation directly with the service user. In the above example, it would be upsetting for Jack to realise that some of the staff feel frustrated to the point of wanting to discharge him straight away, although from the team perspective these reactions need to be included so that they can be worked with and not simply acted out. At the same time, it is not comfortable to 'feel as if the team are talking behind the client's back' (Whomsley, 2009; 117). For these reasons, careful consideration needs to be given to which aspects of the formulation will be shared with the client and how this is to be done. One possibility is to inform the service user that when their care plan has been reviewed, the team will be sharing their thoughts and ideas with him/her in a letter and asking for feedback. The content and tone of the letter also needs to be guided by the formulation; for example, in Jack's case, direct reference to sexual abuse may feel too exposing or intrusive at this point. The letter might look something like this:

Dear Jack,

As you know, now that you have been in hospital for a while, the team has met to discuss how we understand your difficulties and how we can best help you. We would like to share our thoughts so far, and we would very much appreciate your feedback.

We know that at school you were seen as talented and popular. Life seemed to be full of promise, and you probably assumed that one day you would take over your father's business. Unfortunately, things started going badly wrong when the business ran into trouble. This led to a chain of events including your father's drinking and violence, your parents' divorce and the family's forced move to Swindon. You still miss your father, despite his behaviour, and you are deeply concerned about your family's well-being and the struggle to survive financially. It is not surprising that you found it hard to do your best at school, and that you took refuge in drug use and alcohol. However, this seems to have led to so many arguments that your mother threw you out. At this point you must have felt that you had lost everything. You were given a diagnosis of depression, but perhaps this also stands for despair, anger, guilt and a sense of failure as well.

Just as life started to improve a bit, your mother developed serious health problems. We wonder if this seemed like the final straw. It was around this time that you became very worried about Robbie Williams and the money that you believe he owes you. As you know, our view is that this is very unlikely to be true. At the same time we appreciate that given everything you have been through, it is understandable that you have been left with a feeling that the world is unsafe, and that you have been unjustly deprived of what is owing to you. Many people who have been through traumatic events develop similar kinds of fears and beliefs. Perhaps this kind of explanation might make more sense to you than a diagnosis.

We have the impression that it is very hard for you to face all the painful feelings and memories of the last 15 years. In particular, we are aware that you had some very distressing experiences as a teenager which you have not yet been able to talk about. Most people find that they need to be living reasonably stable lives and to have trusting relationships with the professionals and the team before they are able to re-visit such events and eventually come to terms with them. You and Caroline have agreed that you are not yet ready to do this work, and we respect this decision.

In the meantime, we think it is very important that you try to achieve some structure and stability in your life. We would like to help you plan for life after you leave hospital. This might include social activities and taking up some of your musical activities again. We also wonder if it would be a good idea to arrange some meetings with your family and try to overcome some of the tensions in your relationships with them.

Because of all the ups and downs in your life, we think it is very important that we can provide some consistency and continuity. You know your core team, Dr Robinson, Shabnam and Tony, quite well now and you also know the staff on Juniper Ward. We all want to support you as best we can while you re-build your life. This will take determination and persistence on your part as well as on ours, but you have many gifts and strengths and we are confident you can do it.

Best wishes,
Shabnam and the team

Reflection on the team formulation and intervention plan

It may be objected that this process simply describes good practice, and that much of it happens anyway through the CPA (Care Plan Approach) process, whereby the care co-ordinator takes responsibility for summarising and overseeing the delivery of the treatment package. To some extent this is true. However, there are many traps for a team that does not base their work on the crucial first step of an explicitly shared understanding of a service user's difficulties, based in psychological theory. In Jack's case these traps might be:

'Splitting' in the team, as half of the staff become fed up with him while the other half is tempted to try and 'rescue' him (Dunn and Parry, 1997; Meaden and Van Marle, 2008; Walton, 2011). If the former dynamic wins, Jack may be abruptly discharged – effectively thrown off the ward in the same way as he was thrown out of home. He will thus have chalked up another devastating rejection. If the latter wins, then it may become too easy for him to slide into a 'mental patient' role and abdicate responsibility for himself.

Medicalising of Jack's difficulties – an ongoing risk in any mental health setting (see below for further discussion of this issue). If there is no coherent psychological understanding of Jack's core difficulties and he does not seem to 'improve' sufficiently quickly, additional diagnoses may be suggested, along with more powerful medications. He will then be well on the way to becoming a long-term psychiatric patient, and probably one at war with the team because he disputes his diagnosis – which in turn may lead to a more coercive approach that increases his distrust and may be experienced as re-abuse.

Less dramatically, Jack may simply be offered a series of interventions which, while well-intentioned, are not part of a coherent formulation-based package and therefore do not address his central difficulties in a way that will help him to make progress. We might then see this kind of pattern:

- Problem: the medication has not reduced Jack's delusional beliefs. Solution: Increase the dose and/or try different medications. This pattern can continue for years.

- Problem: Jack has started drinking again. Solution: refer him to the drug and alcohol service. However, if this new team does not have a shared understanding of *why* Jack is drinking, he is unlikely to be able to stop, and the only effect will be to reduce the consistency of the approach by introducing yet more professionals into his life.
- Problem: Jack says he is too afraid of Robbie's minders to leave the house. Solution: ask the occupational therapist to do a graded exposure programme, i.e. taking gradual steps towards going to the shops. Unfortunately, if the nature and meaning of his core fears is not understood, Jack will not feel able to put these skills into practice.

Typically, the lack of an explicit and shared psychological formulation leads to an accumulation of diagnoses, medications and unsuccessful interventions delivered by a growing army of professionals, while Jack becomes more and more entrenched in the psychiatric system and both he and staff gradually lose hope for his recovery. The way out of this trap is not complicated – none of the interventions suggested by the team formulation is beyond the professionals' skills – but it is unlikely to happen without the crucial first step in place.

The moral is that instead of the routine psychiatric procedure of:

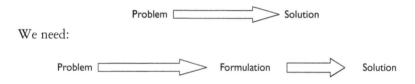

We need:

The team formulation approach is likely to be less controversial in the child primary care service attended by Janet. Typically the culture is more therapeutically-based in such settings, with the psychiatrists and other staff often having further training in family therapy. Joint working is routine, and clinicians tend to think in terms of developmental stages and systemic perspectives, although labels like 'conduct disorder' may be used. The debate about the validity of diagnoses such as 'ADHD' has been discussed at length (Timimi, 2005). Chapter 4 describes the kind of systemic formulation that might be developed for Janet within the team working with her.

Essential characteristics of a team formulation

As with individual formulation, there is no prescribed method for developing a team formulation; some of the different models have been described and referenced above. As discussed in chapter 8, the DCP (2011) checklist of good practice argues for an integrative approach based on personal meaning as the starting point for all formulations, even if simple or single-model versions are the most appropriate for particular circumstances. The kinds of difficulties that are presented to mental health teams are by definition extremely complex, and formulations are unlikely to be sufficiently sophisticated if based on one model only.

My personal checklist of aspects that should also be included in every team formulation is as follows.

Transference and counter-transference between service user and team

'Transference' refers to feelings derived from early relationships which may be re-played in the present in relation to carers and others, and 'counter-transference' reactions refer to carers' responses (see chapter 3). Transference and counter-transference reactions run riot in all mental health settings, as a number of team formulation studies have noted. If, as is usually the case, there is no opportunity to understand and process these feelings, they may lead to 'staff re-enacting punitive, withholding or abusive roles in relation to enraged, overwhelmed or helpless clients ... The team can be split, with mistrust and misunderstanding between colleagues' (Dunn and Parry, 1997: 20). 'Staff may inadvertently re-enact early patterns of abuse and become enmeshed in unhealthy, destructive interactions' (Meaden and van Marle, 2008: 44). (A similar focus on counter-transference is encouraged by Davenport, 2002; Martindale, 2007 and Lake, 2008). In Jack's case, we hypothesised that he feared and distrusted professionals in the same way that he feared his father (and perhaps the man who abused him). We also guessed that staff reactions to Jack reflected his own feelings and dilemmas. We tried to anticipate and avoid the 'transference trap' whereby staff might end up re-creating the kind of relationships that brought Jack into services in the first place.

An attachment perspective on the way the client uses/ interacts with the psychiatric service as a whole

Although attachment theory has been extremely influential ever since its development in the 1960s, surprisingly little has been written about the kinds of attachments that service users develop towards teams and services (Adshead, 1998; Ma, 2007). Nevertheless, it is clear that such patterns often echo the relationships with early caregivers (e.g. Dunn and Parry, 1997; Whomsley, 2009). We hypothesised that Jack was, at some level, seeking from the service the kind of consistent attachments that his family were unable to provide, but that his fear and distrust created an anxious-ambivalent style of relating which made it hard for him to engage, and which risked splitting the team. In order to be able to offer Jack a different kind of attachment experience within services, staff themselves need to feel secure and contained – something which is difficult to achieve in a typical clinical environment of constant re-organisation and upheaval. Team formulation can promote a sense of containment and mutual support.

Psychological framing of medical interventions

Psychologists in particular are inclined to believe that decisions about medication, admission and so on are beyond their remit. Whether or not this is true, it is certainly the case that such interventions have *psychological* meanings and effects which need formulating along with other aspects of the care package. For Jack, medication may represent a hope that an outside agent will 'make me better' and/or it may be seen as a passport to the safety of the psychiatric system. (See Martindale, 2007 for further discussion of the subjective meanings of medication.) If he reaches the point of wishing to work on the trauma, it may impede access to his feelings. Other medical decisions – giving a diagnosis, admitting someone to hospital, and so on – also have psychological impacts and meanings that need to be included in the formulation.

Similar considerations apply in relation to the growing tendency to prescribe medication to children, especially those who are said to display symptoms of 'ADHD'. In addition to the physical effects, this can convey unhelpful messages about failure, inadequacy, abnormality and the location of the problem within the child, diverting attention from more systemic interventions.

Psychological framing of 'symptoms' including 'psychosis'

The biomedical model of psychiatry assumes that certain categories of experience, including 'delusions' and hallucinations, should be seen as 'symptoms' of an underlying illness. A psychiatric formulation of Jack might therefore take the form of 'schizophrenia triggered by the stress of family ill-health'. In contrast, as described in the DCP Guidelines, psychologists see such experiences as meaningful, although not necessarily immediately understandable, in the context of the person's life (DCP, 2011: 16–17). Jack's formulation therefore describes his experiences in non-medical terms (e.g. 'unusual beliefs') and hypothesises about their personal significance to him. Although controversial in AMH settings, this kind of understanding would be common in child and adolescent services when encountering problems such as those presented by Janet.

Awareness of social factors, such as class, gender, housing, employment etc

It is too often taken for granted that service users and their families will be poor, unemployed, living in inadequate housing and so on, all of which are very significant stressors in their own right. Moreover, poverty and its consequences may be experienced as a powerful sense of unworthiness, exclusion and stigma (see chapter 6). Jack's formulation attempts to remind the team of these very real difficulties and their likely impact on Jack.

Influence of the 'mental patient' role

In my view, this is a central but usually overlooked aspect of the formulation for any service user. Giving someone a psychiatric diagnosis is a very powerful act that may shape their entire life. Entry into the 'sick role' also conveys strong messages about lack of responsibility and agency (Johnstone, 2000, chapter 3). These messages nearly always interact unhelpfully with the service user's existing difficulties. In Jack's case we can see that he risks falling into the very common trap in which the mixed benefits of a psychiatric career (provision of accommodation, structure, social contact and support coupled with escape from expectations and responsibility) may be chosen, consciously or unconsciously, as a false solution to the overwhelming challenges (both internal and external) that he faces. The letter to Jack attempts to balance these medical messages with a clear statement that recovery depends on all parties working together.

Children of Janet's age are unlikely to be referred for residential treatment, although such facilities do exist. However, it is still important to be aware of the effect of identifying one person in the family as 'the problem'. Family therapists are very sensitive to this kind of dilemma (see chapter 4).

Last but certainly not least is an aspect that is receiving an increasing amount of attention in theory and practice, and which applies to individual and team formulations across the specialties; the possible role of trauma and abuse.

Possible role of trauma and abuse

A growing body of research suggests that a history of trauma and abuse is associated with all types of mental health problems, not forgetting psychosis, which would include the kind of experiences that Jack reported. Up to 85 per cent of people with a diagnosis of psychosis report a history of trauma, broadly defined to include sexual and physical abuse, witnessing or being subjected to domestic violence, emotional neglect, and bullying (Read et al., 2005; Larkin and Morrison, 2006; Read and Bentall, 2012). This appears to be a causal link: there is evidence of a dose-dependent relationship between the severity, number, and number of types of traumatic episodes, and the likelihood of psychosis. People abused as children are 9.3 times more likely to develop psychosis; the risk rises to 48 times for the severest abuse (Janssen et al., 2004); people who have experienced 3 kinds of abuse are 18 times more likely to be psychotic; with 5 types of abuse, the risk rises to 193 times (Shevlin et al., 2007). The relationship holds in prospective studies and after controlling for gender, ethnicity, education, substance abuse, etc. In addition, there is some evidence linking particular kinds of abuse with particular 'symptoms' (for example, child sexual abuse seems to be a stronger risk factor for hearing voices than child physical abuse). It has been noted that the content of unusual beliefs is often closely related to actual experiences of abuse (Read et al., 2005).

These are shocking figures, and raise profound questions about how professionals have managed to be unaware of the epidemic of trauma in our midst. They also raise very fundamental questions about the role of psychiatry and the biomedical model on which it is based (Read and Bentall, 2012). How much sense does it make to treat people as though they were suffering primarily from illnesses with biological causes, rather than traumas with psychological effects?

> There is growing evidence that the experiences that service users report (unusual beliefs, distressing voices etc) are, in many cases, a reaction to the abuses they have been subjected to. There is the abuse, and there are the responses to the abuse. There is no additional 'psychosis' that needs explaining.
>
> (Johnstone, 2011: 106)

The implication is that we need a paradigm shift in our model of mental health problems, one that is based on the accumulating evidence about the effects of trauma on the mind and body (see Dillon et al., 2012 for a summary).

For reasons of space, I will simply note here that formulation in any mental health presentation, child or adult, individual or team, should be trauma-informed. If there is a known history of trauma, the presenting difficulties should be considered as possible trauma effects. If the formulation does not seem to account for the difficulties, trauma (perhaps undisclosed) should be the first consideration as a candidate to fill the gap.

Clinicians in child and adolescent services will be aware of the possibility of developmental trauma, as we saw in Janet's case, and are on the whole less likely to reach for a medical explanation of distress. This awareness tends to be lost by the time someone reaches adult services. Even where there is a known history of trauma, it may be months or years before a service user is ready to work on these issues. In such cases, one of the central purposes of the formulation is to provide a framework for staff that explains the need for supportive waiting, and thus reduces the risk of increasingly controlling medical interventions in the meantime. This is certainly a risk in Jack's case. We can easily see how compulsory medication injected into his buttocks would be experienced as a repeat of earlier abuse. Such re-enactments are very common in psychiatry.

Another essential consideration in team formulations is therefore acknowledgement of the possible re-traumatising role of services.

Possible re-traumatising role of services

In training, I illustrate this process through a 'One-size-fits-all formulation for long-term service users' which looks like this:

> Service user X has unmet attachment needs and unresolved trauma from their early life. X tries to meet these through the psychiatric services, but fails, since services are not set up to do this. Still needy, but unable to achieve enough emotional security to move on, X ends up trading 'symptoms' for whatever psychiatric care is on offer. Staff are initially sympathetic but become increasingly frustrated at X's lack of progress. The resulting dynamic may end up repeating X's early experiences of neglect, rejection or abuse. Both parties become stuck, frustrated and demoralised in this vicious circle.

Interestingly, no group of staff has ever disputed the accuracy of this all-purpose formulation. On the contrary, it is always greeted with rueful recognition. In fact research shows that psychiatric interventions are frequently traumatising, although the response is to suggest therapy for this iatrogenic PTSD rather than abandon the 'treatments' that have caused it (Lu et al., 2011). As already noted, we can see how such a process might be played out in relation to Jack in the form of rejections and coercive interventions from the service. He is likely to experience this as repeated abuses by powerful people who are not able to see his real needs. Perhaps his suspicion of professionals is justified, despite the fact that each individual staff member is genuinely trying to help.

This cycle of re-traumatisation is not an individual problem but a systemic one, the inevitable result of basing a service on fundamentally false principles, in which service users are seen as 'patients with illnesses' rather than 'people with problems'. I have discussed the damaging consequences in more depth elsewhere (Johnstone, 2000). For the purposes of team formulation, we can note that this is a sensitive area, best approached from the assumption that all staff are doing their best within a system that is not suited to their or the service users' needs. The staff in the formulation meeting are likely to be those who are most open to a change in practice and in the strongest position to minimise or undo the damage. Like service users, they need support and new ways of looking at things, not blame. The team formulation for Jack tries to anticipate and avoid the common trap of re-traumatisation.

Team formulation in practice

As already discussed, evaluations suggest that team members value formulation highly. The approach has the advantage of being both simple and complex. At one level, formulating is something that we all do as human beings; we try to make sense of people's relationships, feelings, behaviours and motives. This makes it very easy for staff of all levels of training and experience to contribute to a team formulation meeting. There is no such thing as a 'wrong guess', and the hunches of a newly arrived student or support worker are likely to be at least as valuable as the opinions of the highest-status staff. All professionals are implicitly formulating in their work, and the process is perhaps most acceptable to them if described as a more explicit, structured and shared version of what they are doing already.

At another level, pulling together the complex mixture of information, feelings and intuitions into a coherent, integrated, theory-based narrative that is acceptable to staff and service user is a sophisticated and demanding task that may well end up falling to the psychologist, although it is desirable to share this round the team as people gain in confidence.

Useful concepts in team formulation

I have found it helpful to introduce the concept of formulation to teams in low-key training sessions, using practice examples. I have also found it useful to introduce certain key concepts and ideas to the team so that they become part of the common language which can be drawn upon during formulation meetings. My own favourites are:

- Parallel process (how staff reactions reflect the service user's problems).
- Transference/counter-transference.
- Symbolic meanings (especially in psychosis).
- Cycles of re-victimisation.
- Splitting (polarisation of staff attitudes).
- Attachment styles.
- Rescuer/Persecutor/Victim triangle (a concept from Transactional Analysis; e.g. Lapworth and Sills, 2011.)
- Core beliefs/schemas (see chapter 2).
- 'Reciprocal roles (from cognitive analytic therapy: e.g. Ryle and Kerr, 2002).
- 'Sick role' messages.

The first five concepts derive from psychodynamic theory, and are discussed further in chapter 3 as well as in introductory textbooks (e.g. Malan, 1995; Bateman et al., 2010).

Facilitating a formulation meeting

Facilitating a team formulation meeting is, like formulation itself, both simple and complex, exciting and demanding. It is much easier to construct a formulation as a group than as an individual. Drawing on the ideas of the whole team, a broad outline can usually be generated in 15–20 minutes. It is the process aspects of the meeting that may need most attention. The team will bring to the meeting not only their thoughts and information, but their feelings as well. Since these emotions reflect those of the service user, compounded by the inevitable challenges of working in the psychiatric system, they can be very powerful. It means that a team formulation meeting can have a very different flavour to that of a routine care planning meeting or ward round – it may be dominated by feelings of anger, stuckness, hopelessness, sadness and so on, and conflicts that reflect the service user's dilemmas may emerge in the form of disagreements and 'splitting' between team members. All this is useful material to work with, but it means that facilitation may sometimes feel more like group therapy, and may need to draw on the same skills. It is helpful to have a co-facilitator who can keep an eye on the process if this is likely to be challenging. It is also helpful to allow time at the start of the meeting for staff to express their feelings about working with the service user. The message is that no feelings are taboo – we are all human beings, and feelings are information. However, as professionals we are expected to reflect on and use our feelings to help the service user, not simply act them out.

In Jack's case, we might anticipate any of the following scenarios in the team formulation meeting:

- Staff adopting opposite positions about Jack's discharge date.
- Expressions of anger and frustration with Jack.
- A strong desire to 'rescue' and take care of Jack.
- Insistence that Jack is 'ill' and needs more medication.
- A dispute about the relevance of diagnosis.
- Avoidance of the subject of trauma.
- A general feeling of hopelessness and 'stuckness' about Jack's progress.

Any combination of the following strategies might be useful in such situations:

- If diagnoses or 'symptoms' are described, encourage translation into formulation terms; for example, 'When you say he is paranoid/ schizophrenic, what leads you to that conclusion? Is it because he has some unusual beliefs? How else could we understand the beliefs he holds?' For obvious reasons do not challenge the whole concept of 'schizophrenia' or other diagnoses, but suggest that there may be alternative ways of understanding *this particular case.*
- Similarly if medical solutions are dominating, ask: 'What are we hoping we might achieve by increasing medication/putting him on a depot/ prescribing ECT? And what are the possible disadvantages? Are there other ways of achieving the same aims?'

- Notice, allow space for and validate staff feelings of frustration, anger, despair and so on ...
- ... but encourage 'I' language ('When she does X, I feel Y') not 'He makes me furious/she is manipulative' ...
- ... and then relate it to the service user: 'What does that tell us about Jack?' (but do not be tempted to 'psychologise' the team member).
- Watch out for parallel process – for example, Jack's argument with the consultant about his diagnosis may be reflected in a team disagreement about diagnosis. Relate this back to Jack's situation. For example, 'Perhaps this difference of opinion is re-playing Jack's battle with the team – how could we resolve it?'
- In the case of splitting – validate both perspectives as containing part of the truth, and invite the team to find a middle ground.
- Try to find something useful in every contribution; for example, 'He's just using the ward as a hotel – we should discharge him tomorrow': 'I can understand your feelings of frustration, and I suspect they are shared by others. Maybe we need to discuss the reasons for these feelings. And of course you are right that we need to be planning for discharge at some point'.
- Encourage staff to hypothesise – there are no 'correct' answers.
- Notice what the team is *not* discussing. If we cannot acknowledge the horrific nature of the events in most service users' lives, we will not be able to help them, and our avoidance may reinforce theirs.
- Comment on the atmosphere in the room. A feeling of heaviness and despair needs to be acknowledged, because it may inform us about how Jack feels inside. Identifying this will help the team to retain a sense of hope, rather than being drawn into Jack's hopelessness.
- Notice quieter members of the team, make a point of trying to draw them in.
- Offer, not impose, your own views.
- Perhaps hardest of all – accept that your own view (whatever that is) may not prevail. It is not always possible to divert teams from interventions that you may see as grossly inappropriate and damaging. It may be a case of losing a battle or two, but trying your best to maintain a good relationship with the team in order to win the war – in other words, to shift a whole team in a more psychologically-aware direction, as discussed below.

Team formulation for culture change

One of the claimed benefits of team formulation as listed in the DCP Guidelines is 'facilitating culture change in teams and organisations' (DCP, 2011: 9). Clinicians have reported that 'Using formulations may help in shifting staff culture' (Summers 2006: 343). A key clinical psychology document, *New Ways of Working in Teams*, recommends team formulation as 'a powerful way of shifting cultures towards more psychosocial perspectives' (Onyett 2007: 23).

The culture that is in need of this shift is, as already discussed, the dominant biomedical one which assumes that patients are suffering from 'illnesses' with primarily biological causes. The team power struggles and mixed messages that arise out of unresolved tensions and contradictions between competing models have been extensively documented (e.g. Johnstone, 1993, 2000; Colombo et al., 2003), and are bound to be played out in the formulation meeting as well.

Part of the appeal of formulation to staff may lie in their frustration with the current model and the hope for an alternative. This emerged as a strong theme in the study by Hood et al. (2013) in which staff members made a number of comments along the lines of:

> I think services now are full of people who wouldn't be here if people had taken a little bit longer to think about what brought them to the service and how we can help them and be more proactive and help them to recover, I think we're just stuffed full of people who've been given various diagnoses and medication and that hasn't actually achieved that much.
>
> (Hood et al., 2013)

Within this culture they saw formulation as 'still fighting for recognition as the useful way of understanding the person's issues' (Hood et al., 2013).

The issue of whether a formulation should be an addition to, or an alternative to, a psychiatric diagnosis is discussed further in chapter 12. The former position is apparently unproblematic for some of those using a team formulation approach (e.g. Davenport, 2002; Meaden and van Marle, 2008; Berry et al., 2009; Martindale, 2007) although others (e.g. Kennedy, 2008) believe that the biomedical model and diagnosis play a major role in creating and perpetuating the difficulties that need formulating. This is also my experience – and it accords with the testimony of many service users (e.g. Rogers et al., 1993). The DCP Guidelines state that psychological (as opposed to psychiatric) formulation should not be premised on psychiatric diagnosis (DCP, 2011: 16–17), a view that was shared by some of Hood's participants:

> I don't think you can complement a diagnosis [with formulation]. I don't think it works. I think it's useless. I think it's really damaging. I think it's really awful. I mean you know you put that diagnosis of paranoid schizophrenia, of borderline personality disorder, of manic depression on someone, they've got it for life, end of story.
>
> (Hood et al., 2013)

The combination of diagnosis with formulation conveys a mixed message about personal responsibility and the service user's capacity to take control of their lives. As Kennedy puts it: 'simultaneously, the messages received by the patient include that they are helpless, out of control, unable to manage without being (forcibly if necessary) detained and drugged, while being asked to explain their own behaviour, take responsibility for their actions and "get better"' (Kennedy, 2008: 42). In other words, service users are effectively told, 'You have an illness which is not your fault BUT you retain responsibility for it and must make an effort to get better BUT you must do it our way because we are the experts in your illness'. Muddled thinking leads to muddled practice. Should Jack take more medication to get rid of his 'delusions' or should we encourage him to talk about his beliefs and relate them to the traumas in his life? Is his distress when he talks about his family a sign that he is more 'depressed' or more in touch with his feelings? – 'worse' or 'better'? Should he accept his diagnosis of 'mental illness' and take more medication, possibly for life, or should he stop hanging around in hospital and make more effort to get on with his family and find a job? Both staff and service users find themselves stuck in this trap, which generally originates from the first contact with the psychiatric services when psychosocial difficulties are re-defined and diagnosed as 'illnesses'.

At a pragmatic and strategic level it is important for the facilitator to be pro-formulation rather than anti-diagnosis. This is in the spirit of formulation itself, which is about offering, not imposing, ideas and viewpoints. In the example of Jack, I have assumed that after the formulation discussions, the consultant was willing to entertain the possibility that in Jack's particular case the difficulties could be understood as a response to trauma. The phrasing of this section of the hypothetical intervention plan is deliberate ('Jack is adamant that he does not suffer from "paranoia" or "delusional disorder", and his strong feelings about this are creating a barrier to working with the team'). While this tends to imply that it is Jack's attitude rather than the team's failure to understand him that is the impediment to progress, it may make a reduced focus on diagnosis more acceptable to the team.

The trauma perspective has led to suggestions for new subcategories of diagnosis such as 'traumatic psychosis' (Callcott and Turkington, 2006) which can perhaps be seen as a kind of halfway house between formulation and diagnosis, and for this reason do not present a direct challenge to the biomedical model. It may also be possible to persuade teams to re-designate someone as suffering from 'dissociative disorder' rather than 'schizophrenia', 'bipolar disorder' or 'paranoia'. This diagnosis describes a pattern of response to extreme trauma and thus implies a psychological origin of the person's difficulties.

Summary

The alternative to the one-size-fits-all formulation would look like this:

> Service user X has unmet attachment needs and unresolved trauma from their early life. X tries to meet these through the psychiatric services.........

Formulate here!

A formulation-based approach, embedded with the service and implemented from first contact in order to guide the whole care pathway, can provide an exit from this trap.

Within a non-medical model, the central task of every mental health professional would be to *create meaning out of chaos and despair*. Team formulation is one way of doing this.

Much remains to be done in developing, promoting, implementing and researching the team formulation approach. However, at minimum it provides a space in the team for both *thinking* and *processing feelings*. In busy teams these opportunities are rare, squeezed out by the constant crises and demands and not valued by the dominant model of treatment. The 'thinking' consists of the information, experience, theory and evidence that staff bring to the meetings, while the 'feelings' derive from the service users' distress and the professionals' emotional reactions to it. These two aspects of the therapeutic work, thinking and feeling, can be integrated via the team formulation process, and framed in terms of personal meaning.

In this way, team formulation can provide an alternative, indeed an antidote, to the limitations and damage of the traditional psychiatric approach. It is a powerful instrument for culture change. It puts back what psychiatry takes out, and restores meaning, agency and hope, for staff and service users.

Acknowledgements

Thanks to Rudi Dallos, Richard Down and Neil Harris for their helpful comments on the applicability of this model to child and adolescent work.

References

Adshead, G. (1998) Psychiatric staff as attachment figures: understanding management problems in psychiatric services in the light of attachment theory. *British Journal of Psychiatry*, 172: 64–69.

Bateman, A., Brown, D. and Pedder, J. (2010) *Introduction to Psychotherapy: an Outline of Psychodynamic Principles and Practice*, 4th edn, Hove: Routledge.

Berry, K. (2007) Psychology services in psychiatric rehabilitation: service user needs and staff perceptions, *Clinical Psychology and Psychotherapy*, 14, 244–248.

Berry, K., Barrowclough, C. and Wearden, A.J. (2009) A pilot study investigating the use of psychological formulations to modify psychiatric staff perceptions of service users with psychosis, *Behavioural and Cognitive Psychotherapy*, 37, 39–48.

Borrill, C. and West, M. (2002) *Team Working and Effectiveness in Health Care: Findings from the Health Care Team Effectiveness Project*, Birmingham: Aston Centre for Health Service Organisation Research.

British Psychological Society (2010) *Accreditation through partnership handbook: Guidance for clinical psychology programmes*, Leicester: British Psychological Society.

Callcott, P. and Turkington, D. (2006) CBT for traumatic psychosis. In W. Larkin and A.P. Morrison (eds) *Trauma And Psychosis: New Directions For Theory And Therapy*, Hove, New York: Routledge, pp. 222–238.

Charlesworth, G. (2010) Commentary, *PSIGE newsletter*, 112, 4–6.

Christofides, S., Johnstone, L. and Musa, M. (2011) Chipping in: clinical psychologists' descriptions of their use of formulation in multi-disciplinary team working, *Psychology and Psychotherapy: Theory, Research and Practice*. DOI: 10.1111/j.2044-8341.2011.02041.x

Clarke I. (2008) Pioneering a cross-diagnostic approach founded in cognitive science. In I. Clarke and H. Wilson (eds) *Cognitive Behavior Therapy for Acute Inpatient Mental Health Units: Working with Clients, Staff and the Milieu*, Hove UK: Routledge, pp. 65–77.

Colombo, A., Bendelow, G., Fulford, B. and Williams, S. (2003) Evaluating the influence of implicit models of mental disorder on community-based multi-disciplinary teams, *Social Science and Medicine* 56, 1557–1570.

Craven-Staines, S., Dexter-Smith, S. and Li, K. (2010) Integrating psychological formulations into older people's services – three years on (Part 3): staff perceptions of formulation meetings, *PSIGE newsletter*, 112, 16–22.

Davenport, S. (2002) Acute wards: problems and solutions, *Psychiatric Bulletin*, 26, 385–388.

Davies, L. (2010) *Consultation to a local residential children's home: the process of service development, implementation and evaluation, illustrated with a case study.* Unpublished report of clinical activity, Cardiff Doctorate in Clinical Psychology.

Dexter-Smith, S. (2010) Integrating psychological formulations into older people's services – three years on, *PSIGE Newsletter*, 112, 8–22.

Dillon, J., Johnstone, L. and Longden, E. (2012) Trauma, dissociation, attachment and neuroscience: a new paradigm for understanding severe mental distress, *Journal of Critical Psychology, Counselling and Psychotherapy*, 12(3), 145–155.

Division of Clinical Psychology (2011) *Good Practice Guidelines on the Use of Psychological Formulation*, Leicester: The British Psychological Society.

Down, R. (2010) CAMHS Residential Care Consultation Service: 4 month review to April 2010, *Internal Trust report*, Hywel Dda Health Board.

Dunn, M. and Parry, G. (1997) A formulated care plan approach to caring for people with borderline personality disorder in a community mental health service setting, *Clinical Psychology Forum* 104, 19 –22.

Health Professions Council (2009) *Standards of Proficiency: Practitioner Psychologists,* London: Health Professions Council.

Hewitt, O. (2008) Using psychological formulation as a means of intervention in a psychiatric rehabilitation setting, *The International Journal of Psychosocial Rehabilitation,* 12, 1, 8–17.

Hollingworth, P. and Johnstone, L. (2013) *Team formulations: what are the staff views?* Clinical Psychology Forum (in press).

Hood, N., Johnstone, L. and Christofides, S. (2013) *The hidden solution? Staff experiences, views and understanding of the role of psychological formulation in multi-disciplinary teams*, Journal of Critical Psychology, Counselling and Psychotherapy, in press.

Ingham, B. (2011) Collaborative psychological case formulation development workshops: a case study with direct care staff, *Advances in Mental Health and Intellectual Disabilities,* 5 (2), 9–15.

Janssen, I., Krabbendam, L., Bak, M., Hanssen, M., Vollebergh, W., de Graaf, R. and van Os, J. (2004) Childhood abuse as a risk factor for psychotic experiences, *Acta Psychiatrica Scandinavica*, 109, 38–45.

Johnstone, L. (1993) Psychiatry: are we allowed to disagree? *Clinical Psychology Forum*, 56, 30–32.

——(2000) *Users and Abusers of Psychiatry: A Critical Look at Psychiatric Practice,* 2nd edn, London, Philadelphia: Routledge.

——(2011) Can traumatic events traumatise people? Trauma, madness and 'psychosis'. In M. Rapley, J. Moncrieff and J. Dillon (eds) *De-medicalising Misery: Psychiatry, Psychology and the Human Condition*, Basingstoke: Palgrave Macmillan, pp. 99–109.

Kennedy, F. (2008) The use of formulation in inpatient settings. In I. Clarke and H. Wilson (eds) *Cognitive Behavior Therapy for Acute Inpatient Mental Health Units; Working with Clients, Staff and the Milieu,* Hove UK: Routledge, pp. 39–63.

Kennedy, F., Smalley, M. and Harris, T. (2003) Clinical psychology for in-patient settings: principles for development and practice, *Clinical Psychology Forum,* 30, 21–24.

Lake, N. (2008) Developing skills in consultation 2: a team formulation approach, *Clinical Psychology Forum,* 186, 18–24.

Lapworth, P. and Sills, C. (2011) *An Introduction to Transactional Analysis: Helping People Change*, London: Sage.

Larkin, W. and Morrison, A.P. (eds) (2006) *Trauma And Psychosis: New Directions For Theory And Therapy*, Hove, New York: Routledge.

Lu, W., Mueser, K.T., Shami, A., Siglag, M., Petrides, G., Schoepp, E., Putts, M. and Saltz, J. (2011) Post-traumatic reactions to psychosis in people with multiple psychotic episodes, *Schizophrenia Research*, 127, 1, 66–75.

Ma, K. (2007) Attachment theory in adult psychiatry. Part 2: Importance to the therapeutic relationship, *Advances in Psychiatric Treatment*, 13, 10–16.

Malan, D. (1995) *Individual Psychotherapy and the Science of Psychodynamics*, 2nd edn, London: Hodder Arnold Publications.

Martindale, B.V. (2007) Psychodynamic contributions to early intervention in psychosis, *Advances in Psychiatric Treatment*, 13, 34–42.

Meaden, A. and van Marle, S. (2008) When the going gets tougher: the importance of long-term supportive psychotherapy in psychosis, *Advances in Psychiatric Treatment*, 14, 42–49.

Onyett, S. (2007) *Working Psychologically in Teams*, Leicester: The British Psychological Society.

Palazzoli, M.S., Boscolo, L., Cecchin, G. and Prata, G. (1980) Hypothesising–circularity–neutrality: three guidelines for the conductor of the session, *Family Process*, 19, 3–12.

Read, J. and Bentall, R.B. (2012) Negative childhood experiences and mental health: theoretical, clinical and primary prevention implications, *British Journal of Psychiatry*, 200, 89–91.

Read, J., van Os, J., Morrison, T. and Ross, C.A. (2005) Childhood trauma, psychosis and schizophrenia: a literature review with theoretical and practical implications, *Acta Psychiatrica Scandinavica*, 112, 5, 330–350.

Rogers, A., Pilgrim, D. and Lacey, R. (1993) *Experiencing Psychiatry*, London: Macmillan/MIND.

Ryle, A. and Kerr, I.B. (2002) *Introducing Cognitive Analytic Therapy: Principles and Practice*, Chichester: John Wiley and Sons.

Shevlin, M., Dorahy, M.J. and Adamson, G. (2007) Trauma and psychosis: an analysis of the National Comorbidity Survey, *American Journal of Psychiatry*, 164(1), 166–169.

Shirley, L. (2010) Sharing formulation with care staff using the Newcastle Model – group problem-solving, *PSIGE newsletter*, 112, 55–61.

Skinner, P. and Toogood, R. (eds) (2010) *Clinical Psychology Leadership Development Framework*, Leicester: British Psychological Society.

Summers, A. (2006) Psychological formulations in psychiatric care: staff views on their impact, *Psychiatric Bulletin*, 30, 341–343.

Timimi, S. (2005) *Naughty Boys: Anti-social Behaviour, ADHD and the Role of Culture*, Basingstoke: Palgrave Macmillan.

Wainwright, N. and Bergin, L. (2010) Introducing psychological formulations in an acute older people's inpatient mental health ward: a service evaluation of staff views, *PSIGE newsletter*, 112, 38–45.

Walton, M. (2011) Complex case consultation forums: a thematic analysis, *Clinical Psychology Forum*, 223, 10–14.

Whomsley, S. (2009) Team case formulation. In C. Cupitt (ed.) *Reaching Out: The Psychology of Assertive Outreach*, London: Routledge.

Chapter 11

Using integrative formulation in health settings

Samantha Cole

This chapter aims to give a flavour of the kind of integrative formulation that psychologists might use with individuals and teams in physical health care settings. The application of formulation to the medical context entails the same principles and strategies outlined in the earlier chapters but with the obvious difference that a central aspect of the service user's difficulties will always be related to an actual or potential experience of physical threat (whether an illness, condition, injury, disability or symptom, such as pain). Some differences of emphasis and process follow from this central shift of focus, as will be discussed below, before Janet's case is presented from the health perspective.

Challenges and considerations in formulation in health settings

It is now generally accepted that the biomedical model cannot operate efficiently without attending to psychological processes and holistic *care*, as distinct from physical *treatment*. However, the history of mind–body dualism has shaped research into psychological aspects of physical health and the model of delivery of services to meet these identified 'additional' needs (Salmon, 2000). Psychological care can still be seen as a parallel but relatively unconnected activity attended to by specialists who often work as an adjunct to the physical health care team with few effective channels of communication, rather than as an integral aspect of the entire care pathway. For obvious reasons, priorities will almost always be framed in terms of the physical wellbeing of the service user, and the medical intervention aimed at improving it will invariably continue regardless of any ongoing psychological assessment, formulation and intervention cycle. A cancer patient for whom chemotherapy is indicated is likely to receive it irrespective of a psychological formulation, although this may help guide the way the patient is prepared for the treatment and the specific arrangements for administering it.

This context has potential advantages and disadvantages for psychologists in healthcare settings. On the one hand, colleagues are less likely to be able to draw readily upon concepts such as 'attachment', 'transference' and 'negative schemas', which to some extent can be assumed when communicating with allied professionals in mental health services. On the other, this means that even relatively simple formulations can offer valuable insights to multi-disciplinary team discussions about the management of a patient (e.g. why they might not be 'complying' with medical advice). Indeed, a preliminary research study that colleagues and I conducted with an acute inpatient staff group suggests that simply having the offer of a psychologist's support to develop a team formulation for a 'difficult' patient during integrated care meetings may be enough to reduce staff's self-reported feelings of frustration and increase their felt competence to deal with the challenges. It seems that merely giving the implicit message that, at some level, it all makes sense may be valuable support for stressed nurses working with confusing presentations.

A related consequence of working with professionals who do not necessarily have any training in mental health or health psychology, is that most formulations are in effect team formulations with more than one 'client' (the patient and the medical team). Each is seeking to negotiate a shared understanding of the difficulties which may indicate the necessity for change in either or both sides in relation to each other. The psychologist is, therefore, often in the position of mediating between the understandings of stakeholders at all levels of the health service and the service user – understandings that do not always coincide. For example, the medical team may refer a patient with 'mental health issues' who attributes their distress to the (mis)management of their medical care or their consultant's style of relating and who, therefore, situates the needed change in the process of healthcare delivery. This means that parallel formulations may be developed with the team and service user, with neither being shared with the other in its entirety if that is not likely to be helpful (e.g. staff and patient's judgements of and emotional responses to each other). However, in general the process is likely to involve the wider system as opposed to being primarily developed and used within a dyadic therapy relationship, as is more common in mental health settings. Formulations need to be co-constructed with healthcare colleagues as tentatively and respectfully as with the individual service user, as discussed in the chapters on systemic working and team formulation in chapters 4 and 10.

As noted in the DCP 'Good practice guidelines on the use of psychological formulation' (2011: 16), a medical diagnosis will often, though not always, play an important role in a formulation in a physical health setting where the medical model is not 'metaphorical' (Boyle, 2002: 233), as in mental health services, and the legitimacy of a truly *bio*psychosocial formulation, taking account of the psychological effects of biological factors (e.g. depression in stroke), is far less controversial. However, the use of psychiatric diagnoses in this context remains contentious and it is no more conceptually coherent to premise a health formulation on them. For example, viewing cancer as a 'trigger' of underlying vulnerability to depression tends to further reduce the agency of a patient who may think that it is in the hands of the doctors to 'treat' the secondary diagnosis of a 'mood disorder' as well. This may in turn increase their sense of hopelessness since they are now unfortunate enough to be suffering from two illnesses concurrently. This can be avoided if the experiences themselves, for example, tearfulness and lack of interest in or enjoyment of activities, are understood as obviously meaningful and valid psychological reactions to an overwhelming set of circumstances.

In general, my impression is that patients' distress is often understood by healthcare professionals as a response to the personal impact of medical/ organic factors, rather than from within an illness model that assumes that it too is primarily caused by biological dysfunction. Indeed, it may be that the potential role of a psychologist in supporting the adjustment of a physically ill patient whose distress is easy to empathise with is often overlooked. However, medical professionals tend to hold (often unstated) norms about how distressed someone 'should' be about having a particular illness, injury or symptom. When a patient's reaction seems to be out of proportion to the expected impact, a formulation is likely to be more helpful in explaining the gap, and less stigmatising than a psychiatric diagnosis with its implicit normative judgements about the appropriate degree of sadness or fear in the situation. Health formulations also have the advantage over psychiatric diagnoses of being able to address and thus pre-empt difficulties *before* a potentially distressing event has occurred (for example, when developed as part of a pre-transplant assessment), enabling psychological care in medical settings to be pro-active and preventative in a way that is often not possible in mental health services.

Knowing that a user of healthcare services already has a psychiatric diagnosis of, say, schizophrenia does not tell us much about how they and their family members will respond to a diagnosis of, and treatment for, a life-limiting or life-threatening illness or how they will cope with chronic pain or disability. However, if Jack, for example, were to become physically ill it would be relevant to consider the personal meaning he has constructed about his psychiatric diagnosis, his experiences of being 'ill' and a 'patient' within this context, and how, if at all, he relates these experiences to his physical health status.

The distinction is still sometimes (implicitly) made between illnesses that are physical (and therefore 'real') and those that are psychosomatic or 'in the mind' (and therefore 'unreal'). Even when there is an understanding on the part of healthcare professionals that the interaction between the physical and psychological aspects of a presentation is more complex than that, service users may assume that this distinction has been made if the involvement of a psychologist is suggested. The potential for service users to feel dismissed or judged is even greater if referral to psychological health services is the only intervention offered, as is often the case with diagnoses of exclusion such as chronic fatigue syndrome or chronic regional pain syndrome. The psychologist then needs to carefully negotiate a shared view about where the 'problem' resides so that barriers to engagement are overcome and constructive change can occur.

However, the pressure to 'prescribe' immediate solutions that often pervades medical settings can persist, especially if the available time for first developing a meaningful understanding is limited due to, for example, shortened life expectancy, urgency of the medical treatment schedule, the burden of existing hospital appointments which take priority, or patient fatigue. The process of assessment–formulation–intervention in health may, therefore, tend to be even more recursive than in mental health settings, often constituting a series of evolving 'on-the-spot' solution-focused reformulations as new assessment information emerges and medical interventions proceed. For example, a brief, extemporary formulation of a child's fears in relation to an imminent invasive procedure may be offered to the parent and nurse in the treatment room to ensure that an essential medical test can proceed with minimal distress to the family. The family may then have a longer follow-up appointment with the psychologist at a less pressured moment to 'flesh out' the assessment and formulation so that further medical investigations or treatments can be planned in a way that avoids escalation of the child's anxiety. At any particular moment during this process, the 'working' formulation may be a transitory, contingent one allowing certain aspects of the service user's experience to be fore-grounded for the purposes of, sometimes urgent, targeted interventions. This means that a 'full' written formulation is probably less likely to be routinely offered to service users or colleagues than might be the case in mental health services.

Medicine and nursing are very solution-focused professions for obvious reasons, and this tends to go hand-in-hand with implicit understandings about expertise: patients and health professionals tend to share assumptions that the 'expert' will generally lead interactions, decide what information is relevant, assess it independently of the patient in order to arrive at a diagnosis, and then advise on a plan of action, which they are also likely to assume responsibility for implementing. Many service users value clinical paternalism or authoritarianism since it can reduce uncertainty and unpredictability, and relieve them of responsibility for understanding and responding to a possibly frightening situation. If this has been an individual's experience of the help they have already encountered in the hospital or primary care clinic, they may reasonably also approach psychological support with hopes or expectations that the psychologist will offer immediate 'expert' solutions to their problems. There will often be contextual cues to reinforce expectations that the same passive 'patient' role is appropriate in the therapeutic relationship, such as some clinical psychologists' use of the 'doctor' title. Similarly, if the setting in which the psychologist works is a medical consulting room, for example, it may suggest the same 'script' as for a doctor's appointment. These expectations can be initial barriers to fostering a genuinely collaborative approach to formulating, although once overcome the process can ameliorate the subtle negative implications of the wider expert model.

For similar reasons, 'decentred' therapies such as narrative therapy, which seek to avoid pathologising stories that further decrease service users' sense of control, can be attractive for psychologists working in health settings. However, they can be difficult to communicate to medical colleagues (and sometimes resisted by patients) who expect an 'expert' view. Furthermore, more collaborative practices are not always facilitated by physical healthcare systems and processes that are predicated on a hierarchy. For example, clinical letters often have a standard format, starting with a diagnosis, and addressing the referring GP rather than the patient. There is also the potential for formulations to be unhelpful, or even harmful, if the patient's control in health matters is emphasised too much, giving the impression that illness is preventable and that if it occurs, it represents a personal failure to keep healthy. Longitudinal formulations linking people's psychological history to their current health and emotional state, or which describe the power of emotional events to influence physiological ones, may leave the patient feeling to blame for the onset or maintenance of their health problems (e.g. for not leaving a 'stressful' job earlier). This can perhaps be mitigated by theories that consider stress and illness as, at least partly, a function of environmental demands and resources (such as those discussed in more detail in chapter 6). Attention to socio-cultural health inequalities is another aspect that will generally inform a health formulation. These and other relevant issues in formulation in healthcare settings are discussed in more detail below.

Additional theoretical influences on health formulation

In principle, formulating in health settings could draw upon any of the theoretical models described in the preceding chapters. As with work in other settings, a fully integrated formulation is not always necessary and it may be more useful to draw primarily from one conceptual framework at a given point in the process to illustrate a particular aspect of the problem to a service user. For example, a cognitive behavioural model of a panic cycle may be drawn out with a service user with chronic obstructive pulmonary disease to explain how misinterpretation of the symptom of breathlessness (e.g. as a sign of imminent collapse) leads to anxiety and an escalation of physical discomfort due to the body's stress response. In some areas of health, particular models may be favoured for their utility in conceptualising the psychological issues most commonly associated with the condition. For example, 'third wave' cognitive behavioural therapies, such as acceptance and commitment therapy and mindfulness-based cognitive therapy, are often used in pain services. In many health settings, systemic perspectives are likely to be a focus since, as discussed above, formulations are not only likely to need to include the impact of illness and/or disability upon relational processes within the service user's social network, but will also need to account for the context of the healthcare system itself in relation to the family's experience. However, the process of formulating within medical settings is almost always integrative in the sense that it will combine psychotherapeutic models with an understanding of the causal role of the physical health condition and theoretical concepts from the health psychology literature, some of which are outlined below.

Health beliefs and illness representations

Our attitudes and beliefs about physical health are shaped in part by our previous experiences of, or exposure to, illness and/or injury. This learning influences our long-term health-related behaviour and will affect the reception, retention of and reaction to new information relating to our physical wellbeing. In order to make sense of health experiences and guide responses, individuals actively construct cognitive and emotional representations of health threats organised around several dimensions: beliefs about what actually constitutes the threat (the illness *identity*); perceived *causes* (e.g. hereditary, external, internal); perceived trajectory or *time-line* (e.g. acute, chronic, cyclical); assumed *consequences* (Leventhal et al., 1997); anticipated *severity* (a combination of the magnitude of perceived consequences and expected time course); ideas about *susceptibility* (how vulnerable a person thinks they are to a particular health threat; Becker, 1974); illness *coherence* (i.e. meta-cognitions evaluating the meaningfulness or usefulness of the representation: Weinman et al., 1996); and *emotional* representations (Moss-Morris et al., 2002).

Individuals' engagement in preventative health behaviours, and their behavioural response to health advice once a health threat has been realised, are likely to be influenced by the following set of appraisals: their judgements about *curability and controllability*, including the extent to which the individual plays a part in this (i.e. their personal control and self-efficacy beliefs) and their belief in the treatment or recommended advice (i.e. outcome expectancies: Lau and Hartmann, 1983); determinations of the *necessity* of the proposed treatment (whether its medication, surgery or behaviour change: Horne et al., 1999); a *costs-benefits* analysis of different ways of responding (e.g. whether it is expected to be painful, to worsen quality of life or to be degrading); the individual's *health motivation* (i.e. their readiness to be concerned about health matters); *cues to action* (either internal or external: Becker, 1974); and *subjective norms* (i.e. their perception of the norms of their social environment in relation to a health behaviour and their evaluation of whether they are motivated to comply, weighted by the importance they attribute to social opinion: Ajzen and Fishbein, 1980). All of these factors would need to be explored with users of psychological services in a health setting and are likely to need reformulating over time as their beliefs are modified by their experiences.

Coping theory

When someone has an acute or chronic illness or condition, their whole family may need to adjust their expectations, roles and daily lives. For most people, it takes time to make sense of what has happened and get used to new, and therefore sometimes worrying, experiences, including treatments. This process of change is almost always stressful and illness and treatments present formidable challenges. According to Moos and Schaefer (1984), the situation engendered by illness and injury can be conceptualised as a crisis because it is often unpredicted, and entails considerable ambiguity and uncertainty, and yet often demands a quick response to be formulated, probably drawing on limited prior experience (since most people are healthy most of the time). Furthermore, illness and injury may pose threats to an individual's identity and future as well as necessitating often abrupt changes in their roles, social support and environment (for example, becoming confined to a bedroom and being cared for by family members who are normally dependent on you for care).

For these reasons, understanding how people tend to respond to unexpected challenges, change and stress in general may help us to understand or predict their responses to illness and treatment. Coping theory has provided a taxonomical framework for exploring the various actions taken by people facing threats to their health in order to reduce the stressfulness of the challenge when the internal and/or external demands of the situation are appraised as overwhelming their resources (Lazarus and Folkman, 1984). Broadly speaking, people can respond by tackling the issue 'head on' (known as problem-focused coping) or by addressing its emotional effects (known as emotion-focused coping). Behaviourally, problem-focused coping strategies may be limited in the context of serious health concerns but people may still be able to confront the issue cognitively (e.g. by engaging in self-talk or mentally rehearsing a coping or health-maintaining skill). Emotion-focused coping strategies such as relaxation or distraction may be more accessible to acutely unwell people. However, they often entail reactions (e.g. denial, repression or rationalisation) that can disconcert or challenge the clinicians who are engaged primarily in managing the problem. 'Coping' is, therefore, an interactional and dynamic process in which the individual and the environment each affect the other and one which a clinician would want to reformulate as it evolves when working with family members such as Mary and Janet.

Cultural/societal context

Illness and *disability* are social constructs that relate to the person as a whole in the context of their social environment, as opposed to disease process or *pathology*, and so it is important to bring a critical awareness of the wider cultural and political context to the process of health formulation. There is substantial evidence that factors such as socioeconomic status, social support and networks, occupational status (particularly unemployment and retirement), social cohesion and religious belief have significant effects on health outcomes (Wilkinson and Marmot, 2003). Furthermore, illness and disability are not generally socially neutral, with some conditions attracting a great deal of stigma and moral opprobrium (e.g. HIV/AIDS), or diagnoses of exclusion (such as chronic fatigue syndrome being characterised as 'yuppie flu'), and obesity or smoking-related conditions. Even when the diagnosis tends to be viewed more sympathetically, those who are given the diagnosis with it can feel that their responses to their own health predicament are constrained by prevailing discourses about 'thinking positively' and 'bravely battling'. For example, Susan Sontag's observation from over thirty years ago that the combative metaphor of 'fighting' cancer contains the implicit accusation that some patients' will to resist the disease is not strong enough, is still keenly felt by some people (Sontag, 1978).

Although unlikely to be explicitly included in every health formulation, the process should include an attempt to understand the health beliefs of the service user in the context of the historically, socially and culturally specific constructs of illness and health that the service user lives within – including any apparent health norms related to ascribed characteristics such as gender, race, ethnicity, and class – and how these sit with wider discourses about health and illness within any minority or socially marginalised groups that the service user may identify, or be identified, with.

Cognitive development and health-related understanding

An awareness of how understanding of the concepts of health and illness develop should inform formulations of health-related difficulties for children and young people, and perhaps also for adults with significant learning difficulties. Research suggests that children's concepts of illness and health change in fairly predictable directions with age and/or cognitive development and in ways that broadly correspond to Piagetian theory (Bibace and Walsh, 1980). During the earliest developmental stage, generally between two and six years of age, children make links, often expressed in terms of proximity or magic, between an illness and external cues in the environment that may coincide spatially or temporally with it (e.g. cold air). This has been termed 'associational contagion' (Rozin et al., 1985). Younger children's spontaneous accounts of illness often have a moral dimension: they tend to believe that 'boys and girls who misbehave get sick more often than those who are good' (Brodie, 1974); and the idea of illness (and treatment) as punishment for wrongdoing is common, particularly amongst hospitalised children (Brewster, 1982).

Children who are functioning at the concrete operational stage, usually between seven and ten years of age, begin to revise their ideas about the aetiology of illness. They initially believe that one becomes ill by being in physical contact with an external 'contaminant': a person, object or activity that is thought to be harmful in some way. More sophisticated conceptualisations of the method of transmission from the contaminant through internalisation (e.g. swallowing or inhaling) begin to develop later, although illness is usually still only vaguely located within the body (Bibace and Walsh, 1980).

With the transition to formal operational thinking from around 11 years of age, young people become more aware of the body as a system of organs and of basic internal mechanisms and transformations (e.g. food is for energy, waste is excreted; Carey, 1985). Consequently, illness is construed increasingly in terms of failures of these internal physiological structures or processes, which may be the result of a sequence of events triggered externally or internally. More mature interpretations may also acknowledge psychological factors, that is, that one's thoughts or feelings can affect functioning of the body (Bibace and Walsh, 1980).

A clinician formulating with a child or young person would need to have an understanding of their phase of cognitive development so that they can help to make sense of the particular health beliefs and illness representations they have constructed, and to be able to communicate this in a way that does not extend too far beyond their current mental model. For example, when formulating with Janet, who would normally be expected to be at the concrete operational stage, one could not assume that she would share the psychologist's assumption that psychological factors such as her thoughts or feelings would be relevant to her physical health, and guidance is likely to be needed to help Janet make these links.

Janet: a perspective from the health context

As in the previous chapters, a formulation based on written information without access to Janet and Mary's accounts of their concerns will always be limited and somewhat speculative. However, their story as it has been presented provides a good opportunity to illustrate how physical, psychological and social factors can interrelate to create and maintain problems and how this might look as a tentative integrative formulation.

As discussed above, a formulation for Janet from a health psychology perspective would include an understanding of the personal meanings of, and beliefs about, health, illness and the healthcare system of Janet and those in her social network. This would certainly include Janet and Mary but may also need to reflect upon relevant health-related assumptions, judgements and beliefs of the other people involved in attempting to understand the situation: the school nurse, social services, accident and emergency staff, the paediatric consultant, and Janet's wider family. Although organic causes have been ruled out as an explanation for the persistence of Janet's poor food intake and weight loss, and so doctors do not consider her 'ill', chronic food refusal has potentially serious physical consequences for Janet's apparently already delayed development and growth, and so she may not be considered 'healthy' either. It is sometimes difficult for families who present to healthcare services with ostensibly physical symptoms (in this case weight loss and limited mobility) to understand or accept that 'no physical problems were evident' to the clinicians; they may feel disbelieved or disregarded or they may think that the doctors have not yet successfully identified the cause. This can be reinforced if healthcare professionals remain concerned and involved, offering follow-up appointments and continuing to regularly assess the symptoms, as in Janet's case. Mary is likely to be picking up mixed messages about the basis for Janet's problems, whether she is 'ill' or not, and who, therefore, is responsible for initiating change or intervening. If Mary does not have a coherent framework for understanding Janet's low weight and mobility problems, it is unlikely that Janet has had a clear understanding conveyed to her.

Similarly, it would be useful to gain an insight into Mary's understanding of her own health conditions (angina and arrhythmia), which are cursorily mentioned in the referral, and how much, if any, of this has been shared with Janet and in what way. For example, is the brevity with which her imminent heart surgery, an event which would reasonably be expected to be a considerable stressor in any family, is introduced into the referral merely an artefact of the focus on Janet as the 'index patient'? Or does it reflect a wider (avoidant) coping strategy for Mary of distracting herself from the considerable health challenges she faces by focusing her attention on Janet's physical wellbeing? The main symptom of angina is pain, primarily in the chest, that can be triggered by physical activity or stress and can also develop after eating a meal. Obesity and a high-fat diet are risk indicators and people with this diagnosis are often given advice about dietary changes and paced activity. However, patients, particularly women, are more likely to cite uncontrollable causes such as stress or family history for their angina (as opposed to personal behaviour, such as diet, exercise levels and smoking; Furze and Lewin, 2000).

If Mary experiences pain and exhaustion upon exertion she may have come to see herself as vulnerable to physical threat (perhaps even death) if she engages in more than minimal physical activity. If she has then generalised this association, it could explain why she requested a wheelchair for Janet, perhaps assuming that over-exertion could similarly further damage Janet's health. It is also possible that Janet may have formed some understanding of a link between her mother's eating and her poor health (perhaps if she observed an episode of pain after her mother ate or if she has heard conversations at home or at school indicating the importance of a balanced diet to reducing the risk of coronary disease) and this may be contributing to her refusal to eat the food that Mary prepares for her.

The family's strong Romany identity may also provide some insights into the kind of issues that might be explored during the process of formulation. For example, discourses about illness within Romany culture sometimes make a distinction between those that originate from within their own ethnic group, which can only be helped by their own healers, and those which are attributed to non-Roma society, and which are amenable to conventional western medicine (Jesper et al., 2008). Self-reliance, stoicism and a sense of urgency in relation to problem-solving all tend to be highly valued qualities for a travelling lifestyle but may also contribute to avoidance of, or late presentation to, healthcare services (Department of Health, 2004). The limited available evidence suggests that Roma in the UK are less likely to be registered with a GP than the majority of the population and are more likely to encounter, or perceive, barriers to service access or use (e.g. geographical distance from healthcare providers and communication difficulties). Moreover, when they do access services, whether due to mutual lack of understanding or familiarity with areas of potential conflict in health beliefs, attitudes and practices, or to experiences of discrimination, Roma often report negative or unhelpful interactions with healthcare providers (DoH, 2004; Mladovsky, 2007). Perhaps for a combination of these reasons, it is common for Roma to seek medical care only when it is deemed to be immediately necessary, often resulting in acute presentations at accident and emergency departments, rather than in what might be perceived by healthcare professionals as more 'appropriate' use of primary, secondary and preventative healthcare services (Jesper et al., 2008; Mladovsky, 2007).

All of this may be relevant to understanding Mary's pattern of engagement with healthcare services on Janet's behalf. If so, this might provide an alternative construction to one which might pathologise her repeated 'unnecessary' presentations as indicative of parental abuse (either by construing her as consciously or unconsciously wanting medical staff to identify the signs of physical or sexual abuse by Janet's father or by viewing her as inducing or fabricating symptoms in her daughter to meet her own psychological needs, as in the diagnosis of factitious disorder by proxy mentioned in chapter 6). These are not necessarily mutually exclusive hypotheses, of course, but an awareness that there may be contributing factors that would not be given due weight in a normative assessment of parental behaviour in relation to their child's health in the UK must surely provide a sounder basis for assessing any current risk.

Within Romany culture, *marime*, a concept of physical and moral impurity which is usually related to a feeling of shame, must be avoided by cleaning, food preparation and hygiene practices (e.g. washing hands between contacts with the upper and lower body) that are not usually adhered to or facilitated within the NHS (Larkin, 1998). Enclosed public places where the majority of people can be presumed not to act according to these beliefs, such as hospitals, public toilets, schools and offices, are consequently sometimes viewed as 'unclean' and potentially contaminating. This could be another factor that may be influencing Janet's attendance history; perhaps Mary needs to feel that it is an emergency before exposing Janet to such an environment. It is also plausible that the concept of *marime* may contribute to Janet's fear of public transport, which may be viewed as best avoided as a potential source of disease, and to her refusing to eat food prepared for her by Mary, which she may consider 'contaminating' in some way, perhaps because her mother is ill herself.

The empirical data to date suggests that, for the most part, the development of children's concepts of health and illness is more similar than not across cultures (Burochovitch and Mednick, 1997). Therefore, it might be reasonable to assume that Janet is at a stage of cognitive maturation that would incline her towards explanations of illness based upon a theory of contamination. It is plausible that cultural ideas such as *marime* would have particular salience for a child at this stage of development and may be interpreted in quite a literal way, losing some of the nuances. It would be important to explore with Janet how she construes 'health' and 'illness' and what aspects of her environment and behaviours are associated with each. The significance of eating and dietary habits to these two states would also need to be understood in Janet's own terms.

Sharing food in Romany culture implies an acknowledgement of each others' 'cleanliness' and so conveys respect and trust; refusing to eat with someone expresses the opposite and would usually be taken as an affront. Interviewees in a UK research study saw providing food as 'an important nurturing role for mothers and an important aspect of being a good parent' (DoH, 2004: 49). Greater physical size is associated with greater health and wellbeing, which are closely allied concepts to good fortune: someone who is overweight compared to populations norms might be perceived as happier, healthier and luckier than those who would be considered of 'ideal weight' by doctors. Poor appetite in children is commonly perceived to be worrying (DoH, 2004; Jesper et al., 2008). If these beliefs were shared by Mary or her wider community, they would be likely to heighten her emotional responsiveness to Janet's resistance to eating and increase the likelihood that she would interpret it as a rejection. Interactional patterns have been observed in mothers and daughters who show food refusal whereby as perceived parental pressure to eat more increases, so does the child's dietary restraint and distress, which tend to elicit more verbal and physical control behaviours from the mother, and so on, culminating in an aversive eating experience for both (Carper et al., 2000; Lindberg et al., 1998). Formulation with Mary and Janet would need to map out their particular pattern of reciprocal responses at mealtimes to see what processes might be perpetuating Janet's reluctance to eat certain meals.

For Roma, illness is often seen as a concern for the wider community and rallying around the ill person, often in relatively large groups that NHS visiting policies are not designed to accommodate, is a common response (Jesper et al., 2008). It would be important to find out what response Janet's weight loss and/or presentations at the accident and emergency department had elicited from their wider family and community. It may be that these cultural norms operate to focus a lot of concerned attention upon Janet and perhaps make available resources that would not be offered otherwise. Given that Janet and Mary live in an area of social deprivation and have become increasingly isolated due to Mary's limited mobility, this could be welcomed by both of them. It may be particularly gratifying to Janet who may feel that she receives less attention from her mother than her siblings and their children do. Being 'ill' may function as a way of achieving a comparable 'special' status to the brother who became a schoolteacher whilst perhaps simultaneously reducing any expectations that Janet should reach the same level of educational attainment. She may also have observed that her mother's ill health drew caring responses from those around them. If the 'sick role' elicits attention that might otherwise be withheld, then Janet's eating habits may be inadvertently reinforced by her mother and/or members of her wider social network.

Towards intervention

It is possible, as speculated earlier, that the involvement of a number of healthcare professionals is reinforcing unhelpful or conflicting messages about what constitutes the problem and who is responsible for finding a solution. Given the apparent attachment issues and the possibility of cultural distrust of healthcare professionals, it may be helpful to avoid recruiting further 'experts' into the family's network that may become interpolated between Mary and Janet. Being mindful of these possibilities, as well as of the reality of resource and time constraints for psychological services in healthcare, it would probably be most appropriate for the psychologist to support the existing healthcare team to formulate with Mary and Janet and to help them to make any changes that are suggested by this process.

For example, the school nurse could perhaps be enlisted to explore what Mary and Janet currently understand about each other's health and what meaning they attribute to each other's behaviour in relation to that. The overall aim of the exploration would be to support them to make sense of their situation and concerns in ways that facilitate adapting to and managing them within the context of their lives generally. Basic educational information on, for example, child nutrition and paced activity, may be offered if clear misconceptions are identified. The psychologist could consult to the nurse in supporting Mary to find developmentally appropriate ways of explaining her scheduled surgery to Janet so as to minimise anxiety, and of communicating with Janet about her own somatic experiences. The process of sharing their understandings fully with someone who is respectful and interested might be expected to provide emotional relief in itself as well as developing potentially new perspectives as they examine their concerns and clarify the issues they face.

Assuming that the jointly shared understanding to emerge from that process bore any resemblance to that outlined above, then the school nurse might be ideally placed to work with Mary on a plan for introducing target foods in small quantities to Janet at home that she could also encourage consistency with during school mealtimes. For example, she could perhaps help Mary to develop a wider repertoire of strategies such as providing clear, direct prompts; using verbal and physical praise and other rewards (e.g. preferred foods, interactive games) for cooperating with eating; and ignoring disruptive behaviours such as verbal refusals.

Reflections

Reflecting upon this formulation for Janet, I am aware that some difficulties that were persuasively accounted for in previous chapters in terms of psychotherapeutic models have now been recast as psychological consequences of her experience and understanding of physical health difficulties (such as her fear of public transport). It goes without saying that both might be valid in the sense of having a good 'fit' for the service users, and indeed the health formulation has made reference to some of the hypotheses in earlier chapters such as attachment issues. In the many cases where a person is experiencing physical as well as emotional problems, both specialties may benefit from the other's perspective in order to create an effective and comprehensive formulation. In this way we can attempt to bridge the mind–body split that, as discussed at the start of the chapter, has often limited our practice. However, usefulness, rather than satisfying narrative coherence, should always guide the extent to which physical and psychological experiences are linked into one formulation.

I am also reminded of the need, when formulating from a health perspective, to remain aware of one's own thoughts, feelings and attitudes in relation to illness and disability, and one's perception of one's own health status, and how these may be impacting upon the process. We perhaps more readily assume a continuum of physical health experience than we do mental health experience; most people can access a memory of what it is like to be in pain with greater cognitive ease than they might be able to access an experience which appears to be on a continuum with hearing voices. Whilst this may enable us to empathise and 'be alongside' service users more easily, it may also leave us at greater risk of extrapolating unhelpfully from our own experiences. For example, I have experienced 'exhaustion' and so I may need to guard against assuming too much understanding of how Mary's angina affects her and make a conscious effort to remain curious.

Moreover, the illness representations of people working in physical health settings will inevitably be influenced and modified by their exposure to their service users' experiences. Over time, representativeness biases (Tversky and Kahneman, 1974) are likely to affect our appraisals of how prevalent, severe, or threatening chronic or acute illnesses and injuries are, depending on the particular specialties we work in. It is therefore sometimes beneficial to consciously 'recalibrate' our perspectives with people less professionally familiar with those physical health areas and to reconnect with the 'naive' experience of entering medical environments with possibly minimal experience of the processes and systems we work within.

Key characteristics of formulation in health settings

- Will always, obviously, be a biopsychosocial formulation which includes physical health problems as a core element.
- Can be pro-active and preventative, that is, before events that might cause an increase in psychological distress have occurred.
- Are generally, at some level, team formulations seeking to incorporate the understandings of the wider healthcare team as well as the service user's views and to communicate each to the other.
- Do not usually fit the traditional 'stage' model of the assessment–formulation–intervention cycle and may be more recursive and 'on-the-spot' as medical interventions proceed.
- Will always be integrative in the sense that they address the impact of disease and disability, and draw on theoretical constructs and ideas from health psychology as well as psychotherapeutic models.

References

Ajzen, I. and Fishbein, M. (1980) *Understanding Attitudes and Predicting Social Behavior*. Englewood Cliffs, NJ: Prentice-Hall.

Becker, M.H. (ed.) (1974) *The Health Belief Model and Personal Health Behavior*. Thorofare, NJ: Slack.

Bibace, R. and Walsh, M.E. (1980) Development of children's concepts of illness. *Pediatrics*, 66, 912–917.

Boyle, M. (2002) *Schizophrenia: A Scientific Delusion?* (2nd edn) Routledge: London.

Brewster, A.B. (1982) Chronically ill hospitalized children's concepts of their illness. *Pediatrics*, 69 (3), 355–362.

Brodie, B. (1974) Views of healthy children toward illness. *American Journal of Public Health*, 64, 1156–1159.

Burochovitch, E. and Mednick, B.R. (1997) Cross-cultural differences in children's concepts of health and illness. *Journal of Public Health*, 31 (5), 448–456.

Carey, S. (1985) *Conceptual Change in Childhood*. Massachusetts, USA: Massachusetts Institute of Technology (MIT) Press.

Carper, J.L., Orlet Fisher, J. and Birch, L.L. (2000) Young girls' emerging dietary restraint and disinhibition are related to parental control in child feeding. *Appetite*, 352, 121–129.

Department of Health (2004) *The Health Status of Gypsies and Travellers in England*. London: Department of Health Publications.

Division of Clinical Psychology (2011) *Good Practice Guidelines on the Use of Psychological Formulation*. Leicester: British Psychological Society.

Furze, G. and Lewin, B. (2000) Causal attributions for angina: results of an interview study. *Coronary Health Care*, 4 (3), 130–134.

Horne, R., Weinman, J. and Hankins, M. (1999) The beliefs about medicines questionnaire: the development and evaluation of a new method for assessing the cognitive representation of medication. *Psychology and Health*, 14 (1), 1–24.

Jesper, E., Griffiths, F. and Smith, L. (2008) A qualitative study of the health experience of Gypsy Travellers in the UK with a focus on terminal illness. *Primary Health Care Research and Development*, 9 (2), 157–165.

Larkin, J. (1998) The embodiment of marime: living Romany Gypsy pollution taboo. *Electronic Doctoral Dissertations for UMass Amherst*. Available: http://scholarworks. umass.edu/dissertations/AAI9909179 (accessed 4 September 2012).

Lau, R.R. and Hartman, K.A. (1983) Common sense representations of common illnesses. *Health Psychology*, 2, 185–197.

Lazarus, R.S. and Folkman, S. (1984) *Stress, Appraisal, and Coping*. New York: Springer.

Leventhal, H., Benyamini, Y., Brownlee, S., Diefenbach, M., Leventhal, E., Patrick-Miller, L. et al. (1997) Illness representations: theoretical foundations. In K.J. Petrie and J.A. Weinman (eds), *Perceptions of Health and Illness*, pp.19–46. Singapore: Harwood Academic Publishers.

Lindberg, L., Bohlin, G., Hagekull, B. and Palmérus, K. (1998) Interactions between mothers and infants showing food refusal. *Infant Mental Health Journal*, 17 (4), 334–347.

Mladovsky, P. (2007) Research Note: To what extent are Roma disadvantaged in terms of health and access to health care? What policies have been introduced to foster health and social inclusion? The London School of Economics and Political Science [Electronic]. Available: http://academos.ro/sites/default/files/biblio-docs/112/mladrom.pdf (accessed 4 September 2012).

Moos R.H. and Schaefer, J.A. (1984) The crisis of physical illness: an overview and conceptual approach. In R. Moos (ed.) *Coping with Physical Illness: New Perspectives*, vol. 2, New York: Plenum Press.

Moss-Morris, R., Weinman, J., Petrie, K.J., Horne, R., Cameron, L.D. and Buick, D. (2002) The revised illness perception questionnaire (IPQ-R). *Psychology and Health*, 17, 1–16.

Rozin, P., Fallon, A. and Augustoni-Ziskind, M. (1985) The child's conception of food: the development of contamination sensitivity to 'disgusting' substances. *Developmental Psychology*, 21, 1075–1079.

Salmon, P. (2000) *Psychology of Medicine and Surgery: A Guide for Psychologists, Counsellors, Nurses and Doctors*. Chichester, UK: John Wiley & Sons Ltd.

Sontag, S. (1978) *Illness as Metaphor*. New York: Farrar, Straus and Giroux.

Tversky, A. and Kahneman, D. (1974) Judgment under uncertainty: heuristics and biases. *Science*, 185, 1124–1131.

Weinman, J., Petrie, K., Moss-Morris, R. and Horne, R. (1996) The illness perception questionnaire: a new method for assessing the cognitive representation of illness. *Psychology and Health*, 11, 431–445.

Wilkinson, R. and Marmot, M. (2003) *The Solid Facts*. Copenhagen: World Health Organization.

Chapter 12

Controversies and debates about formulation

Lucy Johnstone

Jack and Janet: the formulations

The reader who has reached this point may well be feeling overwhelmed by the numerous ways of understanding Jack's and Janet's difficulties. There are certainly striking differences between the formulations: some are based on individual work with Jack and Janet, others on seeing the family; the formulation may be built primarily about their thoughts, or their feelings, or their relationships, or their social contexts, or the narratives they have woven about their lives; it may be constructed largely by the therapist, or jointly with the individual or family, or perhaps not exist in a traditional form at all; it may co-exist with a psychiatric diagnosis, or be seen as an alternative to a diagnosis, or else both the concepts of diagnosis and formulation may be regarded with suspicion; it may be an absolutely central or a very peripheral part of the underlying theoretical approach; and it may lead to very different kinds of intervention, or perhaps none at all. In all cases, our authors have emphasised the need to work as collaboratively as possible and to be open to re-formulation as necessary. The two chapters on Integration have, we hope, given the reader some pointers towards putting together the ideas from different models, and have also highlighted the need to work sensitively and reflectively in real-life settings.

We are now in a position to return to the themes outlined in the very first chapter and explore some of the issues, debates and controversies in more detail, before coming to some tentative conclusions and finding out about how the real Jack and Janet have fared.

Formulations: are they evidence-based?

As we saw in chapter 1, the location of formulation within a scientific, experimental framework as 'a central process in the role of the scientific practitioner' (Tarrier and Calam, 2002: 311) has been widely accepted by psychiatrists and clinical psychologists, especially those of a cognitive-behavioural orientation. The earlier chapters show that such assumptions are by no means universal, and the application of a positivist model of scientific enquiry to human problems and relationships is problematic in itself. However, if one does start from this position then as Bieling and Kuyken (2003) have pointed out, formulation ought to stand up to scientific investigation into its reliability, validity and outcome. In other words, we ought to be able to point to evidence that case conceptualisation (as it is increasingly referred to in CBT circles), hailed as the 'heart of evidence-based practice' (Bieling and Kuyken, 2003: 53), is itself supported by the evidence.

Unfortunately 'current evidence for the reliability of the cognitive case formulation method is modest, at best' while 'there is a striking paucity of research examining the validity of cognitive case formulations or the impact of cognitive case formulation on therapy outcome' (Bieling and Kuyken, 2003: 52). While the effectiveness of cognitive therapy as a whole has received support from the evidence, the same cannot be said for the individualised case formulation. For example, although clinicians show reasonable levels of agreement when asked about the descriptive elements of a formulation, this breaks down as more inference is introduced (Bieling and Kuyken, 2000; Tarrier and Calam, 2002; Kuyken et al., 2009). There is very little research looking at the question of validity, or whether case formulations are meaningfully related to a client's presenting problems, for which reliability is a pre-requisite. Nor is there any clear link between case formulation and improved outcome. This has mainly been tested by comparing manualised CBT treatment packages with individualised ones; worryingly, and perhaps surprisingly, the latter do not seem to be any more effective than the former (Kuyken et al., 2009).

Investigations into psychodynamic formulations have been a little more productive (see summaries in Eells, 2010; Bieling and Kuyken, 2003; Messer, 1996; Weerasekera, 1995), although early attempts were unpromising (Malan, 1976). One of the most extensively researched methods is the Core Conflictual Relationship Theme, in which key themes are inferred from clients' descriptions of their relationships and used to develop a formulation expressed in a standardised format (Luborsky and Crits-Christoph, 1990). Interestingly, there is reasonable evidence of reliability between trained judges. There is also some limited evidence that interpretations which are in line with the CCRT themes are positively related to therapeutic alliance and to outcome. In a frank appraisal of the evidence, Kuyken et al. (2009) have argued that a more rigorous and principle-based approach to CBT case conceptualisation, similar to the work on CCRT themes, is needed as a basis for further evaluation. For example, they suggest that we need a psychometrically robust measure of the quality of case conceptualisations which might include such aspects as comprehensiveness, coherence, parsimony, explanatory power and so on (2009: 320).

This debate raises some interesting questions. It will be apparent that the above studies are based on a view of 'formulation-as-an-event' – an object or 'thing' that can be disentangled from the therapy and assessed independently. As we have seen in earlier chapters this assumption fits some therapeutic approaches, including CBT, better than others. However, it is hard to see how any mainstream therapy could proceed without the therapist having some hypothesis, explicit or not, about the reasons for the problem. Divested of all such speculations, the therapy would be reduced to a series of nods and basic reflections. On the other hand, if it is more accurate to see formulation as a shared activity which is embedded within the whole process of the therapeutic relationship, in other words 'formulation-as-a-process' (as in systemic formulation, chapter 4), the question of how to assess it as a specific entity becomes extremely complicated. Interestingly, team formulation offers one way out of this dilemma, since in this the formulation is, by definition, separate from the therapy – indeed, therapy may not be part of the intervention at all.

Other questions arising from the debate about research into formulation include: whose judgements should we use in order to assess a formulation's quality, reliability or validity? All the studies to date seem to assume that these decisions fall to the therapist – as if the client's views are irrelevant (although Kuyken et al., 2009 have recently argued that therapist–client agreement is the key test). Presumably this is related to another unstated assumption, that the formulation is something produced and owned by the therapist, rather than co-created with the client (or team) – which sits oddly with the strong claims for the collaborative nature of CBT. And what is 'validity' as applied to a formulation, and how, if at all, could it be measured? (See Barber and Crits-Christoph, 1993 and Messer, 1991 for a discussion of this complex issue.) Could both CBT and psychodynamic formulations, for example, be shown to be reliable and valid in a given case? If so, which would be the 'correct' or 'true' one? Or are we actually talking about usefulness, not truth (as systemic, narrative and personal construct formulations emphasise, chapters 4, 5 and 7), in which case there could be a number of equally effective routes to solving the same problem?

In summary, the gap between the claims made for formulation and the evidence to back up those claims is only partially filled. The Division of Clinical Psychology 'Guidelines on the use of psychological formulation' list 19 hypothesised benefits of formulation ranging from 'Minimising decision-making biases' to 'Strengthening the therapeutic alliance' (DCP, 2011: 8). An additional 17 benefits, including 'Achieving a consistent team approach to intervention' and 'Raising staff morale' are claimed for team formulation (2011: 9). As discussed in chapter 10, emerging evidence about the effectiveness of team formulation is cautiously promising, although this has yet to be corroborated in terms of impact on the service user and specific measures such as improved outcomes, reduced admissions and so on. Clearly, practitioners are firmly convinced of the value of formulation. However, evidence to support this conviction is lacking. Moreover, there are numerous conceptual and methodological obstacles to gathering it.

Before discussing these issues further, it is important to note that there is considerable empirical evidence in support of many of the theories and psychological principles that formulations draw upon; for example attachment theory, developmental psychology, and the therapeutic relationship, as well as specific bodies of knowledge about the effects of trauma, bereavement, poverty, discrimination, domestic abuse and so on. Thus, while a specific formulation may or may not be accurate or useful for a particular individual, its inferences can still be solidly evidence-based. Secondly, evidence of the potent healing effects of creating narratives lends indirect support for employing the particular kind of narrative that we call 'formulation'. For example, adults who are able to give a coherent and consistent account of their childhood relationships with their parents, even if these were difficult, are more able to attune themselves sensitively to their own children (Hesse, 2008). An intervention called Narrative Exposure Therapy has been found to reduce severe post-traumatic stress in adults and children who have experienced torture and other atrocities in war-torn countries (e.g. Neuner et al., 2008).

Formulations: truth versus usefulness

Butler, a clinical psychologist and author of a thoughtful overview of the subject, starts from the premise that formulation is 'the lynch pin that holds theory and practice together' (Butler, 1998: 1), a broad definition that allows her to claim agreement from 'proponents of most major therapeutic traditions' including behaviour therapy, family therapy, cognitive therapy, cognitive analytic therapy and interpersonal therapy. She appears to be a little ambivalent on the question of whether formulations can be said to be 'correct' or 'true'. On the one hand she asserts that 'formulations can never be shown to be right as they are hypotheses not statements of facts ... Like other scientific hypotheses, formulations can only be shown, conclusively, to be wrong' (Butler, 1998: 20). This appears to locate the process of formulation alongside other scientific investigations which do assume that there are 'facts' and 'truths' about the way the world is, even if we can never reach a final account of them. On the other hand, she later says: 'it is not necessary to believe that there is such a thing as a "correct" formulation', and quotes Messer: 'There is no one version of the truth because we largely construct our realities, which inevitably leads to multiple perspectives on that reality' (Messer, 1996 in Butler 1998: 21). For example, different family members are likely to have their own individual understandings, or formulations, of their difficulties. This view leans more towards a social constructionist perspective such as that expressed in chapters 4 (systemic formulation) and 5 (narrative formulation). Indeed, it is hard to see how any given formulation can be said to be the 'correct' one given that it is possible to formulate the same case from any number of different models – unless one assumes that some therapeutic models are 'truer' than others.

The chapters in this book represent different positions along this continuum, from those that see the notion of a 'correct', 'true' or 'accurate' formulation as relatively unproblematic in principle (which as above usually leads to attempts to research and validate it along traditional scientific lines), to those which reject any such assumptions. The latter position would lead to a very different kind of research, more likely to be qualitative in nature and to focus on the *client's* perspective (one that is notably lacking from the investigations described above).

Although the tension between these two very different perspectives is not resolved in Butler's article, it does lead her to suggest that 'a formulation does not have to be correct, but it does have to be useful' (Butler, 1998: 21). This allows us to take a step back from the debates about reliability, validity and so on outlined above. Usefulness itself has to be evaluated, of course, though perhaps according to less stringent criteria than truth, and Butler suggests that a 'useful' formulation will help to organise and clarify the information, develop an internal supervisor, and communicate with the client. She also puts forward a list of 'Ten tests of a formulation' (Butler, 1998: 21):

1 Does it make theoretical sense?
2 Does it fit with the evidence? (symptoms, problems, reactions to experiences)
3 Does it account for predisposing, precipitating and perpetuating factors?
4 Do others think it fits? (the patient, supervisor, colleagues)
5 Can it be used to make predictions? (about difficulties, aspects of the therapeutic relationship, etc.)
6 Can you work out how to test these predictions? (to select interventions, to anticipate responses and reactions to therapy)
7 Does the past history fit? (with respect to the person's strengths as well as weaknesses)
8 Does treatment based on the formulation progress as would be expected theoretically?
9 Can it be used to identify future sources of risk or difficulties for the person?
10 Are there important factors that are left unexplained?

Similar checklists of the usefulness of a formulation have been suggested by others including Persons (1989).

Formulations: useful to whom?

Useful to the client?

To argue that a formulation should be useful immediately raises the question: 'Useful to whom?'

Ideally, of course, one would hope that formulations would be useful to the client, although clients do not generally come to see us asking explicitly for formulations. Arguably, though, they *do* come to us asking for help in making sense of their experiences, which amounts to much the same thing. I will return to this point later. As we have seen, there is little evidence that formulations in general have a beneficial effect on outcome, which could be taken as a broad indication of whether they are useful to clients. Indeed, there is virtually no research at all on clients' views of formulations. One exception is Chadwick, et al. (2003), who assessed the impact of case formulation on symptoms of anxiety and depression and found no significant effect. Semi-structured interviews revealed that nine clients found the formulation helpful by enhancing their understanding of their problems, and six felt reassured and encouraged. Six others reported that they found the formulation saddening, upsetting and worrying, for example: 'My problems seemed so longstanding, I didn't realise they went back to my childhood'.

As the authors note, it is not possible to draw any longer-term conclusions from this; perhaps initial dismay was followed by a greater commitment to the therapeutic process, for example. Such an interpretation is supported by Evans and Parry (1996) who looked at the impact of re-formulation, a central feature of Cognitive Analytic Therapy, on four 'difficult to help' clients. Re-formulation did not seem to have any immediate effect on the client's perceived helpfulness of the sessions, on the therapeutic alliance, or on individual problems, and in interview clients used words like 'frightening' and 'overwhelming' to describe its impact. However, this seemed to be related to a recognition that they had been faced with painful material that they had tried to block off, and they also commented that they now believed that the therapist had really listened to and understood them. Similar findings emerged from Redhead (2010) in which participants made statements such as: 'I knew that it upset me, realising that it was all about having that abortion, but you do have to process it, and you do have to talk about it, and, you know, find some sort of outlet'.

Two studies have found more positive client reactions. Team formulation was endorsed by the clients in one project, with participants reporting that they felt 'normal' and had a new understanding of their problems (Kennedy et al., 2003). Individual formulation, in Redhead's (2010) interviews with 10 clients who had been referred for CBT for anxiety and depression, was described overall as increasing understanding and trust, and enabling clients to move forward. Participants made comments such as:

'It all just made sense. I got it, because it was true.'
'It was bang on, so I trusted that she understood.'
'She just got where I was coming from, and to have someone else understand, well, I just thought, I can't be a complete freak.'
'I just felt empowered that I could do something about them (the problems).'

However, some clients had experienced lasting distress from facing the origins of their difficulties and the associated painful feelings.

This research, limited as it is, does highlight the important point that to give a formulation to a client, perhaps particularly if it is done in an expert-derived way, is a powerful action which for this very reason may be experienced as distressing and damaging. 'It raises the possibility that CF might be a point of unrecognised therapist–client distance for those clients with negative emotional reactions' (Chadwick et al., 2003: 675). Attention to the process of formulation (collaboration, reflectiveness, sensitivity and so on) is a central theme of systemic and narrative approaches, among others, and one might imagine that a gradual shared evolving story is much less likely to be experienced as upsetting or damaging. The DCP Guidelines (2011: 30) include a checklist of good practice in formulating (as distinct from formulation).

Harmful to the client?

The possibility of negative emotional reactions is even more relevant in situations where the formulation is – in the client's view – simply wrong. For example, an anonymous client reported, 'My therapist simply ignored what did not fit into her theory ... Worst of all, she dismissed abusive elements from my past ... It's as if she has plundered my very being and soul and rewritten my life history according to what *she* thinks has affected me' (Anon quoted in Castillo, 2000: 42). Some particularly disturbing examples come from Jeffrey Masson's book *Final Analysis*:

> I was fascinated by the fact that in less than one hour, a person's life was being summed up ... And when Dr Garbin read us his summary, in the somber tone he gave it, it sounded more like a judgement, a final judgement, than an interpretation, and I could just imagine how stunned, or stupefied, or mortified that patient would be to hear it:
> 'The "truth" which dominated this patient's life', he said, 'was her discovery that she did not possess a penis and so had nothing to feel important about or to show off.'
> (Masson commented) 'I pity that woman ... her truth has been boxed in, sealed tight, unalterable forever.'
> (Masson, 1990a: 67, 70)

A service user who interviewed other service users for her research made a similar point, describing 'a man who was insulted to have been referred for any kind of psychiatric help as the disasters in his life of the last few years were quite sufficient to explain his somatic symptoms ... Another person went for psychological problems, by his definition, and was given a social worker to work with him. He was insulted by the fact that what he had said about himself, and his idea of what the trouble was, had been ignored' (Lindow, personal communication, April 2002). While it is not clear whether these clients had explicitly been offered a formulation as per the standard definitions, there was evidently a damaging clash between their and the professionals' broad understanding of the nature of their problems. Proctor (2002: 119) has vividly described how her therapist's consistent unwillingness to revise her interpretations 'had the effect of completely trapping me as someone unable to trust her own knowledge'.

A mismatch between the psychosocial understandings that service users often have of their problems, and the medical model of standard psychiatric treatment that is offered to them, has been widely documented (Rogers et al., 1993; Barham and Hayward, 1995; Mental Health Foundation, 1997). This can happen in reverse too – for example, individuals or families may hold strong 'illness' beliefs that contradict the professional viewpoint (as discussed in chapter 4). Disagreements between service users and professionals about *psychological* models and formulations have been much less discussed or explored. An exception is Madill et al.'s (2001) conversation analysis of a case in which client and therapist disagreed about their psychological understanding of the core problem, with the therapy ultimately having an unsuccessful outcome. This suggests that even if we cannot demonstrate that 'correct' formulations lead to good therapy outcomes, we may at least be able to show that 'not-useful' formulations lead to poor outcomes.

Formulation should be an on-going process rather than a one-off expert pronouncement (see chapter 7), and therefore one would hope that re-formulation based on the client's feedback would ensure that unhelpful formulations are revised or abandoned. Unfortunately, this does not always happen. Dumont (1993) provides an early example of Freud's refusal to give up a general formulation that, as he himself acknowledged, met with considerable disagreement from his patients. When 3-year-old Hans's mother threatened that the family doctor would cut off his penis if he touched it again, Freud noted that he was 'obliged to infer' a castration complex, although his patients 'one and all struggle violently against recognising it' (Freud in Dumont, 1993: 198).

In the same vein, Masson (1990b) provides a tragic re-reading of the famous case of Dora, who determinedly resisted Freud's interpretation that she was secretly in love with Herr K., a friend of her father. In fact, as Masson shows, Dora was repelled by Herr K.'s advances, and legitimately furious that her father had tried to promote this liaison as a pay-off for his own affair with Frau K. She ended up being betrayed not only by her father but also by Freud, who was determined to impose his own view of reality on her.

Such travesties are not confined to dead psychoanalysts. Dumont (1993: 197) argues that theories are mindsets that not only dispose us to select and configure the innumerable data that clients proffer over several sessions, but in subtle ways tendentiously elicit those data in the first place ... Rogerians, rational emotive therapist, Horneyans, behaviourists, existential therapists, Freudians, Gestaltists, among many others, rather consistently formulate ... the same kinds of problems for the most diverse clients and disorders.

Having done this, they are all likely to make 'the fundamental error in problem solving ... thinking that the "givens" of the problem are facts when indeed they are more or less fallible inferences' (Dumont, 1993: 196). We tend to be extremely resistant to revising our initial explanations of phenomena, even in the face of contradictory evidence. In systemic therapy this reluctance to give up on a formulation has been termed 'marrying one's hypothesis'. While a little dating and courtship is permitted, the general advice is to be as promiscuous as possible with one's hypotheses (Dallos and Draper, 2000).

Social psychology research has established that our judgements are characteristically distorted by a whole range of attributions that operate largely outside our awareness. Kuyken (2006) has summarised the biases that may affect the process of case formulation, especially at times of uncertainty and time pressure: the tendency to interpret new information as an example of something else that we already know about (representativeness bias); the tendency to draw on information that is more easily available to us (availability bias); and the tendency to assimilate new information into a core initial hypothesis (anchoring and adjustment bias).

The general point seems to be that professionals need to maintain a difficult balance between the theory and formulations that their work is based on, and the suspension of these ideas that allows them to listen properly to their clients. They must also find a balance between applying the evidence and maintaining reflective awareness about the influence of their own views, feelings and experiences. Without this, there is the danger of 'a diagnostic style of formulation which is just a list of problems ... an inflexible and concrete bunch of ideas' (Ray, 2008). Butler notes: 'Being on the receiving end of a formulation can feel like being weighed up, evaluated, or judged – like being "seen through" or "rumbled" rather than understood' (Butler, 1998: 2). The examples cited above suggest that if the therapist insists on imposing a formulation that is actually wrong, or that is strongly rejected by the client, the consequences can be even more devastating. Masson notes that 'We know that even torture victims often find the fact of not being believed as painful as the torture itself' (Masson, 1990b: 96).

The fundamental issue here is power, and specifically, the power of one person, in an expert position, to impose their viewpoint on another. In her introduction to Masson's *Against Therapy*, Rowe says: 'In the final analysis, power is the right to have your definition of reality prevail over other people's definition of reality' (Rowe in Masson, 1990b: 16).

There is no space to repeat or explore the wider debates about power in psychotherapy here, although they are obviously relevant to formulation since it is a central process in most therapies. Viewpoints range from Masson's assertion that all therapy is inevitably abusive because it always involves an imbalance of power (Masson, 1990b), to Proctor's (2002) more sophisticated analysis of the different kinds of power, both positive and negative, that may form part of the therapeutic relationship. For the purposes of this book, we can note that formulation is less likely to be damaging if it 'is presented questioningly and collaboratively ... It should be presented as a hypothesis, not as fact ... Formulation thus goes hand-in-hand with re-formulation' (Butler, 1998: 22). In other words, the tentative and provisional nature of the formulation must always be borne in mind, and it should be a joint exercise.

Rosenbaum (1996) is also aware of the dangers: 'Formulation can slide too easily into "fitting something to a known formula"'. His 'manifesto for avoiding formulation' describes how:

> Whenever I see a client, my first step towards formulation is to take the walk from waiting room to office one relaxed step at a time. Once I get back to the office, I have the client precede me into the room while I stand outside and try to let go of everything I have ever heard, hoped for, expected or wanted – what Bion (1967) calls entering the session 'without memory and without desire'. I pause and make an active effort to cultivate compassion, kindness, acceptance, and joy for the client.
>
> (Rosenbaum, 1996: 110)

Attaining Rosenbaum's Zen-like position of detachment, although a worthy aim, is likely to be difficult or impossible for most of us. We cannot separate ourselves completely from our own assumptions and judgements and those of the culture we are part of, and it may be naive to tell ourselves that we can.

This brings us onto the question of formulations and culture. Clearly, cultural misunderstandings are one possible source of mistaken or unhelpful formulations. The DCP Guidelines note that 'Western models of psychology and psychological therapy, and, therefore, the formulations that are based on them, often privilege ideas of independence and self-actualisation ... and focus on the individual as the basic unit of therapy ... Formulations may, therefore, need adaptation for use in a culturally appropriate way'. The Guidelines also note that 'the concept of formulation itself, especially one that prioritises internal causal factors, is itself culturally-based' (2011: 18).

These are complex and unresolved issues. Perhaps it is worth remembering that our own culturally sanctioned explanatory constructs are not necessarily more 'true' or more 'useful'; and that we need to respect a variety of ways of conceptualising and coping with distress even if we do not fully share them. We will need to inform ourselves about the cultural meanings of certain beliefs in order to do this effectively, and there may be a need for quite a bit of 'negotiating for shared … meanings' (Butler 1998: 20). A parallel can be drawn with the case of Jack. We may not understand or agree with the highly unusual ideas expressed by someone like Jack, but we can at least respect them as personally meaningful (see May, 2011 for an example of working in this way). Sometimes this means searching for a symbolic rather than literal meaning. This applies within as well as across cultures.

The Hearing Voices Network is a self-help campaigning organisation that challenges the view of voice-hearing as pathological and promotes various non-medical ways of coping with them. It uses 'constructs', which are very similar to formulations, to co-create an individual understanding of the meaning and origins of a person's voices. The HVN takes an interesting perspective on these issues, with its willingness to step right outside conventional psychiatric and psychological explanations and acknowledge entirely different frameworks that may be held by voice-hearers such as mystical, religious, metaphysical and paranormal beliefs. A conviction that voices are, for example, due to telepathy or reincarnation or gods or ghosts is treated with as much respect as any other belief system, and valued for its importance and usefulness to the voice-hearer. 'Accepting the experience and the belief system is a prerequisite of effective therapy' (Romme and Escher, 2000: 108).

Useful to the therapist?

Most of Butler's (1998) 'Ten tests of a formulation' seem to apply more directly to the therapist than to the client. He/she will be enabled to organise material, make predictions, identify risks, select interventions and so on. Her 'Summary of the purposes of formulation' (see chapter 1) is also mainly therapist-focused, covering factors such as clarifying hypotheses and questions, planning treatment strategies and predicting responses to strategies and interventions.

One would hope, of course, that what is beneficial to the therapist would also be beneficial to the client. Once again, there is little experimental evidence to support this. Chadwick, et al.'s (2003) study found that it was powerful and validating for therapists to have clients endorse a case formulation; that it made the therapists feel more hopeful about therapy and increased their sense of alliance and collaboration; and that it increased their confidence in the choice of therapy. However, as noted above, there was no identifiable change in the *clients'* distress or alliance scores. The authors note the possibility that 'at least some of the faith therapists have in the potency of CF might be due to the impact it has for them personally' (Chadwick et al., 2003: 675).

Any practitioner can appreciate the feeling of relief at arriving at a formula that seems to offer an explanation and a possible way forward, in the face of the overwhelming pain and confusion that clients bring to us. In Yalom's words, our theories are 'self-created, wafer-thin barriers against the pain of uncertainty' (Yalom in Dumont, 1993: 203). However, there is a danger that this is meeting our emotional or intellectual needs and not those of the client. There may be less risk of this in approaches such as systemic where, as we saw in chapter 4, the team may generate multiple formulations, which are offered to the family and judged in terms of their usefulness to them.

Useful to professions?

There is another important way in which formulations may primarily serve the interests of the therapist rather than the client, and that is via the benefits that may accrue to the therapist's profession by adopting a formulation-based approach. As discussed in chapter 1, formulation does not originate with, and is not used exclusively by, any single profession, and it is listed as a skill in the regulations for health, educational, forensic, counselling and sports and exercise psychologists as well as clinical psychologists and psychiatrists. This does not fit with a statement about formulation from the Division of Clinical Psychology's 'The core purpose and philosophy of the profession' (DCP, 2010: 6): 'What makes this activity unique to clinical psychologists is the information on which they draw. The ability to access, review, critically evaluate, analyse and synthesise psychological data and knowledge from a psychological perspective is one that is unique to psychologists.'

These rather grandiose claims have been greeted with scepticism by other clinical psychologists (Harper and Moss, 2003; Crellin, 1998). Harper and Moss feel that formulation 'had a minimal influence on our development as clinical psychologists and it is perhaps testament to our profession's ability to regularly reconstruct its identity that formulation, barely heard of a decade ago, is now seen as a central defining characteristic' (Harper and Moss, 2003: 6). Crellin argues that claims about formulation have served the key political purposes of, in the early years, achieving professional independence from psychiatry, and more recently justifying increases in grading and training places.

The DCP statement appears to rest on clinical psychologists' claim to be drawing on research and evidence as a basis for formulation – an 'elegant application of science' as Kinderman (2001: 9) puts it. According to the DCP, clinical psychologists are 'more than psychological therapists; they are scientist-practitioners' because they are 'rooted in the science of psychology' (DCP, 2010: 2–3). Detailed discussion of these claims is beyond the scope of this chapter (but see Bem and de Jong, 1997, and Jones and Elcock, 2001 for debates on the status of psychology as a science).

The DCP 'Good practice guidelines' (DCP, 2011: 13, 15) take a somewhat different perspective on the characteristic features of formulation in clinical psychology. They state that 'the fullest use of clinical psychologists' professional skills implies a broad-based, integrated and multi-model perspective which locates personal meaning within its wider systemic, organisational and societal contexts'. In other words, 'A narrower or single-model formulation needs to be a conscious and justifiable choice from a wider field of possible models and causal influences'. The key terms here are *multi-model, integrated*, and *personal meaning*. While this implies the ability to evaluate and apply the evidence, there is an equally strong emphasis on reflexivity, or the recognition that 'the subject nature of our discipline, human beings and human distress ... requires a kind of artistry that also involves intuition, flexibility and critical evaluation of one's experience' (2011: 7).

Boyle (2001) has some interesting arguments to make about the possible role of formulation as an alternative to psychiatric diagnosis (see below); a less self-interested, though not unproblematic, way for clinical psychologists to make political use of the concept of formulation. Psychiatrists are also showing increased interest in formulation in parallel with the international controversy about the proposals for the Diagnostic and Statistical Manual 5, in which psychiatric diagnosis has come under sustained criticism. As one author has noted: 'These limitations to ... diagnosis, if true, are serious. Consequently clinicians and professional training standards have argued that case formulation is a better way to guide selection of the most effective treatment' (Sturmey, 2009: 6). While this is in some ways a welcome development, it also has potential drawbacks, depending on how formulation is defined.

Formulation versus psychiatric diagnosis

The various therapeutic approaches have taken different views on whether formulation is a replacement for, or an addition to, psychiatric diagnostic systems such as DSM. As we saw in chapter 1, early behaviour therapists, as part of establishing their credibility in relation to psychiatrists and their right to work independently from them, promoted functional analysis (subsequently developed into case formulation) as a more useful alternative to diagnosis, since it did not rely on unobservable mental entities and had clear implications for intervention (Eells, 2010). Contemporary CBT therapists are more likely to see the two systems as able to co-exist (see chapter 2). Turkat, an influential figure in the development of case formulation, argued that 'diagnosis and formulation complement each other' (Bruch and Bond, 1998: 3). Tarrier and Calam, clinical psychologists and CBT therapists, argue that 'it is feasible to use case formulations within a disorder-based classification system' (Tarrier and Calam, 2002: 315).

Early psychoanalysts did not include psychiatric diagnosis as part of their understanding of their patients (Eells, 2010: chapter 1) although contemporary psychoanalytic and psychodynamic clinicians may well do so (Malan, 1995). According to one psychodynamic therapist, 'diagnosis and formulation have different and complementary functions'; both are said to be useful, especially in neurosis and 'personality disorders' (Aveline, 1999: 199).

Some CBT therapists have reached a kind of halfway house on this issue, using psychiatric diagnostic terms such as histrionic or narcissistic personality disorder as a short-hand general formulation for certain groups of individuals who express their problems in characteristic ways. In a similar way, psychoanalytically oriented clinicians may refer to 'psychoanalytic character diagnosis', which uses diagnostic terms such as 'paranoid personality', 'depressive personality' and 'manic personality' to describe certain character structures and the typical defences and transference reactions that accompany them (Weston, 1990). The intention here, again, is to provide a general formulation of certain types of psychological difficulty together with indications for therapeutic intervention. This would be supplemented with a formulation constructed to fit the particular individual.

This is a somewhat confusing use of language. All therapists are likely to have at their disposal certain broad-level formulations that describe common patterns of difficulty (for example, 'bereavement reaction' or 'trauma reaction'). These help therapists to look out for typical responses (denial, shock, flashbacks and so on) and to suggest therapeutic interventions that are often found useful in such cases. However, it introduces an extra layer of confusion to use *medical/psychiatric* concepts in order to describe something that is actually being conceptualised in *psychological* terms. As discussed below, the two models, medical and psychological, have very different assumptions and implications.

Systemic therapists have always seen families in social and relational, as opposed to medical, terms. They start, by definition, from the fundamental assumption that difficulties never reside within one individual, as is implied by a psychiatric diagnosis. And, as described in earlier chapters, social inequalities and narrative therapists, along with some family therapists, are sceptical not only about diagnosis but about some versions of formulation as well, particularly in its more concrete sense. Their focus is not 'the problem' (or 'the formulation') as such; rather, it is the views of 'the problem' held by the identified client, his/her family, and by the systems in which both client and therapist live and work.

Some of the best-known writers on formulation take the view that combining psychological formulation with psychiatric diagnosis is unproblematic. Eells, for example, suggests that 'a case formulation provides a pragmatic tool to supplement and apply a diagnosis to the specifics of an individual's life. It also serves as a vehicle for converting a diagnosis into a plan for treatment' (Eells, 2010: 25). Weerasekera's grid in which formulations from various models can be combined with psychiatric diagnosis to produce a comprehensive treatment plan, has been described in chapter 8. Thus, for example, in the case of

an individual suffering from depressive and anxiety symptoms in the presence of chronic, severe marital distress may benefit from individual (medication plus cognitive behavioural therapy) and systemic (marital)

> therapy … A pharmacological treatment of depression can be integrated
> with marital therapy, whereby the same therapist administers the
> medication and conducts the marital therapy.
>
> (Weerasekera, 1995: 357)

These suggestions have much in common with the multi-axial classification
of DSM, whereby information about personal and social context is added on
to the main psychiatric diagnosis. However, as we have seen, such views are
not unique to psychiatrists. A debate on the subject in *The Psychologist*
(Pilgrim, 2000; Letters to the Editor, 2000) drew supporters from both
sides.

It is worth noting that formulation is strongly emphasised as a skill in
current psychiatric training, in both written work and presentations. In
evaluating these developments, we need to be clear what is meant by
'formulation'. The DCP Guidelines draw a distinction between psychiatric
formulation and psychological formulation. Whereas trainee psychiatrists are
required to 'demonstrate the ability to construct formulations of patients'
problems that include appropriate differential diagnoses' (Royal College of
Psychiatrists, 2010: 25), the Guidelines define psychological formulations in
clinical psychology as 'not premised on a functional psychiatric diagnosis'
(DCP, 2011: 29). For example, while a psychiatric formulation might take
the form of: 'Schizophrenia, probably with a genetic component as indicated
by the family history, triggered by the stress of bereavement', the equivalent
psychological formulation might be: 'Hearing the voice of your abuser, as a
result of unprocessed feelings and memories stirred up by his death'. While
psychiatric formulation acknowledges the impact of psychosocial factors to
some extent, it is seen as an addition to, not a replacement for, the diagnosis.
Rather like the currently popular biopsychosocial model of mental distress, a
psychiatric formulation retains a primary role for (unevidenced) biological
causal factors, while reducing other life events to the status of 'triggers' of a
disease process. In political terms, it puts psychiatrists in the strong position
of claiming expertise in both these essential skills, diagnosis and formulation.
However, there are serious disadvantages to this conceptually incoherent
position.

In chapters 4 (systemic formulation), 8 (integrative formulation) and 10
(team formulation), it was pointed out that professionals and institutions are
likely to be working from fundamentally medical assumptions and thinking
in terms of diagnosis, medication and so on, and that in Jack's case this may
have both benefits and costs. For example, Jack's medication may help both
him and his family to cope at present – but on the other hand, it may reinforce
the message that he is inadequate and a failure. A 'formulation fight' between
professionals is not going to help anyone, least of all the client, and the authors
give some useful ideas about how to avoid this. The disadvantages of
combining the two systems will now be explored in a little more detail.

For a start, there are the many documented shortcomings of psychiatric diagnosis as a form of classification: low reliability, lack of validity of diagnostic concepts, overlap between categories, and unclear links with aetiology, prognosis and treatment. It can also have a number of other undesirable consequences such as the obscuring of personal, social and cultural contexts; the individualising of problems; stigma and disempowerment; removal of responsibility; omission of the client's viewpoint; objectification of the client; and most worrying of all, the loss of personal meaning (Boyle, 2002; Follette and Houts, 1996; Johnstone, 2000, Johnstone, 2008; Kirk and Kutchins, 1992; Pilgrim, 2000; Honos-Webb and Leitner, 2001; Mehta and Farina, 1997). These criticisms have recently re-surfaced in heated debates about the latest edition of DSM (see www. dxrevisionwatch.wordpress.com). Formulation could, at least in principle, be seen as a possible way of re-introducing personal meaning, personal and social contexts and mutual collaboration into mental health work. If the meta-messages of psychiatric diagnosis are that the service user's difficulties have no personal significance, are not within his/her control, and may last a lifetime, psychological formulation can restore a sense of meaning, agency and hope, for both service users and staff (Johnstone, 2008).

Arguing against the use of both systems concurrently, Boyle (2001) points out that if psychiatric diagnosis did what it aims and claims to do, and provided a valid, coherent and reasonably complete account of someone's difficulties with clear indications about effective treatment, then psychological formulation would be redundant. The same is also true the other way round. If a convincing formulation can be developed, meeting Butler's (1998) criteria for accounting for the facts, indicating the intervention and so on, then an extra explanation that says, in effect, 'Oh and by the way, they have a mental illness too' becomes redundant. As argued in the DCP Guidelines, a psychological explanation of 'symptoms' such as hearing voices, low mood and so on eliminates the need for concepts such as 'schizophrenia' or 'bipolar disorder'. With a dual system, we are being offered incompatible explanations from conflicting models: 'You have a medical disease with primarily biological causes' versus 'Your problems are an understandable emotional response to your life circumstances'. In essence, a formulation says that the nature and content of your distress is *personally meaningful*, while a psychiatric diagnosis says that it is *meaningless*. These assumptions cannot both be true.

Moreover, the adoption of both models at the same time leads to damaging contradictions in clinical practice, as discussed in chapter 10 (team formulation). With Weerasekera's anxious and depressed client, for example, the medication, unless carefully explained, carries the message that 'the problem is a biological one lying within you as an individual, and the pill will rectify it'. On the other hand, the marital therapy will not make progress unless the couple are able to accept that 'the problem is a function of the relationship you have with each other, and you both need to accept responsibility for working on it'. This is a recipe for stalemate (Johnstone, 2000).

Thus formulation can, Boyle argues, be offered as a genuine alternative to diagnosis and its many shortcomings. Pilgrim agrees, asking:

> Do we not have a professional responsibility to challenge and expose the shortcomings of a diagnostic approach? ... Surely our main duty is ... not to shore up medical reifications, but to demonstrate why formulations about specific presenting problems in specific contexts are more useful and compelling.

He attributes the failure to do this to clinical psychology's 'ambivalent position towards psychiatry – wanting full professional independence but, at times of selective convenience, co-opting a medical knowledge base' (Pilgrim, 2000: 304). In a recent and radical shift, the profession has answered this call by issuing a Position Statement calling for the abandonment of functional psychiatric diagnosis ('schizophrenia', 'bipolar disorder', 'personality disorder' and so on) and the development of formulation-based systems instead (DCP, 2013).

However, it is not a simple matter of jettisoning one system for the other. For a start, 'the issue is that "problem" is not an objectively identifiable natural category, and it is often not possible to see any particular behaviour or experience as inherently problematic' (Boyle, 2001: 2). This is an issue that has been explored most thoroughly within systemic, social constructionist and social inequality approaches, with their willingness to ask, 'Who has the problem?' and to deconstruct some of the current discourses around what is viewed as problematic behaviour (being a lone parent, being a working mother, and so on).

Another danger is that formulations can be open to some of the same criticisms as diagnosis – for example, that by uncritically accepting the view of the service user or client as the site of the problem, formulations individualise distress and ignore social context. And, as we have already seen, there is no guarantee that formulations will not be used in a stigmatising, objectifying, un-collaborative way as well. Moreover, service users may find formulation a more complex way of accounting for their difficulties to others, in contrast to the apparently stronger justification provided by diagnosis, which thus represents both 'salvation and damnation' (Leeming et al., 2009). Perhaps the best that can be said is that these dangers are not intrinsic to the process of formulation (and the earlier chapters have discussed a number of ways of trying to avoid these risks), whereas they are, arguably, an almost unavoidable consequence of psychiatric diagnosis.

Even if we accept psychological formulation as a valid alternative to psychiatric diagnosis at an individual or family level, there is still the problem of replacing the various functions that diagnosis serves – or seems to serve – at a broader clustering level. In general medicine, a diagnosis is used to indicate which category the patient's complaints fall into and hence to give indications about aetiology, prognosis and treatment and provide a basis for communication and research. The fact that psychiatric diagnosis does all of these very poorly, or not at all, does not eliminate the need for some kind of clustering system so that we do not have to treat every individual service user as a 'first instance'. Psychiatric diagnosis also retains its central position because it performs, or seems to perform, a variety of administrative functions such as deciding who should be offered a service, who should be held responsible for their actions (e.g. in the criminal justice system), and who should receive benefits.

It may be useful to discuss these issues in more depth.

Are formulations individualising?

It is certainly true that formulations *can* be individualising, ignoring personal and social contexts and replicating the damage that has been attributed to psychiatric diagnosis. The early women's movement abounded with accounts of women whose despair at being trapped within traditional roles had been met with mystifying psychoanalytic formulations from their (male) psychotherapists:

> The loss of her father when she was six was assumed to be the cause of Mrs O's depression, and her unresolved Oedipal conflict was thought to underlie her husband's complaints of her frigidity. Mrs O ... was totally responsible for the 24 hour a day, 7 day a week care of three pre-school children. Her husband's demanding job as an air traffic controller ... precluded any help from him. Mrs O felt trapped, tired, overwhelmed, resentful and seething with anger towards her husband. Because of her socialisation she thought she should be happy, could not acknowledge her feelings as expectable in the situation, and agreed with her doctor that she was depressed, neurotic and had sexual problems.
> (Penfold and Walker, 1983: 179)

Davis's (1986) in-depth qualitative analysis shows how the task of re-formulating a female client's initial version of her problems as stemming from her role as full-time housewife and mother, into an individual deficit (she is not good at expressing her feelings), is achieved via the therapeutic conversation.

A central claim of David Smail's extensive critiques of therapy is that psychotherapies are concerned with individual internal psychological states viewed in isolation from their social and political context (Smail, 1993, 1996). Another noted critic of psychotherapy, Jeffrey Masson, contends that by focusing on the individual, 'every therapy I have examined displays a lack of interest in social justice' (Masson, 1990b: 285). The result of formulating social and political problems as individual pathology is mystification about the true origins of one's distress (Smail, 1993, 1996) and 'an implicit acceptance of the political status quo' (Masson, 1990b: 285), which, for some people, betrays the true purpose of the therapy industry: 'The rise of a purely psychological view of human difficulties is a handy way of mystifying social reality' (Kovel, 1981: 73). The DCP Guidelines on formulation remind us that 'service users are almost always survivors of immensely difficult personal and social circumstances. Interventions will be ineffective if wider causal factors are located at an individual level, thus pathologising the service user and increasing their sense of hopelessness' (2011: 20).

The key question is whether formulations are *inevitably* individualising. A number of attempts have been made to reduce this risk.

Systemic therapists, by definition, seek to formulate problems from a broader than individual perspective, including as appropriate the couple, family, school, workplace and so on. They are likely to be aware of competing views about whether there is a problem and what the problem is, from the individual, the family, agencies such as the police and social services, the school, the legal system, professionals and the wider culture (Dallos and Draper, 2000). This may lead to a complex, multi-layered intervention of the type described in chapter 4.

Community psychology is a movement within clinical psychology which, as we saw in chapter 6, aims to develop an understanding of people within their social worlds and to use this to reduce mental distress through social action. A well-known example of this comes from community psychologist Sue Holland, who has developed an approach that she calls Social Action Psychotherapy (Holland, 1992). In this, women move, as and when they are ready, from 'Step one: Patients on pills' through the various stages of person-to-person psychotherapy, talking in groups and taking action in their community. The formulation or understanding of their difficulties thus proceeds in layers, with the second step most closely resembling traditional psychotherapy and the last two adding in the social and political dimension. Holland calls this 'a progression from private symptom to public action' (Holland, 1992: 5).

There have, then, been a number of attempts to integrate wider relational, social and political factors into the understanding of people's problems, although it should be noted that simply asking the family along does not in itself guarantee such a formulation. (See, for example, the Family Management approach to psychosis which is based on the philosophy that 'we do *not* view the family as being in need of treatment ... our aim is to help the family to cope better with the sick member who is suffering from a defined disease', Kuipers et al., 1992: 4). Nor, as Sue Holland observes, does working in the community necessarily indicate a willingness to acknowledge the role of inequality and injustice in the people's difficulties: 'The present trend towards "hospitalising the community" ... using new means but old models ... is a backward step' (Holland, 1992: 7).

Equally, it has been argued that individual therapy need not necessarily imply an individualising formulation of the client's difficulties. Roy-Chowdhury contends that Smail draws a false dichotomy between the practice of individual psychotherapy and the acknowledgement of the social world. While 'the socio-cultural constraints of poverty and disadvantage ... should not be psychologised away' (Roy-Chowdhury, 2003: 8), there is still the possibility (although it is certainly under-developed in many mainstream therapies) of using the psychotherapeutic conversation to make the links between the individual and the society of which they are a part (for examples, see McNamee and Gergen, 1992). This is a position that Smail also appears to acknowledge at times when he talks of the role of individual psychotherapy as 'to side with the person rather than the social world, helping to drag out his or her *internalised* norms ... At the very least this gives people the freedom to think and feel what they like, to examine their experience for its significance rather than simply for its "abnormality"' (Smail, 1987: 401). The implication is that even within one-to-one therapy, it is possible both to challenge assumptions about the nature of the 'problem' and to construct formulations which link the person and their social context.

The starting point must be 'a critical awareness of the wider societal context within which formulating takes place, even if this dimension is not explicitly included in every individual formulation' (DCP, 2011: 20). This is even more crucial in the light of recent compelling evidence that a society's level of social inequality is causally related to (among many other undesirable outcomes) its rates of 'mental illness'. 'If Britain became as equal as the four most equal societies ... mental illness might be almost halved' (Wilkinson and Pickett, 2009: 261).

Clearly, the implications of these findings go well beyond formulation. Some of them are drawn out below.

What would a formulation-based system look like?

We can see that the use of formulation as an alternative to psychiatric diagnosis is far from straightforward if we want to avoid simply reproducing some of the latter's more damaging aspects. It is, however, perfectly possible to work with individual clients without using diagnosis at all, as many clinical psychologists have done for years. The issue becomes very much more complex if we move from individual work to a broader clustering level. What general terms could be used to replace diagnoses such as 'schizophrenia', 'psychosis', 'bipolar disorder', 'ADHD', 'personality disorder' and so on, and the functions that they serve, or seem to serve? In another sign of the inadequacy of the existing system, various alternatives such as 'traumatic psychosis' (Callcott and Turkington, 2006) and 'dissociative' subtype (Ross, 2008) have been suggested for 'schizophrenia', while 'complex PTSD' has been put forward as a replacement for 'personality disorder' (Herman, 2001). These terms can perhaps be understood as occupying a halfway position between formulation and diagnosis, incorporating some acknowledgement of psychosocial causal factors while retaining the concept of 'disorder'. In this respect they are similar to some existing DSM diagnoses such as bereavement reaction, adjustment disorder and dissociative disorder.

While these proposals do indicate a paradigm under threat, it is important to note that they stop well short of challenging its core assumptions. They still imply some kind of dysfunction located within an individual rather than, say, a desperate attempt to employ survival mechanisms to cope with traumatic relationships and situations. They also imply a cut-off point between 'well' and 'ill', 'normal' and 'abnormal', rather than a spectrum. More specifically, they still make the bizarre assumption that human emotional distress – which is what we are talking about – can be divided into the neat categories associated with classification in the natural sciences.

One of the reasons that it is so difficult to think outside the 'DSM mindset' is that its assumptions (which, as noted, can tarnish formulation as well) are deeply embedded in Western culture as a whole, with its emphasis on the separation of thought from feeling, the individual from the community, the mind from the body, and humankind from the natural world. Stepping back from all this implies the very different philosophical position that human beings are not (potentially faulty) machines carving an individual path through their lives, but are fundamentally meaning-making creatures, whose subjective experiences are 'a way of being in the world … relationally, societally and materially *co-constituted*' (Cromby and Harper, 2009: 335–336, italics in the original). Although this may be an unfamiliar way of thinking, it is in fact much better supported by the evidence than the traditional psychiatric one (see, for example, Brown and Moran, 1997; Warner, 2004; Fernando, 2003; Wilkinson and Pickett, 2009 for some of the well-established links between subjective meanings, emotional distress, and relational and social/material circumstances). Rather than *causes*, as in the medical model of distress, we need to look for *grounds* or *reasons* for human behaviour. Human beings are agents and their actions are intentional and functional, albeit mediated by biological processes (Ingleby, 1981; Cromby and Harper, 2009). The painstaking and painful process of re-discovering these connections and patterns (as in the large body of recent research on trauma and abuse, Read and Bentall, 2012) is the best hope for providing us with a body of knowledge to support the co-construction of individual formulations.

It is too soon to say what kind of general patterns might emerge from this project. It is possible that the majority of psychiatric diagnoses could be replaced with something similar to the broad-level terms that, as already noted, most therapists already draw on implicitly in their work – perhaps 'unresolved trauma in the context of social isolation and unemployment' and so on. In philosophical terms these would be 'fuzzy concepts' without exact boundaries, cutting across traditional psychiatric diagnoses, but precise enough to fulfil one of the core purposes of categorisation, i.e. to reduce complexity by grouping similar types of experience together. This would provide a basis for carrying out further research, as has happened very successfully with the term 'hearing voices' as used by the Hearing Voices Network. These terms could then be used to indicate the relevant evidence and resources that specific individual formulations should draw upon. They would not on their own answer administrative questions about responsibility, eligibility for benefits and so on, but psychiatric diagnosis does not do this in any satisfactory way either. These issues and debates will increasingly come to the fore as psychiatry is forced to deal with the fall-out from the DSM-5 disaster.

Can anyone construct formulations? Do we need them at all?

Despite the many claims made for formulation, it is not seen as essential by everyone; indeed some would dispute that it constitutes a special skill at all. 'Every time you cross a road you are formulating. It is hardly a higher skill ... Why a person in their mid-twenties with a postgraduate psychology qualification would be better at this than, say, a journalist, a reasonably well-read union member, a social historian or my mum, is beyond me', in the view of one clinical psychologist (Newnes, personal communication, April 2002).

The understanding and creation of meaning is certainly not unique to therapists; indeed it is central to what it is to be human. Personal construct therapy (chapter 7) argues that we are essentially meaning-creating creatures; we are engaged in a constant process of hypothesising about the world around us, and creating and elaborating a personal system of meanings which will enable us to survive in it. We are, in this sense, 'formulating' our experiences all the time. Thus it is not surprising if we can find examples of what could loosely be called 'formulations' in all aspects of our daily lives – including, perhaps, crossing the road – and anywhere that is concerned with exploring what it is to be human, such as novels.

The construction of stories, or narratives, also seems to be 'a ubiquitous and fundamental characteristic of human nature ... essential for psychological survival, enabling us to arrive at a coherent sense of identity through providing a vehicle by which we can understand the past, explain the present and prepare for the future', (Corrie and Lane, 2010: 106–107; and see chapter 5).

Some therapeutic approaches explicitly reject the use of formulation in its usually understood sense, as we have seen in the chapters on narrative and social inequalities approaches. Carl Rogers saw formulation, or as he referred to it 'psychological diagnosis', as unnecessary and even damaging, since it implied the use of power and expertise by the therapist with the consequent danger of the client relinquishing responsibility for themselves (Rogers, 1951 in Eells, 2010). However, his writings make it clear that something rather similar, that is, finding the meanings of the client's experience, is a central aspect of being empathic, albeit with a very person-centred emphasis on caution, sensitivity and non-judgementalism:

> It (being empathic) involves being sensitive, moment to moment, to the changing felt meanings which flow in this other person … By pointing to the possible meanings in the flow of his/her experiencing you help the person to focus on this useful type of referent, to experience the meanings more fully, and to move forward in the experiencing.
>
> (Rogers, 1975: 4)

The Hearing Voices Network, as we have seen, talks in terms of creating 'constructs' rather than formulations, but does not see this as a task that necessarily involves a professional; it can also be facilitated by a friend, partner or another voice-hearer. However, it does believe that making links between voices and life experiences, whether those links are historical, psychodynamic or metaphorical, can relieve distress (Romme and Escher, 2000).

It could be argued, then, that even those constructionist, humanistic or self-help approaches which reject the use of formulation as such, and object to the idea of a professional producing this kind of summary, are in fact using techniques or strategies which have the aim of helping clients reach a psychological understanding, or formulation, of their distress. The key difference seems to be an over-riding emphasis on respecting the client's own views – a welcome antidote to some of the abuses described earlier in the chapter.

So what are formulations then?

As noted earlier, clients do not typically come to us requesting a 'formulation' of their problems. In the sense suggested above, though, it can be argued that they do approach us asking for *explanations*, and for help in *constructing meaning* and *making sense* of their distress.

Butler (1998: 2) suggests that the key assumption underlying all formulations is that 'at some level it all makes sense'. Towards the end of her review she describes formulation as 'a way of summarising meanings, and of negotiating for shared ways of understanding and communicating about them'. This may be a flag under which therapists of different persuasions, and their clients, can all unite – despite the other differences outlined in this chapter.

Harper and Moss make a similar point when they describe formulation as, in essence, 'a process of ongoing collaborative sense – making' (2003: 8). Although it may draw on theory – as well as on numerous other sources – this construction of what might be called a shared story does not fit comfortably within the traditional rhetoric of the scientist-practitioner and evidence-based practice. It does, however, allow for reflexivity and an awareness of all the potential pitfalls discussed above.

Is formulation, on this definition, a special skill? Could our mothers do just as well? The answer is both yes and no. We are all constantly engaged in a process of creating theories about the world and the people in it, and a great many non-professionals (as well as novelists, poets, philosophers, priests and others whose subject matter is human nature and human suffering) are extremely good at this. On the other hand, as Roy-Chowdhury (2003) has argued, we can acknowledge this without falling back into the 'therapy/ formulation is no more than a chat with a friend' camp. Like the authors quoted above, he sees the core aim of therapy of all brands as 'to seek to understand and make sense of another's experience and to offer these provisional and tentative understandings to the other for consideration' (Roy-Chowdhury, 2003: 8). However, his discourse analysis of therapy conversations suggests that this is a highly skilled procedure. While drawing on basic human warmth, the therapist must also 'listen not only to what is ostensibly signified in the therapee's speech but also to the hidden and disguised significations'. The therapist who is not 'tuned into the nuances of the talk, the multiplicity of discourses evoked in each sentence, who does not seek to enter the lifeworld of the client and to communicate an understanding of that lifeworld using a language congruent with the expectations of the client' (Roy-Chowdhury, 2003: 9) will risk losing the client. We might add that the therapist must also be reflective about his or her own assumptions and feelings, aware of the developing relationship with the client, and sensitive to differences in each other's formulations. He or she will bring to the relationship a body of knowledge and theory as well as accumulated 'practice-based evidence' from clinical experience, and these need to be woven into the therapeutic process in ways that respect the client's own feelings and meanings.

This book has presented the argument that there are significant benefits – along with some risks – to employing the particular kind of narrative that has come to be referred to as a formulation. In a broader sense, making stories and sense out of our experiences is a fundamental characteristic of what it is to be human.

Summary

The potential criticisms and limitations of formulation echo the potential criticisms and limitations of therapy itself. This is hardly surprising if formulation is conceived, at least by most schools of therapy, as central to the process of therapeutic intervention. Both pose enormous problems for evaluation; both raise questions of truth versus usefulness; both can be damaging; both can be used for professional and political ends; both contain implicit assumptions and value judgements; both have a problematic relationship to psychiatric diagnosis; both can be individualising, ignoring social and cultural contexts; both are open to analogies about the emperor's clothes. On the bright side, both are requested and (often) found helpful by service users (if we use formulation in its 'meaning-seeking' sense); both can offer an alternative to psychiatric diagnosis and intervention with all its well-documented damage; and both, arguably, demand a high level of skill, though not one that is unique to any particular profession or indeed any particular group of human beings.

If we wish to maximise the benefits of formulations for clients, teams and services and minimise the potential damage, the lessons seem to be that we must:

- Be reflexive about our own role in the formulation and the values and assumptions we bring to it.
- Offer formulations tentatively, to individuals and teams.
- Construct formulations collaboratively, with individuals and teams.
- Use personal meaning as a central integrating factor.
- Be constantly open to re-formulating.
- Express formulations in ordinary language.
- Ensure that formulations are culturally sensitive.
- Always consider the possible role of trauma and abuse.
- Respect client and team views about the accuracy and usefulness of the formulation.
- Be aware of stakeholder interests.
- Be willing to acknowledge the possible role of services in compounding the difficulties.
- Take systemic and wider social/political factors into account.

(NB: see also the checklist for best practice formulations in the DCP Guidelines, 2011: 29.)

If we wish to promote the use of formulation more widely as a route to understanding and intervening in mental distress, and perhaps as a basis for a whole different paradigm that is not premised on psychiatric diagnosis, we must:

- Be cautious about entering debates on the reliability and validity ('correctness' or 'truth') of formulations.
- Carry out more and different types of research, including qualitative methodologies and collaboration with service users, into the effects of formulation on the client, the team, the therapist and the therapy.
- Collect hard data on outcome measures such as cost, admissions, use of medication, staff morale, recovery rates and so on, in relation to individual and team formulation.

- Abandon unsupportable claims about the uniqueness of formulation to any one profession, and (particularly as clinical psychologists) be willing to share these skills as widely as possible.
- Be willing to speak out about the short-comings of psychiatric diagnosis (while 'highlighting the social and moral issues which diagnosis has helped to obscure', Boyle, 2001: 5).
- Develop coherent formulation-based alternatives to the use of psychiatric diagnosis as a clustering and administrative tool.
- Be realistic, but confident, about the usefulness of formulation.

Jack and Janet: an update

Jack was discharged from hospital in a slightly more settled state after a few weeks. He never really engaged in individual therapy, due to his erratic time-keeping and tendency to disappear into fantasy. A family meeting appeared to help all parties to appreciate each others' positions a bit better. Jack received a lot of practical support from a male community psychiatric nurse, with whom he had a good relationship, and later from an occupational therapist. A year on, he was very proud of the flat that had been found for him, and had made contacts in the local community. After numerous relapses into drinking, he had finally committed himself to an access course to higher education, and intended to take a degree in marketing in the future with the aim of going into the music business. He was still quite pre-occupied with Robbie Williams but seemed to have decided that 'If he was going to get me he would have done so by now', and was mostly able to put these worries out of his head. Jack was in friendly contact with his mother and sisters.

Janet is doing reasonably well. She is attending school and getting on better with her mother. Although she still has anxieties about public transport, her mother is less concerned about this and believes that Janet will eventually overcome her worries. Family work seems to have helped Mary to feel more confident as a mother and less to blame for Janet's difficulties. The fact that Andrew, Janet's brother, is continuing to do well at school is a further boost to Mary's confidence as a parent. Janet has not resumed contact with her father.

Acknowledgements

Many thanks to Rudi Dallos for his thoughtful comments on this chapter.

References

Aveline, M. (1999) The advantages of formulation over categorical diagnosis in explorative psychotherapy and psychodynamic management, *The European Journal of Psychotherapy, Counselling and Health*, 2, 2, 199–216.

Barber, J.P. and Crits-Christoph, P. (1993) Advances in measures of psychodynamic formulations, *Journal of Consulting and Clinical Psychology*, 61, 4, 574–585.

Barham, P, and Hayward, R. (1995) *Relocating Madness: From the Mental Patient to the Person*, London: Free Association Books.

Bem, S. and de Jong, H.B. (1997) *Theoretical Issues in Psychology: An Introduction*, London: Sage.

Bieling, P.J. and Kuyken, W. (2003) Is cognitive case formulation science or science fiction? *Clinical Psychology: Science and Practice*, 10, 1, 52–69.

Boyle, M. (2001) Abandoning diagnosis and (cautiously) adopting formulation, Paper presented at British Psychological Society Centenary Conference, Glasgow.

——(2002) *Schizophrenia: A Scientific Delusion?* (2nd edn), London: Brunner-Routledge.

Brown, G.W. and Moran, P. (1997) Single mothers, poverty and depression. *Psychological Medicine*, 27, 21–33.

Bruch M. and Bond F.W. (1998) *Beyond Diagnosis: Case Formulation Approaches in Cognitive–Behavioural Therapy*, London: Wiley.

Butler, G. (1998) Clinical formulation in A.S. Bellack and M. Hersen (eds) *Comprehensive Clinical Psychology*, Oxford: Pergamon.

Callcott, P. and Turkington, D. (2006) CBT for traumatic psychosis in W. Larkin and A.P. Morrison (eds), *Trauma and Psychosis: New Directions for Theory and Therapy*. London: Routledge, pp. 222–238.

Castillo, H. (2000) 'You don't know what it's like', *Mental Health Care* 41, 2, 42–58.

Chadwick, P., Williams, C. and Mackenzie, J. (2003) Impact of case formulation in cognitive behaviour therapy for psychosis, *Behaviour Research and Therapy*, 14, 6, 671–680.

Corrie, S. and Lane, D. (2010) *Constructing Stories, Telling Tales: A Guide to Formulation in Applied Psychology*, London: Karnac.

Crellin, C. (1998) Origins and social contexts of the term 'formulation' in psychological case – reports, *Clinical Psychology Forum*, 112, 18–28.

Cromby, J. and Harper, D. (2009) Paranoia: a social account, *Theory and Psychology*, 19, 335–361.

Dallos, R. and Draper, R. (2000) *Introduction to Family Therapy: Systemic Theory and Practice*, Oxford: Oxford University Press.

Davis, K. (1986) The process of problem (re) formulation in psychotherapy, *Sociology of Health and Illness*, 8, 44–74.

Division of Clinical Psychology (2010) *The Core Purpose and Philosophy of the Profession*, Leicester: The British Psychological Society.

——(2011) *Good Practice Guidelines for the Use of Psychological Formulation*, Leicester: The British Psychological Society.

——(2013) *Position Statement on the Classification of Behaviour and Experience in Relation to Functional Psychiatric Diagnoses: Time for a Paradigm Shift.* Leicester: The British Psychological Society.

Dumont, F. (1993) Inferential heuristics in clinical problem formulation; selective review of their strengths and weaknesses, *Professional Psychology: Research and Practice*, 24, 2, 196–205.

Eells, T.D. (ed.) (2010) *Handbook of Psychotherapy Case Formulation* (2nd edn), New York, London: The Guilford Press.

Evans, G. and Parry, J. (1996) The impact of reformulation in cognitive-analytic therapy with difficult-to-help clients, *Clinical Psychology and Psychotherapy*, 3 (2), 109–117.

Fernando, S. (2003) *Cultural Diversity, Mental Health and Psychiatry: The Struggle Against Racism*, Hove, New York: Brunner-Routledge.

Follette, W.C. and Houts, A.C. (1996) Models of scientific progress and the role of theory in taxonomy development: a case study of the DSM, *Journal of Consulting and Clinical Psychology*, 64, 6, 1120–1132.

Harper, D. and Moss, D. (2003) A different kind of chemistry? Reformulating formulation, *Clinical Psychology*, 25, 6–10.

Herman, J. (2001) *Trauma And Recovery*, New York: Basic Books.

Hesse, E. (2008) The adult attachment interview: protocol, method of analysis and empirical studies in J. Cassidy and P.R. Shaver (eds) *Handbook of Attachment: Theory, Research and Clinical Applications*, London, New York: The Guilford Press, pp. 552–598.

Holland, S. (1992) From social abuse to social action: a neighbourhood psychotherapy and social action project for women in J. Ussher and P. Nicholson (eds), *Gender Issues in Clinical Psychology*, London: Routledge.

Honos-Webb, L. and Leitner, L.M. (2001) How using the DSM causes damage: a client's report, *Journal of Humanistic Psychology*, 41, 4, 36–56.

Ingleby, D. (1981) Understanding 'mental illness', in D. Ingleby (ed.) *Critical Psychiatry: The Politics of Mental Health*, Harmondsworth: Penguin, pp. 23–71.

Johnstone, L. (2000) *Users and Abusers of Psychiatry: A Critical Look at Psychiatric Practice* (2nd edn), Philadelphia, London: Brunner-Routledge.

——(2008) Psychiatric diagnosis, in R. Tummey and T. Turner (eds), *Critical Issues in Mental Health*, Basingstoke: Palgrave Macmillan, pp. 5–22.

Jones, D. and Elcock, J. (2001) *History and Theories of Psychology: A Critical Perspective*, London: Arnold.

Kennedy, F., Smalley, M. and Harris, T. (2003) Clinical psychology for in-patient settings: principles for development and practice, *Clinical Psychology Forum*, 30, 21–24.

Kinderman, P. (2001) The future of clinical psychology training, *Clinical Psychology*, 8, 6–10.

Kirk, S.A. and Kutchins, H. (1992) *The Selling of DSM: The Rhetoric of Science in Psychiatry*, New York: Aldine de Gruyter.

Kovel, J. (1981) The American mental health industry in D. Ingleby (ed.) *Critical Psychiatry: The Politics of Mental Health*, Harmondsworth: Penguin.

Kuipers, E., Leff, J. and Lam, D. (1992) *Family Work for Schizophrenia: A Practical Guide*, London: Gaskell.

Kuyken, W. (2006) Evidence-based case formulation: is the emperor clothed? in N. Tarrier (ed.) *Case Formulation in Cognitive Behaviour Therapy: The Treatment of Challenging and Complex Cases*, London: Brunner-Routledge.

Kuyken, W., Padesky, C.A. and Dudley, R. (2009) *Collaborative Case Conceptualization: Working Effectively with Clients in Cognitive-Behavioral Therapy,* New York, London: The Guilford Press.

Leeming, D., Boyle, M. and Macdonald, J. (2009) Accounting for psychological problems: how user-friendly are psychosocial formulations? *Clinical Psychology Forum*, 200, 12–17.

Letters to the Editor (2000) *The Psychologist*, 13, 8, 390–392.

Luborsky, L. and Crits-Christoph, P. (1990) *Understanding Transference: The Core Conflictual Relationship Theme Method*, New York: Basic Books.

Madill, A., Widdicombe, S. and Barkham, M. (2001) The potential of conversation analysis for psychotherapy research, *The Counseling Psychologist*, 29, 3, 413–434.

Malan. D.M. (1976) *Toward the Validation of Dynamic Psychotherapy*, New York: Plenum Press.

——(1995) *Individual Psychotherapy and the Science of Psychodynamics* (2nd edn), London: Hodder Arnold.

Masson, J. (1990a) *Final Analysis: The Making and Unmaking of a Psychoanalyst*, London: HarperCollins.

——(1990b) *Against Therapy*, London: Fontana.

May, R. (2011) Relating to alternative realities in M. Romme and S. Escher (eds), *Psychosis as a Personal Crisis: An Experience-Based Approach,* London, New York: Routledge, pp. 140–152.

McNamee, S. and Gergen, K. (1992) *Therapy as Social Construction,* London: Sage.

Mehta, S. and Farina, A. (1997) Is being 'sick' really better? Effect of the disease model of mental disorder on stigma, *Journal of Social and Clinical Psychology*, 16, 4, 405–419.

Mental Health Foundation (1997) *Knowing Our Own Minds*, London: Mental Health Foundation.

Messer, S.B. (1991) The case formulation approach: issues of reliability and validity, *American Psychologist*, December, 1348–1350.

——(1996) Concluding comments. Special section: Case formulation, *Journal of Psychotherapy Integration*, 6, 135–137.

Neuner, F., Catani, C., Ruf, M., Schauer, E., Schauer, M. and Elbert, T. (2008) Narrative exposure therapy for the treatment of traumatized children and adolescents (KidNET): from neurocognitive theory to field intervention, *Child and Adolescent Psychiatric Clinics of North America*, 17 (3), 641–664.

Penfold, P.S. and Walker, G.A. (1983) *Women and the Psychiatric Paradox*, Montreal, London: Eden Press.

Persons, J.B. (1989) *Cognitive Therapy in Practice: A Case Formulation Approach*, New York: W.W. Norton.

Pilgrim, D. (2000) Psychiatric diagnosis: more questions than answers, *The Psychologist*, 13, 6, 302–305.

Proctor, G. (2002) *The Dynamics of Power in Counselling and Psychotherapy*, Ross-on-Wye: PCCS Books.

Ray, A. (2008) *Understanding reflective practice as part of the process of formulation*, unpublished doctoral thesis, Bristol Clinical Psychology Doctorate.

Read, J. and Bentall, R.B. (2012) Negative childhood experiences and mental health: theoretical, clinical and primary prevention implications, *British Journal of Psychiatry*, 200, 89–91.

Redhead, S. (2010) *Clients' experiences of formulation in cognitive behaviour therapy*, unpublished doctoral thesis, Bristol Clinical Psychology Doctorate.

Rogers, A., Pilgrim, R. and Lacey, R. (1993) *Experiencing Psychiatry*, London: Macmillan/MIND.

Rogers, C. (1975) Empathic: an unappreciated way of being, *The Counseling Psychologist*, 5, 2, 2–10.

Romme, M. and Escher, S. (2000) *Making Sense of Voices*, London: MIND Publications.

Rosenbaum, R. (1996) Form, formlessness and formulation, *Journal of Psychotherapy Integration*, 6, 2, 107–117.

Ross, C. (2008) Dissociative schizophrenia in A. Moskowitz, I. Schäfer and M. Dorahy (eds), *Psychosis, Trauma and Dissociation: Emerging Perspectives on Severe Psychopathology*, Oxford: Wiley-Blackwell, pp. 281–295.

Roy-Chowdhury, S. (2003) What is this thing called psychotherapy? *Clinical Psychology* 29, 7–11.

Royal College of Psychiatrists (2010) *A competency-based curriculum for specialist core training in psychiatry*. Retrieved 5 October 2011 from www.rcpsych.ac.uk/training/curriculum2010.aspx.

Smail, D. (1987) Psychotherapy as subversion in a make-believe world, *Changes*, 4 (5), 398–402.

——(1993) *The Origins of Unhappiness: A New Understanding of Personal Distress*, London: Secker and Warburg.

——(1996) *How to Survive without Psychotherapy*, London: Constable.

Sturmey, P. (ed.) (2009) *Clinical Case Formulation: Varieties of Approaches*, Chichester: Wiley-Blackwell.

Tarrier, N. and Calam, R. (2002) New developments in cognitive–behavioural case formulation, *Behavioural and Cognitive Psychotherapy*, 30, 311–328.

Warner, R. (2004) *Recovery from Schizophrenia: Psychiatry and Political Economy* (3rd edn), Hove and New York: Brunner-Routledge.

Weerasekera, P. (1995) *Multiperspective Case Formulation: A Step Towards Treatment Integration*, Malabar, Florida: Krieger Publishing Company.

Weston, D. (1990) Psychoanalytic approaches to personality in L. Pervin (ed.) *Handbook of Personality: Theory and Research*, New York: Guilford Press.

Wilkinson, R. and Pickett, K. (2009) *The Spirit Level: Why More Equal Societies Almost Always Do Better*, London: Allen Lane.

Index

Figures are shown with an *italic* page number and tables are shown with a **bold** page number.

practice, 233–6; usefulness of
formulation, 265
team working, 109, 216–39
technical eclecticism, 176
Tees Esk and Wear Valleys NHS
Foundation Trust, 218–19
terminology: *see* language
therapeutic alliance, 177, 184–5,
265, 283; *see also* therapeutic
relationship
therapeutic conversations: *see*
narrative therapy
therapeutic documents, 108–9
therapeutic formulation, 214
therapeutic letters, 109; for Jack,
110–12; to Janet and Mary,
115–16
therapeutic relationship, 2, 183,
193–8, *213*, 262; existing
integration, 178–9; integrative
formulations, 186–7, 191–2;
see also therapeutic alliance
therapists, 71, 270–2, 281–3; CBT
(Cognitive Behavioural Therapy),
33–4; integrative approach,
210–11; psychodynamic
approach, 62–4; systemic family
therapy, 67–9; *see also* therapeutic
relationship
therapy outcomes, 184–5, 283–4
Trailblazer Project, Hackney, 109
transference, 51, 52, 229
trauma, 31, 231–2, 280, 284; post-
traumatic stress disorder, 31, 263;
re-traumatisation, 233

Traveller community, 134, 161;
view of illness, 253, 254–5
'Tree of Life,' 109
triadic relationships, 68–9, 153,
167
'triangle of conflict,' 47, *48*
Triangle of Person, 10, 51
triggers, 30–1

unconscious processes, 45, 46, 47,
52–4
unique outcomes, 106–7, 113–14
usefulness of formulation, 263–72

validation, 156, 163
validity of approaches, 260–3
values, 35; *see also* beliefs
vicious cycle, 23, 68
vigilance, 34

Weerasekera's framework, 179–84,
182, 273–4, 275
wellbeing, 125
White, Michael, 96–100, 105,
108–9
witnessing, 129–31
women: feminist theories, 127;
health context, 252;
individualising formulation, 277;
mothers, 134–5; society and
beauty, 99–100
working-class communities,
125

young people, 126